Anja Kervanto Nevanlinna
INTERPRETING NAIROBI

BIBLIOTHECA HISTORICA 18

Anja Kervanto Nevanlinna

Interpreting Nairobi
The Cultural Study of Built Forms

Suomen Historiallinen Seura ■ Helsinki

Cover: Aerial view of Nairobi city center.

© Anja Kervanto Nevanlinna 1996

ISSN 1238-3503
ISBN 951-710-049-3

Hakapaino Oy
Helsinki 1996

Contents

	Preface and acknowledgements	7
	List of illustrations	11
PART ONE	THE FRAME OF INTERPRETATION	
	1 Urban built form as an object of study	19
	2 The cultural study of built forms	25
	3 The conceptual network	36
	4 Interpreting built forms	54
PART TWO	RE-PRESENTING NAIROBI	
	5 Beginnings	61
	6 Settings	75
	7 Footings	79
PART THREE	HISTORIES OF URBAN FORM IN NAIROBI	
	8 The birth of the railway town, 1895-1902	89
	9 Power disputes and sanitation problems, 1902-1910	105
	10 Segregation plans and practices, 1910-1919	115
	11 The municipality takes form, 1919-1940	126
	12 Establishing the colonial capital, 1940-1963	157
	13 Modernizing the African metropolis, 1963-1983	204
PART FOUR	DWELLING FORMS IN NAIROBI	
	14 Colonial European dwelling forms	257
	15 African dwelling forms	275
	16 Asian dwelling forms	280
	17 "Universal" dwelling forms	296
	18 Dwelling practices in Nairobi, 1983	318
PART FIVE	CULTURAL INTERPRETATIONS OF BUILT FORMS	
	19 Interpreting the built forms of Nairobi	337
	20 Towards cultures	345
	Appendixes	348
	Illustration sources	354
	Sources	355
	Name Index	365
	Place Index	369

Preface and acknowledgements

Built forms have been studied either as planned instruments for well-being, relating to the philosophy of modernity, or as expressions of ideals and intentions, relating to the philosophy of romanticism. In this study, built forms are approached as producers of cultures, relating to the philosophy of hermeneutics; here, the concept of culture is defined as any urban community with its particular values and practices in the historically changing, ununiform context of other cultures "living" the same city. Built forms are perceived as the domain within which the practices and meanings of some cultures are established while those of others are rejected. The interpretation of built forms involves understanding their meanings in relation to a particular context, necessitating a real historical object of study, here, Nairobi.

This is a study of built forms in two senses: it is an inquiry into the cultural study of built forms in general and into the built forms of Nairobi in particular. The first could be described as a philosophical, theoretical, and methodological inquiry, the second as an empirical one. As texts, the theoretical sections form the envelope within which the empirical sections are placed. The structure of the text thus grows out of the main aim of the study: to explore the potential of a new approach to built forms, here identified as the cultural study of the built forms of the city. The theory is developed in connection with one city, Nairobi, through the process of interpreting its particular histories of practices involving built forms.

The concept of culture implies interpretation: translation from one culture, one language, one mode of representation into another. Cultural interpretation carries not only the notion of re-presentation but also the notion of dis-location; in this sense, a cultural study of built forms is problematic. First, there arises the issue of cultural differences between the contexts of research and the objects of study, the problem encountered by anthropologists: how to represent within one culture, one frame of interpretation, an "other" culture? The issue is further complicated by the notion that processes of cultural translation cannot be detached from systems of domination, either locally or globally. Second, there is the issue of the cultural differences between contemporary and historical horizons of understanding, the problem confronted by historians: how to retain the past as "other," distinct from the present? Third, there is the issue of cultural translation from a non-textual to a textual mode of representation, the problem encountered by both art historians, urban historians and anthropologists: how to read visual materials – such as built forms and maps, plans, drawings and photographs of them – and translate them into text? And in the context of historical textual material possibly distorted by the colonial presence, can visual material be used not only as illustrations but as historical sources, as a passage towards culturally multiple representations of the past?

Interpretation is produced as text, as writing. The language used – both verbal and visual – carries a specific network of meanings and is connected to particular cultures. This study, for example, was influenced by the fact that it was written in English, which carries European (or Euro-American) systems of meaning, and by my own background as an internationally-oriented person who belongs to several cultural communities in Finland. Within this frame, it may be difficult to convey the wide extent of the culturally multiple meanings connected to the built forms and urban practices of Nairobi, but, I believe, it is not impossible to suggest some of these meanings for "other" people. More important is to open the possibility of built forms as producers and reproducers of a multitude of cultures, not only in one particular case such as Nairobi, but as a philosophical point of departure with practical consequences.

The textuality of the representation of the city carries a contradiction. Writing normally presupposes a coherence of the text. In the context of the cultural study of the built forms of the city, however, the notion of coherence must be questioned: within the cultural concept, the city is perceived as a dis-unified, dis-uniform – therefore incoherent – collection of cultures. To present a dis-unified interpretation of the city, the text cannot be confined to one voice, for example, my voice; more voices need to be heard within the text, as well. This kind of a text resembles Mikhail Bakhtin's notion of a polyphonic novel with its plurality of independent, separate voices and consciousnesses. In analyzing Feodor Dostoyevski's novels, Bakhtin has emphasized that he does not present a multitude of characters and destinies in a unified objective world and explained through the consciousness of one person, but a plurality of several equally significant consciousnesses – a plurality of worlds – attached to the singularity of an event, the consciousnesses remaining separate. In a similar manner, a text presenting a cultural interpretation of the city can become the site for the reproduction of different and contradictory meanings. In this text, I have wanted to preserve the plurality of the voices of the different cultures. As polyphonic, the text may be perceived as a culturally true representation of the built forms of the city. The built city also is polyphonic and "speaks with many voices."

***

The support of one person has been essential to the completion of my work. During the crucial phases of transforming the research process into a book, I have had the great privilege of receiving criticism and encouragement from Professor Riitta Nikula. The intellectual standards she set and the opportunities she provided for me to attempt to reach them have influenced the work in no small measure. To her I gratefully give my thanks. Professor Keijo

Virtanen and Docent Pekka Korvenmaa read the final version of the manuscript; I want to thank them for their useful comments and suggestions. My thanks are also due to the post-graduate group of the Department of Art History: the discussions helped me clarify many of these pages.

During the years I have been involved in my topic, I have been working with many persons and in several institutions in different parts of the world. For the initial phase, I am grateful to Professor Ahti Korhonen of the Institute of Urban Design and Planning at the Helsinki University of Technology for the enthusiasm with which he met my independence in the formulation of the problem.

In Nairobi, the Department of Architecture and the Housing Research and Development Unit at the University of Nairobi provided facilities and assistance during my field study phase. A large number of people from the faculty, both teachers and students, shared their local knowledge with me. I would especially like to thank Neelkanth Chhaya, who perceptively presented the different layers of the city to me and whose involvement in the study opened many doors which otherwise would have remained closed. Kenya Railways kindly allowed me to consult its plan archives and conduct part of the field study in its staff housing; for this, I want to thank the management and the many helpful members of the staff. My special thanks go to all the families who let me into their homes: without their participation, an important part of the study could not have been completed. At their request, their names are not mentioned. I would also like to thank the students of architecture, who prepared the measured drawings: Samson Akara, Anzaya Akatsa, David Kimani, Christopher Korir, Nathan Kureba, Rajinder Mahajan, Hitesh Mehta, Mervyn Moniz, and Paul Mpungu. In Nairobi, Ann and Bruce Creager, Professor A. Maleche of the Department of Land Development, Kamau Karogi, Zahir Ismael, Helena Horelli (now deceased), Leena and Jarkko Juselius, and Jorma Ruotsi helped in many ways.

During my eight years of teaching in the Master Program in Architecture and Urban Design of the Institute of International Studies in Architecture at the Helsinki University of Technology, I could explore the issues central to this study. For our discussions, I want to the thank all my 65 graduate students and the other participants. Kurula Varkey, Madhura Prematilleke, and Vithushani Kokuleraj drew the final versions of the maps, site plans, and dwelling plans. I am also indebted for exchanges and disputes with colleagues within the NOFUA network of the Nordic schools of architecture; the opportunities to present aspects of my work in several conferences were fruitful.

In Paris, I am grateful to Professor Marion Segaud for her support during my work at the Institut Parisien de Recherche: Architecture, Urbanistique, Société. I would also like to thank Professor Marcel Roncayolo of the Ecole des Hautes Etudes en Sciences Sociales and Professor Charles Goldblum of L'Institut Français d'Urbanisme, as well as the Maison des Sciences de l'Homme for providing me with a base at Maison Suger and access to their excellent library.

At the University of Helsinki, the Department of Art History has offered an intellectually inspiring community; I want to thank my colleagues and the staff members for all their support.

During the extent of my work, I received various kinds of help from a number of other friends and colleagues. In particular, my thanks are due to Riitta Launonen, Marja-Liisa Swantz, Anja Niera, Riitta Kuoppamäki-Kalkkinen, Annick Osmont, Finn Barnow, Antti Veltheim, Jerker Lundequist, Annick Sjögren-de Beauchaine, and Päivikki Suojanen.

I am grateful to the institutions which have financially supported my study: the Academy of Finland (the Research Council of Technology, the Sub-Committee for Development Studies, and the Central Board of Research Councils), the National Committee for Architecture, the Leo and Regina Weinstein Foundation, and the Finnish Cultural Foundation. The Gallen-Kallela Museum has kindly given me permission to publish the photograph taken by Akseli Gallen-Kallela in Nairobi in 1909.

I would like to thank the Finnish Historical Society for publishing my study and Rauno Endén, Secretary General of the Society, for his assistance in preparing the manuscript for printing. My thanks are also due to Nely Keinänen, who corrected my language.

Through the years, my family has supported my endeavors; I can only thank my mother and sister for this. A true cosmopolitan, my father Josef Kaartinen held a keen interest in cultural issues all through his life, but he died before seeing the realization of some of these ideas in my approach.

My husband Arne has lived through the whole process – Nairobi, the interpretation, and the writing – and never failed to stand by me. The range of his knowledge and the precision of his criticism have been invaluable to my work, his support fundamental to its completion. I dedicate this book to him.

■ Illustrations

In the captions, the street names refer to the contemporary usage, often differing from the names used today. Many of the names – but not all – were changed in connection with independence. Names of streets in the city center frequently mentioned in the text:

Earlier name(s)	*Name(s) today*
Station Road, Government Road	Moi Avenue, the northern part, Harry Thuku Road
Sixth Street, Delamere Avenue	Kenyatta Avenue
Bazaar Street	Biashara Street
Hardinge Street	Kimathi Street
Eliot Street	Wabera Street
Portal Street	Banda Street

Two major hotels have been part of Nairobi's history from the beginning:
the Norfolk Hotel, located north of the city center on Harry Thuku Road
the Stanley Hotel, located at the corner of Kenyatta Avenue and Kimathi Street

Cover: Aerial view of Nairobi city center

PART II RE-PRESENTING NAIROBI

    5. *Beginnings*
5.1 Moi Avenue to the north at Kenyatta Avenue
5.2 Harambee Avenue
5.3 Tom Mboya Street
5.4 Jamia Mosque and the ICEA Building
5.5 Traffic headed towards the city center
5.6 The Municipal Market and a local mosque
5.7 Kirinyaga Road near the Nairobi River
5.8 Shan Cinema, Ngara Road
5.9 Lamu Road, Pumwani
5.10 Kiosks off Peponi Road
5.11 Kaloleni residential area
5.12 Karen Blixen house, Karen

5.13   Residential area, Eastlands
5.14   Playground, Buru Buru
5.15   Map: Nairobi city center, 1978

PART III HISTORIES OF URBAN FORM IN NAIROBI

   8. The birth of the railway town, 1895-1902
8.1   Plan of survey at foot of hill and edge of plains, 1898
8.2   Uganda Railway Plan of Staff Quarters, 1899
8.3   Map: Nairobi, c.1900
8.4   Map: Nairobi, c.1900
8.5   Uganda Railway General Plan of Nairobi, 1901
8.6   General view of Nairobi, 1899
8.7   Government Road from Market
8.8   Sixth Avenue to the west, at Eliot Street
8.9   Bazaar Street, 1904

   9. Power disputes and sanitation problems, 1902-1910
9.1   Map: Nairobi, c.1905
9.2   View from the second floor window of the Stanley Hotel, 1909

   10. Segregation plans and practices, 1910-1919
10.1   Map: Segregation Proposals, 1913
10.2   Government Road to the north, 1913

   11. The municipality takes form, 1919-1940
11.1   Government Road, eastern side, 1919
11.2   Traffic jam, Sixth Avenue and Government Road, 1918
11.3   Government Road, western side, 1920s
11.4   Government Road, eastern side, 1927
11.5   Map: Roads, 1927
11.6   Map: Planned roads
11.7   Nairobi railway station
11.8   Norfolk Hotel, 1928
11.9   Government Road, western side, 1920s
11.10 Sixth Avenue, northern side, at Hardinge Street, 1920s
11.11 Aerial view: Nairobi city center to the north, 1930s
11.12 Aerial view: Nairobi city center to the southwest, 1930s
11.13 Map: Railways area and Law Courts, 1940s

   12. Establishing the colonial capital, 1940-1963
12.1   Aerial photograph: City center, 1940s
12.2   Population of Nairobi, 1906, 1926, 1936 and 1944
12.3   Map: Buildings and open spaces distribution

12.4   Master Plan, 1948
12.5   Master Plan: Roads, 1948
12.6   Master Plan: Central area
12.7   Master Plan: Kenya Center
12.8   Master Plan: Kenya Parkway
12.9   Comparative plans
12.10 Master Plan: TW neighborhood unit
12.11 Map: Existing residential density zoning
12.12 Buildings of Nairobi, 1940s: Law Courts and Secretariat, Railways Headquarters, East African Lighting Company offices, and an African family housing area.
12.13 Delamere Avenue to the east, 1940s
12.14 Delamere Avenue to the west, 1950s
12.15 Portal Street with McMillan Library, Jamia Mosque and the City Market, 1950
12.16 Government Road to the north
12.17 Nairobi street view during the Emergency, 1950s

13. *Modernizing the African metropolis, 1963-1983*
13.1   Map: Central area
13.2   Map: Uncontrolled settlements in central Nairobi
13.3   Karura Forest uncontrolled settlement
13.4   Dwellings, Karura Forest
13.5   Pumwani residential area
13.6   Map: Existing roads, 1972
13.7   Metropolitan Growth Strategy for 2000
13.8   Map: Central area land use, 1972
13.9   Map: Proposed transport network in the central area
13.10 Company housing in Mathare Valley
13.11 Layout plan: Dandora area, phase I
13.12 Dandora area
13.13 Map: Physical structure
13.14 Map: Residential densities
13.15 Map: Nairobi city center in 1973
13.16 Nairobi city center from the Hill, 1973
13.17 Moi Avenue, southern part, 1980s
13.18 Kenyatta Avenue with Hotel Stanley and the ICEA skyscraper, 1983
13.19 Biashara Street and City Market, with Koinange Street to the right, 1980s
13.20 Law Courts and the Kenyatta Conference Center, 1987
13.21 Maps: The built structure of Nairobi, 1900, 1920, 1940, 1950, 1960, and 1970
13.22 The city center, 1980s

PART IV DWELLING FORMS IN NAIROBI

14. Colonial European dwelling forms
14.1 Railways housing for Europeans, the Hill, site plan
14.2 Railways housing: detached house for Europeans, the Hill, dwelling plan
14.3 Railways housing: detached house for Europeans, the Hill
14.4 Railways housing for Asians, Ngara, site plan
14.5 Railways housing: row house for Asians, Ngara, dwelling plan
14.6 Railways housing: row house for Asians, Ngara
14.7 Railways housing: semi-detached house for Asians, Ngara, dwelling plan
14.8 Railways housing for Africans, Muthurwa, site plan
14.9 Railways housing: landhies for Africans, Muthurwa, dwelling plan
14.10 Railways housing: landhies for Africans, Muthurwa
14.11 Employer-built flat, Spring Valley, dwelling plan
14.12 Employer-built flat, Spring Valley
14.13 Employer-built flat, the Hill, dwelling plan
14.14 Employer-built flat, the Hill
14.15 Privately-built detached house, Spring Valley, dwelling plan
14.16 Privately-built detached house, Spring Valley
14.17 Privately-built row house, Upper Hill, dwelling plan
14.18 Privately-built row house, Upper Hill

15. African dwelling forms
15.1 Self-built residential area, Pumwani, site plan
15.2 Self-built dwellings, Pumwani, majengo house, dwelling plan
15.3 Self-built dwellings, Pumwani, majengo house

16. Asian dwelling forms
16.1 Privately-built courtyard house by Asians, Ngara, dwelling plan
16.2 Privately-built courtyard house, Ngara
16.3 Privately-built courtyard house area, Eastleigh, site plan
16.4 Privately-built courtyard house, Eastleigh, dwelling plan
16.5 Privately-built courtyard house, Eastleigh
16.6 Privately-built courtyard house area, city center, site plan
16.7 Privately-built courtyard house, city center, dwelling plan
16.8 Privately-built courtyard house, city center
16.9 Privately-built detached house, Parklands, site plan
16.10 Detached house converted into courtyard house, Parklands, dwelling plan
16.11 Privately-built detached house, Parklands
16.12 Privately-built semidetached house, Nairobi South, dwelling plan
16.13 Privately-built semidetached house, Nairobi South

17. "Universal" dwelling forms

17.1 Public sector housing, Kibera, site plan
17.2 Public sector courtyard house, Kibera, dwelling plan
17.3 Public sector courtyard house, Kibera
17.4 Public sector housing, Umoja, aerial photograph
17.5 Public sector row house, Umoja, dwelling plan
17.6 Public sector row house, Umoja
17.7 Public sector row house, Buru Buru, dwelling plan
17.8 Public sector row house, Buru Buru
17.9 Private sector flat, city center, dwelling plan
17.10 Private sector flat, city center
17.11 Private sector housing, Kileleshwa, site plan
17.12 Private sector row house, Kileleshwa, dwelling plan
17.13 Private sector row house, Kileleshwa
17.14 Private sector detached house, Lavington, dwelling plan
17.15 Private sector detached house, Lavington

18. Dwelling practices in Nairobi, 1983

18.1 Living room of African family in the Hill
18.2 Living room with dining area of African family in Buru Buru
18.3 Bedroom and storage of clothes of African family in the Hill
18.4 Master bedroom of African family in Upper Hill
18.5 Kitchen of African family in Kibera
18.6 Courtyard of Asian family in Ngara
18.7 Living room and master bedroom of Asian family in the city center
18.8 Formal living room of Asian family in Parklands
18.9 Shrine of Asian family in Nairobi South
18.10 Rooms with connecting doors of Asian family in the city center
18.11 Kitchen of Asian family in Lavington
18.12 Terrace of European single person in Kileleshwa
18.13 Living room and dining area of European family in Spring Valley
18.14 Children's bedroom of European family in Spring Valley
18.15 Kitchen of European family in Spring Valley (flat)
18.16 The gate pattern
18.17 The chain pattern
18.18 The wing pattern

Appendixes

A.1 Map: Topography and boundary changes, 1900, 1920, 1927, and 1963
A.2 Map: Locations in Nairobi, 1983

PART ONE

THE FRAME OF INTERPRETATION

1 Urban built form as an object of study

The city: social form or built form?

The study of cities holds a major position in research on contemporary societies within a multitude of fields including sociology, anthropology, philosophy, geography, history, and art history. But when cities have been studied, what precisely has been the object of study? In this respect, the approaches common in the social sciences seem to differ from those conventionally applied in fields oriented to the city as a built form, the former emphasizing the social and cultural reality, the latter the physical and material reality. In anthropology, for example, Clifford Geertz has illustrated the marginality of the built environment:

> The locus of study is not the object of study. Anthropologists don't study villages (tribes, towns, neighborhoods . . .), they study *in* villages.[1]

Even when the physical characteristics have been recognized in social studies, they nevertheless seem to have been placed into a mechanistic and passive position within the relationship: built forms have been seen as the setting, the stage for the social action, not as an element essential to the social reality. In other words, the built city has been perceived as a "given" with little significance in the social sphere. Equally, some of the research within fields focused on the physical dimension of cities such as geography, town planning, and architecture (in relation to urban form), has been criticized for suppressing the social aspects of cities.[2]

In the last decades, the differences in points of view have been reduced between disciplines oriented towards social reality and towards physical reality. Within sociology and geography, and, to a lesser extent, anthropology, cultural studies, and philosophy, theoretical work has evolved on the interdependence of the social and the spatial. Social relations have been perceived as both space-forming and space-contingent, spaces and built forms as simultaneously social products and instruments for social reform.[3] In this

---

1 Geertz 1973, 22. For related comments on urban anthropology, see e.g. Fox 1975, 59ff.
2 See e.g. Morris 1979, vii; Choay 1988, 152ff. On urban morphological studies in architecture and geography, see Merlin 1988, Slater 1990.
3 On the socio-spatial interdependence in sociology, Lefebvre 1991, Giddens 1984, 355-368;

respect, the researchers in the Sociology Department at the University of Chicago in the early decades of the 20th century were forerunners; in their studies on human ecology which they understood as a sociology of space, the spatial dimension was seen as essential for knowledge about social phenomena.[4]

The Sociology Department at the University of Chicago was the first one in the United States, but their studies have also been recognized as pioneering in other, partly overlapping fields like modern urban studies, ethnology, urban anthropology, social studies, and social history. For the study of built forms, social reality has emerged not only as a means of understanding the physical reality better, but as something even more fundamental, what Anthony D. King described as a paramount necessity:

> If we are to understand buildings and environments, we must understand the society and culture in which they exist. With this approach, by focusing our attention on built form and spatial organisation, we can understand much more about the society in which such forms exist – much, indeed, that might otherwise escape us. In this way, the relationship between society and its built environment could be explored and clarified.[5]

Within the study of history, the interconnections between social forms and built forms have long been seen from a more concrete perspective and as less problematic: histories have been about both. For example, Daniel Roche attributed the attraction the town holds for French historians to its comprehensive character: the ways in which the city "brings together the whole gamut of questions posed by the development of our system of civilization over the centuries."[6] He connected the emergence of the "new urban history" in France with the rise of social history in the 1950s. The concept of urban history in the sense of a new kind of urban history was established in the 1960s in Britain and the United States, and in the 1970s in Germany.[7] Elements of social history have also been incorporated into urban research within art history, as in the art historian Gregor Paulsson's

---

in geography, Harvey 1988, Soja 1989; in anthropology, Rabinow 1989; in cultural studies, Jameson 1991, chap.1; in philosophy, Foucault 1979.

4   However, Grafmeyer and Joseph (1984, 34) have argued that in the Chicago School studies, space was never presented as the explanatory principle or as the privileged object of analysis. On the Chicago School, see Hannerz 1980, 19-118; Grafmeyer and Joseph 1984.
5   King 1980, 8.
6   Roche 1980, 12ff.
7   For the history of urban history in Britain, see Rodger 1992, 9; in the United States, Mohl 1983, 19ff.; in Germany, Reulecke and Huck 1981, 44ff. Rodger's perspective was attached in particular to the *Urban History Newsletter*, first published in 1962; it may be seen, perhaps, as a reflection of H.J. Dyos' view that "urban history is the most newly discovered continent" (Dyos 1968, 6). Significantly longer histories have been identified within French urban history. For example, Roche (1980, 12ff.) dated the beginnings of urban historiography to medieval urban communities, and Bedarida (1968, 49ff.) in the late nineteenth century with disciplines other than history, particularly geography. Cf. Dyos 1968, 19-25.

study on the Swedish town, first published in 1950.[8] Paulsson advocated an approach based on the notion that spaces and buildings receive their character from the "actions, social positions, sentiments and valuations of the people that fill them"[9]; indeed that, quoting the geographer Max Sorre,

> to understand a city, beyond its monuments, beyond the history inscribed in its stones, is to recover the particular way of life of its inhabitants.[10]

In contrast with histories of urban form advocating the idea of the – only partly planned – evolution of city forms, planning history can be seen specifically as the history of modern conscious urban planning. A large corpus of studies of cities from the late nineteenth century to our own times seems to have been directed to urban planning in practice or its analysis in theory; in both, the notion of built form as planned seems to dismiss any other aspects of urban change.[11] In this sense, studies in planning history diverge from those in urban history. Comparing the approaches of the different historians, François Bedarida has distinguished the approach of planning historians and art historians from that of urban historians as one where the study of towns not only excludes the inhabitants, but also includes only forms with aesthetic or functional qualities; "requirements so alien to [the historian's] ethic," as Bedarida noted.[12]

Built forms as histories

Bedarida also emphasized the difference in the points of view between geographers' and architectural historians' interest in spatiality and the urban historians' pursuit of temporality.[13] A similar juxtaposition was presented by the urban historian Richard Rodger. In describing the focus of urban history retrospectively in comparison with what he identified as well-defined

---

8   Paulsson 1971. In a conference report *Perspectives on "Svensk stad,"* Ingrid Hammarstrom and Thomas Hall (1983, 75) noted that it later became a canonical text in urban studies in Sweden.
9   Paulsson 1959, 85.
10 "Comprendre une ville, c'est, par dela ses monuments, par dela l'histoire inscrite dans ses pierres, retrouver la manière d'être particulière de ses habitants." (Max Sorre, *Les Fondements de la géographie humain*, vol.III, 1952, 287, quoted in Paulsson 1959, 87.)
11 Many of the early and contemporary historical approaches to cities have emphasized the perspective of planning, including, for example, Camillo Sitte's *Der Städte-Bau nach seinen künstlerischen Grundsätzen* of 1889 (1986), Patrick Geddes' *Cities in Evolution: An Introduction to the Town Planning Movement and to the Study of Civics* of 1915 (1968), Lewis Mumford's *Culture of Cities* of 1938 (1970), Edmund N. Bacon's *Design of Cities* of 1967 (revised edition 1975), and Peter Hall's *Cities of Tomorrow* (1988); see also the sections on cities in Leonardo Benevolo's *History of Modern Architecture* (1971a, 1971b) and Sigfried Giedion's *Space, Time and Architecture* of 1941 (fifth, revised edition 1967).
12 Bedarida 1968, 52. Bedarida's examples in this section were from the early decades of this century.
13 Bedarida 1968, 51.

disciplines, he maintained that

> Planning and architectural historians were interested in the buildings, historical geographers with their spatial distribution, and social historians in the families living within them, but only urban historians were interested in the interaction of the urban fabric with the social fabric.

He went on to urban history as a symbiosis of different components:

> Urban history is not, therefore, merely the sum of its constituent parts – cultural, physical, organizational and behavioral – but more accurately an analysis of their interaction in a unique spatial setting.[14]

Both Bedarida and Rodger, then, perceived spatiality – urban built forms – as an unhistorical characteristic of cities.

The notion of built forms as essentially unhistorical has to be questioned. If we want to understand built forms as part of society – not only as a setting or stage – the built forms must also necessarily be perceived as temporal, that is, as processes, involving both the notion of different times of origin and the notion of alterations within time. A particular built form, then, can be seen to contain its origin and any later changes. For the study of built forms in cities, however, the notion of temporality suggests a multi-layered concept of spatiality: several spatialities. As processes, the spatialities can be compared to the temporalities developed by Fernand Braudel in his study of the Mediterranean. Braudel approached his object within three time levels: the almost imperceptible history of the relationship of the people to their geographical and urban environment, the slowly changing social history of groups, economic systems, states, societies, and civilizations, and, finally, the traditional rapidly changing history of individuals and events.[15] Applied to urban built forms, the spatialities could include, for example, first, the geographical location which imperceptibly affects both the organization of the built forms and the ways of "living" them, secondly, the continuous evolution - construction, modification, expansion, and demolition - of the built city as a social and physical entity on the basis of the already existing urban forms and the establishment of their participation in social life, and, thirdly, the rapidly changing spatial processes involving the planning and construction of mostly individual buildings or areas.

An even more direct parallel may be drawn between the nature of history and the nature of urban forms. History rarely "begins": there is always a past before it. Similarly, although some cities are founded on places which can be described (but only in terms of existing buildings) as "tabula rasa," the concept of the city does not "begin": there are always already concepts of the city, and their realizations, which precede the founding of the real city.

---

14 Rodger 1992, 9.
15 Braudel 1986, 20f.

In existing cities, the built forms which are already there influence the introduction of new built forms. Thus in terms of built cities, the histories of urban forms contain not only the linear history of forms which exist or have existed but also a more invisible and more complex spatiality. In this context, the potential of art history as a field of study attached to the material and visual reality has not been exhausted. Evidently, for an approach integrating society and built forms, to some extent a redefinition of art historical concepts is necessary; at the same time, the traditions of art history offer useful footings.

Interdisciplinarity

King identified approaches relating to society and its built environment as "essentially interdisciplinary."[16] The notion of interdisciplinarity – the combination of different fields of study, for example, social sciences and art history, to approach a particular object – raises some problems. Within each field of study, the traditions of research have involved particular ways of defining the objects of study, particular methods of analysis, and particular terms of interpretation. The notion of interdisciplinarity suggests two alternative paths. One is to follow the existing traditions of each field of study; in this case, the interdisciplinarity would refer to a group of parallel but autonomous approaches to a common topic. However, cleavages between different fields of study may make it impossible, for example, to define a common object of study in other than very general terms. The other alternative is to develop new approaches, detached from the segmented traditions of research; in this case, the interdisciplinarity would refer to essentially new research methods, and, as Roland Barthes has maintained, a new object of study:

> Interdisciplinary work, so much discussed these days, is not about confronting already constituted disciplines (none of which, in fact, is willing to let itself go). To do something interdisciplinary it's not enough to choose a "subject" (a theme) and gather around it two or three sciences. Interdisciplinarity consists in creating a new object that belongs to no one.[17]

Whether this is possible is somewhat open to question. The newness may result in methods without the theoretical foundation which a tradition of research normally provides, and, in extreme cases, with little potential for generalizations beyond the particular material.

In this study, the apparent contradiction of the two alternative paths has been resolved by the construction of an object of study which has been

---

16 King 1980, 8.
17 Barthes, "Jeunes Chercheurs," (*Communications*, 1972) quoted in Clifford 1986, 1; for the complete text, see Barthes 1986, 72.

developed within the frame of art history but does not completely conform to its traditions of research. At the same time, the approach shares a theoretical and philosophical foundation with approaches within other fields of study. The art historical footing has been here seen as primary because the physical characteristics (the material and visual reality) are essential to the approach. Thus, in relation to art history, the object of this study is the urban built form, understood as a fundamental element of social reality, here defined as cultural.

For the purposes of this study, Ivan Gaskell's expanded version of the definition of the objects of art history may also be helpful. Gaskell renamed the field of study the "history of images" because art historians, exceptionally among historians in general, use visual material, and defined the objects of study as comprising, in addition to art,

> those constituents of the human-made visual environment which are or have been valued for reasons other than their ostensible practical purpose (if they have one), whether by design from the outset (for instance, the chair not simply designed to be sat on), or retrospectively (the "found object" or "collectable" invested with new significance by designation).[18]

Thus the objects of art history may include not only designed or planned built forms, but also forms which were built without the intervention of designers or planners. For this context, then, the object of study may initially be defined as urban built forms, planned or unplanned, carrying the values of the society and culture which built them and for which they were erected.

---

18   Gaskell 1991, 168f.

2 The cultural study of built forms

The definition of the object of study as built forms carrying the values of society and culture necessarily also involves the theoretical and philosophical frame within which the study occurs. To define an object of study within art history is also to define the concept of art history: what art historical objects can be understood to be about. In this sense, the object of this study could be defined not only as the built forms of the city but also as the concept of the city.[1] The concept of the city may be described as the particular way of understanding the city: what a city is seen to be about. Thus the concept of the city is a frame of interpretation within which urban practices can occur, containing presuppositions on reality in general (that is, philosophical presuppositions) and on urban built forms in particular (that is, architectural/ spatial presuppositions connected to the philosophical presuppositions). The urban practices may include activities such as researching, planning, and "living" the city; here, only the research aspect is discussed. In this study, the built forms of the city are approached as cultural, through the cultural concept of the city which may be connected to the hermeneutic tradition of philosophy.

A philosophical introduction to frames of interpretation

Our understanding of reality is based on a frame of interpretation which carries philosophical presuppositions of reality. Human communities can and frequently do produce frames of interpretation which are incommensurable with each other, which do not have concepts, practices, or meanings corresponding to those of another community. In studying the city, the researcher does not need to refer to a frame of presuppositions explicitly; particular ways of understanding the city carry these presuppositions implicitly. Our knowledge of reality is always based on a pre-existing frame which we normally do not notice or question: the existence of the frame is the condition of our understanding. In his book *On Certainty*, Ludwig Wittgenstein described the role of a "system" within which understanding occurs:

---

[1] Here, "city" is used to refer specifically to the city as a physical reality. On objects of study in art history, see also Tagg 1992, 42ff.

> All testing, all confirmation and disconfirmation of a hypothesis takes place already within a system. And this system is not a more or less arbitrary and doubtful point of departure for all our arguments; no, it belongs to the essence of what we call an argument. The system is not so much the point of departure, as the element in which arguments have their life.[2]

The frame of interpretation is based on presuppositions which are by nature beliefs. It may be compared to the sense of reality, *doxa*, which Pierre Bourdieu has described as the experience of self-evidence in the correspondence between the natural and social worlds; in his drawing, the universe of discourse – which he also defined as the locus of the confrontation of competing discourses – was surrounded by the universe of the undiscussed and undisputed.[3] The presuppositions inherent in the frame are ultimately impossible to prove, to quote the philosopher Georg Henrik von Wright:

> The evidence which we produce for the truth of a proposition which we claim to know consists of propositions which we accept as true. If the question is raised, how we know these latter propositions, further grounds may be offered to show how we know them and further evidence given for the truth of the propositions thus claimed to be known. But the chain of grounds (evidence) has an end, a point beyond which no further grounds can be given.[4]

This frame of presuppositions nevertheless continuously directs our thinking and actions. The frame is not universal, the same for everyone, nor is it subjective, individual, but attached to a community which has its own identifiable system of values, its own traditions, and its own practices; in this sense, it can be compared with Wittgenstein's concept of world view,[5] Clifford Geertz' concept of culture,[6] Thomas S. Kuhn's concept of paradigm,[7] or Roy Bhaskar's concept of tradition in the philosophy of science.[8] The language used in the community also carries the same presuppositions. Thus, the frame constitutes some of the conditions on which the propositions concerning reality are based.

---

2 Wittgenstein 1974, para.103.
3 Bourdieu 1977, 164-170.
4 von Wright 1972, 51, in reference to Wittgenstein 1958, para.326, 485; 1974, para.471.
5 In discussing Wittgenstein's *On Certainty*, G.H.von Wright (1972, 56) wrote: "The bulk of our propositions belonging to our *Vor-Wissen* can also be said to constitute a world-picture, *Weltbild*. This latter expression is used frequently by Wittgenstein himself. It does not mean a view of the world in the esoteric sense of a philosopher's *Weltanschauung*. It is not a private possession, but bound up with the notion of a "culture" and with the fact "that we belong to a community which is bound together by science and education" (298). One could also say that it is the common ground which we must share with other people in order to understand their actions and words and in order to come to an understanding with them in our judgements."
6 Geertz 1973, 45.
7 Kuhn 1970, 10f.
8 Bhaskar 1978, 24ff.

Because of the character of the frame, the presuppositions are normally not articulated, as Charles Taylor described:

> we remain . . . captured in the force field of a common sense which frustrates all our attempts to take a critical stance towards its basic assumptions. The field distorts the alternatives, makes them look bizarre or inconceivable. To take some distance to this, we have to formulate what is now unsaid.[9]

To be able to define and analyze the frame of the unsaid, it is necessary not only to formulate the unarticulated but also to relate it to other frames of interpretation, here, to other concepts of the city. Different concepts of the city are not determined on the basis of differences between disciplines or fields of study, but on the differences of the fundamental presuppositions relating to reality in general and to the city in particular, essentially other philosophical and spatial points of departure.

Concepts of the city

The concepts of the city may be seen as frames of interpretation. To set the concept of the city used as the basis of this study in its theoretical and philosophical context, I propose a model of three concepts of the city, each of which may be linked to a particular tradition of philosophy:

- the city as an instrument for well-being, related to the tradition of modernity, here identified as the modernist concept of the city;
- the city as a creation of art, related to the tradition of romanticism, here identified as the romanticist concept of the city; and
- the city as a producer of cultures, related to the tradition of hermeneutics, here identified as the hermeneutic concept of the city.

The first two are only referred to briefly, through a presentation of some of the presuppositions concerning reality in general and the city in particular. The third, the hermeneutic concept of the city – also called the cultural concept of the city – is developed in comparison with the other two. The conceptual network attached to it is presented in chapter 3.[10]

Since the three concepts of the city are by definition based on different traditions of philosophy, they cannot be seen as variations of one unified

---

9   Taylor 1984, 24.
10 On the three concepts of the city, see also Nevanlinna 1992b, 1993a and 1993b; cf. concepts of architecture, Kervanto 1987. "Modernity" is here used to refer to the tradition of philosophy which was founded on the philosophy of Enlightenment and which has dominated much of western thinking during the last centuries, understood in the same sense as in Toulmin 1990. On the distinction between "modernité" as an ideology and "modernisme" as a technological practice, see Lefebvre 1981, 52. "Romanticism" is used here to refer to the tradition of philosophy in the same sense as in Berlin 1990, 175-206; and "hermeneutics" to the tradition of philosophy in the same sense as in Taylor 1987, 33-81.

world view or of one paradigm; instead, they may be perceived as parallel traditions of urban philosophy or as parallel ideologies in urban research. It must be emphasized that the presentation of the presuppositions inherent in modernity, romanticism, and hermeneutics is in no respects intended to be exhaustive; the brief and simplified references to each of the traditions of philosophy are used as a means to illustrate the essential differences between the three concepts of the city. The three concepts of the city should be perceived as a set of ideal-types in the Weberian sense, that is, as condensed theoretical constructions with which reality may be studied. They do not have empirical correspondents in reality; in this sense, they may be seen as conceptual tools in research.[11] Equally, the comments on the selected studies of urban built forms are here intended merely as examples to demonstrate and clarify some of the issues attached to each frame of interpretation.

The modernist concept of the city. The concept of the city as an instrument for well-being – or the modernist concept of the city – is based on presuppositions related to the philosophy of modernity, central in the development of scientific and technological thinking, and its precedent, the philosophy of Enlightenment. These presuppositions have included

- the belief in the fundamental unity of the world: in the notion that all phenomena of reality are united within the same universal structure and goals;
- the belief in the capacity of human beings to attain correct, objective, and reliable knowledge through observation and experimentation;
- the belief in "natural" and inevitable progress;
- the belief in the directing of progress rationally with science and technology, including technological, economic, and administrative systems of experts;
- the belief that true values could not conflict with each other.[12]

The modernist concept of the city as an instrument for well-being has contained the notion of the city as the concentration of pathological aspects of urban life – problems of, for example, sanitation, social behavior, or traffic – with the solution of these problems seen as progress towards well-being. Within the modernist concept of the city, the history of a city has been perceived as the history of its continuous improvement socially, politically, economically, and technologically.[13] In this, the role of conscious planning

---

11 Weber 1949, 90-93.
12 For presuppositions inherent in the tradition of modernity, see e.g. Toulmin 1990; Berlin 1990, 175-213; Dumont 1985; Habermas 1973 and 1987; Touraine 1992, esp. Première partie; Escobar 1992. Toulmin emphasized the shared assumptions about rationality as the basis of modernity (p.9); on rationality, see e.g. Gellner 1992. On the concept of progress, see e.g. Crampe-Crasnabet 1985. The concept of progress has been used parallel to the concepts of evolution, development, modernization, and growth, each with a slightly different emphasis; for a discussion of these, see e.g. Wallerstein 1984, 173-185; Boudon and Bourricaud 1986, 168-175, 396-404; Esteva 1992.
13 For similar observations in urban history, see e.g. Conzen 1980, 281; Olsen 1986, x.

and control conducted by specialist institutions and implemented through model plans has been seen as essential. Within the modernist concept of the city, the issue of urban built forms has been an issue of universal categories and models of physical forms, the issue of the history of the built forms of a city the history of its urban plans. At the extreme, the physical plan of the city has been perceived as determining the character of the society. In other words, the built city has been seen as an instrument for the generation of well-being. This concept of the city may be described as plan-oriented and universalizing.

In research on urban built forms, the modernist concept of the city seems to have suggested approaches emphasizing urban planning; this has included both theoretical works and studies of particular cities. For example, in analyzing and assessing the ideas which have provided the basis for urbanism, Françoise Choay defined urbanism as the field oriented towards solving the problems of cities scientifically and critically. Her distinction between progressist, culturalist and naturalist models, which superficially may appear to be related to the concepts of the city employed in this study, are in fact subdivisions within the frame of interpretation where the notion of urbanism as conscious planning of the city is the unquestioned basis of the study.[14] In another work subtitled *On the theory of architecture and urbanism*, Choay analyzed texts produced by persons who she claimed had established the discipline of urbanism and had become part of its hegemony. She described the character of each text to be either a doctrine (a set of rules) or a utopia (a model) of architecture, with both alternatives presupposing urbanism as an instrument for changing the city.[15] In Choay's definition, then, urbanism was about cities as objects of planning.

A similar orientation can be perceived in some historical studies of cities. For example, in his introduction to a collection of articles on metropolitan cities between 1890 and 1940, Anthony Sutcliffe defined the issue of giant cities as one of urbanization, more precisely as the problems of urbanization, to be approached through analyses of its planning.[16] As another example, Norma Evenson's study of the changes in the built forms of Paris in 1878-1978 involved specifically tracing the evolution of the planning efforts in Paris, with planning understood to include "also major government policies and programs that have affected the development of the city."[17] Evenson's study contained some presentations of the social conditions of the inhabitants and on the artistic experiences of the townscape, but these served to justify the contents of the plans; the general emphasis of the study was nevertheless on planning.

Research on urban built forms within the modernist concept of the city,

---

14 Choay 1965, 8f.
15 Choay 1980, 9, 16f.
16 Sutcliffe 1984, 1ff.
17 Evenson 1979, xv.

then, seems to have been focused on planning as a self-evident point of departure both for theoretical and historical studies. This has entailed a concentration on not only the fairly recent period of time attached to processes of industrialization, urbanization and modernization and their pathological consequences in urban contexts, but also on the institutionalized means of control over built forms. Aspects of urban life perceived as unproblematic or outside institutional interests seem to have been neglected. Within the modernistic frame of interpretation, moreover, the research on built forms seems to have emphasized those aspects which have been perceived as the same in various cities, while neglecting aspects distinguishing the particular urban forms from those in other cities.

The romanticist concept of the city. In comparison, the concept of the city as a creation of art – or the romanticist concept of the city – has been based on presuppositions which may be drawn from the philosophy of romanticism and particularly from its foundation of opposing the notion of universal and absolute truths promoted in Enlightenment philosophy. These presuppositions have included

- the belief in the singularity of phenomena, individuals, peoples, and periods of time: in the absolute individuality of each of these realities;
- the belief that each individual, people, or age must realize its historically determined goal, to seek to attain its own purpose;
- the belief in the capacity of individuals, through their personal and authentic experience and intuition, to fulfill their inner vision of reality;
- the belief in art as the means of reaching basic truths, but also the belief that these truths are fundamentally impossible to reach through consciousness or conscious efforts;
- the belief in the archetypal character of the basic truths: in that they are fundamentally simple entities which unify the world of experiences and which are at once beyond thinking, time and memory.[18]

In the romanticist concept of the city, it has been perceived primarily as the expression of ideals and ideologies. Its history has been understood as the search for its origin and the discovery of its basic character. The paths in the creation of the urban built forms – planned or unplanned, "organically" evolved – have been assessed as less significant than the result, the visually accessible artefact. Within the romanticist concept of the city, the issue of urban built forms has been an issue of the expression of the ideals and of the history of the individual conditions which created the urban built forms. The appearance of the totality of the city has been approached as the symbol

---

18 For presuppositions inherent in romanticism, see e.g. Berlin 1976 and 1990, 175-206; Dumont 1985; Gellner 1987, 75-90; Finkielkraut 1987, première partie; Hauser 1962, 168ff. On the inaccessibility of truth, cf. the myth of the tree of knowledge in the Bible, von Wright 1992, 132f., and the theme of forbidden knowledge, Ginzburg 1989, 63.

and embodiment of the values of the society. This concept of the city may be described as visually oriented and totalizing.

In research on urban built forms, the romanticist concept of the city seems to have involved approaches focusing on the existing townscape: the visual reality is understood as an expression of the circumstances which generated it. For example, in his history of urban design in western Europe in 900-1900, Wolfgang Braunfels described the city as an object of art history, emphasizing that to understand the processes which changed cities,

> visual examination . . . is the more exact truth . . . Cities do not merely report their history. By the forms that served for their physical manifestation, cities provide the motives for the building of every house and every street. Written sources may contribute information; as far as art-historical research is concerned, they become tags which promise to take some of the work out of looking; but no other source can inform us as well as the building itself. No other historical process instructs us in the same totally undeceitful manner. We are present as eyewitnesses. Suppositions, obstacles, goals, and ideals are all visible to us.[19]

According to Braunfels, the successful architectural image of a city reflected the political, economic, and sociological conditions of its time: his examples from history only included urban built forms where political success corresponded to aesthetic success.[20]

Another version within the romanticist concept of the city has involved the notion of the origins as essential to the explanation of the urban forms. For example, in his study of London (first published in the 1930's), Steen Eiler Rasmussen delved into the beginnings of the city, using two thirds of the text to describe that part of its past extending beyond a hundred years. For Rasmussen, the uniqueness of London was in its individual visual and historical genesis.[21] On a more theoretical level, Christian Norberg-Schulz has developed the concept of the genius loci – the spirit of a place – to indicate how built forms can be perceived as the visualizations of the spirit: the symbols of the genius loci. According to Norberg-Schulz, the spirit gives the place its identity, and is not invented but discovered.[22] Both Rasmussen and Norberg-Schulz perceived urban built forms as the embodiments of the identity of the place and the community inhabiting it.

Research on urban built forms within the romanticist concept of the city, then, seems to have been oriented towards the visual aspects of the built forms and their role as symbols. The self-evident point of departure has been the notion of the built forms as an organic part of the social entity and as the expression of its ideals. This has also involved the appraisal of some built

---

19 Braunfels 1988, 9f.
20 Braunfels 1988, 5f.
21 Rasmussen 1960.
22 Norberg-Schulz 1980, 5, 18-23, 170. See also Langer 1953, 92-103.

forms as more true – more successful – reflections of the society, therefore as aesthetically more valuable; in this sense, the descriptions of built forms have implied prescriptive aspects. Within the romanticist frame of interpretation, the research on built forms has seemed to be more oriented towards cities with a long history and towards traditions of urban forms, while contemporary elements have held less interest. In general, approaches within the romanticist concept of the city seem to have emphasized aspects which distinguished a particular built form from those connected to other societies and other periods.

The hermeneutic concept of the city. The concept of the city as a producer of cultures is based on presuppositions which may be linked to the philosophy of hermeneutics. The presuppositions of both modernity and romanticism may be perceived as expressions of a single system of values: in modernity, the coherence of the system of values was presupposed to be universal, common to all of humanity, in romanticism, it was seen as the characteristic of one people or time period presumed to be homogeneous. In contrast with both, within hermeneutical thinking the presupposition of the unity of systems of values has been rejected. The presuppositions attached to hermeneutics have included

- the belief in the fundamental differences between systems of values (that is, cultures), in their incommensurability, but at the same time, the belief that the alterity – otherness – of the other systems of values is possible to understand to an extent;
- the belief that systems of values are produced by communities (not by individuals);
- the belief in discursive and non-discursive practices as the producers and reproducers of systems of values and social structures;
- the belief in research on meanings as the means to increase understanding of otherness and its basic values;
- the belief that all forms of life and ways of thinking are fundamentally attached to a system of values, and that an external or objective approach is not possible, not even within research.[23]

In discussing the modernist and the romanticist concepts of the city, to distinguish presuppositions concerning built forms was to refer to a wealth of material: both concepts of the city have been established as viable approaches in contemporary urban research and planning. With the hermeneutic concept of the city, the situation is different. Although approaches displaying characteristics which could be identified as related to the tradition of hermeneutic philosophy may be distinguished both within urban research and urban planning, the notion of a hermeneutic concept of the city cannot be said to be established or even generally acknowledged, except, perhaps, within some institutions or groups. Thus the description of

---

23 For presuppositions inherent in hermeneutics, see e.g. Taylor 1987; Vattimo 1988, chap.9. See also Gadamer 1976, chap.2.

the hermeneutic concept of the city here is, indeed, the construction of the concept for this context. In the development of the hermeneutic concept of the city, its relation to the other concepts of the city is essential: a description of the hermeneutic concept of the city includes analyses of the other concepts of the city; therefore it can be said in a sense to "contain" them. If assessments of the modernist and the romanticist concepts of the city are accepted as potential fragments towards the development of a cultural concept of the city related to hermeneutic philosophy, the body of research and planning approaches relevant in the context is enlarged.

Within modernity, built forms have been perceived as material objects, as elements which can be observed and measured objectively with exact scientific methods: that is, the city has been understood as its physical forms, resulting from planning and the norms and conventions which regulate it. Within romanticism, the fundamental character of the built forms has not been their materiality, but their capacity to evoke emotions in the minds of those who experience the forms: that is, the city has been understood as its image, reflecting subjective experiences, common symbols, archetypes, or the spirit of the place or time. In both, the concept of the city has involved the physical form, but the difference was whether the form has been seen as a goal itself or as the means to convey something immaterial. Both concepts have also implied a particular concept of human being, usually not problematized, carrying the presupposition that in relation to built forms, human beings are alike, individual experiences perceived as reflections of a symbolic universe shared by all of humanity.[24] Within hermeneutics, however, the concept of human being is defined by differences, human beings seen as members of (sub)cultures,[25] each with its particular interpretation of the spatial. The idea of plurality also contains the idea of alterity, of otherness, of contradictions, and of structures of domination which have been employed to conceal cultural differences. In each historical context, the meanings of the built forms for the (sub)cultures vary.

Within the concept of the city as a producer of cultures, then, the built city is perceived not only as the stage for social action but as an elementary part of the society, one of the domains within which social relations are constituted. The city is seen as part of the process of producing meanings, without an "end." The built forms of the city carry cultural codes which are understood by the people and which form the basis for their culturally defined ways of life in the city. In the historically formed and continuously changing (sub)cultural practices of the city and in their interpretation, the network of cultural meanings is produced and reproduced every day over and over again. The built forms support some practices, hinder others, and possibly reject some practices altogether. Through the meanings attached to the urban

---

24 On archetypes and symbols, see e.g. Jung 1964, 57ff.; Cassirer 1944, 25ff.; Langer 1953, 82ff., 98ff.
25 For a more detailed discussion of the concept of culture, see below.

practices and their interpretations, the city is seen as the producer of cultures. This concept of the city may be described as difference-oriented and particularizing.

In research on urban built forms, the hermeneutic concept of the city seems to have involved approaches focusing on how built forms have served to support particular cultural practices and reject others. For example, in analyzing the socio-spatial structure of the colonial city, Anthony D. King indicated how within one urban system, separate spatial units, different physically but offering disparate spatial provisions, were developed to the advantage of the colonial cultural group. In reference to the physical-spatial forms manifest in British colonial cities in India and specifically in Delhi, King emphasized the long processes of acculturation through colonialism within which not only the political, technological, and cultural factors, but also the institutions attached to them, influenced the structure of the city and its individual built forms.[26] In other words, built forms were analyzed in particular historical contexts related to a specific society, but, unlike approaches within the romanticist concept of the city which have cultivated the notion of social coherence, King identified the differences and the contradictions between the cultural groups living the city (e.g. colonial vs. indigenous, "European" vs. "Indian") and between their cultural traditions, activities, and values.

The issue of cultural contradictions in urban built forms was also central in James Holston's anthropological critique of Brasília, the modernist capital of Brazil. In his analysis, Holston juxtaposed the intentions embodied in the architects' designs and those motivating the government's plans with the social and cultural reality of the people, in conflict with the hidden agenda of the designs and plans.[27] Both King and Holston approached the built forms as vehicles used by one cultural group to control and reform the ways of life and values of another cultural group, within systems of domination.

Research on urban built forms within the hermeneutic concept of the city, then, although still relatively recent, seems to contain an orientation towards differences and conflicts between cultures simultaneously present in a particular urban context. The point of departure has been the notion of built forms not as the expression of the values of a coherent society, but as a fundamental element in the formation of social processes. Built forms in multicultural contexts such as metropolises in general and Third World cities in particular seem to have been identified as fruitful objects of study. The disciplinary footings also seem more often to be plural.

This study is based on the concept of the city as a producer of cultures, which is connected to the hermeneutic tradition of philosophy and implies a criticism of both the presuppositions and the practices of those concepts of

---

26 King 1976, esp.33-40.
27 Holston 1989, 289.

the city which may be connected either to modernity or romanticism. The cultural approach to the city, as it is conceived here, is at once a study of the built forms and of the conditions within which it is possible to study cities.

In this study, the conceptual network attached to the concept of the city as cultural includes five concepts:

– *culture*, used to refer to a (sub)culture, that is, to any urban community with its particular practices and meanings within the disunified context of other (sub)cultures;

– *otherness*, used to refer to the incommensurable differences between cultures;

– *context*, used to refer to the frame of interpretation, that is, to the particular histories and spaces within which cultural practices and meanings are produced and which make the culture intelligible;

– *meanings*, used to refer to the shared network of signification, rooted in the social practices within a context, a culture; and

– *practices*, used to refer to the network of relations – including both discursive and non-discursive practices – which produce and reproduce the network of meanings and, therefore, the culture.

3 The conceptual network

Culture / (sub)cultures

In defining the concept of culture for this study, we may identify two related but nevertheless differing meanings, depending on whether the reference is to "culture" in the singular or to "cultures" in the plural.[1] As Norbert Elias has shown, the distinction between "culture" and "cultures" may be connected to the historical differences in the usage of the concept: the concept of culture in the singular to the English and French concepts of "civilization/civilisation," and the concept of culture in the plural to the German concept of "Kultur." Elias compared the usages of the two concepts:

> To a certain extent, the concept of civilization plays down the national differences between peoples; it emphasizes what is common to all human beings or – in the view of its bearers – should be . . . In contrast, the German concept of *Kultur* places special stress on national differences and the particular identity of groups . . . Whereas the concept of civilization has the function of giving expression to the continuously expansionist tendency of colonizing groups, the concept of *Kultur* mirrors the self-consciousness of a nation which had constantly to seek out and constitute its boundaries anew, in a political as well as a spiritual sense.[2]

Discussing the concept of culture in the *Dictionnaire de l'ethnologie et de l'anthropologie*, John Galaty and John Leavitt related the concepts to different traditions of philosophy. Thus in the singular, the concept of culture can be traced back to Enlightenment thinkers who conceived culture as opposite to nature: for them, culture distinguished human beings from all other species – it was what made beings human – and carried the ensemble of knowledge acquired by societies in different phases of development.[3] In this context, the concept of culture was understood not merely as the spiritual aspect of human beings but as its progress: the process of the conscious cultivation of the spirit and its products. Among the products of humanity, the arts and the sciences

---

[1] For discussions on the different usages of the concept of culture, see Elias 1978, 3-10; Wallerstein 1990, 31-55; Bonte and Izard 1991, 190-196; Eco 1995, 155-172. See also Williams 1981, 10-16; Williams 1983, 87-93. For bibliographies, see the entry "culture" in Bonte and Izard 1991. On the different usages of the concept of culture in the context of research in architecture, see Nevanlinna 1992a.
[2] Elias 1978, 5f.
[3] Galaty and Leavitt 1991, 193.

were seen as its finest achievements, as illustrations of the perfectibility of the human mind; in essence, they were (the) Culture (with a capital c). The arts and the sciences were conceived as the embodiment of characteristics considered to be exceptional, superior to everyday life. Thus the concept of culture carried not only the aspect of values, "uncultivated" as barbaric and inferior to "cultivated," but also the aspect of norms, what every cultured person should know.[4] True to the general spirit of modernity, both meanings referred to the idea of the historical self-development of humanity. Within this frame, the differences between peoples were explained as different stages on the same ladder of development towards perfection. In other words, peoples who were not perceived as civilized in the "universal" sense of the concept were defined to be at an "earlier" phase of development: they were "savage," "barbaric," or "primitive."[5] Used in the singular, then, the concept of culture implied that both the process of development and its direction towards perfection were to be understood as universal.

In the plural, the concept of culture can be attributed to romanticism, and perhaps in particular to J.G. Herder, the most famous among the romantics who revolted against the Enlightenment idea of a reality comprised of universal, absolute, and objective laws.[6] Since the Renaissance, western thought has been dominated by the view that all achievements of humanity were fundamentally "branches of the same great tree of enlightenment."[7] This approach was questioned by historians, lawyers, and writers who emphasized the differences between the societies of the past and of the present, and between the peoples of Europe and Asia, in whom new interest had risen with the Renaissance and with the discovery of the new continents. The idea of the differences between cultures was essentially against universality and for plurality.[8] Within the frame of romanticism, humanity was seen to be comprised of cultures not only separate but different from each other: a culture was defined as a group of significant discontinuities in relation to the rest of humanity.[9] The unity of an ensemble of characteristics defined it as a culture, as a cohesive entity. The cultural totality was seen as a complex system of relations, a system in which no aspect can be understood devoid of the others, all the phenomena "at the same time juridical, economic, religious, and even

---

4   See "usage II" of the concept of culture in Wallerstein 1990, 32ff, and the discussion of high and elite cultures in LaCapra 1985, 73ff.
5   See e.g. Tylor 1974, esp. Chapter II. Tylor's study was first published in 1871.
6   Berlin 1990, 55. Herder's *Auch eine Philosophie der Geschichte* (Yet Another Philosophy of History) was first published in 1774. The concept of culture, in the plural, as a group of characteristics distinguishing one society from another, had been developed already in the early eighteenth century by Giambattista Vico; his work, however, remained largely unknown until Jules Michelet advocated it in early nineteenth century France (Berlin 1976, 93). Vico's *Scienza Nuova* (New Science) was first published in 1725. For an extensive study on the ideas of Vico and Herder, see Berlin 1976.
7   Berlin 1990, 54.
8   Berlin 1990, 54-59.
9   See also Lévi-Strauss 1963, 295.

aesthetic and morphological, etc."[10] The approach implied the rejection of the idea of universal progress and the acceptance of the value of each culture on its own terms: there are no uncivilized or uncultivated people, just people of different civilizations or cultures. Thus each culture was seen as unique within the diversity of humanity and, as such, esteemed and preserved.

The idea of the culture of a people carried not only the notion of particularity, therefore of value,[11] but also the notion of naturalness, of nature.[12] This connotation legitimated the notion of a people as an organic form of social life, its religion, language, and art growing out of immemorial customs and responses to common experiences.[13] As an organism, a group of people was identified as a community held together by more fundamental reasons than mere contractual obligations. In other words, the social groups forming a culture in the romanticist sense of the concept were seen as "natural" communities, "Gemeinschafts," and not as rational associations, "Gesellschafts."[14] The particularity of a culture therefore involved both the idea of difference from the others and the idea of the originality of the source of this difference, hence its essential nature. In the plural, then, the concept of culture carried the notion of particularity: cultures were not about universal, objective, or absolute categories, but about unique, contextual, and relative entities which contained values possibly fundamentally incompatible with those of other cultures. Thus the concept of culture in the plural referred to a particular way of life, to meanings and values imbedded not only in intellectual and artistic expressions (as the concept of culture in the singular implied) but also in the diverse forms of social life on the everyday level, involving a particular system of collective ideas and all the institutions, ways of acting, habits of thought, and manifestations arising from it.[15] As a way of life, culture was understood to be an entity comprised of aspects which were not autonomous but which were in constant interaction with each other, which formed the particular whole.

In many respects, the two concepts of culture differed: while the approach claiming culture to be universal rejected the possibility of different value systems, the approach maintaining cultures to be incompatible denied the possibility of objective cultural values. However, both concepts of culture contained the notion of uniformity. Cultural universalists saw all aspects of humanity as ultimately uniform: of the same origin and evolving into an integrated unity, the apparent differences between cultures explained as different stages on the ladder of progress, as more or less civilized or more

---

10 Mauss 1990, 79. Cf. also Lévi-Strauss 1963, 358f., 365.
11 Herder quoted in Berlin 1979, 11. See also Gellner 1987, 78.
12 Gellner 1987, 86ff.
13 Cf. Berlin 1979, 11-13.
14 The concepts of Gemeinschaft and Gesellschaft refer to the ideal-typical concepts developed by Ferdinand Tönnies (*Gemeinschaft und Gesellschaft*, first published in 1887; transl. *Fundamental Concepts of Sociology*, 1940).
15 Cf. Williams 1963, 313ff.

or less advanced. This implied both the presupposition of the uniformity of culture as a reality, and the presupposition of the universality of the categories for the study of this reality. Cultural relativists perceived each culture not only as particular and distinct, with its own origins and divergent phases of development, but also as coherent, internally homogeneous and harmonious; inherent in this was the norm of a consensus, an agreement, in the face of outsiders. By definition, discontinuities were identified only between cultures.[16] In both the universalistic and the relativistic conceptions, then, the emphasis was on the idea of culture as a whole: among the universalists, the totality was all of humanity, among the relativists, it was all of a particular culture, understood as homogeneous. For both, the concept of culture has implied coherence.

Derived from the concept of culture in the plural, the concept of subculture has been mainly used in sociology for the study of divergent groups of people living in an integrated setting, typically a large western city. Within sociology, however, the concept of subculture has involved a challenge to the notion of coherence implied in the historical usages of the concepts of culture: in the sociological usage, the totality – the city – was seen as basically heterogeneous and as containing the potential for conflicts between subcultures.[17] Contemporary usages of the concept of subculture have roots in several traditions of research. For this study, three kinds of meanings of the concept of subculture may be distinguished: subculture as class, as ethnicity, and as distinction.

The concept of subculture as class, developed in the mid-nineteenth century by Karl Marx and Friedrich Engels especially for the study of capitalist industrial cities, has more recently also been used in the study of big cities in "less-developed," that is, Third World countries where the processes of industrialization coincided with those of extremely rapid urbanization, detribalization, and sometimes decolonization. Oscar Lewis used the concept of "the culture of poverty" to describe the subculture as an anthropological entity, to see poverty as a way of life which, despite being conditioned by the scarcity of resources, provided rationales and strategies for survival, passed down as traditions from generation to generation.[18] In the second meaning, subcultures as urban ethnic groups comprised of people from different countries and with distinct ways of life, the concept was used in the early twentieth century to study the immigrants from various parts of the world who populated the large industrial cities of northeastern United States. The Chicago School of sociologists used the concept of subculture to analyze the city as the mediator in a process of acculturation from a "mosaic" of

---

16 Within the structuralist approach, the discontinuities are categorized, on the conceptual level, as invariants present in all cultures, that is, as different examples of the same "objective" categories of culture; see e.g. Lévi-Strauss 1963, 295f. Extreme relativists also deny the possibility of any universal categories of study.
17 Cf. Worsley 1984, 51-60.
18 Lewis 1961, xxiv-xxviii. See also Lewis 1975.

different languages, cultures, races, and religions to a "melting-pot" of peoples, where the diversity of the cultures was seen to be, with sufficient time, transformed into a more sophisticated and rational urban way of life.[19] The third meaning, subculture as distinction, has been connected to the notion of the city as the place where unconventional behavior is tolerated more than in non-urban societies. This concept of subculture has not been used to define class or ethnicity, but to refer to a more consciously selected behavior, sometimes even in opposition to a particular way of life, as a "counter-culture" or an "underground" culture. In this definition, the concept of subculture has been conceived as deviation from the behavior of the majority: of conventions followed by "normal" people, not necessarily defined explicitly.[20] The strangeness of the deviant subcultures was perceived as the source of the fascination of the city and as the essence of urbanity; the marginal became valued because it distinguished the city from all other places. Thus the third meaning of the concept of subculture involved a constant tension between the dominant culture and the subordinated cultures distinct from it and challenging its position.

In all three senses, however, the prefix "sub" defined the concept of subculture as a relatively distinguishable social formation within a wider social system: a segment of a larger culture, of a parent culture or a super-culture.[21] The parent culture was seen as a whole in which the subculture is at the same time embedded but of which it also, in a particular way, is distinct. While subcultural studies focused on the characteristics which distinguished the subculture from the larger totality, the content of the parent culture was taken as more or less unproblematic.[22] However, the notion of the parent culture may be questioned, because it implies a whole seen, on some level, as homogeneous, and the subculture as a part of it. Written as (sub)culture, the concept implies the plurality of the communities, with the prefix written in parenthesis to indicate that each community is seen as a totality in itself, not as a formation dependent on a parent culture. The context of these (sub)cultures, then, is not formed by a unified culture conceived as homogeneous, but the disunified collection of all the other (sub)cultures.

---

19 Wirth 1975, 33. Criticizing this, Herbert J. Gans (1968, 34-52, in particular 36ff.) maintained that urban subcultures were not about individuals with ethnic or racial distinctions, but consisted of relatively homogeneous groups each with their particular combination of features relating to ways of life. In his study of an Italian-American area in Boston, Gans (1982, 24-36) identified the subculture in terms of both class and ethnicity as well as in terms of the particular place. On the Chicago school, see above, chapter 1.
20 These deviations included either specific digressions from lawful activities (by delinquents or professional criminals, see e.g. Hannerz 1980, 35-40), from settled life (by urban nomads or "hobos," e.g. Hannerz ibid., 31-35), or from conventional sexual interests (by gays or lesbians, e.g. Wilson 1991, 61-62), or unconventional behavior in general, attached to various groups including artists, snobs, intellectuals, avant-garde musicians, motorcycle enthusiasts, and others. For a discussion of different kinds of subcultures, see e.g. Fischer 1976, 192-197; Sennett 1978, 191; Hebdige 1979; Brake 1980; Davis 1990, 64ff.
21 On the concept of subculture, cf. Fischer 1975, 1323; 1976, 36ff; Hannerz 1980, 294ff; 1982, 55; 1992, 68-81; Clarke et al. 1981, 55.
22 Hannerz 1992, 69.

In this study, the concept of culture is defined as (sub)culture, used to refer to any urban community with its particular values, histories, ways of life, and practices, distinct from other communities. These communities may be formed on the basis of any shared activity or interest, including characteristics like the place of habitation, place of work, occupation, religious or political affiliations, ethnicity, field of interest, or social status, income level, or membership in an association; but in addition to the manifestly common characteristics, the members also share an underlying network of meanings. Each member of a (sub)culture can belong and usually belongs to several (sub)cultures at the same time.

For the study of built form, the concept of subculture also implies that particular built forms are included in the cultural practices and meanings of a community. In other words, members of different subcultures not only "live" built forms in different ways, but within each subculture, the meanings it attaches to the built forms differ from those attached to the same built forms by another subculture: what varies is how built forms are related to the cultural totality, how built forms are about different issues for different subcultures. If this view is accepted, the art historical object of study cannot be built forms as separate physical entities, but the meanings given to the built forms within the (sub)cultures which produce and "live" the built forms.

Otherness

The concept of culture – regardless of whether referring to culture as universal, culture as particular, or subculture – has contained the idea of unity: culture has been about coherence, about characteristics which comprise a whole; but the notion of coherence, of continuity, has also contained the notion of difference, of discontinuity: coherence internally, towards the Self, and difference externally, towards the Other. Within a culture, the identity of a smaller unit or even a single person is defined by its difference towards the others. Thus the Other is not only external to the Self but part of it. Each culture carries an alterity within itself. We may perceive a particular phenomenon as a coherent cultural entity, but its unity is not only contextual and therefore temporary, but also, in a very fundamental sense, produced and conceived by us. In the production of the coherence of the Self, therefore, the concept of difference is essential: the Self is that which is different, what the non-Self, the Other, is not.

Also, the concept of difference is complex. Within modernity, difference was understood in the context of progress as difference from western civilization: an earlier and lower stage of culture, with western civilization defined as the most advanced stage of humanity. "Different" cultures were seen as primitive and archaic, displaying the origins of the universal history of civilization, or as backward and exotic, in need of civilizing control.[23] In essence, the idea of difference carried a dichotomized version of human existence: a generalization in which the internal differences within the Other were reduced to a homogeneous "difference" from the Self. However, just as the Self is never completely coherent, neither is the Other. There is always more than one Other. Instead of a dualistic Self/Other distinction, the concept of difference carries the idea of more than two poles, of multiple distinctions. Thus the idea of culture contains at the same time the notion of the Self as different from the non-Self, the Other, and the notion of the Other as plural, as alterities. The conception of the plurality of cultures opens up the possibility of otherness, as Paul Ricoeur wrote:

> When we discover that there are several cultures instead of just one and consequently at the time when we acknowledge the end of a sort of cultural monopoly, be it illusory or real, we are threatened with destruction by our own discovery. Suddenly it becomes possible that there are just *others*, that we ourselves are an "other" among others.[24]

That is, our values can be perceived as no more universally true than those of any others. The otherness, in a sense, makes the cultures incomparable.

Thus the concept of culture is contextual: a culture is not about autonomous or universal characteristics, but about its relation to other cultures.[25] For the concept of culture, the notion of otherness, of alterity, is fundamental. To define a culture is to distinguish its differences from others in a particular, historically changing, and non-uniform context. A culture exists only through its network of interdependent relationships with its non-homogeneous context of other cultures. Thus, the concept of subculture as a smaller formation within a larger social system, a parent culture, may also be questioned, because it presupposes the existence of a uniform – universal, national, regional – culture. Therefore there are no subcultures, only cultures. Hereafter the concept of culture as otherness, alterity, is used to refer to the concept of (sub)cultures as it was defined for this study.

The notion of the Other, of a discontinuity of the Self, may be seen not

---

23   For example, in 1871, Edward B. Tylor (1974, 23f.) wrote: "Civilization actually existing among mankind in different grades, we are enabled to estimate and compare it by positive examples. The educated world of Europe and America practically settles a standard by simply placing its own nations at one end of the social series and savage tribes at the other, arranging the rest of mankind between these limits according as they correspond more closely to savage or to cultured life . . . Few would dispute that the following races are arranged rightly in order of culture: - Australian, Tahitian, Aztec, Chinese, Italian." Edward W. Said (1983, 264) has argued that contemporary academic Orientalists, for example in the United States, seem to continue to perceive Orientals as essentially backward, illustrated, for example, in the analyses of the Islamic mentality during the October 1973 war.

24   Ricoeur 1965, 278. The concepts of the Other and of alterity have been widely discussed in contemporary cultural and social studies, see e.g. Foucault 1970, 328-335; Said 1978; de Certeau 1986; Vattimo 1988, 145-163; Spivak 1988; Todorov 1989; Baudrillard and Guillaume 1992. The idea of an inner other in individuals has been discussed in the Freudian notion of the subconscious; see e.g. Hauser 1962, 169f; Kristeva 1988, 268f.

25   Cf. Foucault's notion that things do not exist except as relations, Veyne 1978, 228n6.

only as an object of study, but also, at the same time, as an instrument for it. Conventions of writing history in modernity have been founded on the notion that history is about a coherent path of logical development, about the continuity of the process and of the concepts used in describing and explaining it. Romantic historians maintained that the discontinuity represented by Others – like Rousseau's savages – can be overcome with compassion and imagination, by attempting to think as they think.[26] This was based on the idea that fundamentally, all human beings are alike; that is, their otherness could be and was reduced to similarity, their differences were seen as comparable. To use the concept of alterity as an instrument of study, then, requires the reversal of the earlier point of view: instead of perceiving the Other as something we already know, we need to conceive of things we think we know as different, as Carlo Ginzburg maintained:

> The essential instrument is that of alienation, of distancing oneself, the ability to see well-known things as incomprehensible – and not the reverse, as historians do.[27]

Understanding a culture, then, involves the act of becoming an Other, an intellectual exile from our own cultural frame, from the horizon of our understanding which we have not questioned before.

In discussing the concept of culture as otherness, we may refer to cultural anthropology which Gianni Vattimo has described as the encounter with cultures that are Other. To understand a culture is to conceive it as an Other. However, as Vattimo indicated, cultural anthropology is not a domain external to cultures, not a value-free point of objective observation; it is part of the western system of knowledge, carrying particularly formulated western conceptions of otherness.[28] In other words, the alterity of the other cultures is defined on the basis of western ideas in a western context. Within western systems of knowledge, this context is always already there and contains both the object of study – the culture – and the researcher. In this sense, an intellectual exile into otherness from the frame of understanding is problematic.

Cultural anthropology involves the presupposition that although cultures differ from each other, there are structural similarities which recur in each culture, making the ensemble of phenomena into a culture. The presupposition contradicts the idea that all cultures are others and incommensurable. If the concept of culture is understood as fundamental alterity, the otherness of cultures implies an ultimately untranslatable content. That is, the presuppositions of modernity have to be rejected. There is no coherent overview of

---

26 Cf. Lévi-Strauss 1976, 36ff. See also Geertz 1973, 357.
27 "Das grundsätzliche Instrument ist das der Entfremdung, der Fremdmachung, die Fähigkeit, bekannte Dinge als unbegreifbar anzusehen - und nicht umgekehrt, wie es die Historiker machen" (Ginzburg 1983, 22; my translation).
28 Vattimo 1988, 147, 151ff.

reality, no objective point of observation, no external positions of truth, no common rationality nor a unifying language into which all discourses of otherness would be translatable.[29] Culture as otherness is based on the idea that discourses are incommensurable. In this, the definition of culture is located within hermeneutics as a philosophy of understanding. Defined as otherness, then, the concept of culture carries the notion of contextuality, of relations between cultures and the notion of incomparability, of fundamental and untranslatable differences between cultures in terms of values and meanings.

For the study of built forms, the notion of otherness implies that built forms not only relate to different cultures in different ways but that these ways may be and often are incommensurable; moreover, research on built forms occurs within one particular cultural frame and external to other frames. This may be seen to involve a paradox. Access to the researcher's own frame may prevent consciousness of characteristics taken as self-evident, but at the same time, access to the external 'other' frames is restricted because of their incommensurability. For the study of built forms, this could suggest, for example, that researchers from western countries were unable to study both western built forms (because of their inability to perceive their own cultural presuppositions) and "other" (non-western) built forms (because of their western bias). However, the notion of otherness may help in resolving the paradox: there is no unified "western" built form, there is always more than one voice, more than one culture within an object of study.

Contexts

In theories of interpretation, the concept of context has been essential: understanding an event or action has been based on placing it in its context. In the philosophy of language, for example, Charles Taylor, in discussing how we can grasp particular uses of words, stressed that we have to see the word within the context; to find the historical meaning of a text, we have to

> read the text as action in context.[30]

Context, then, gives meaning to an action. This context is comprised not only of the immediate surroundings – for a text, other texts; for a built form, other built forms – but of the shared background of practices, both the said and the unsaid. For anthropology, Clifford Geertz has developed the concept of *thick description* with which he referred to the use of culture as the basis of interpretation:

---

29 Rorty (1980, 3-9, 315-356) has noted that for Cartesian-Kantian philosophers, epistemology has been the unifying language. Cf. Vattimo 1988, 145-163.
30 Taylor 1988, 219; see also Taylor 1985a, 280.

culture is not a power, something to which social events, behaviors, institutions, or processes can be causally attributed; it is a context, something within which they can be intelligibly – that is, thickly – described.[31]

For the interpretation of built forms within the concept of the city as culture, this implies that the understanding of built forms involves their own cultural context within which they can be intelligibly described. However, the cultural context is not to be perceived as unified, but as plural, that is, as contexts, including not only the culture which produced and gives meaning to the built form, but the other cultures. Moreover, these contexts include the historical and spatial contexts – the histories and spaces – of these cultures. An interpretation of particular built forms – a city, for example – therefore involves the contextual frame of understanding, comprised of cultural, historical, and spatial aspects, all three perceived as plural. For this kind of interpretation, no privileged point of observation is available, no context-free study is possible: the researcher is also embedded within a frame of understanding.[32]

In relation to the concept of culture as otherness, contextuality involves the problematization of the concept of history. Within modernity, history was the necessary and continuous process of development towards the perfection of humanity: history was seen as History, following a single course and carrying universal meanings. National histories appeared as local versions of the universal history. Within hermeneutics, however, this notion of history has been challenged. The idea of history as the one true description of a sequence of events following the course of progress has been dissolved and replaced by the idea that histories are many, that they contain narrative aspects ("stories"), and that they are ideological in character. In essence, the dissolution of the universalizing view of history has signified, in Gianni Vattimo's words, the "end of modernity."[33] Instead of an unbroken continuity of the present with the past and to the future, history is to be conceived of as discontinuities, incoherencies, a plurality of histories, a genealogical approach to the past, as Michel Foucault defined it.[34] From this point of view, we may also argue against the idea of a coherent history in relation to the concept of subculture. A unitary history has not only contradicted the notion of the plurality of histories, but has been used to legitimate the sectional interests of one group,[35] a history of victors, the dominant subculture against the dominated others. In this sense, the idea of a plurality of histories corresponds to the notion of a plurality of cultures.

Similarly, contextuality also involves the problematization of the concept

---

31 Geertz 1973, 14.
32 See Taylor 1985a, 280; Rabinow 1977, 150ff.
33 Vattimo 1988, 8ff. See also Eley 1992, 182ff.
34 Foucault 1972, 7-11. See also Foucault 1979, 146ff.
35 Giddens 1979, 188.

of space, of built forms. Within modernity, space was perceived as a material reality: objective, exact, universal, and essentially unambiguous. Within romanticism, spaces, territories, and places were seen as self-evident parts of the coherence comprising a people, a culture. In both, the physical characteristics of the built forms were identified, in a sense, as "given," fixed, and autonomous objects. Michel Foucault questioned the notion of space as an innocent category, emphasizing the influence of spaces in the disposition of power:

> Space is fundamental in any exercise of power.[36]
> A whole history remains to be written of *spaces* – which would at the same time be the history of *powers* (both of these terms in the plural) – from the great strategies of geo-politics to the little tactics of the habitat, institutional architecture from the classroom to the design of hospitals, passing via economic and political installations. It is surprising how long the problem of space took to emerge as a historico-political problem. Space used to be either dismissed as belonging to "nature" – that is, the given, the basic conditions, "physical geography," in other words a sort of "prehistoric" stratum; or else it was conceived as the residential site or field of expansion of peoples, of a culture, a language or a State. It took Marc Bloch and Fernand Braudel to develop a history of rural and maritime spaces. The development must be extended, by no longer just saying that space predetermines a history which in turn reworks and sediments itself in it. Anchorage in a space is an economico-political form which needs to be studied in detail.[37]

Spaces and built forms, then, were seen as instruments for social control, the organizers of the spaces and the built forms as agents in the processes of spatially implemented domination. Analyzing colonial Delhi, Anthony D. King indicated how spatiality was used:

> The segregation of areas performed numerous functions, the first of which was to minimize contact between colonial and colonized populations. For the colonial community they acted as instruments of control, both of those outside as well as those within their boundaries. They helped the group to maintain its own self-identity, essential in the performance of its role within the colonial social and political system . . . The extensive spatial provision within the colonial settlement area, as well as the spatial division between it and the indigenous settlement, are to be accounted for not simply in terms of cultural differences but in terms of the distribution of power. Only this can explain why labor and urban amenities were available in the spacious, cultivated areas in the colonial settlement, but not in the indigenous town.[38]

---

36 Foucault 1984, 252.
37 Foucault 1980, 149.
38 King 1976, 39f.

In the Delhi described by King, the built forms were not the same for members of different cultures: the spatial organization served the cultural and social policies of the colonizers. But this complex network of relations was not only about how the colonial culture could form spaces to control the other cultures. If the concept of cultures as incommensurable alterities is accepted, the spaces – albeit physically unambiguous – are about different issues for different cultures. That is, different groups of people, different cultures, attach different meanings to a particular space, a particular built form. In this sense, the otherness of cultures implies the otherness of spaces.

For the study of built forms, the notion of context implies that the idea of universal theories of built form (architecture, urban space, etc.) must be dismissed. If built forms are perceived as cultural, their contexts are formed by practices with histories. In the study of built forms, then, the histories of the cultural practices within which the built forms were produced are fundamental.

Meanings and practices

The concept of culture involves values, as Max Weber indicated:

> The concept of culture is a *value-concept*. Empirical reality becomes "culture" to us because and insofar as we relate it to our value ideas. It includes those segments and only those segments of reality which have become significant to us because of this value-relevance. Only a small portion of existing concrete reality is colored by our value-conditioned interest and it alone is significant to us. It is significant because it reveals relationships which are important to use due to their connection with our values.[39]

Events or objects are seen as part of (a) culture only if they carry meaning for and within (the) culture. The definition of the concept of culture, however, has essentially been connected to what can be taken as significant in relation to the culture: the definition of the concept of culture has also been a definition of the values and of the meanings of what is understood as culture. In this, the concepts of culture as universal, of culture as particular, and of culture as otherness fundamentally differed from each other.

For the concept of culture as universal, differences among people were perceived ultimately as obstructions of what is truly human: "the constant, the general, the universal."[40] Within modernity, this was based on the presuppositions – reflecting the Platonic ideal – that the values of human beings can be objectively defined, that they are universal, and that true values must necessarily be compatible with each other and form a single whole.[41]

---

39 Weber 1949, 76.
40 Geertz 1973, 35.
41 Berlin 1990, 183f., 5f.

In other words, within the concept of culture as universal, values were seen as absolute, carrying meanings which are objective and the same for all of humanity. For the concept of culture as particular, each culture has been seen as containing its own autonomous values and its particular view of the world. Each culture could be understood by others only in terms of the meanings the members of the culture themselves attached to what they did and what was done to them.[42] The self and the idea of the intellectual autonomy of the individual was even seen as a more real source of values than the external reality.[43] Thus the concept of culture as particular has carried the idea of values unique to each culture, and, in their differences, as perhaps fundamentally incommensurable.

For the concept of culture as otherness, values are based on meanings within a context; there are no universal or unique meanings without a relation to their context. Thus values are seen as contained within a social reality of meanings where each meaning presupposes the context of the meanings of other things. Within interpretive hermeneutics, these kinds of realities cannot be reduced to the subjective realities of individuals' values or beliefs, nor to the presumed objective reality of physical descriptions, but have to be approached through meanings which are shared. The social reality and the language used to describe it are inseparable: the language both constitutes the social reality and is constituted by it.[44] Thus the concept of culture as otherness also involves the conceptual organization of the systems of meaning, that is, of language. In the discussion of meanings, the concept of language is essential.

Within modernity, the idea of language has been that of a tool: a means of flawlessly reflecting the non-verbal reality. Scientific language – purified of its singularities and standing passively at a distance from the reality to be conveyed – has been seen as a neutral vehicle describing strictly that which was known. Thus, language has also carried the idea of universality characteristic to modernity as the objective and undistorting mirror of reality. The idea of language as a mirror is in its complete detachment both from its context and from its content: the detachment makes it universal.

Within romanticism, language has had a totally different role. Instead of being the universal mirror of a reality, as in modernity, it has been seen as a shared symbolism: the expression of "the collective experience of the group."[45] Symbols have been understood as not merely one of the vehicles for thinking, but as the only possible means of access to thoughts, attitudes, and feelings. Isaiah Berlin has referred to the philosophical ideas of Giambattista Vico:

---

42 Berlin 1990, 75f.
43 Hauser 1962, 167-172.
44 Taylor 1987, 53-63.
45 Herder (*Sämtliche Werke*, ed. B. Suphan, Berlin, 1877-1913, IX, 225) quoted in Berlin 1976, 169.

> Ideas, and the symbols in which they are expressed, are not, even in thought, separable. We do not merely speak or write in symbols, we think and can think only in symbols, whether words or images; the two are one.[46]

Language has been seen as the essential medium of making a group into one: a people, a culture, a nation; it has carried the traditions and the memories of a culture. It has been historically developed, inherited, and could not have been made out of nothing, as in Isaiah Berlin's description of Johann Gottfried Herder's views on language:

> Words, by connecting passions with things, the present with the past, and by making possible memory and imagination, create family, society, literature, history.[47]

Within romanticism, then, language has in no sense been neutral or detached as it has been within modernity, but quite the opposite: language has been seen as the very embodiment of the particularity of a culture. Like language, art as a symbolic language has been seen within romanticism not only as a representation of reality but as an incarnation of that reality;[48] according to Ernst Cassirer, art,

> like all the other symbolic forms . . . is not the mere reproduction of a ready-made, given reality. It is one of the ways leading to an objective view of things and of human life. It is not an imitation but a discovery of reality.[49]

By romanticists, art has been perceived as the expression of the personal feeling of an artist, but because artistic creation has involved symbols, the ideas presented through the work of art have been understood to transcend individual experience and to be connected to the collective experience of the group, just like myth and language.[50] Art has been seen as a kind of language, a medium to gain access to the fundamental truths of humanity, the collective experience from the past which was beyond thought, time, and memory. This has involved the belief that although fundamental truths cannot be reached – nor should this be attempted – through conscious pursuit, art and the subconscious operating in its creation were the means of overcoming the difficulty.[51]

For the philosophers of hermeneutics, language has referred to meanings:

---

46   Berlin 1976, 42.
47   Berlin 1976, 168.
48   Cassirer 1944, 168.
49   Cassirer 1944, 143.
50   Langer 1953, 390. Because of their capacity to express the collective subconscious through forms, artists have been perceived as exceptional and vitally important to the community. C.G. Jung (1964, 57f.) linked myths to the subconscious in his concept of the archetype which he defined as the tendency of the unconscious mind to form mythic representations.
51   See above, chapter 2.

not only meanings of words but also of things which could be "read" like words. The concept of language has been connected to include all forms of being which can be understood.[52] Thus the idea of language has been extended to comprise all expressions of life which carry meaning, that is, all meaningful action. To read a thing is to understand the meaning it carries: to read the meaning as articulated within and by the traces of the action.[53] These meanings are neither universal nor objective in the sense that their validity could be confirmed by empirical data only; they always presuppose specific values and are, as such, founded on a particular culture. For the concept of culture as otherness, then, language has been the essential medium for producing and understanding meanings.

In hermeneutics, social reality cannot be identified detached from the language used to describe it, operate it, or act on it: language constitutes reality.[54] Language contains not only the concepts used to describe reality but also the meanings attached to them. Meanings are the essence of language. Language is formed within and by a culture: to understand a language is to understand a culture.[55] Meanings are not pre-determined but are connected to language through use, through social practices.[56] These practices are culturally based, that is, they are not individual actions but modes of social relation, they carry meanings which are not subjective but mutual to human subjects, intersubjective, and they are not absolute or universal but contextual. To understand a language, therefore, is to understand the shared background of practices which may not be explicitly informed but which forms the context of the language.

Practices are forms of continuing social life: what human beings do. Practices include both actions and words. More precisely, practices are about social realities: about the ways of doing things. The concept of practice is central to the discussion of the relationship between social reality and meaning. The concept contains the idea of the practices as a network: the system of relations that can be established between practices. Thus the system of practices occurring in a particular situation is not about detailed instances of categories assumed to be universal, but about meanings specific to the culture. By constituting the objects and the events of the culture, the network

---

52   Gadamer 1976, 99-104.
53   Ricoeur 1981, 206f.
54   Taylor 1987, 54ff. However, following Quentin Skinner (1988, 250), I do not deny the existence of a mind-independent world but maintain that observational evidence is always to an extent shaped by our concepts and thus our language. Cf. also Roy Bhaskar's (1978, 25ff.) description of transcendental realism.
55   Cf. Wittgenstein (1958, I, para.19, 18e): "to imagine a language means to imagine a form of life."
56   According to Dreyfus (1991, 219), Martin Heidegger (*Being and Time*, 1927) saw meanings in the background of social practices: "language is used in a shared context that is already meaningful, and it gets its meaning by fitting into and contributing to a meaningful whole." Wittgenstein's concept of language-games - which are also forms of life - conveyed the idea that language and action presuppose and define each other reciprocally (Wittgenstein 1974, para.204, 28e; see also para.229, 30e; Wittgenstein 1980, 85e).

contributes to the generation of that culture. This network of urban practices, like Michel Foucault's formulation of the concept of "dispositif" implies, is

> a thoroughly heterogeneous ensemble consisting of discourses, institutions, architectural forms, regulatory decisions, laws, administrative measures, scientific statements, philosophical, moral and philanthropic propositions – in short, the said as much as the unsaid,[57]

and most importantly, the different ways of "living" a city: the different urban cultures, the different "lived" interpretations of the city. In this context, built forms themselves are seen as representations of the practices. The coherence of the network of practices implies the existence of a totality, a culture. Within the culture, the coherence generates actions, objects, and concepts which are consistent with the values of the culture, that is, they are foreseeable, and which can be understood by the members of the culture, that is, they are intelligible in the particular context, thus "normal."

Within the concept of practices, the notions of otherness, contexts, and meanings converge. The practices of the present do not constitute a completely coherent totality, but are comprised of differences, of pluralities, and of contradictions, forming cultures which are fundamentally other. Moreover, practices carry the past within them in that they are based on tradition, on the histories of the practices, although, as Hans-Georg Gadamer emphasized,

> the confrontation of our historic tradition is always a critical challenge of this tradition . . . Every experience is such a confrontation.[58]

Finally, practices are recursive, that is, they presuppose and are generated within a frame of meaning, a culture, and, at the same time, they serve to constitute the social reality as a frame of meaning. Pierre Bourdieu used the concept of *habitus* to describe the recursive character of practices:

> The homogeneity of habitus is what – within the limits of the group of agents possessing the schemes (of production and interpretation) implied in their production – causes practices and works to be immediately intelligible and foreseeable, and hence taken for granted . . . the habitus, the product of history, produces individual and collective practices, and hence history, in accordance with the schemes engendered by history. The system of dispositions – a past which survives in the present and tends to perpetuate itself into the future by making itself present in practices structured according to its principles, an internal law relaying the continuous exercise of the law of external necessities (irreducible to immediate conjunctural constraints) – is the principle of the continuity and regularity which objectivism discerns in the social world without being able to give them a rational basis.[59]

57　Foucault 1980, 194. According to Dreyfus and Rabinow (1982, 120ff.), Foucault's concept "dispositif" has no satisfactory equivalent; they suggested the "grid of intelligibility." It has also been translated as the "apparatus" (see e.g. Foucault 1980, 194ff.).
58　Cf. Gadamer 1987, 87.
59　Bourdieu 1977, 80, 82.

Through practices we produce meanings. Meaning and significance are not "found in" or "deduced from" events or objects; they are conferred on reality by human beings.[60] But meanings cannot be produced in a void: they are always preceded by a context which already contains meanings. A person is born into a community and becomes its member by adopting the existing tradition of meanings of the community through language and non-discursive practices. Language can be used as an example of this. As a discursive practice, language is an expression of meanings relating to both history – what has been already said[61] – and experience – how we appropriate the ongoing reality, as Hans-Georg Gadamer wrote:

> language ... is the reservoir of tradition and the medium in and through which we exist and perceive the world.[62]

If practices are perceived as not simply repetitions of history but as phenomena with a potential for genuine originality, language becomes a field of tension between two opposite forces. As the locus of tradition, of the unspoken habits of thought, language, in Michel Foucault's words, "accumulates an ineluctable memory which does not even know itself as memory,"[63] that is, it carries meanings which are implicit and which remain unchanged because they are taken for granted. As the locus of practices, language is related to everyday life and to our self-reflection of it in specific contexts of meaning, that is, it carries meanings which are explicit and which are continuously challenged with demands to constitute the changing practices.

Meanings are given within a context, a particular frame of understanding. In this frame, meanings are produced not by events or objects in isolation but by their relations to each other, by the relations into which the events or objects are entered. Like practices, meanings exist through their network of interdependent relationships with their context, comprised of other meanings.[64]
To understand a phenomenon in a culture, then, is to understand it in the context of a network of meanings. The connection is not about a logical (formal) relation between the phenomenon and its context, but about the coherence of all the relations within the context, in a sense the coherence of the network of meanings within the culture. This overall organization of meanings could be compared to the "web of signification" identified by Max Weber,[65] the "hidden grammar" described by Paul Veyne,[66] or the "grid of intelligibility" suggested by Hubert L. Dreyfus and Paul Rabinow.[67] The

---

60 Cf. Weber 1949, 81.
61 Cf. Foucault 1973, xvi.
62 Gadamer 1976, 29.
63 Foucault 1970, 297. See also Geertz 1973, 45.
64 Taylor 1987, 41ff.
65 Geertz 1973, 5, referring to Weber.
66 Veyne 1978, 215.
67 Dreyfus and Rabinow 1982, 120f.

network of meanings forms a frame which implies immediate intelligibility within the frame and unintelligibility – otherness – from the outside. In this sense, the concept of culture as otherness can be conceived as a network of meanings.

Finally, in the study of built forms, the researcher is also involved in the network of meanings and practices. The object of study formulated, the concepts selected, the data referred to, the methods employed – all carry a particular frame of understanding which is not value-free or context-free. In this sense, the theories of built forms are part of the practices which serve to establish, maintain and strengthen a particular frame of understanding and, therefore, to question or subordinate other frames of understanding. In essence, then, in research on built forms practices are seen as more fundamental than theories.

■ 4 Interpreting built forms

Theoretical implications

In the writing of art history, built forms have sometimes been approached as objects designed by an author. Inherent has been the presupposition of the coherence of the object and of the author, with the built forms seen as expressions of various influences. Art historically, the interpretation of the built forms has related to the recovery of the intentions of the author.[1] For the study of cities, for example, Spiro Kostof has suggested that we can

> "read" [city-]form correctly only to the extent that we are familiar with the precise cultural conditions that generated it.[2]

In this, the earlier notion of the designer as the author of the object has been replaced by the notion of cultural conditions, but the idea of physical forms as expressions of the origins has been retained, the "correct" reading to be recovered by the architectural historian.

However, if built forms are perceived as meaningful action, we may study them as texts. To approach built forms as texts involves processes of interpretation, of reading. The reading of built forms may be compared to the interpretation of texts. Paul Ricoeur has called the object of understanding depth semantics:

> The depth semantics of the text is not what the author intended to say, but what the text is about, i.e., the non-ostensive reference of the text. And the non-ostensive reference of the text is the kind of world opened up by the depth semantics of the text. Therefore what we want to understand is not something hidden behind the text, but something disclosed in front of it. What has to be understood is not the initial situation of the discourse, but what points toward a possible world. Understanding has less than ever to do with the author and his situation. It wants to grasp the proposed worlds opened up by references of the text. To understand a text is to follow its movement from sense to reference, from what it says, to what it talks about.[3]

The notion of built forms as texts grows out of the construction of the object of study in art history. When urban built forms are conceived of as texts, the

---

1   See, for example, Porphyrios 1981; Wolff 1993, chapter 6.
2   Kostof 1991, 10.
3   Ricoeur 1981, 128.

art historical object is not physical entities but the network of urban practices which have produced and continues to reproduce the meanings of the urban forms. As texts, built forms are plurivocal; we may say that they are open to several readings, or, that they carry different meanings for different groups of people, communities, cultures. Built forms, then, are seen as representations of the different networks of practices of the cultures: they may be studied as traces of the meanings the various urban cultures have attached to them. These traces contain histories of urban practices. In this study, then, the object of study is the networks of practices and meanings within which urban built forms, planned or unplanned, are produced.

The relationships between social practices and built forms have earlier been investigated in several fields of study. In his introduction to a collection of essays on the social development of the built environment, Anthony D. King identified three main bodies of research. In the first, the physical environment and buildings have been related to social and cultural variables; these approaches have been used in cultural geography and social and cultural anthropology. According to King, within anthropology and architecture, these studies have usually concentrated on "exotic" and non-western cultures and on dwellings. In the second, the city was studied as a social entity, but the actual built forms were mostly dismissed from the analyses; this approach has been identified within urban sociology. As King noted,

> the attempt to relate other, non-domestic elements in the built environment . . . to forms of economic, social and political organisation in a broader sociological understanding of social development seems to be relatively rare.[4]

In the third body of research, the built environment has been studied historically; this approach has included urban, social and economic history, urban and historical geography, the history of housing and planning, and architectural and building history. King maintained that approaches of architectural history have often been selective, the studies focused on objects assessed to contain aesthetic value, with the relation to the built form to the social or economic basis of the culture neglected.[5]

Philosophy was not mentioned in King's description, although he did refer to the work of Michel Foucault, best described, perhaps, as a historian of philosophy. For the discussion of the relationship between society and space, Foucault has injected important new openings. Foucault studied how from the seventeenth century onwards, particular built forms – from individual buildings to towns – were used as laboratories for social experiments:

> A whole problematic then develops: that of architecture that is no longer built simply to be seen (as with the ostentation of palaces), or

---

4 King 1980, 5.
5 King 1980, 3-8.

to observe external space (cf. the geometry of fortresses), but to permit an internal, articulated and detailed control – to render visible those who are inside it; in more general terms, an architecture that would operate to transform individuals: to act on those it shelters, to provide a hold on their conduct, to carry the effects of power right to them, to make possible to know them, to alter them.[6]

Foucault questioned the notions of architecture and space as socially neutral elements, perceiving built forms as political technologies of power. For this study, Foucault's concept of built forms has been useful. Yet Foucault's avoidance, in relation to the concept of power, of the notion of agency – of power as interventions by communities, institutions, or individuals – conveys the idea of power as un-localized, as devoid of cultural context. In this sense, Foucault's notions of architecture and space are problematic. In this study, then, Foucault's concept of built forms is employed with cultural differences as the point of departure. Built forms are perceived of as instruments of control not by power in general, but within a particular urban context in terms of the relations of power between different cultures. Built forms are approached as elements which serve to establish particular cultural practices and to reject others. Through the built forms of a particular culture, the practices of that culture, that community, are presented as self-evident and obvious, while those of other cultures are silenced. In this way, the built forms serve to naturalize particular ways of "living" the city, particular interpretations of the built forms of the city.

Practical implications

To interpret built forms is to understand their meanings within their particular context. This implies that the meanings cannot be reconstructed on the basis of universalities, in theory, but only through particular urban practices in conjunction with specific built forms and their histories, in practice. In this sense, the notion of a real historical object of study is fundamental. In this study, the built form selected was Nairobi. For a cultural study of urban form, Nairobi was exemplary. As capital of Kenya in eastern Africa, Nairobi was in 1983 (when the field study was done) a metropolis of around a million inhabitants growing at an enormous rate. Its history reaches to 1899 when British colonialists established in the middle of nowhere a tiny railway town on the railway line being constructed between the coast at the Indian Ocean and the central parts at Lake Victoria. From the very beginning, its population has been multicultural, the major groups being the "Africans," the "Asians," and the "Europeans," as they are commonly formulated in Nairobi. These groups have not integrated into each other, but have retained their distinctions;

---

6   Foucault 1979, 172.

at the same time, each culture of Nairobi differs from that of its "origin."[7]

Colonial cities have been a particular object of interest among researchers who have developed approaches relating the cultural and the spatial aspects of societies. Some researchers have suggested that by enlarging the scope from western cities, a study of colonial cities provides possibilities for more global generalizations on both fundamental social processes and universally applicable urban theory.[8] For others, the object of study has been the colonial society; according to them, the history of western urban planning can be better understood by analyzing its colonial implementations, sometimes perceived as laboratories of experimentation.[9] In some studies, the argumentation has been based on the notion that the "origin" of the city could somehow provide explanations for its present problems, the time frame restricted to the colonial phase or part of it.[10] Although several researchers have emphasized that a typology for *the* colonial city cannot be constructed because of the diversities involved,[11] the concept has nevertheless been employed. It must be pointed out, however, that both the concept of the colonial city and the concept of post- or neo-colonial city contain presuppositions on the primacy of the colonial phase in understanding the history and present of the city, and suggests, at least for an extent of time, its economic, political, and cultural dependence on a western power.

In this study, Nairobi is not approached as a colonial city in the sense as in the studies referred to above. Nairobi is here perceived primarily as a multicultural city like other metropolises of the world, a capital with its own history. Although part of its history has been colonial – as are the histories of many major cities, including Paris, London, New York, Rio de Janeiro, Bombay, Saigon, and Helsinki – the orientation of the study is based on contemporary Nairobi. In this respect, the intentions of the study correspond with those expressed by Janet Abu-Lughod for her study of Rabat in Morocco:

> This book . . . is not an antiquarian exercise in reconstructing the past. It is an attempt both to explain the present and to pose a moral problem for the future.[12]

To interpret the urban built form of Nairobi, then, is to study the histories of contemporary Nairobi, or, more precisely, the histories of the urban practices in Nairobi and their interpretations. For this study, the beginning is the description – or diagnosis – of Nairobi as it appeared when the field study was made, that is, in 1983.

---

7   For a more detailed discussion of the cultural distinctions, see below.
8   See, for example, the studies quoted in King 1976, 13-15.
9   See e.g. Ross and Telkamp 1985, 2; Rabinow 1989, 289; Wright 1991, 3. In 1934, the Parisian art critic Léandre Vaillat wrote of Morocco that it is a "laboratory of Western life and a conservatory of oriental life" (*Le Périple marocain*, p.55, quoted in Wright 1991, 85).
10 The notion of "origins" has in some studies been replaced by the idea of major changes which are still evident, see e.g. Dossal 1991, xiii, 1ff.
11 See e.g. de Bruijne 1985; King 1985; King 1990.
12 Abu-Lughod 1980, xviii.

PART TWO

RE-PRESENTING NAIROBI

■ 5 Beginnings

To present the Nairobi of 1983, that is, of the time of my field study, is to locate the idea of Nairobi within a pre-existing universe of meanings. Each description involves words which carry particular pre-existing connotations both to the one who writes the description and to the ones who read it. In this sense, a presentation of Nairobi is always also a re-presentation: a repetition of something already written. But a presentation of Nairobi is also a representation in another sense. To present Nairobi as an object of study in art history is to transform non-textual (including visual) material into text, to use words as representations of a reality. This representation of a reality involves a reduction of the complexity of the reality to produce a coherence within the text. In essence, the textualization of a reality is about translation, about the conversion of events, objects, and relations into a coherent system of meanings. The system of meanings attached to the context of the text not only affects what can be represented but may also convert the experience of the reality. In a very fundamental sense, then, a representation of Nairobi also involves its reproduction: the creation of Nairobi in a particular context for a particular end, in this case, as an object of study in art history.

Approaching Nairobi for the first time cannot occur in the context of an unwritten sheet, a "tabula rasa," neither for me in 1980 when I first visited the city nor for the readers, regardless of their relation to Nairobi. In texts, Nairobi has conventionally been seen as an urban conglomerate in a developing country with a colonial history, the core words being "developing" and "colonial." Both concepts have implied the western countries as the point of reference. The notion of development has referred not only to the path of progress seen as universal but also to the "developed" western countries (and the United States in particular) as the model. Conceptually, development has involved the notions of the economic growth as well as the political, social and cultural change of societies perceived to be dominated by poverty, inequalities and ignorance, development connoting essentially their modernization or, as Wolfgang Sachs put it, westernization:

> From the start, development's hidden agenda was nothing else than the Westernization of the world.[1]

---

1   Sachs 1992, 3f. On the concepts of development and modernization, see e.g. Esteva 1992, 6-25; Worsley 1984, 16ff.; Boudon and Bourricaud 1986, 396-404.

The notion of colonialism has referred to the political and military control of a distant area or country by a (usually European) empire; from the point of view of the imperial power, this has included the development of the colony.[2] In this sense, the concepts of development and colonialism have been connected. Today, references to the colonial history of a country emphasize that aspect of the country's past related to the history of its colonizer and reject aspects outside of it; at the same time, they also carry the connotation of a dependency – economic, technological, and cultural, even if no more political – which still continues. To conceive Nairobi as a post-colonial city in a developing country, therefore, is to perceive it as a city which historically has been dependent on the "developed" world but which may eventually, with help from the "developed" countries, be able to become more like them. It is in this context that studies on the built forms of Nairobi have usually been conducted.

With emphasis on the concept of development, two main lines of inquiry, closely related, may be discerned: one linked to urbanization and urban growth as a spatial phenomenon, the other to housing in general and to unauthorized squatter settlements in particular. In studies on the spatial development of Kenya, Nairobi has been perceived as the at once most modernized center of Kenya and a very urban European "island." For example, in his spatial analysis done after independence, Edward W. Soja described the morphology of towns in Kenya as reflecting the "lack of participation by Africans in urban culture," that is, the recentness of permanent urban African communities, regardless of the fact that Africans formed the bulk of the urban population through most of the colonial period.[3] A similar orientation based on the colonial past of Kenya and the position of Nairobi within it can be observed in a variety of studies on urban spatiality, including Samson M. Kimani's "The Structure of Land Ownership in Nairobi" where the patterns of land ownership were seen as the result of the colonial policies, and R.A. Obudho's "Urbanization and Development Planning in Kenya" where the spatial organization of central places in Kenya was perceived to have been developed and consolidated during the colonial period. In a geographical study of African cities, Anthony O'Connor identified the physical form of Nairobi as colonial and European in origin.[4] Many, if not most, of the spatial studies of Nairobi, then, seem to have focused on aspects seen to be derived from its past as a colonial city. References to the west seem to have dominated urban research in Nairobi regardless of whether the interest of the researchers has been that of seeing the built form of Nairobi as part of European history, as part of the country's colonial history, or as both, as G.A. de Bruijne described the

---

2   On the concepts of colonialism and imperialism, see e.g. Said 1993, 7f., 128ff.; Izard 1991, 160-163.
3   Soja 1968, 48f.; see also 107. For his own reappraisal of the approach, Soja 1979.
4   Kimani 1972, 398; Obudho 1979, 245ff.; O'Connor 1983, 193-195, 198ff.

developing (post-)colonial cities of today.[5]

Moreover, the more systematic analyses of the urban form of Nairobi seem mostly to have been attached to planning, either on a general level, such as Dorothy M. Halliman's and W.T.W. Morgan's study of the city at independence, or as part of the preparation of a particular plan, such as the historical and descriptive sections of the *Nairobi Master Plan* of 1948 or the studies made by the Urban Study Group for the *Nairobi Metropolitan Growth Strategy* of 1973. Thus the studies have usually included either the identification of planning problems, a discussion of planning strategies, or planning recommendations.[6] In this respect, a noteworthy exception among the urban studies of Nairobi was the analysis by Sören Emig and Zahir Ismael of the four official town plans in 1900-1980 they assessed as the most important, studied in relation to the political-economic conjunctures of each period[7]; although critical towards the political implications of the plans, Emig and Ismael saw the planning of Nairobi in the context of its colonial history, the western conceptions of development and planning accepted as self-evident presuppositions.

Studies on housing areas in Nairobi have focused on two topics: unauthorized settlements and land utilization patterns. Of these, research on unplanned squatter areas – sometimes also referred to as slums – has been connected to their improvability and to development plans. David Etherton's study of Mathare Valley, the largest area of uncontrolled housing in Nairobi, contained a physical survey of the site development, house types and construction as well as a social survey of the households, and was intended as background material for planning by the City Council and for proposed improvement schemes.[8] These kinds of studies have not only supported planning, but to an extent have also begun to make the unauthorized forms of habitation more legitimate. Describing squatter areas in Zambia, three planners even noted that the built forms could be perceived as derived from a particular – African and urban – lifestyle and not from the imposition of foreign (colonial) legal systems.[9] In his study of the "other face of two-faced Nairobi," its "self-help city," Andrew Hake identified these areas of temporary dwellings and marginal employment as having an "immense potential for creative development" for the transformation of the society.[10] Land use patterns have been investigated in surveys of Nairobi housing areas. George Gattoni and Praful Patel, for example, described and compared twelve "localities" representing the five types of residential development they had

---

5   de Bruijne (1985, 231) did not refer directly to Nairobi.
6   Halliman and Morgan 1967; MP 1948. On the studies related to the *Metropolitan Growth Strategy*, e.g. Kimani 1972, 1981.
7   Emig and Ismael 1980.
8   Etherton 1971, iv. For other studies of informal settlements in Nairobi, see e.g. Morrison 1972, Chana and Morrison 1973, Memon 1982, Amis 1987; for discussions of solutions to the unauthorized housing problem, see e.g. Weisner 1976, Soni 1980, Chana 1984.
9   Andrews, Christie and Martin 1973.
10 Hake 1977, 9, 250ff.

recognized in Nairobi: suburban, rural village, tenement, squatter, and municipal housing; their categorization was based on differences in population density, modes of development, user income, control of open space, and dwelling unit types.[11] Gattoni and Patel's study was also used at the Massachusetts Institute of Technology in the compilation of an *Urbanization Primer* intended as a reference framework, "addressed to questions of urbanization, specifically, land subdivision and the provision of services for the most needy sectors of the population."[12] In the Primer, seven Nairobi residential localities were described.[13] Although manifestly advocating an approach based on actual practice under widely different conditions, the proposed design criteria were universal: technical and cost-oriented, with emphasis on utilities, circulation, and uniform geometric land use models.

Thus the studies on urbanism and housing in Nairobi have contained a definite bias within which universal models have been applied to both the problematization of the issues and to the methodological approaches. In the studies, the idea of "less-developed" countries and "the most needy" groups within the city has dominated, but the proposed solutions have been based on mathematical calculations and geometric models presented as universal. Technological progress and cost minimization have been perceived as essential, but the influence of the changes on the lives of the people has not been discussed. In describing the areas, the physical characteristics of the built forms have been seen as central, while their relation to the ways of life have hardly been mentioned. The scope of the studies has been the future, with the present and sometimes historical details described only to support the idea of improvement.

However, with emphasis on the concept of colonialism, other kinds of studies of Nairobi's built forms may be identified. In these studies, Nairobi's built forms have not referred to the city as a whole nor to housing areas, but to individual buildings, particularly those constructed by and for the colonizing power. In the context of colonial or British colonial architecture, examples from Nairobi have been few. For example, the over 1600 pages of Banister Fletcher's massive *A History of Architecture* contained references to just seven cases of Nairobi architecture, three of which had been designed by the famous architect Herbert Baker prior to the Second World War, one "impressive achievement" not designed by an architect at all (nor was it completed according to the design), a mosque "faithful to tradition" (i.e. not "designed" in the western sense of the word) and two post-Independence

---

11 Gattoni and Patel 1973, 8-12.
12 Caminos and Goethert 1980, 7. The approach was developed at the program in Urban Settlement Design in Developing Countries, carried out at the School of Architecture and Planning, Massachusetts Institute of Technology, the notes compiled in 1976 in a Primer for site and services projects, prepared at the request of the International Bank for Reconstruction and Development (World Bank), Washington D.C. (p.4).
13 Caminos and Goethert 1980, 94f., 208-219.

constructions with forms relating to the climate and built forms of Africa.[14] Compared to the extensive presentation of the architecture of, for example, South Africa, Nairobi nearly did not appear on the map of architecture. David Aradeon's quotation from the *Architectural Review* and comment suggest one reason:

> "The tropical territories are the less developed areas of the world; they are inhabited by colonial or ex-colonial peoples vigorously emerging into nationhood and faced, while they do so, with the problem of assimilating European techniques and ideas of progress." In 1960 the *Architectural Review* had no doubt that such assimilation and Westernization was the way forward for the newly independent African states, while recognizing that although "in due course each territory will no doubt become self-sufficient architecturally, for most of them this will be a long process, and they are only now beginning to acquire their own architectural professions and architectural schools. Not till they have done [it], perhaps, can they expect to achieve a consistent architectural style recognizably their own."[15]

Each "less-developed" country, then, was to generate an architectural style of its own to express its individual character. Architecture as an expression and symbol of a people's unity had been Herbert Baker's governing idea when he designed buildings for the British Empire, as Derek Linstrum, referring to the Union Buildings of Pretoria (South Africa), wrote:

> As an imperial symbol it achieved what Baker intended when he wrote about the parallels between architecture, which "within the limits of order, true science and progress" provides scope for self-expression, and British colonial rule, which conferred "order, progress and freedom within the law to develop national civilizations on the lines of their own tradition and sentiment."[16]

In the study of Nairobi's built forms, then, histories of architecture were of little use. Like the analyses of urbanism and housing, the histories of architecture were biased in favor of points of view which could be described as "western" or "Euro-American." Visual representations of Nairobi have supported such a perspective. Photographs in professional books and journals, newspapers, travel books, postcards, films in television news and documentaries, and similar material, often used to illustrate texts, have conventionally presented Nairobi – its physical form – with images either of dilapidated squatter areas, of the modern but anonymous skyscraper center, or, sometimes, of the Kenyatta Conference Center, the contemporary architectural landmark of the city. These presentations of Nairobi have functioned as re-presentations which satisfy one's expectations, operating much in the same way Edward W. Said described the work of the Orientalist:

---

14 Fletcher 1987, 1189, 1385f., 1390, 1393.
15 Aradeon (Section "Post-Independence" in chapter 42) in Fletcher 1987, 1389.
16 Linstrum (chapter 33) in Fletcher 1987, 1205.

> For what the Orientalist does is to *confirm* the Orient in his reader's eyes; he neither tries nor wants to unsettle already firm convictions.[17]

The images evoked both by texts and by pictures not only presented a view of Nairobi as an "ex-colonial" city in a "developing" country, but also produced this view as a prescription: they served to make Nairobi into that particular kind of city. To question the approaches used to present and represent Nairobi as a built form, then, is to question the already constituted field of discourse, essentially, to question the presuppositions inherent in the earlier approaches. What this could involve may be illustrated by two quotations, two descriptions of a "colonial city" by two non-European writers.

Franz Fanon saw the colonial world as a world divided in two, the native town and the settlers' town confronting each other:

> The settlers' town is a strongly-built town, all made of stone and steel. It is a brightly-lit town; the streets are covered with asphalt, and the garbage cans swallow all the leavings, unseen, unknown and hardly thought about. The settler's feet are never visible, except perhaps in the sea; but there you're never close enough to see them. His feet are protected by strong shoes although the streets of his town are clean and even, with no holes or stones . . . The settlers' town is a town of white people, of foreigners.
>
> The town that belongs to the colonised people, or at least the native town, the negro village, the medina, the reservation, is a place of ill fame, peopled by men of evil repute. They are born there, it matters little where or how; they die there, it matters not where, nor how. It is a world without spaciousness; men live there on top of each other, and their huts are built one on top of the other. The native town is a hungry town, starved of bread, of meat, of shoes, of coal, of light. The native town is a crouching village, a town on its knees, a town wallowing in the mire. It is a town of niggers and dirty arabs.[18]

In his novel *In a Free State*, V.S. Naipaul described an African city:

> It was like another Sunday in the capital, which, in spite of the white exodus to South Africa and in spite of deportations, remained an English-Indian creation in the African wilderness. It owed nothing to African skill; it required none. Not far from the capital were bush villages, half-day excursions for tourists. But in the capital Africa showed only in the semi-tropical suburban gardens, in the tourist-shop displays of carvings and leather goods and souvenir drums and spears, and in the awkward liveried boys in the new tourist hotels, where the white and Israeli supervisors were never far away. Africa here was décor. Glamour for the white visitor and expatriate; glamour too for the African, the man flushed out from the bush, to whom, in the city, with independence, civilization appeared to have been granted complete. It was still a colonial city, with a colonial glamour. Everyone in it was far from home.[19]

---

17   Said 1978, 65.
18   Fanon 1963, 32.
19   Naipaul 1973, 103f.

Although hardly representative of the wide variety of "colonial" cities, the quotations nevertheless demonstrate the possibility of withdrawal from "western" concepts and references in describing non-western cities.

My personal encounters with Nairobi and its built forms put to question the descriptions of Nairobi by others. Entering the city in reality was an opening towards a different approach. The geographical entry is unforgettable. From Europe, after hours of flight over Saharan sand, passing Mount Kenya hidden behind clouds, the airplane starts to descend and the first signs of Nairobi appear: the parched plain extending to the horizon, some giraffes visible in relief from the flat base, the blue range of the Ngong Hills outlined on one side. Writing about the scenery from her coffee farm, the Danish writer Karen Blixen described the Ngong Hills – rising eight thousand feet above the sea and two thousand feet above the surrounding landscape – as "crowned with four noble peaks like immovable darker waves against the sky."[20] Then the first view of the city: a cluster of buildings reaching towards the sky, white against the yellow earth, still visible after the plane has landed.

The visual entry is sudden: the modern airport, the clear and warm air, the glaring equatorial sun straight above, the highway to the city center, row houses splattered on both sides of the road, small scale industries, the occasional roundabout, and, finally, crossing the railway on a bridge, the center, bigger than it looked from the air, busy with cars and people, the streets lined with blooming trees. Then the lush suburbs, stretching endlessly, the roads climbing up and down and over ridges. Eventually, disparities: glass-covered skyscrapers and worn wooden structures side by side on the main street, luxury apartment blocks with gardens and a pool just some kilometers off a huge squatter area with constructions made of cardboard and canvas, a pink Art Deco cinema next to anonymous shops, a tiny cottage with low eaves shrunk from the road raised to serve a large Spanish-style villa fenced with a two-meter wire-netting, a cozy but decayed hotel serving five o'clock tea for gray-haired couples and the bar of the Intercontinental Hotel full of noisy car freaks celebrating the Safari Rally. (*Figs. 5.1 - 5.15*)

The cultural entry is more gradual and more concealed. At first the unexpected details catch the eye: the potholes on the road, the mosque turned towards Mecca, the display of used books and magazines for sale spread on the sidewalk, all enhancing the feeling of being in a foreign country. Next, the discovery of characteristics reminding one of home: the logic of traffic and parking, the modern clean office buildings, the Italian restaurants with their customary menus, the roomy suburban houses with well-tended gardens, each making the city more familiar to the European visitor. After a while, the fluctuation between the foreign and the familiar is replaced by the development of distinctions. Some parts of the city and some buildings gain identities of their own and begin to be connected to particular kinds of

---

20   Blixen 1954, 14.

activities, ways of life, people. For the European visitors – expatriates and tourists – there are three Nairobis. In the city center, the European Nairobi with its banks, hotels, restaurants, libraries, specialty shops, cinemas, and souvenir shops is found around the most expensive hotels and one of the main streets, Kenyatta Avenue with its 1960s atmosphere. The African Nairobi flows on the streets, but may also be encountered near the offices and ministries on two other main streets, the supermodern Harambee Avenue and Tom Mboya Street, reminiscent of the 1940s, at the post offices and travel agents, in coffee shops and parks during lunch hour. The Asian Nairobi with its temples, restaurants, and shops for all purposes, is more concentrated around streets portraying something of a 1920s character: River Road, Biashara Street and in the older part of Moi Avenue. Similar distinctions also begin to appear in relation to the areas outside the city center.

What Nairobi as a built reality opened was more than a collection of diverse identities: it opened whole universes of multiplicities. The built forms of the city, initially appearing as lack of coherence, even chaos, gradually began to emerge as a complex of several layers of differences which included not only the variation of the built forms as physical elements, but the variation of the ways in which they were connected to peoples' lives and the variation of meanings attached to them. The built forms started to appear not only as representations of the histories of the diverse cultures within a particular city, Nairobi, but also as elements which continue to sustain the cultures, which participate in re-producing the networks of cultural practices and meanings. In this context, the built forms emerged as urban practices.

Fig. 5.1 Moi Avenue to the north at Kenyatta Avenue

Fig. 5.2 Harambee Avenue

Fig. 5.3 Tom Mboya Street

CHAPTER 5 BEGINNINGS ■ 69

Fig. 5.4 Jamia Mosque and the ICEA Building

Fig. 5.5 Traffic headed towards the city center

Fig. 5.6 The Municipal market and a local mosque

Fig. 5.7 Kirinyaga Road near the Nairobi River

Fig. 5.8 Shan Cinema, Ngara Road

Fig. 5.9 Lamu Road, Pumwani

CHAPTER 5 BEGINNINGS ■ 71

Fig. 5.10 Kiosks off Peponi Road

Fig. 5.11 Kaloleni residential area

Fig. 5.12 Karen Blixen house, Karen

*Fig. 5.13
Residential area,
Eastlands*

*Fig. 5.14
Playground, Buru
Buru*

CHAPTER 5 BEGINNINGS ■ 73

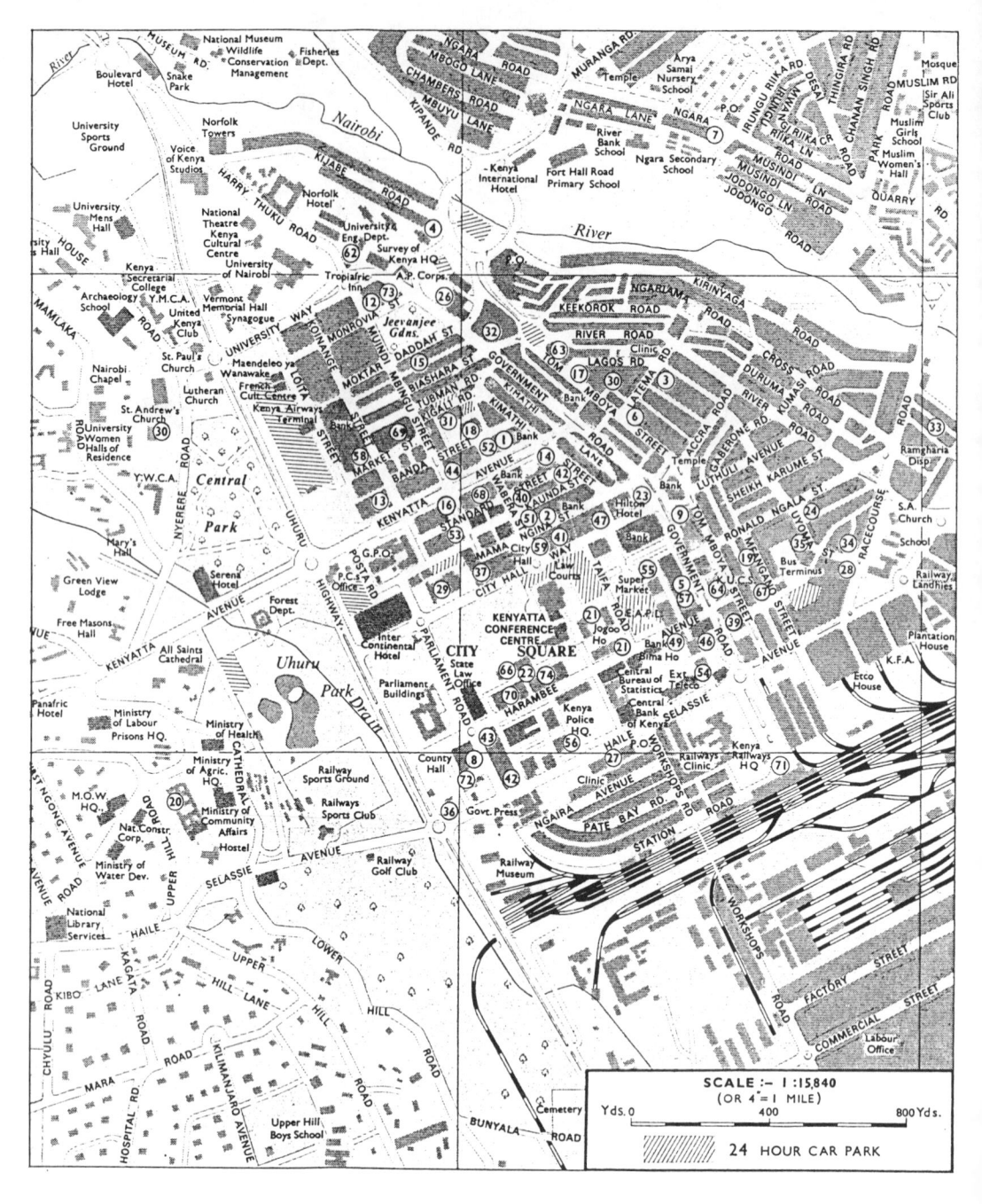

Fig. 5.15 Map: Nairobi city center, 1978

6 Settings

An interpretation of the built forms of Nairobi, then, involves a study of the changes in the urban practices of different cultures within history: in essence, the genealogy of the networks of cultural practices occurring in Nairobi. In this study, the notion of genealogy refers to "writing the history of the present" much in the same sense as Michel Foucault used it. Hubert Dreyfus and Paul Rabinow have described Foucault's approach as diagnosing a current situation and tracing it back in time. According to Dreyfus and Rabinow, Foucault was not trying to capture the significance of a past epoch, to get the whole picture of a past institution, or to find underlying laws of history. The orientation was contemporary, rejecting the intentions of both "presentist" and "finalistic" histories.[1] A genealogy of built forms of Nairobi, then, is about the networks of cultural practices – including built forms, administrative measures, philosophies, institutions, regulations, plans, discourses etc. – which have produced contemporary Nairobi as a combination of different cultural practices and meanings.

In relation to the study of cultural practices, both the historical and the cultural contexts are fundamental. Historically, Nairobi has been and continues to be part of the global economic, social, and ideological system;[2] this also encompasses its built forms. Nezar AlSayyad has formulated assumptions on which the relationship between the global system and the built forms has been based:

> A first assumption is that urban form can only be understood in the context of the colonial past; a second is that urban form is part and parcel of the global system of production. Of course, both of these are predicated on a third assumption – that built form is socially produced and is consequently a product of global processes.[3]

Although Nairobi can be perceived as part of a global system, the point that its urban form could only be understood in the context of the colonial past must be questioned within the genealogical approach. References to the colonial past as the key to understanding the present imply that the dependency in one form or another still continues – an oversimplification of

---

1 Dreyfus and Rabinow 1982, 118ff.
2 On the world-system, see e.g. Wallerstein 1991, chapter 5: Societal Development, or Development of the World-System?
3 AlSayyad 1992, 4, referring to King 1990.

more complex and more diverse relations.[4] Even if the notion of the global system connotes dependencies, it does not automatically refer to the same kinds of dependencies as during colonialism. For a genealogical study of the urban forms of Nairobi, then, the present cultural practices have to be the point of departure.

Culturally, Nairobi contains an unhomogeneous mixture of different (sub)cultures. Some of these cultures may be seen as connected to contexts outside Nairobi, including cultures of rural Kenya, coastal ("swahili") urban Kenya, East Africa or sub-Saharan Africa, western India, Britain, the British Commonwealth, western Europe, and North America. Other cultures may be seen as originating inside Nairobi, as more intensely local versions of various influences, often linked to particular dwelling areas, such as the Kibera of the "Somalis," the Pumwani of the "Swahilis," or the Muthaiga of the "wa-Benzi."[5] Moreover, the cultural mixture has varied historically. The contemporary cultures have been preceded by other cultures, not necessarily continuous to the present, but discernible as traces in the urban forms of the city. Thus the role of the railway organization, for example, one of the initiators of Nairobi during the first decades in the history of the city, can be perceived in the contemporary urban form of the city. In this sense, the cultural multiplicity also contains historical multiplicity.

The histories of the cultural practices within a particular city may be connected to built forms in two mostly alternative, but sometimes overlapping ways. Different cultures may share a territory, built in a form corresponding to a specific culture, later possibly changed for another, but nevertheless also used by other cultures, each culture generating their own distinct ways to "live" the built form. Culturally shared territories may include the city center, central locations within a residential area, and the urban structure as a whole. Or, different cultures may each be attached to their own territories, developing their own built forms in accordance with their ways of life. These culturally privileged territories comprise homogeneous residential areas and, traditionally, dwellings. For the study of built forms, the two kinds of cultural territories pose different kinds of problems. As a built form, the culturally heterogeneous city center is more difficult – perhaps impossible – to connect with any specific culture. While residential areas and individual dwellings may offer more direct evidence of the ways of life of a culture, even then the links may be diffuse. In both cases, the existing built form as a physical object can reveal only part of the relationship: the cultural connection to those who initially produced the form and the conditions which enabled the building. More important for the "history of the present," however, is how the existing built forms belong to the networks of urban practices of the

---

4   See above, chapter 5.
5   "Somalis" and "Swahilis" are in quotes to indicate that they refer to communities existing in Nairobi for generations, not to recent immigrants; "wa-Benzi" - a local expression - to indicate people who can afford to drive a Mercedes Benz car.

different urban cultures and what meanings they carry for each culture. Thus a house in Nairobi may be studied primarily not as a dwelling built by the colonial powers for an Indian clerk in the 1920s but as a dwelling – albeit having that history of production – which is lived in and carries meanings for a Kenyan African family of today.

In this study, the built forms attached to the city as a whole and to the city center – the two initially emerging as one – and those attached to dwellings are discussed separately, even if their development has been interdependent. The urban forms have conditioned the selection of possible dwelling forms, but have also been influenced by the cultural concepts of dwelling used as points of reference. Both the urban forms and the dwelling forms were influenced by contextual aspects. Because of the dual presentation, some repetition has been unavoidable.

The histories of the urban forms of Nairobi are discussed first, in Part III. The genealogy of the urban forms is divided into phases arranged chronologically. On a general level, the periodization is related to the changing roles not only of Nairobi but of Kenya and East Africa within the British Empire and the global systems of power. In the period studied, major imperial and global transformations involving East Africa occurred around the turn of the century when European powers competed over control of the inner parts of Africa, during and after the First World War when British power in East Africa was consolidated, during and after the Second World War when the strategic position of the country was rediscovered, and, finally, during the early 1960s when the East African countries became independent. In the periodization of the histories of urban forms in Nairobi, the time preceding the First World War is discussed in three phases to emphasize the rapidly changing situations of the initial years.

In the histories of urban form, each phase suggests a particular frame of conditions within which the urban forms were produced; each phase also presents the kinds of groups – the social agents – involved in forming Nairobi. Thus the histories of Nairobi's urban forms are discussed in six chapters:
– the birth of the town from around 1895 to 1902 when the Railway Committee in London and the railway authorities in Kenya were the main agents, in chapter 8;
– the initial shaping of the town from 1902 to 1910 when the town started to grow and when British government officials and sanitation experts began to intervene, in chapter 9;
– the organization of the main areas from around 1910 to 1919, involving an increasingly diverse population administered by both British government officials and local settlers, in chapter 10;
– the development of the municipality between 1919 and 1940, when the effects of the First World War had altered the relations of power among the different groups in Nairobi, in chapter 11;
– the introduction and extension of the concept of Nairobi as a colonial capital, from 1940 to 1963, when the hold of the British government on

the city was strengthened and when the positions of the different groups – the settlers, the British, the Kenyan Asians, and the Kenyan Africans – began to grow further apart, illuminated during the Mau Mau activities, in chapter 12;
- the changes produced by the Independence of Kenya, from 1963, until the time of my field study in 1983, during which colonial concerns were discontinued, diverse interests in development and modernization were introduced, and new social agents appeared, such as national policy organizations, an emerging African middle class, large numbers of rural immigrants, expatriates from different parts of the world, and international "aid" agencies, in chapter 13.

Dwelling forms in three Nairobi cultures are discussed in Part IV. The genealogy of the dwelling forms is divided into four sections, three arranged on the basis of the notion of culturally privileged territories planned for a particular culture and the fourth on the notion of culturally un-privileged – i.e. universal – territories. Each section identifies a frame of conditions within which the dwelling forms were produced. Nairobi has had a history of cultural diversity where any distinctions are bound to be only approximations. Historically, three main cultures have been identified, conventionally called Africans, Asians, and Europeans. In contemporary contexts, these concepts have been used to refer to Kenyan Africans, Kenyan Asians (who originated from India and Pakistan) as well as both Kenyan Europeans and expatriates (who mostly originate from Europe and North America); these concepts are also used here. The distinction, sometimes together with Arabs as the fourth group, was originally utilized in the colonial administration but in 1983 continued to be employed, although it obviously excluded groups like non-Kenyan Africans (such as Tanzanians and Ugandans) and non-Euro-American expatriates. In the section describing the field study of the twenty dwellings, the concept of Africans is used to refer to Kenyan Africans originating from different parts of Kenya not identified separately, the concept of Asians to refer to Kenyan Asians originating from Gujarat in western India and Hindu by religion, and the concept of Europeans to refer to expatriates originating from Europe and specifically from Finland.

The dwelling forms are discussed in four chapters:
- the colonial European dwelling forms which include dwellings built by the colonizers for themselves and for other cultures, in chapter 14;
- the dwelling forms built by the Kenyan Africans for themselves, in chapter 15;
- the dwelling forms built by the Kenyan Asians for themselves, in chapter 16;
- the dwelling forms conceived as universal, built by the public and the private sectors, in chapter 17.

The dwelling practices observed in 1983 are described in the final chapter of this part, chapter 18.

7 Footings

Written material

The written sources used in the study included not only studies of the built forms of Nairobi and studies from related fields, but also less theoretically formulated material like biographies, recollections, letters, diaries, and even fictional material. The diversity of the material was a consequence of the scope of the study, to understand the practices relating to the built forms of Nairobi. Although this range of sources is not unusual within the comprehensive approach of cultural history,[1] it nevertheless posed some problems. In terms of method, the approach involved the re-analysis and interpretation of earlier studies within a new theoretical frame. Thus some of the research which formed the basis of the critical argument against earlier approaches to the built forms of Nairobi was used as sources in this study; in a sense, they were re-exploited.[2] Some of the material may be perceived as primary, including, for example, unpublished reports on housing in Nairobi. To assess the relation of the sources to the reality of their own time, descriptions of their original purposes have been included. The section on sources only includes documents directly referred to; sources quoted from other documents are indicated in the notes.

In the study of Nairobi built forms, some written material focused primarily on the urban forms, others on dwelling forms. The most useful material for the purposes of this study was related to both built forms – urban and dwelling – and included three publications: the *Nairobi Master Plan for a Colonial Capital* by L. Thornton White, L. Silberman and P. R. Anderson;[3] Dorothy M. Halliman's and W.T.W. Morgan's geographical article "The City of Nairobi";[4] and Andrew Hake's *African Metropolis: Nairobi's Self-Help City*.[5] The *Master Plan* of 1948 represented the views of the Europeans involved in the administration of the city, Halliman's and Morgan's study an overtly non-political approach, however, with a bias in favor of rapid modernization, while Hake's study on life in a self-help city could be described as sympathetic to ways of life the colonizers would have seen as undesirable. All three contained a historical section and utilized historical material such

---

1 See e.g. Virtanen 1987, 93ff.
2 See above, Chapter 5.
3 Abbreviated as MP 1948.
4 Halliman and Morgan 1967.
5 Hake 1977.

as administrative reports, economic surveys, population census results, and minutes of the municipal council proceedings and legislative council debates in addition to references to other research.

With some reservations, two other publications need to be included among useful sources for both urban forms and dwelling forms. In their *Notes on the Urban Planning of Nairobi*, published in 1980, Sören Emig and Zahir Ismael analyzed four Nairobi town plans from 1898, 1927, 1948 and 1973, offering views deviating from the other sources in terms of the extent of visual material.[6] The usefulness of the maps was somewhat diminished because they were mostly redrawn versions, the usefulness of the analyses because of the strong political orientation. From the same institution, *Urban Development in Kenya: The Growth of Nairobi 1900-1970*, compiled by Finn Barnow and others, published in 1983, presented empirical material, that is, maps, drawings and statistical data for 1900, 1920, 1940, 1950, 1960, and 1970, but, as the authors admit, "does not enter into an analysis of this material."[7] The collection was valuable for this study particularly because data on the built forms of Nairobi is generally difficult to reach, to quote the authors:

> This ... does not mean that reliable information on urban development in Kenya is readily available. On the contrary, a lot of necessary information is unavailable or non-existent. A lot of information has simply not been collected, a large amount of reported figures are incommensurable or imperfect, and entire records have been destroyed.[8]

In this study, the collection also served as a necessary cross reference for evaluating the accuracy of data given elsewhere. It contained material relating to both the urban forms and the dwelling forms of Nairobi, in addition to providing population census figures on parts of the city. Maps indicating the physical, the functional and the social structures of the city had been constructed for each target year. For the maps, plans, and figures compiled, the sources were given, and their reliability assessed. Some reservations, however, have to be noted. The usefulness of the series of maps for this study was reduced by the absence of the road network at each time period; the base of all the maps was the situation of around 1970/80. The omission of Kibera, a residential area with inhabitants from the 1910s, from the maps before 1970 puts some doubt on the general accuracy of the maps, even if the omission may have been justified because of Kibera's location outside the city boundary until 1962; this restriction, however, was not indicated by the authors. Barnow's book on urban planning in the third world, *Kolonistens by*, which

---

6   Emig and Ismael 1980.
7   Barnow et al. 1983, 3.
8   Barnow et al. 1983, 3.

included a 1913 plan of Nairobi, not published earlier, was also helpful.[9]

Other material relating both to the urban forms and to the dwelling forms of a specific area in Nairobi included, for example, an unpublished administrative report on Pumwani and a thesis on the River Road area.[10] Material not directly addressing the built forms but touching the subject, included studies on Kenyan and African history,[11] nationalism in Kenya,[12] political behavior in Nairobi and the working class,[13] economic history,[14] and regional development.[15] With few exceptions, the approaches expressed Euro-American points of view. For more local perspectives, C. Ojwando Abuor's book *White Highlands No More*, despite its strongly political emphases, was helpful.[16] For Asian interpretations, two studies were useful: *Portrait of a Minority: Asians in East Africa*, a collection of articles edited by Dharam P. Ghai and Yash P. Ghai, and Dana April Seidenberg's *Uhuru and the Kenya Indians: The Role of a Minority Community in Kenya Politics 1939-1963*.[17]

Material relating to the urban forms of Nairobi included both studies and other written material. For placing the early decades of Nairobi in the context of the construction of the railway, M.F. Hill's *Permanent Way*, the official history of the building of the Kenya and Uganda Railway, was valuable, Charles Miller's *The Lunatic Express: An Entertainment in Imperialism* providing a more diversified perspective of the early years.[18] Elspeth Huxley's *White Man's Country: Lord Delamere and the Making of Kenya*, originally published in 1935, is simultaneously Delamere's two-volume biography covering the years from 1870 to 1935 and an inside view of the community of settlers; Delamere was one of the country's central figures until his death.[19] For other European perspectives on Nairobi, illuminative observations could be found in the 1902-1906 diary of the military officer Richard Meinertzhagen, in the letters of 1914-1931 and essays by the Danish coffee farmer, later well-known writer Karen Blixen/Isak Dinesen, in the recollections of Nairobi around 1910 in the biography of the famous Finnish painter Akseli Gallen-Kallela by his daughter Kirsti and in her autobiography, in the book by Errol Trzebinski, based on interviews, diaries and letters of Kenya pioneers of the first two decades, and in the adventurous Swede Hjalmar Frisell's depictions of life in the Nairobi of the 1920s.[20] A more

---

9 Barnow 1990. Barnow was an advisor in Emig and Ismael's study.
10 Farnworth 1964; Moniz 1984.
11 Davidson 1978; Ogot 1974.
12 Rosberg and Nottingham 1966.
13 Ross 1975; Stichter 1975.
14 Zwanenberg 1975; Zwanenberg and King 1975; Obbo 1980; Swainson 1980.
15 Soja 1968; Obudho 1979 and 1981.
16 Abuor 1973.
17 Ghai and Ghai 1970; Seidenberg 1983.
18 Hill 1949; Miller 1971.
19 Huxley 1968a and 1968b.
20 Meinertzhagen 1983; Dinesen 1983; Blixen 1954; Gallen-Kallela 1992 and 1982; Trzebinski 1985; Frisell 1939.

critical approach to colonial practices was conveyed by Norman Leys in his book Kenya, first published in 1924, and in a collection of his and J.H. Oldham's correspondence of 1918-1926; Leys was a medical official in the colonial administration, living in various parts of East Africa from 1902 to 1918.[21] In literary works, such as Huxley's and Blixen's novels, references to Nairobi and life in town were only included in a few passages.

For the time after the Second World War until Independence, in addition to the *Master Plan* of 1948, useful material on the Nairobi and Kenya of the 1950s and early 1960s included articles and books by journalists and writers.[22] The previously mentioned books by Abuor as well as by Ghai and Ghai, both published after independence, and by Seidenberg, later, included particularly acute observations on the perspectives of the different groups living in Nairobi at this time. In this sense, Ngugi wa Thiong'o's novels and essays also provided a view differing from that presented in Robert Ruark's colonially-biased adventure novels.[23]

For the urban forms relating to the period after independence, various kinds of written material were available, including research, administrative reports, articles in newspapers, and fiction. For the early 1960s, administrative reports were useful. Studies produced for urban planning and housing from around 1970 offered more detailed information; this also included unpublished reports available at the Housing Research and Development Unit of the University of Nairobi. During independence, perspectives on Nairobi have continued to be diversified in newspapers, travel books, and other informal material; for descriptions of contemporary Nairobi, novels by Meja Mwangi and Thomas Akare were particularly illuminating.[24]

In the material relating specifically to the dwelling forms of Nairobi, descriptions and analyses of unauthorized residential areas dominated; however, since the focus of this study was dwellings of the middle classes, these studies had only limited use for my purposes. Of the areas studied, the Fort Jesus area within Kibera was presented in a professional journal.[25] A number of unpublished reports – mostly on social surveys – concerned some of the areas studied, particularly the newer ones;[26] in some cases, the reports may have been produced as part of the evaluations required by international organizations providing loans or other support. Very little material describing ways of life in Nairobi could be found. The historical material included occasional remarks in letters or other reminiscences by the Europeans of Nairobi, but little by members of the other cultures; of studies providing the

---

21 Leys 1973; Cell 1976.
22 For example, Moore 1950; Cox 1965.
23 Ngugi 1982 and 1981; Ruark 1955 and 1961.
24 Mwangi 1976 and 1979; Akare 1981.
25 Wuensche 1974.
26 For Fort Jesus, Hooper et al 1974; for Buru Buru, Menezes 1978; for Norfolk Towers, Chana and Devji 1981; for Umoja, Hoek-Smit 1983. The studies on Fort Jesus and Norfolk Towers were identified as "user reaction surveys," those on Buru Buru and Umoja as "social surveys."

rural background, Jomo Kenyatta's anthropological study *Facing Mount Kenya: The Traditional Life of the Gikuyu*, first published in 1938, needs to be pointed out.[27] For contemporary dwellings of the Africans in Nairobi, Lucy Jayne Kamau's study of the symbolic aspects of domestic space in one housing area was the only source in which the dwelling forms were analyzed in detail,[28] although aspects of urban life – sometimes in a broad scope of "Africans in general" – were discussed in a number of sources.[29] For contemporary dwellings of the expatriates, Olli Alho's study on Finns engaged in African development projects contained some useful insights.[30] One part of the written material used in the study were the field notes based on communications with the contact persons and inhabitants and on personal observations made in 1983 in Nairobi.

Visual material

In the study, several kinds of visual material were employed. For the study of urban forms, maps, aerial photographs, plans, and other photographs were the main visual sources. The maps (here defined as representations documenting reality) were published maps acquired from the Map Office and included overall maps of the city of Nairobi and its surroundings as well as smaller scale maps of various of its parts. Of these, the overall maps with scales ranging between 1:20,000 and 1:50,000 were fairly recent, from the 1970s and 1980s, while the maps produced in scale 1:2500 were historical, mostly dating from the 1950s; all maps, however, represented the most recent versions available. Some maps out of print could be found in the Map Archives of the Department of Land Development at the University of Nairobi. Some of the maps used were selected from publications; in this sense, the *Master Plan* of 1948 and the collection by Barnow and others were particularly useful. Several publications also contained maps reconstructed from an earlier period. For the more recent urban developments including, for example, the extensive housing areas in eastern Nairobi, only aerial photographs were available; the ones used were produced in scale 1:6000 and were from 1975. The earliest aerial photograph utilized here, of around 1945, was published in the *Master Plan* of 1948. The plans (here defined as representations indicating a possible future reality) used in the study were selected from various publications, especially from the *Master Plan* of 1948 and from Emig and Ismael's analysis of Nairobi plans.

For the urban forms, the analysis of maps was complemented by

---

27 For studies on Africans in rural and traditional contexts in Kenya, Kenyatta 1982, Andersen 1978, Lee Smith and Lamba 1981; on Europeans, e.g. Dinesen 1983; on Asians, e.g. Bharati 1970.
28 Kamau 1978.
29 For example, Marris 1962; Dike 1979; Kayongo-Male and Onyango 1984.
30 Alho 1980. Alho's study was conducted in Tanzania and Zambia.

photographs published in books, journals, and newspapers, and as postcards. One of the earliest views of Nairobi was published in the official history of the Railways; other early views have been published in recollections of settlers' lives, in historical articles, and as material for tourists. In the historical material used, most of the street views documented only the main streets. Among the several tens of photographs Akseli Gallen-Kallela took in Kenya in 1909-1910, only one depicted a street view.[31] A set of historical postcards presented bird's eye views of the city in the 1920s and were valuable in reconstructing an overall image on how the urban form had evolved; they could be compared to similar views of the city center in the 1980s, presented, for example, in postcards and tourist guide books.[32] Contemporary Nairobi between 1980 and 1989, and particularly in 1983, was documented in photographs as part of the study.

For describing Nairobi's dwelling forms, part of the visual material was collected in a field study. Twenty dwellings were selected as the core. The selection process was preceded by a review of the residential areas and forms of dwelling in Nairobi; based on the review, the neighborhoods were chosen from which the dwellings would be sought. In terms of location within the urban structure, the neighborhoods were situated either in the city center, on the ring around it, or in the suburbs. In terms of time, the oldest neighborhoods had been established around the 1910s and the youngest around 1980. Neighborhoods with dwellings constructed on unauthorized sites or from temporary materials – including, for example, squatter areas – were excluded because of the relatively numerous earlier studies focusing on these areas, as were traditional villages located within the city boundary. Thus the neighborhoods selected had been planned for and were lived in by what could be called middle-class families and single persons; locally, the areas were perceived as middle-class areas. In this context, the concept middle-class is used to refer to an internally somewhat heterogeneous group of people and families with similarities in terms of ways of life. Indirectly, middle-class was defined to exclude both the poor, unemployed and disadvantaged groups, and the most affluent, land-owning groups. More directly, the concept of middle-class was used to refer to families with incomes in the middle range. This included family members employed in positions ranging from the lower middle class such as college teachers, nurses, and owners of small shops, to the upper middle class such as university lecturers, self-employed professionals, and owners of small companies.

A network of contact persons was developed to find families and individuals – usually a relative or friend of the contact person – living in each of the neighborhoods selected for the study and willing to allow their dwelling to be studied. These contact persons had a professional interest in

---

31   Gallen-Kallela's paintings of Kenya also included a small oil painting of the simple wooden government buildings located in the town center.
32   See e.g. *Kenya Insight Guide*.

the study and most were lecturers, researchers or students at the Department of Architecture. For the study, the role of the contact persons was essential: it not only allowed the dwellers to discuss the purpose of the study without being committed to accept the request to study the dwelling, but also functioned as a recommendation to the dwellers on behalf of the researcher. Several contact persons were involved, some providing five contacts, some two or three, some only one. Not all the contacts were fruitful, but the required variations in criteria relating to the neighborhoods and to the dwellers were achieved.

In addition to dwellings found through the personal contact network, some dwellings were chosen from units built by the Railways. Unpublished original drawings were selected from the Plan Archives of the Architects' Office of the Kenya Railways in Nairobi. These drawings depicted dwelling plans and site plans made for housing provided by the Railways for their employees in the late 1920s until the 1940s, and in one case, for the redevelopment of an area in the 1980s, concerning four different house types studied in more detail. Other unpublished original drawings were provided by the private archives of five of the owners of other houses studied; the oldest of these houses was built in the late 1940s, with the latest extensions from around 1980.

On each of the twenty dwellings selected, measured drawings were prepared of the plan, including the use and furniture of the rooms. The dwellings were also documented in photographs, both internally and externally. Additional material such as site plans and dwelling plans were acquired from unpublished reports. Published visual data on the specific dwelling forms studied was rare. For comparisons with other contemporaneous dwellings, historical material was used, such as photographs of Karen Blixen's two homes near Nairobi, published in the collection of her letters.

In addition to the visual material of the dwelling forms, their uses were also documented. During the measuring and photography, the arrangements for activities occurring in the dwelling were observed, and the histories of the house, the use of the dwelling and the dwellers were discussed with the contact person and the dweller present; this material, based on direct observations in the dwellings, is discussed in a separate chapter.[33]

Of the twenty dwellings selected for the study:
- three were located in the city center, six in the ring around it, and eleven in the suburbs;
- seven were built in the time period preceding 1940, seven between 1940 and 1963, and six between 1963 and 1983;

---

33 In one dwelling, the occupant did not allow photographing, and in two others, the documentation was incomplete because the owners allowed only partial documentation. With the exception of some of the rooms occupied by tenants, access to all the rooms was allowed, although in some cases, it had to be separately requested; this related to spaces considered private and closed to "normal" visitors, such as bedrooms in some dwellings. For some dwellings, the discussion involved only the contact person, because no adult family members were present.

- originally, five dwellings had been planned for Africans, seven for Asians, and eight for Europeans;
- at the time of the study, twelve were occupied by African, five by Asian and three by European families or single persons;
- eleven dwellings had originally been planned for and were in 1983 inhabited by the same cultural group: five by Africans, three by Asians and three by Europeans;
- seven dwellings were provided by the employer, eight were occupied by the owners, and five were rented;
- among the dwellings studied, most of the Africans (six out of twelve) lived in housing provided by the employer, the Asians owned their dwellings, and most of the Europeans (two out of three) rented their dwellings;
- four dwellings were in detached houses, two in semi-detached houses, six in row houses, four in courtyard houses, three in blocks of flats, and one was a majengo house.[34]

The use of visual material poses some problems. Cartographic material has been used both within urban history and urban geography to represent the physical layout of towns.[35] Even if perceived as representations of a past reality, maps and photographs are subject to presuppositions not necessarily identified but nevertheless inherent in their context.[36] Maps as traces of a past geography may be compared to other maps, but both may have omitted the indication of a particular usage of the land; in Nairobi, the unauthorized settlements – particularly during the colonial period – seem to have been excluded from contemporaneous maps. The intended use of the maps also affects the codes employed; tourist road maps, for example, usually exaggerate the street network and eliminate less important details. For the decoding of aerial photographs, additional knowledge of the areas is usually necessary, particularly if foliage covers large portions of the photographed area, as in parts of Nairobi. In the study of urban forms, the difference between maps and plans is essential: unlike maps, plans are not traces of a reality, but of an envisaged future; in the process, the plans are an instrument for making the future reality. To evaluate the realization of a plan, it must be compared to the reality or a trace of it, such as a map.[37]

For studying urban forms, photographs are priceless. In describing the growth of Chicago into a metropolis, Harold M. Mayer and Richard C. Wade used photographs as evidence, as historical documents, and emphasized their unique potential in the study of physical forms:

---

34   For tables with cross-references of the criteria, see Appendix 4. For a description of the majengo house type, see below, chapter 15.
35   On maps as sources, e.g. Conzen 1968; Carter 1979; Marescotti 1988; Conzen 1990.
36   For a discussion of representations of urban forms, see Nevanlinna 1993b.
37   On the use of the concepts of map and plan as synonyms, see Conzen 1968, 115ff.

Photographic documentation is especially useful in describing the physical growth and internal spatial patterns of cities. In no other way can we see the successive stages of development; no other source shows so clearly the transformation of open land to urban purposes or so well traces the intensification of urban use over a period of time. In a unique way, too, the camera records the changing skyline, from the first court houses and churches to the dominant commercial skyscrapers of the present. An aerial view can convey the pattern of the metropolis; a snapshot can catch the tangled texture of the neighborhood or street.[38]

Yet the use of photographs in the study of built forms has its limitations. Photographs have sometimes been seen as traces of a reality, as transparent evidence of a past, that is, as "neutral" or "pure" documents. This notion must be questioned. Even if a photograph may be a record of something that once existed, it does not carry its meanings in the image: meanings are given to an image not only by the photographer who chooses the topic and the way to frame it, by the context within which it is presented, and by the viewer, but also by its relation to traditions of understanding images. As John Tagg has emphasized,

> Photography is neither a unique technology nor an autonomous semiotic system. Photographs do not carry their meanings in themselves, nor can a single range of technical devices guarantee the unity of the field of photographic meanings. A technology has no inherent value, outside its mobilisations in specific discourses, practices, institutions and relations of power. Images can signify meanings only in more or less defined frameworks of usage and social practice.[39]

Photographs, then, must themselves be identified as historical practices; this applies, of course, to all visual and non-visual material. Thus the photographs of Nairobi, for example, selected for the *Master Plan* of 1948 to further the establishment of a colonial capital, like those taken to demonstrate the character of the squatter areas in a newspaper article, have to be seen in relation to the specific purposes of the intervention. In this sense, photographs were used in the study not only as illustrations but as historical sources.

---

38 Mayer and Wade 1969, viii. For the use of a camera in the anthropological documentation of the visual aspects of cultures, see e.g. Söderholm 1982, 227.
39 Tagg 1992, 143.

PART THREE

HISTORIES OF URBAN FORM
IN NAIROBI

8 The birth of the railway town, 1895–1902

The establishment of Nairobi can be attributed to the decision of the Uganda Railway Committee, appointed by Lord Salisbury in 1895, to build a railway to connect Lake Victoria in the heart of Africa with the coast at the Indian Ocean.[1] The Railway Committee in London decided on the plans, and they were implemented in Kenya by Sir George Whitehouse, the chief engineer. The plans were based on a survey expedition of 1892 which had largely followed the old caravan route.[2] Nairobi, located approximately midway between the port of Mombasa and Lake Victoria, the two terminals of the Uganda Railway, was chosen as the new center of operations because of its advantageous position at the edge of the Athi Plains and at the foot of the highlands. The construction of the first stretch from the coast to Nairobi mostly involved level land and, after the initial phases at the coast, was not particularly complicated. After Nairobi, the construction of the railway would become a more difficult engineering operation: towards Lake Victoria, the topography on the planned railway line included a steep rise of nearly two thousand feet and an almost vertical descent down the side of the escarpment. The construction would have to be controlled from a base as close to the site as possible, and Nairobi was the last level area before the highlands.

Before the arrival of the railway, the Masai people used to water their cattle on the river coming down from the snows of Mount Kenya, passing through the site selected for the new railway town; in Masai, "Enkare Nairobi" means "the place of cold water."[3] According to R.M.A. van Zwanenberg and Anne King, some evidence suggests that the site was earlier used for trading by Kikuyu and Masai women.[4] In 1896, Sergeant Ellis had set up a transport depôt there with stores and stables for caravan traffic.[5] Guildford Molesworth, who had been commissioned in 1898 by the Uganda Railway Committee to write an inspection report on the slow progress of the construction work, assessed the choice of the site:

---

1 *The Uganda Railway*, Vol.1, Origin of Scheme (Colonial Office, London, 1948) quoted in Tiwari 1981, 125. For an extensive description of the political issues and the interests involved, see Hill 1949, Part I (pp.1-138).
2 According to Guildford Molesworth's report of 1899, referred to in Hill 1949, 92f.
3 Tiwari 1981, 123.
4 Zwanenberg and King 1975, 263.
5 MP 1948, 10.

> Nyrobi [sic] has, with great judgment, been selected as the site for the principal workshops. It is about 5,500 feet above the level of the sea, which ensures a comparatively salubrious climate: there is ample space of level ground for all requirements, and excellent sites for the quarters of officers and subordinates, on higher ground above the station site. There is a fairly good supply of water, but reservoirs and tanks will have to be constructed.[6]

The control of land was a crucial issue in the construction of the railway and in the establishment of Nairobi. After the British Government had declared the East Africa Protectorate in 1895,[7] all unoccupied land was considered "Crown land," that is, subject only to the decisions of the government, as the Provincial Sub-Commissioner stated a few years later:

> As the basis of all argument in the matter of land, it has been absolutely laid down that no native in the Province has any individual title to land, and that the land is the common wealth of the people. A native's claim to any land is recognised, even according to native custom, only so long as he occupies beneficially. The present usage is to recognise all unoccupied land as Crown land, and the Administration is free to deal with it as it considers to be to the best advantage. No non-native can acquire land from a native. Vacated land, i.e. land vacated by a native, reverts to the Crown automatically.[8]

This practice was based on the Lands Acquisition Act of 1894, originally defined for India but adopted for the Protectorates of East Africa and Uganda. An Order in Council of 1898 gave the government power to take land, without compensation, for government buildings, roads, and the like, and for the railway, one mile wide on both sides of the line. The power to alienate thus acquired Crown land either by sale or by lease was legalized in an Order in Council of 1901. Terms of alienation were laid down in the Crown Lands Ordinance of 1902. Within this legislation, the issue of land occupied by natives remained vague. Only in the Crown Lands Ordinance of 1915, Crown land was specifically defined to include all lands occupied or reserved for natives. However, by that time, the government had in practice already exercised these powers, granting "to Europeans some 2000 square miles in freehold and some 5500 square miles in leasehold; to Indians, 22 square miles, either freehold or leasehold; to Africans, no land at all."[9] The legislation on land influenced both the allocation of farm land for settlers and the use of land within the townships, controlled by the Protectorate administration and its provincial sub-units. In this context, the Railway organization was a self-contained unit, its legality derived directly from the Foreign Office, and

---

6   Molesworth in his inspection report of 1899, quoted in Hill 1949, 184.
7   Hill 1949, 128.
8   John Ainsworth quoted in Hill 1949, 265.
9   Leys 1973, 93ff., quotation from p.95. See also Hill 1949, 265f.; Zwanenberg and King 1975, 34.

later, from the Colonial Office.[10] The Railways administration interpreted their control over the railway land as concerning not only the planning and use of land for various purposes directly related to the railways, but also the planning and lease of land for commercial purposes to increase the railway's return. In terms of lands in townships, then, the Protectorate administration and the Railway administration had potentially diverting interests and some legal grounds on which to base them.

By the time Molesworth submitted his report with its assessment on the selected site in Nairobi, the first plan for the organization of the railway town had been prepared. The "Plan of survey at foot of hill and edge of plains" is signed by Arthur F. Church, Assistant Surveyor, and dated 30/11/98 (*Fig. 8.1*).[11] The plan indicates the natural conditions of the site – the contours of the land, the forest, the "River Nairobe," and the swamp – as well as the envisaged plan of the railway town with the railway line, the station and the station yard, the sites for permanent offices, caravan camps, cemeteries, houses, the sites to be let for shops in the area marked as bazaar, and the road network, with a cross section of the road shown. In the plan, the town is situated on the plain within a triangle formed on one side by the the edge of the hills and the railway line following it, on another side by the river, and on the third by the railway line and station yard, the railway line turning at a right angle around the town. A handful of individual houses are located on the slopes of the hills overlooking the town. The plan indicates a careful positioning of the station and station yard on the most level area, with the railways housing towards the west on the plain and further on the hill, and the bazaar area towards the north near the swamp. The housing area on the plain is only slightly larger than the area reserved for the bazaar, but the density of the bazaar with its ten streets seems to have been planned to be higher. In the bazaar area, the distance between the streets is less than half than that in the railways housing area next to it; the sites for shops to be let are identified as 75 feet by 75 feet. The roads to the existing Sclaters Road and Kikuyu Road are connected to the station, and an additional loop attaches the houses on the hills to the town road network.

Sören Emig and Zahir Ismail have argued that the first plan of Nairobi, signed by Church, "only took into consideration the European employers of the railway and European and Asian traders . . . [and] completely neglected the Asian labourers or coolies and Africans. Nairobi was going to be a railway town for Europeans with a mixed European and Asian trading post."[12] In other words, they implied that Nairobi was conceived from the very beginning as a town divided by ethnicity and race. However, an analysis of the plan does not support the allegation. On the plan, no distinctions are indicated,

---

10 Zwanenberg and King 1975, 263. In 1905, the administration of the East Africa Protectorate was transferred from the Foreign Office to the Colonial Office (Tignor 1976, 18).
11 Plan from Emig and Ismael 1980, 13; the location of the source was not indicated.
12 Emig and Ismael 1980, 9.

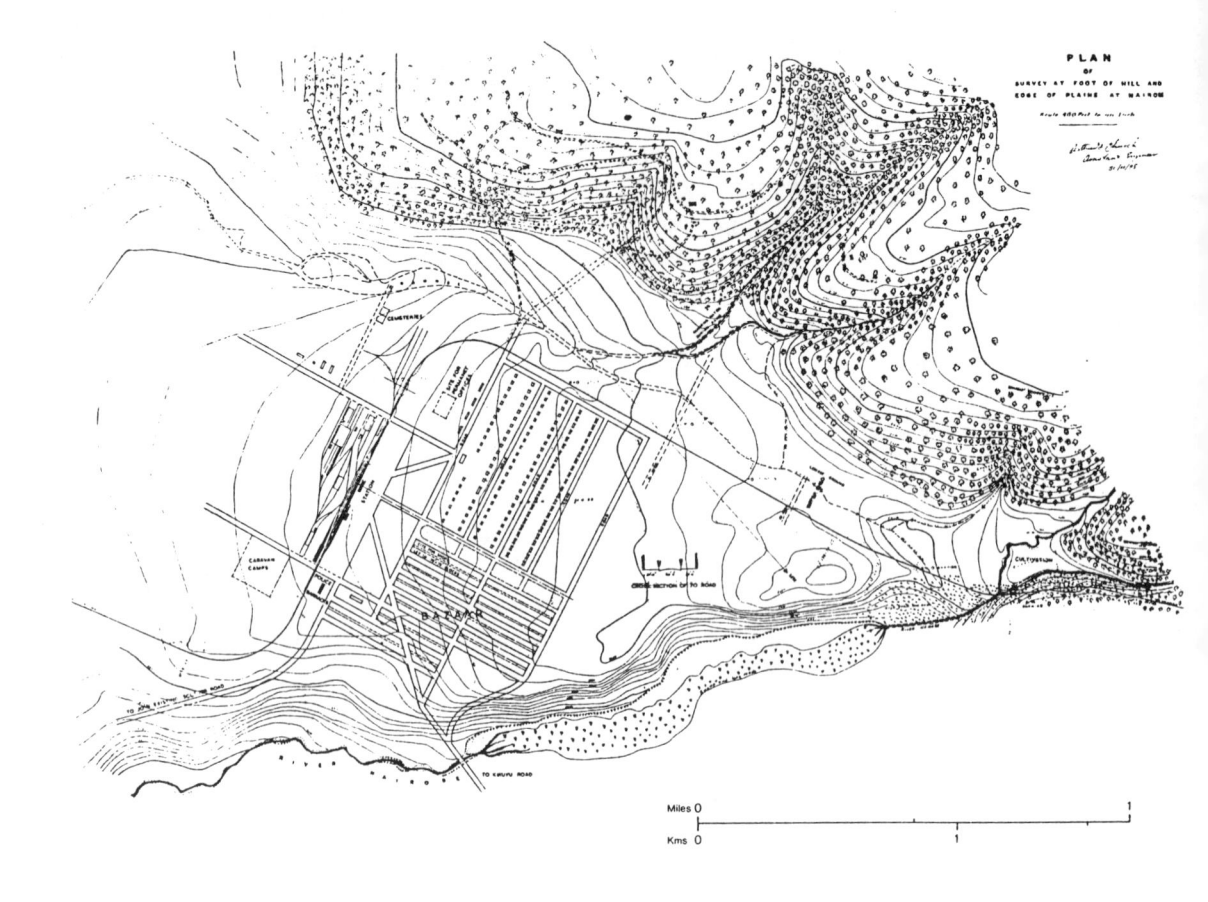

Fig. 8.1 Plan of survey at foot of hill and edge of plains, 1898

not on ethnic characteristics or social positions, neither for housing nor for shops. Neither can the plan be said to have suggested the neglect of Asian and African laborers. During the construction of the Uganda railway, the proportion of European staff members to Asian and African ones was small indeed, and the majority of housing was not built for Europeans but for the other groups. For example, on March 31, 1905, the railway staff consisted of 53 Europeans, 176 Eurasians, 1,254 Indians and 3,050 Africans, with the number of Indian laborers reduced by 1,662 from the previous year after of the completion of the main line;[13] in 1904, therefore, the proportions between the different groups had been around 55 Asians and 57 Africans to each European. The Nairobi plan of 1898 shows some 150 houses, of which seven were on the hills and over 140 on the flat land near the station yard. If the proportions between the different groups of the railway staff in general corresponded to those posted in Nairobi, the housing units shown on the plan had to include Asians and Africans, thus did not "completely neglect" them.

---

13 Hill 1949, 290.

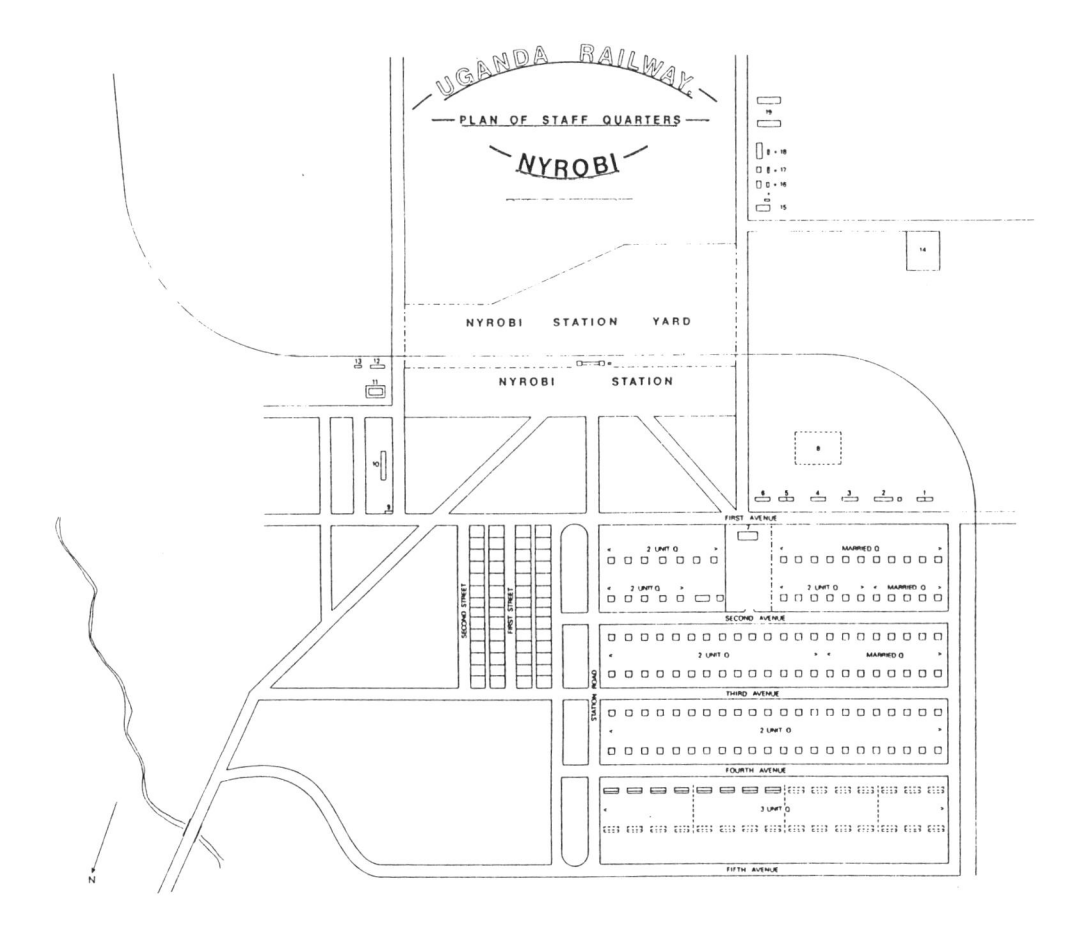

Fig. 8.2 Uganda Railway Plan of Staff Quarters, 1899

A more detailed plan dates from the following year. The "Uganda Railway Plan of Staff Quarters, Nyrobi" is signed by G. Whitehouse, Chief Engineer, and dated 29/10/1899 (*Fig. 8.2*).[14] Earlier in the same year, in a letter discussing the construction of the railway, Whitehouse had remarked that "Nyrobi itself will in the course of the next two years become a large and flourishing place and already there are many applications for sites for hotels, shops and houses."[15] In Whitehouse's plan, neither the contours nor the relation to the surroundings are shown, and the area covered is smaller than in the earlier plan. In addition to the "Nyrobi Station" and the "Nyrobi Station Yard," the different buildings are identified in more detail, and include the offices of the "Supt.of Works, Loco," "Chief Engineer," two for "Accounts," the "D.E.Office, Press," "Traffic," "Site of Ry.Offices," and the "Post Office"

---

14 In a redrawn format in Barnow et al 1983, 14, where it was identified as Nairobi Township Plan No.56 from the Railway Museum, Nairobi.
15 G. Whitehouse to F.L. O'Callaghan, April 20, 1899 (Further correspondence respecting the construction of the Uganda Railway, The Railway Archives, Nairobi) quoted in Tiwari 1981, 126. F.L. O'Callaghan was the Managing Member of the Uganda Railway Committee (Hill 1949, 223).

as well as the "Dak Bungalow," "Police," "Jemidars," "Pointsmen," "Cemetery," "European Hospital," and "Coolie Hospital."[16] Housing is distinguished as "2 unit," "3 unit" or "married" quarters. There are eight roads with names: the Station Road, five avenues numbered from first to fifth, and two streets, First Street and Second Street. Only the plots for letting have been demarcated. Judging from the redrawn format, this plan seems to relate more to the organization of the various railway buildings within a context where the general layout of the town was already taken for granted.

Obviously, the form planned for the railway town at the foot of the hills had been influenced by the fact that the Railway could govern land one mile on both sides of the railway line. The railway line was planned to make two perpendicular turns, before and after the station, thus ensuring that all of the land between the railway line and the Nairobi River would fall within the jurisdiction of the Railway. In both plans, the engineering aspects attached to the construction of the railway line seem to have been of prime importance. The spatial organization of the activities of the railways formed the main content of the plan. The Railways, then, which had both suggested the building of the town and made the plans for its beginnings, perceived Nairobi as a railway town, established for the needs of the Uganda Railway. In this sense, the plans may also be seen as concretizations of the idea of an enlarged railway yard. Contrary to the arguments forwarded by Emig and Ismael that "the plan . . . directly expressed the notions of segregation of the town's functions and moreover segregation by class and race,"[17] the purpose of the plan was simply to organize the area allocated for the railway functions. In the context of the railway center, this also included the bazaar area. It was seen both as a practical necessity and as a valuable asset: with its plots for letting, the rents from the bazaar area were perceived by the Railways administration as contributing towards meeting the interest charges on the capital invested in the construction of the railway.[18] Thus from the Railways' point of view, Nairobi as it was planned was more about a railway center, and less about a town in a more general sense of the concept.

When Nairobi was founded with the railhead reaching the site on May 30 in 1899, the place was almost literally a "tabula rasa": a piece of land with just a few shacks and an old caravan track. The site was later described by R.O. Preston, one of the railway engineers, as

> a bleak, swampy stretch of soppy landscape, windswept, devoid of human habitation of any sort, the resort of thousands of wild animals

---

16　In Kenya, the dak bungalow referred to the building at a railway station, used for rest and refreshment (Huxley and Curtis 1980, 156); cf. British India, where it was a kind of a government guest house (King 1984, 44).
17　Emig and Ismael 1980, 9.
18　The *Report of the Uganda Railway Committee 1899* (Africa, No.6, 1899), quoted in Hill 1949, 190. The issue of land owned by the railway and adjacent to the railway line as sources of revenue had been mentioned already in the *Report on Mombasa-Victoria Lake Railway Survey* of 1893, quoted in Hill 1949, 92.

> . . . Lions were very plentiful in the then papurys swamp [on the Nairobi River] . . . the present Parklands area was one magnificent stretch of impenetrable forest composed chiefly of mohogo. The flat on which Nairobi itself stands did not boast one single tree.[19]

Everything had to be established from ideas and goods brought to the site from elsewhere. Less than ten years later, Colonel Patterson, the Divisional Engineer during the early years of Nairobi's history, wrote in his book *The Man-Eaters of Tsavo*:

> There was an immense amount of work to be done in converting an absolutely bare plain, three hundred and twenty-seven miles from the nearest place where even a nail could be purchased, into a busy railway centre. Roads and bridges had to be constructed, houses and workshops built, turn-tables and station quarters erected, a water supply laid on, and a hundred and one other things done which go to the making of a railway township. Wonderfully soon, however, the nucleus of the present town began to take shape, and a thriving bazaar sprang into existence with a mushroom-like growth.[20]

The citizens of the early Nairobi had come there from different parts of the world. In the early days, the Europeans of Nairobi mostly consisted of colonial officers, either employed by the Railways and involved in the supervising of the construction and later of the running of the Uganda Railway, officials of the Protectorate administration, or army officers. There were also shipping agents, a few contractors and commercial people, and big game hunters; many came from other British colonies. The Asians were usually Indians; altogether almost 32,000 coolies had been recruited from India by the Railways, over 6,700 of whom remained in the Colony, about 2,000 in the service of the Railways. Others became clerks, masons, cabinet makers, leather workers, tailors or gardeners, and a few entered into professions like draftsmen, physicians, lawyers and bankers; most, however, were shopkeepers with "*dukas*" (small shops). The military personnel included members of the Asian community. The Africans were laborers employed by the railway or the government, or working as domestic servants or shop assistants.[21]

In July 1899, the Railways headquarters were moved from Mombasa to

---

19 R.O.Preston (Kenya Graphic, 1922) quoted in Huxley (1935) 1968a, 61.
20 Patterson 1907 (1934 edition, 295f.) quoted in Hill 1949, 191. May 30 is quoted in the official records as the founding date, but according to Patterson, the date was June 5, 1899.
21 MP 1948, 12; Miller 1971, 543. India refers to the present India and Pakistan. Seidenberg (1983, 4f.) has noted that the British had encouraged the emigration of the Indian merchant class because they saw that Indian merchants would be useful in exploiting the resources of the new possession. For the number of Indians involved in the construction of the Railway, see Hill 1949, 240. Involved in the military operations in East Africa around the turn of the century were e.g. the Bombay Infantry, Sikhs and Punjabis and locally-enlisted Africans; some of them were also stationed in Nairobi (pp. 170, 283). According to Leys (Cell 1976, 103), the police and the King's African Rifles were "almost totally recruited from among the 'Mahomedams.'"

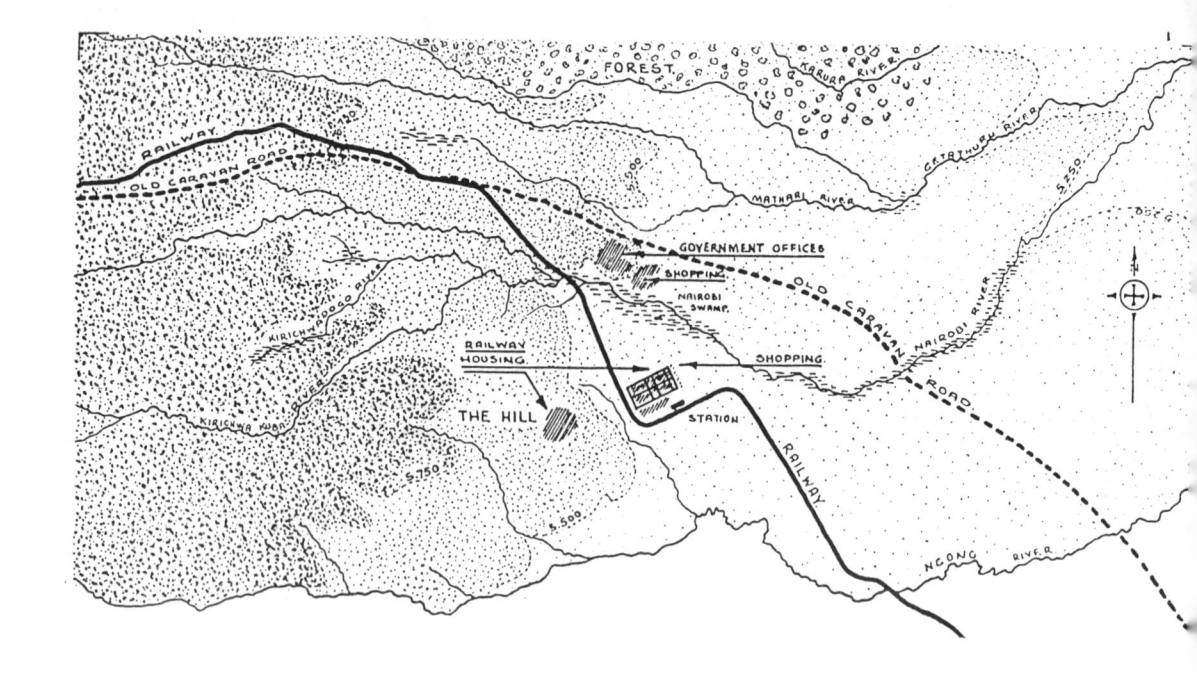

Nairobi, and in August, the railway was opened to the public.[22] In the same month, John Ainsworth, Sub-Commissioner of the Ukamba Province – which included Nairobi – on orders by the Foreign Office transferred the Provincial Headquarters from its earlier location at Machakos to the new railway town, an operation which was received by the Railways with little enthusiasm.[23] From the government's point of view, being located on the railway and not some forty miles off of it enabled the best connections for the administration, but from the Railways point of view, the presence of the government reduced the powers of the Railways administration over the organization of the town, particularly in matters related to land.

Maps presenting Nairobi at the turn of the century all confirm the impression of the centrality of the railway in how Nairobi was perceived. The railway line is shown as the basis of orientation. For example, in the map of "Nairobi (circa) 1900" presented in the brief history of Nairobi as part of the background of the *Nairobi Master Plan for a Colonial Capital*, published in 1948, the line indicating the railway and the station is the most prominent, followed by the line showing the old caravan road north of the Nairobi River

---

22 Hill 1949, 191.
23 Halliman and Morgan 1967, 99f.

Fig. 8.3 Map: Nairobi, c.1900

Fig. 8.4 Map: Nairobi, c.1900

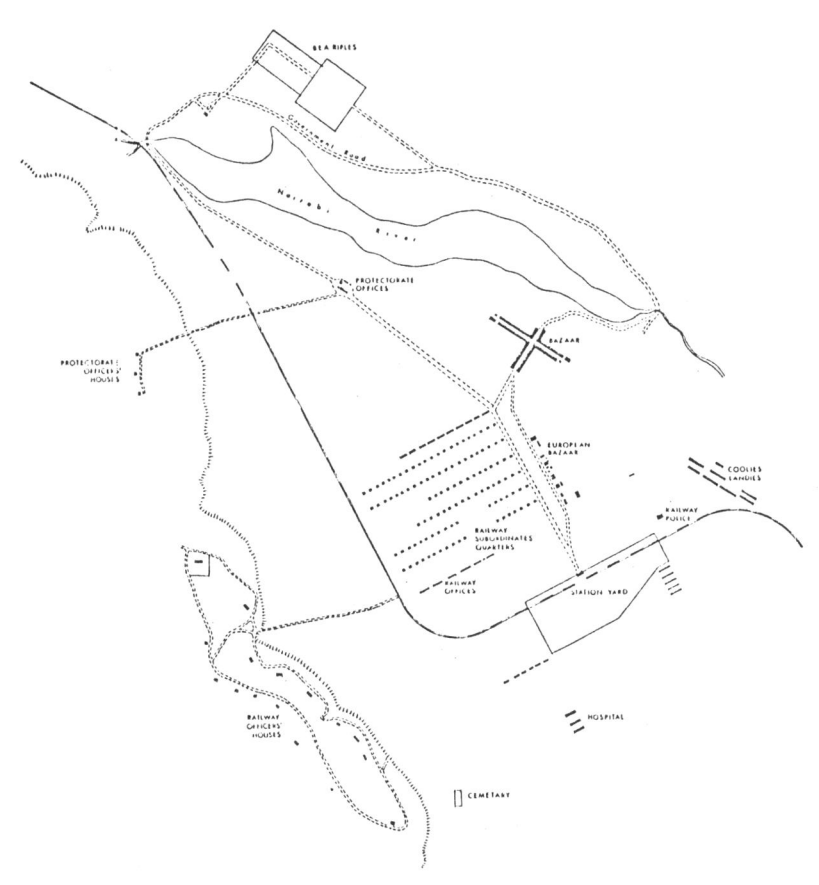

(*Fig. 8.3*).[24] In the map, the town itself is marked with a small gridiron of eight blocks of different sizes next to the station, more as a sign than as a cartographic representation of the existing urban form. The geographical location is shown in more detail, indicating the rivers and their tributaries, the swamp, the topography with contours at 250 feet intervals, and the forest. Arrows and shadings are used to show the position of the Hill, railway housing, shopping, and Government offices.

Similarly, the map marked as "Nairobi, c.1901" presented as part of the description of the historical background and development of Nairobi in Halliman's and Morgan's geographical study of the city and region in 1967, indicates the railway line and the station yard as the main points of reference (*Fig.8.4*).[25] In the map, the Nairobi River with its swamp and the edge of the hill are the only geographical elements shown. The Protectorate offices of the Ukamba Provincial administration, which were not indicated in any of the plans, now appear on the map about a mile northwest of the station, near the Nairobi River. The map shows the main road from the station to the Protectorate offices, and, identified as Government Road, looped around the

---

24 MP 1948, 11. The source of the map is not given.
25 Halliman and Morgan 1967, 101f. The source of the map is not given.

CHAPTER 8   THE BIRTH OF THE RAILWAY TOWN, 1895–1902

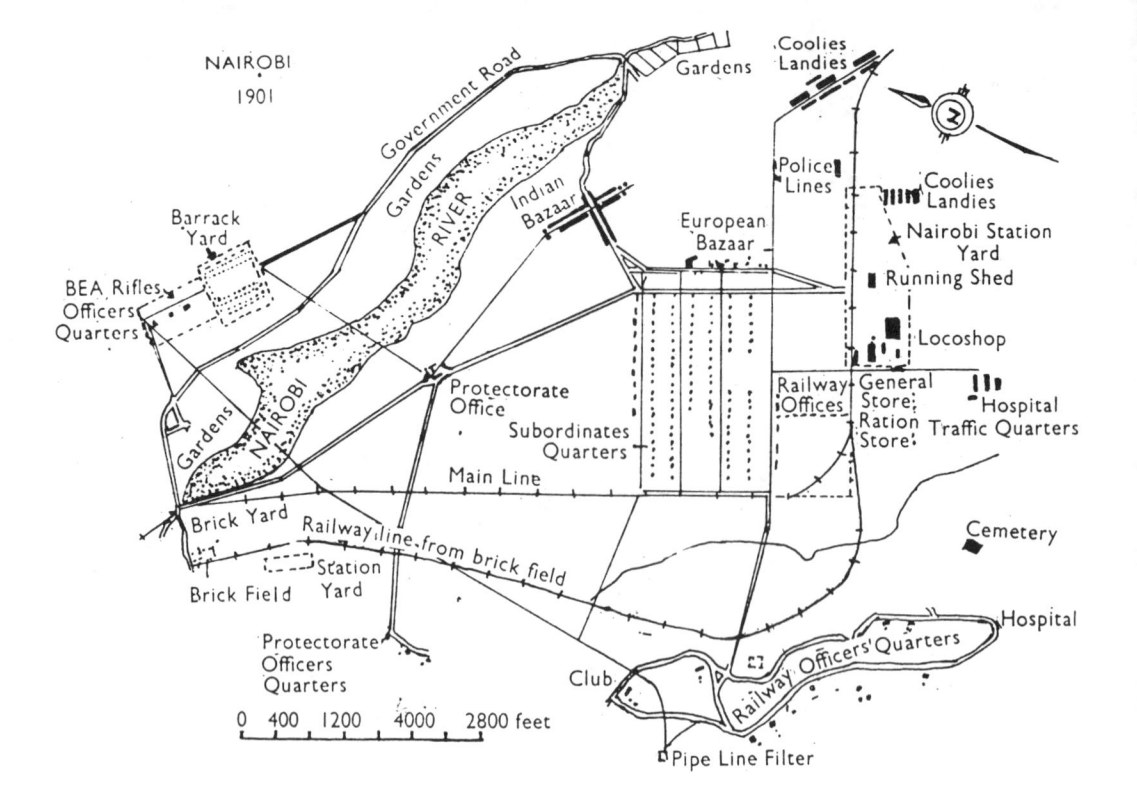

Fig. 8.5 Uganda Railway General Plan of Nairobi, 1901

Nairobi River swamp to the area marked as B.E.A. Rifles and back to the station road through the bazaar. Two roads to the Hill are also shown, one linking the Protectorate officers' houses to the Protectorate offices, and another to the Railway officers' houses. No other roads or streets are indicated, not even in the town center. On the map, the Railway subordinates quarters and Railway offices are located northwest of the station, the European bazaar comprised of individual buildings north of it, and another bazaar of two streets lined with a continuous built edge (unspecified in the map, but obviously the Indian bazaar) further north next to the swamp. The map also shows, near the station yard, the buildings of the railway police and, further northeast, the "*coolies landies*" (Indian workers' housing) as well as the hospital buildings and a "cemetary" to the south.

Another map, identified as the "Uganda Railway General Plan of Nairobi, 1901", shows more extensions (*Fig. 8.5*). New buildings are indicated in the railway yard, including the running shed, the locoshop, traffic quarters, the general store, the ration store, and two areas for coolies landies. In the map, a second railway line traverses between the earlier one and the Hill, connecting the station to the brick field and brick yard at the furthest part of the triangle forming the town. Gardens are marked north and east along the Nairobi River. On the other side of the Nairobi River, behind the gardens, are the B.E.A. Rifles, the Officers Quarters, and the Barrack Yard. With the exception of the river, other geographical elements are not indicated. Again,

Fig. 8.6 General view of Nairobi, 1899

the railway and its buildings dominate the presentation of the town.[26]

Photographs of early Nairobi illuminate something of the character of the initial phases of the town. Two photographs of Nairobi in 1899, taken from the Hill northwest of the station, show a wide extent of flat land with constructions: the first with tents in the foreground and some tens of houses near a railway track (*Fig.8.6*);[27] the second with already a somewhat more orderly outlook with rows upon rows of apparently newly-constructed houses spread in the landscape – the Railways housing area.[28] A short stretch of a kind of a street comprised of maybe six different buildings may be discerned behind them – the European bazaar on the Station Road; further away, more to the left, constructions forming a more uniform group – the Indian bazaar, and in the horizon to the left, the beginnings of the low hills and some tens of scattered trees. In Hill's *Permanent Way*, another photograph, taken a few years later from the same direction more towards the southeast, illustrates the still treeless plain dispersed with the station building, the locomotive sheds,

---

26　In a redrawn format in Tiwari 1981, 127; the source of the map is given as the Uganda Railway General Plan of Nairobi, 1901. Although the drawing is identified as a plan for Nairobi, that is, an envisaged future state of the town, it more probably is a map of it, that is, a representation of its existing state; cf. the maps of Nairobi in c.1901 and c.1905 in Halliman & Morgan 1967, 101f.
27　*Autonews*, October 1983, 22.
28　Miller 1971.

Fig. 8.7 Government Road from Market

Fig. 8.8 Sixth Avenue to the west, at Eliot Street

Fig. 8.9 Bazaar Street, 1904

the workshops, the offices, and some houses: a small railway community, but one which evoked the Railways historian to announce in the accompanying depiction that "a city had been born."[29] An aerial view of the railway town indicates the dominance of the railway workshop buildings in the townscape.[30]

The photographs, obviously originally taken for the Railways to document the history of the construction of the railway line, quite naturally focused on the buildings of the Railways. They may be compared to three photographs of the rest of the town from around the same time. One was identified with a printed text on it as the "Government Road from Market, Nairobi," showing a road lined on both sides with irregularly positioned trees, a few one-story buildings with brick walls and corrugated iron roofs on one side, and some people, among them three men in the foreground, one dressed in Arab-type clothing (*Fig. 8.7*).[31] Another photograph shows Sixth Avenue, apparently near the corner of Eliot Street, with some scattered buildings framing the wide road (*Fig. 8.8*).[32] In the third, Bazaar Street in 1904 was lined with busy shops with high pitched roofs; the streetscape also included oxen and a single street light (*Fig. 8.9*).[33]

The maps and photographs may be complemented by a description of Nairobi from 1902, written in a diary by Richard Meinertzhagen,[34] a young officer attached to the King's African Rifles, later categorized by the editor of the diaries, Elspeth Huxley, as "a killer" – of both animals for sport and tribesmen for duty:[35]

> 1.VI.1902. Nairobi . . . The only shop in Nairobi is a small tin hut which sells everything from cartridges at eightpence each and beer at five shillings a bottle to sardines, jam, tinned food, paraffin, etc. It is run by two bearded brothers called Stewart. The poor fellows say they are doing a roaring trade but that none of their customers will pay their bills and they may have to close down.
>
> The only hotel here is a wood and tin shanty sometimes known as Wood's Hotel and sometimes as the Victoria Hotel; it stands in the only "street," known as Victoria Street. Mr. Jeevanjee has a soda water factory; he also owns several bungalows, including the K.A.R. [King's African Rifles] lines, for which we pay him rent. Then there is also a firm called Boustead and Ridley, General Merchants; they built Nairobi Club.[36]

---

29 Hill 1949, 184a.
30 Blair 1980, 18.
31 Huxley and Curtis 1980, 17; the year 1900 has been handwritten on the photograph. If the description of Nairobi in 1899 as treeless is correct, the height of the trees would suggest that the photograph was taken at least some years later than 1900. In the book, the source of all the photographs, unpublished earlier, is given as private collections of pioneers' families.
32 Huxley and Curtis 1980, 17.
33 City of Nairobi Map and Guide, 1978. The caption notes that the view is from Biashara Street in 1904.
34 Meinertzhagen 1983. Meinertzhagen's diary covers the years 1902-1905 he spent in the East Africa Protectorate.
35 Elspeth Huxley's preface to Meinertzhagen 1983, v.
36 Meinertzhagen 1983, 9.

Neither the maps nor the photographs convey the relationship between those parts of Nairobi controlled by the Railways and the rest, falling under the jurisdiction of the Provincial government. The transfer of the administrative offices to Nairobi did narrow down the freedom of the Railways, but for some time still, the Railways continued to maintain the dominant position in the town. This was particularly evident from the built forms. As the situation was described in the report on the *Master Plan for a Colonial Capital* of 1948:

> A visitor to Nairobi at the beginning of the century would have been struck by the physical disparity of State apparatus and Railway Administration. Considering the scale of those days, the Uganda Railway was a large organization with a developed technical and administrative staff, employing large funds, and having at its disposal its own doctors, magistrates and police force. Its buildings were substantial and impressive in size. On the other hand, the provincial government had a paucity of staff, even unable to cope with the claims made upon it in the way of surveying and land division, and was miserably housed in corrugated iron structures.[37]

In its initial phase, then, Nairobi was conceived as a railway town, born from the needs of the construction of the railway and planned and built by railway personnel. In the process of establishing the town, however, geography also had a large role. Notions of the civilizing effect of the spread of the British imperial administration into the heart of Africa had geopolitical consequences, among them the idea of constructing the Uganda Railway. But the wheres and the hows of the operation were more directly related to the geography of the East African Protectorate, and, in the Nairobi case, more particularly to the engineering aspects of founding and maintaining railway headquarters. Thus the characteristics of the selected site as the meeting-point of the flat plains and the hills established the geographical duality of Nairobi. In this sense, the geography of Nairobi continues even today to influence the production of its urban forms.

---

37   MP 1948, 11.

9 Power disputes and sanitation problems, 1902–1910

Although Nairobi had initially come into being on the basis of a survey and plan, the subsequent changes in the town were more often related to evolving urban practices than to plans prepared in advance. This was particularly clear in the first decades of the century, when the plans prepared were responses to events experienced as problems. In the history of Nairobi, the first of these occurred just weeks after the railhead had reached the town: plague was reported in the Indian bazaar area. Plague had already hindered the construction of the railway line; in 1897, the outbreak of bubonic plague in India had caused a prohibition on the emigration of Indian coolies and subordinate staff and the construction had been crippled for months.[1] With new cases reported, rapid measures had to be taken to prevent the rest of the town from being infected. Colonel Patterson, then Divisional Engineer, described the situation:

> A case or two of plague broke out before very long, so I gave the natives and Indians who inhabited it an hour's notice to clear out, and on my own responsibility promptly burned the whole place to the ground.[2]

After the incineration, the bazaar was rebuilt on the same site.

But in 1902, another outbreak of plague occurred, causing 19 deaths out of the 63 cases recorded. Sir Charles Eliot, who had moved the Protectorate Headquarters from Mombasa two years after the railway line reached Nairobi, described the Indian bazaar where

> the Indians had built their houses so close together that they neutralized the natural advantages of air and light and then allowed the most disgusting filth to accumulate on a small area. To these predisposing causes must be added the presence of a large number of rats.[3]

Although medical opinion differed as to the origin of the plague since, as Hill noted, "no European was afflicted," it uniformly agreed that the remedy was to burn down the infected parts of the town, essentially the Indian bazaar. Some African villages were also burned down. According to rumors, a dead

---

[1] Hill 1949, 158.
[2] Patterson 1907 (1934 edition, 295f.) quoted in Hill 1949, 191.
[3] Quoted from Hill 1949, 227.

plague rat was found in the waiting-room of the railway station, but since the Traffic Manager, who did not wish the railway buildings to be added to those to be burned, removed it unobtrusively, "all was well and saved," as Hill assessed the situation. The owners of the ramshackle buildings in the Indian bazaar, however, had to suffer from the burning of their property, housing in tents, and rebuilding once again – even if they were compensated.[4]

After the second burning, the location of the Indian bazaar was moved to a new "temporary" site, further away from the swampy area towards the west to the present Biashara Street, formerly called Bazaar Street. The new bazaar area consisted of 138 shops, mostly one-storied, and numerous out-buildings on one main street and two back streets. According to Hake, around this time the bazaar began to house essentially only Asians and Africans, although Europeans had also had shops there earlier.[5] Dr. Radford, Medical Officer in 1904, described the area:

> The bazaar was a collection of tin huts, used indiscriminately as dwelling houses, shops, stores, laundries, wash-houses, opium dens, bakeries, brothels, butchers' shops, etc., etc. The amounts of goods stored varied from 800-1,000 tons, rats abounded, and the general conditions of life of the 1,500-2,000 inhabitants were miserable and filthy in the extreme.[6]

Another plague broke out there in 1904, causing parts of the bazaar to be burned down; this was still, as the experts of the *Master Plan* of 1948 commented, "the only method of town improvement known to Africa."[7] The event provoked suggestions for the transfer of the whole town to a more salubrious location; the Railways opposed. Errol Trzebinski later described the prevailing mood during the initial years as one of uncertainty: while the location of the town was open, people were reluctant to commit themselves to investment or development.[8] Discussions about the site continued until 1906, but finally, because of the vested interests involved, the removal of the town was considered impractical.[9] As Winston Churchill later wrote,

---

[4] Hill 1949, 227. The source of Hill's view that no European was afflicted is not given. In her book dealing with the early history of the colony, *White Man's Country: Lord Delamere and the Making of Kenya*, Elspeth Huxley (1968, 87) gives an even more dramatic depiction of the event: "Nairobi, in fact, had been entirely rebuilt [in January 1903]. An outbreak of bubonic plague occurred in 1902 and sixteen people died. The principal medical officer, a thorough man, was as offended as Jehovah had been at the sins of Sodom and Gomorrah; and, following the divine precedent, he burnt Nairobi down - bazaar, native villages, military lines, railway workshops and all. This drastic quarantine measure cost the Government £50,000, a sum equal to about half the total annual revenue." To my knowledge, Huxley's notion of the whole of Nairobi having been burned down is not supported by other sources.

[5] Hake 1977, 174, also noted that only four buildings were two-storied in 1904.

[6] Quoted in MP 1948, 15.

[7] MP 1948, 14.

[8] Trzebinski 1985, 73, also referring to the unpublished biography of Otto Markus.

[9] MP 1948, 12.

> The ground on which the town is built is low and swampy. The supply of water is indifferent and the situation generally unhealthy. It is now too late to change, and thus lack of foresight and of a comprehensive view leaves its permanent imprint upon the countenance of a new country.[10]

Sanitation was to become one of the major areas of interest for the local government. John Ainsworth, Sub-Commissioner of the Ukamba Province, was the promotor of the local government and the first chairman of the Nairobi Municipal Committee. The first Committee consisted of two railway officials, one Protectorate official, three local merchants, and the Sub-Commissioner as the Chairman; later, the composition varied, but throughout all the changes, the role of the Committee was purely advisory, without a real representative content. The decisions on municipal matters remained within the Protectorate Government.[11] In 1904, an ordinance was passed for the Colony concerning matters like streets, roads, the erection of buildings, sanitation, slaughter houses, bakeries, markets, lodging houses, the preservation of order, and many other things. A year later, another ordinance was related to Nairobi, and the following year, one on the Dhobi (washermen) quarters.[12] But there was little control over how the rules were fulfilled; as the first town planning expert consulted, G. Bransby-Williams, noted in 1907 in his report on the sanitation of Nairobi:

> Cases have occurred in Nairobi of houses being built without the plans having been submitted to any authority. The penalty imposed for the offence has been usually a fine for 15 rupees, so that under existing rules it is possible to erect almost any kind of building for a merely nominal fine. The Municipal Authority has no power to pull down buildings erected without their sanction, and this power they certainly should have.[13]

The Nairobi Municipal Regulations had been published on 16 April 1900, with the town established as "that area within a radius of $1\frac{1}{2}$ miles from the present office of H.M.Sub-Commissioner in Ukamba"; Halliman and Morgan described this first boundary of Nairobi as a "completely arbitrary one."[14] The boundary marked the extent of the township's jurisdiction. However, the definition of the boundary was also a statement by the government on the role of the town: Nairobi was to be perceived as a town for Provincial Headquarters, that is, as an administrative center. Its focus was the office of the Sub-Commissioner, irrespective of the railway area. In fact, the location

---

10 Churchill, *My African Journey*, 1909, 19, quoted in Hill 1949, 288.
11 MP 1948, 16f. Hake (1977, 35) noted that the members included, in addition to the Sub-Commissioner, two other officials and three "suitable residents," chosen annually by the Sub-Commissioner.
12 MP 1948, 13.
13 Bransby-Williams, *Report on the Sanitation of Nairobi*, 1907, 11, quoted in MP 1948, 13.
14 Halliman and Morgan 1967, 102.

of the boundary was such that the southernmost parts of the railway officers housing area just barely fit within the municipal boundary, while large areas of land suitable for residential purposes north of the center were included within the boundary, thus offering the government possibilities for selling residential plots for urban habitation.

From the beginning, land was one of the main issues in the formation of Nairobi; the measures taken concerning the plague cases were just symptomatic of the fundamental interests at stake. The Railways and the Protectorate Government disputed over who would have the control over the use of land. The Railways perceived the town area as a place where sufficient land was to be available to them, free of charge, both for the necessary buildings and railway yard, and for the renting of land for commercial purposes to receive revenues on the invested capital; since Nairobi was seen as a railway town, this concerned most of the land in the town center. The government saw the town as the base for the administration of the country and the urban plots as resources which should be offered to enterprising private individuals and companies. Neither expected the town to grow as fast as it did; neither planned for the changes that occurred. The experts of the *Master Plan* of 1948 described the situation as one where

> At first there was a duality of control; later there was evidenced an erroneous respect for the sanctity of private rights of property, including the right to do wrong. At all times there was stringency of money and of technical ability.[15]

The government administration gave plots on freehold, sometimes free of charge, and without conditions regarding their development; as a consequence, the holdings were usually subdivided into small plots and only partially used for building, creating congestion and sanitation problems. The other parts of the plot were left unbuilt in the hope that the value would be increased of the whole holding. At the time, land speculation was common in Nairobi, which a town planning expert noted some ten years later in his report on the question of sanitation in East Africa:

> Serious mistakes were made, such as the granting to individuals of large blocks of land in the township, entailing grave difficulties in regard to town planning, and almost prohibitive expense in respect of public services.[16]

In the bazaar area, most of the plots in the early years had been bought by a handful of wealthy Indian businessmen,[17] among them A.M. Jeevanjee who had made a fortune as a railway contractor and became Nairobi's leading

---

15 MP 1948, 16.
16 W.J. Simpson, *Report on Sanitary Matters in the East Africa Protectorate, Uganda and Zanzibar*, 1914, 5, quoted in MP 1948, 16.
17 Hake 1977, 175.

builder.[18] The owners of the plots in the bazaar area either let them or, if they had sufficient resources, constructed buildings on them for letting. These buildings were used both for shops and as accommodation. Later calculations have suggested that the owner could get as much as a 100 per cent yearly return on the original investment.[19] Finn Barnow has noted that after an Indian company had in 1903 bought 57 hectares of land in the "heart of Nairobi," the colonial administration adopted the practice that sales of property between different racial groups was forbidden, "making the bazaar area into a ghetto for the 1800 Indians of Nairobi."[20] The policy not only restricted habitation, but also investment. In effect, the possibilities of non-Europeans (particularly Asians who had the necessary capital) to make profits on land were fundamentally narrowed, and consequently, those of the Europeans were improved. Nevertheless, in 1905 Ainsworth reported that

> up to within quite recent times, European capital and enterprise have been almost entirely absent. There is, and will be, room for such enterprise, but at present . . . fully 80 per cent of the capital and business energy of the country is Indian.[21]

A map marked as "Central Nairobi, c.1905," presented by Halliman and Morgan in 1967 in their discussion of the town and its surroundings, indicates the first demarcation of the town area, the municipal boundary (*Fig. 9.1*). The map shows how the town had grown in size and how the road network had been developed in the center and in the suburbs, both on the Hill, the first residential area, and in Parklands, the new suburb for government officers behind the Nairobi River. The Indian bazaar was now located west of Government Road. New government offices and public buildings can also be identified: Public Works Department offices, the Roman Catholic Church, the Government House, the (Railway) Club, Gymkhana (a sports club), and a hospital.[22]

East Africa had been promoted as a place for settlement for various groups, both in England and elsewhere. Already in 1893, F.D. Lugard had recommended white settlement in his book *The Rise of Our East African Empire*.[23] In 1901, Sir Harry Johnston wrote: "Indian trade, enterprise and emigration require a suitable outlet. East Africa is, and should be, from every

---

18　Hill 1949, 288.
19　Mary Parker, *Political and Social Aspects of the Development of Municipal Government in Kenya, with Special Reference to Nairobi*, unpublished dissertation, University of London, 1949, quoted in Hake 1977, 175.
20　"Efter at et indisk firma i 1903 havde köbt et areal på 57 ha i 'hjertet af Nairobi', godkendte kolonimyndighederne, at der i sköder på forretningsejendomme indföjedes et forbud mod salg mellem forskellige racegrupper. Dette gjorde byens Bazaar-området til en ghetto for Nairobis 1800 indere" (Barnow 1990, 60, my translation). The source of the statement concerning the changed practices is not given.
21　Quoted in Hill 1949, 286.
22　Halliman and Morgan 1967, 102.
23　Huxley 1968a, 70.

Fig. 9.1 Map: Nairobi, c.1905

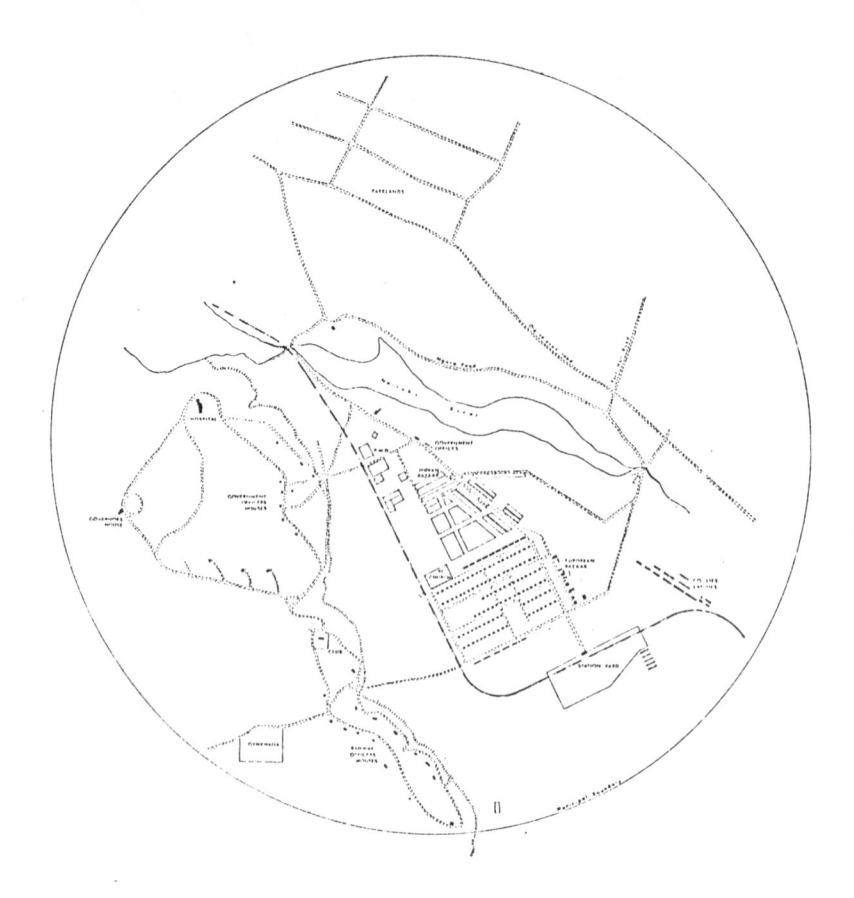

point of view, the America of the Hindu."[24] Around that time, the Highlands were suggested by the Foreign Office as a place for a colony of Finns and parts of the Mau areas for Zionists, but both ideas were later discarded.[25] Activities were also directed at parties closer; for example, the Commissioner of the Protectorate sent a mission to South Africa in 1903 to attract settlers, with hundreds responding to the call.[26] The results of the policies could soon be seen. The first census of Nairobi in 1906 showed that the population of the town had reached 13,500 of whom about 9,300 were Africans, 3,600 Asians, and 600 Europeans.[27]

At this time, the location of Nairobi and its role as an administrative and commercial center had been established to the point that expertise was sought on sanitation and town planning, and in 1906, the Williams Commission was

---

24　Johnston's final report to the Foreign Office (Africa, No.7, 1901), quoted in Hill 1949, 219. Sir Harry Johnston was Special Commissioner in Uganda from 1899 to 1901.
25　Huxley 1968a, 117-125; see also Hill 1949, 275ff.
26　Hill 1949, 268.
27　Political Record Book, Nairobi District (Kenya National Archives, PC/PC 1/8, piece n:o 1) referred to in Barnow et al 1983, 17. Similar figures are presented in the Appendix to the Master Plan of 1948 (p. 84), with two sources of information: the census reported in the Williams Report of 1907 and those in the Feetham Report of 1926.

brought from England. George Bransby-Williams submitted his report in January 1907.[28] By 1906, Nairobi had evolved into a town with seven distinct areas, as Bransby-Williams identified them. They were the Railway Center, the Indian Bazaar, the European Business and Administration Center, the Railway Quarters, the Dhobi (washermen) Quarter, the European residential suburbs, and the Military barracks outside town.[29] Behind the impressive names were areas which in reality appeared insignificant. The Government and European Business Center, for example, consisted of the government offices on the main road from the station northwards, Government Road, which continued over the Nairobi River, and of commercial buildings on plots along it and a parallel road, Victoria Street. The Indian Commercial area covered only 6 acres and contained one main street (Bazaar Street), branching off Government Road, and two back streets; it consisted of one-storied buildings with shops in the front and dwellings for shopkeepers, assistants and lodgers at the back. The 90 acres used for Railway quarters were located between the Station Road and the railway line, containing residential bungalows in six rows; two long rows of landies for laborers were on the other side of the railway station yard. The Dhobi quarter on the other side of Nairobi River, along Ngara Road, contained the houses of government subordinate officials and the washermen's dwellings, as well as the vegetable gardens around the swamp cleared of papyrus. The European residential suburbs spread on the hills around the center, on the west to the Hill and on the northeast to Parklands inhabited by government officials. Outside the municipal boundary, beyond Dagoretti Road were the military barracks of two battalions of the King's African Rifles.[30] Halliman and Morgan have emphasized that to a large extent, the road network of the center of the city – as they saw it in 1967 – was established by 1909, with the central area determined by the railway alignment, the Nairobi River, and the edge of the hills to the west, and the street pattern following from the geometrical relationship of these features.[31]

Early Nairobi described

Three descriptions of Nairobi in the first decade may be quoted here. Richard Meinertzhagen, an officer in the King's African Rifles, who had first arrived in Nairobi in 1902 and had visited the town only a few times after that, wrote in his diary in 1906:

---

28   MP 1948, 12.
29   Tiwari 1981, 128. I have not been able to study George Bransby-Williams' *Report on the Sanitation of Nairobi, British East Africa Protectorate* (London, 1907) but have referred to quotations and summaries of it in the *Master Plan* of 1948 (pp.12-16); Halliman and Morgan 1967, 104; Hake 1977, 36ff, 129; and Tiwari 1981, 128.
30   The description is from MP 1948, 14.
31   Halliman and Morgan 1967, 104.

> 4.IV.1906. Nairobi. Arrived at Nairobi this morning. I naturally expected to find great changes in the place, but was much surprised to see such a transformation scene as I witnessed today. The town has trebled itself in size. Trees have sprung up everywhere, hotels exist where zebras once roamed, private bungalows in all their ugliness now mar the landscape where I used to hunt the waterbuck, impala and duiker. The place is full of strange faces and I felt quite lost. Two years ago I knew every soul of the 20 or 30 Europeans. There are now over 1200 Europeans in the town.
>
> I visited my miserable little 20 acres, now bereft of duiker and guinea-fowl. I was much amused when I was told that the new Government house was going to be built on my property; nobody has asked my permisson, and I shall certainly not broach the subject. I can see a most amusing tangle developing.[32]

The second quotation concerns Nairobi in 1909. Kirsti Gallen-Kallela, daughter of the famous Finnish painter Akseli Gallen-Kallela, lived in Nairobi for over a year from 1909 to 1910.[33] In her father's biography, first published in 1964, she also wrote of her own memories of their stay in Africa when she was thirteen years old:

> At that time, 1909-1910, [Nairobi] was a small village inhabited by about 500 white people, the rest [were] Hindus . . . The main street then ran from one end of the town to the other, from the station to the fine Norfolk Hotel, and thereafter started the primary road across the wilderness to Fort Hall. The street was lined with tall eucalyptus trees . . . Along the main street were the shops of the whites, built of corrugated iron . . . The cross street was entirely a Hindu bazaar; its shanties had been subdivided into cabins with the floor at the level of the buyer's head. The front wall was missing and the sloped floor had been filled with open boxes of rice, maize, peas etc. . . . Further was a roofed market hall from where the white ladies bought their food stuffs, mostly all kinds of fruit and vegetables . . . The Hindu temple was located at the crossing of the main street and the bazaar [street].[34]

And in her memoirs of 1896-1931, published in 1982, she wrote:

> Hotel Stanley in Nairobi was in 1909 a wild west style two-story building with a corrugated iron roof, located on Nairobi's main street, Governement [sic] Road. There were hardly any other streets . . . We stayed in Hotel Stanley for four weeks, until we got our own house outside Nairobi at the edge of the plains.[35]

---

32 Meinertzhagen 1983, 301; compare this with Meinertzhagen's notes on his arrival in the town in 1902, see above. Nb. According to the official census of 1906, the European population of Nairobi numbered about 600 persons.
33 The family arrived in Nairobi in May 1909, lived in the Stanley Hotel for the first four weeks and after that in the "Brickhouse" outside town on the road to Fort Hall, went on a four-month safari between April and August 1910, and left Nairobi in the fall of 1910 (Gallen-Kallela 1992, 463-501).
34 Gallen-Kallela 1992, 463-465, my translation. For the original text in Finnish, see Appendix 3.
35 Gallen-Kallela 1982, 49, my translation. For the original text in Finnish, see Appendix 3.

Fig. 9.2 View from the second floor window of the Stanley Hotel, 1909

A photograph taken by Akseli Gallen-Kallela in June 1909, obliquely downwards apparently from a second-floor window in Hotel Stanley, shows part of the roof and walls of three buildings, one of brick and two of corrugated iron, with covered terraces built on plinths towards the street (*Fig. 9.2*). A sign bearing the text "Tailors" is attached to the front of the nearest building. On the right, some meters away from the buildings, an open drain with the edges strengthened with stonework is visible. In the middle of the photograph is a group of maybe five to ten Africans, seated on the ground, identified in the attached depiction as "natives waiting for work."[36]

The third description of Nairobi at that time emphasizes the difference between the town's ordinary sleepy character and its occasional festive spirit. In her book on Lord Delamere, first published in 1935, Elspeth Huxley, who spent most of her childhood in Kenya, wrote of Nairobi around 1908-1911:

> Nairobi in those days was a queer mixture. It looked like a humdrum little South African dorp, straggling rather listlessly in the sun and occupied, by a handful of European officials and store-keepers, a mob of Indians packed into the insanitary and smelly bazaar, and a drifting population of all breeds of natives. Two or three times a year it would suddenly fill with sunburnt, tattered settlers in broad-brimmed felt hats and revolver holsters. At such times there was something of an eighteenth-century spirit about the place.[37]

---

36 The photographic collection in the Gallen-Kallela Museum Archives. This is the only photograph in the collection which shows buildings or streets in Nairobi, apart from the two houses the family lived in. Kirsti Gallen-Kallela has identified the photographs.
37 Huxley 1968a, 256.

This description cannot be based on Huxley's own observations, since she was only four years old in 1911; it may, however, reflect the views of the Nairobi Europeans in the first decades.

Nairobi was still a small town in 1906. It had grown from a "tabula rasa" at the edge of the plains into a railway and administrative town of some thirteen thousand inhabitants, but its character was dominated by dusty roads and scattered, mostly temporary constructions. Its urban form was by any standards incoherent, with unbuilt plots and areas interrupting any buds of urbanization. Contrary to what was maintained in the *Master Plan* of 1948,[38] this pattern of the urban form of Nairobi was not "the result of spontaneous growth," but had developed on the basis of the initial "Plan of survey" of "Nairobe" prepared by Church in 1898 and the "Uganda Railway Plan of Staff Quarters, Nyrobi" signed by Whitehouse in 1899. Since the center of the town was the area planned, the main central functions of the early railway town had evolved according to these plans. They included the railway line, the station and station yard, the offices, the various railway services like the hospital and police, the residential units for different categories, and the European bazaar. But events not foreseen in the plans had also influenced the town's formation. Three chains of events were particularly important. One of them was the events around the Indian bazaar which, while seen as a normal element of an East African town but not planned for, had nevertheless emerged. Its congestion and lack of sufficient drainage had soon thereafter prepared the ground for the appearance of plague and caused a process during which this part of the town was first burned down, rebuilt, again burned down, and eventually moved to a different location, all without a plan but improving, through practical measures, the salubrious conditions of the town as a totality.

Another chain of events was attached to the transfers of, with the railhead reaching Nairobi, first, the Provincial offices from Machakos and, two years later, the Protectorate Headquarters from Mombasa, to Nairobi; both contributed to the change of the conception of Nairobi from a railway community to an administrative and commercial center within a British Protectorate. Finally, the third chain of events around the rapid population growth was partly attributable to settlement policies commenced even before Nairobi existed, partly to active advocation from the Protectorate, and partly to external events like the end of the Boer War which provoked the emigration of settlers from South Africa. The urban form of Nairobi in its initial phases, then, was the result of both the first survey plans and the later practices of the various groups involved in living in the town. The urban pattern thus established became the foundation of much of central Nairobi as it appeared some eighty years later.

---

38   MP 1948, 14.

10 Segregation plans and practices, 1910–1919

In the first decade of Nairobi's history, the allocation of land was based primarily on ownership: the railways' land was separate from Crown land governed by the Protectorate officials, and both were distinct from land sold to private individuals or companies. The secondary distinguishing element was land use, with the railways workshop area separated from railways housing areas, for example, or the Protectorate administrative offices from military barracks. These kind of functional distinctions, however, were not applied to all areas in the same way: while the railway and Protectorate areas were classified according to each land use, the Indian bazaar contained an integration of functions from shops, warehouses, and dwellings to religious buildings. Ethnic distinctions were only third on the list, and even then only partially. Thus, while Asian shopkeepers were restricted to dwellings located in the Indian bazaar, railways' housing – which included Asians – was not identified ethnically but according to the work the dweller performed for the company. Because of recruitment policies and the characteristics of the employees, in the Nairobi context the employee's position was, indeed, related to ethnicity, but was not as absolute as a purely ethnic criterion would have been. Even then, identification of areas according to the position of the employee may be somewhat misleading. For instance, in the housing area for the (European) railway officials, located on the Hill, the African domestic servants, employed by the railway employee, also inhabited the same plot and neighborhood, albeit in less fortunate conditions. Spatial segregation in early Nairobi, then, was to an extent based on social status, but not purely on ethnicity.

The events relating to the "sanitation" of the Indian bazaar, however, introduced the notion of ethnic segregation into the discussion of Nairobi town planning. In connection with the bazaar area, the first suggestions – like the burning of the bazaar and its removal further away from the town center – involved only the protection of the Europeans from the other groups. It was the European community of early Nairobi which was concerned about the low level of hygiene and sanitation followed especially in the Asian and African areas from where contagious diseases were perceived to spread undiscriminately to areas inhabited by Europeans. Preventive measures were seen as the means to ensure a healthy environment for all; if social control was necessary for this to be fulfilled, so be it. Walter Elkan and Roger van Zwanenberg have argued that in the situation in early Nairobi when plague had occurred several times despite the burning out of the congested areas, there were only two alternatives open to the officials: either to lay down minimal standards for the whole town or to create for the Europeans enclaves of sanitation; of these, the second alternative was chosen. According to Elkan and Zwanenberg, three things commended the strategy to the municipal administration: not only would it combat the contagion of disease, but it would also facilitate control of the African population and of (their) movement into Nairobi.[1]

In fact, although enclaves were created in Nairobi, they were not for Europeans, as Elkan and Zwanenberg maintained, but for the "others," the Asians and Africans. Nairobi was perceived by the colonialists as a European town where European urban practices set the standards and where practices deviating from them could be tolerated only in restricted conditions. Within the town boundary, the restricted conditions referred to spatial limits, to areas reserved for particular groups; in Nairobi, these included the "Indian bazaar" identified as an Asian commercial and residential area and the "native location" for African habitation. The Indian bazaar had emerged, unplanned, with the railway construction reaching Nairobi in 1899, and a site for a native location (on the other side of Nairobi River, downstream from the landies, in present Pumwani) had been chosen by the Sites' Committee of the Township in the first years of the century.[2] In both cases, the idea was to limit the extent of the urban problems seen to be caused by each group by limiting the space within which the group could operate. With the definition of the boundaries of each enclave, the rest of the town would be protected from harmful effects. The separation of the problem areas from the rest of the town was justified by reasons pertaining to sanitation and health. Bransby-Williams' report on the sanitation of Nairobi had contained proposals not only on sanitation, drainage, and the administrative measures needed for sanitary improvements, but also on a new site for the Indian bazaar, a site for a new native location, and the general layout of Nairobi.[3] Although few of his proposals were realized because of lack of funds, the notion of segregation on an ethnic basis had received expert authorization.

Bransby-Williams had estimated that the population of Nairobi would reach 20,000 by 1916, but it had already grown to that level by 1912.[4] Nairobi began to expand and attract investments, with the prices of land within the township or immediately outside it rising. Significant profits could be made

---

1   Elkan and Zwanenberg 1975, 663.
2   Hake 1977, 129. A Native Location Subcommittee was appointed in 1911. The beginning of the discussion on the "native location" has been dated in two different ways: according to Hake 1977, 129, the Sites' Committee had decided on the site in 1906, while Ross 1975, 19, referred to the 1913-14 Annual Report of the District Commissioner.
3   Bransby-Williams, *Report on the Sanitation of Nairobi*, 1907, referred to in Hake 1977, 36.
4   Hake (1977, 38) refers to Mary Parker's unpublished thesis (1949), based on the Annual Reports of the Medical Officer of Health. For 1912, the same figure - broken down into 15,000 Africans, 3,700 Asians, and 1,200 Europeans - is also given in the *Master Plan* (p.84), based on the "Taylor Report," not otherwise identified.

by selling plots bought cheaply earlier and by subdividing larger plots into smaller ones. Control of the subdivision and development of the plots was minimal or absent. Hake gives several examples of the kind of economic activities practiced:

> Muthaiga (754 acres) was sold in 1912 for £20 an acre to Major Morrison who shortly afterwards subdivided it into four-acre plots under no Government control . . . [Eastleigh's] 2,003 acres [located some three kilometers northeast of the center] were bought freehold in two lots at Rs.1 [one rupee] an acre in 1904 and 1905. In 1912, 654 acres of the block were subdivided by the owners into 3,332 plots and it was discovered that the Government had no power to impose any conditions.[5]
> In Eastleigh . . . a member of the Municipal Council . . . with three other Nairobi residents and backers from South Africa, bought land and contractually undertook construction of seven miles of frontage streets and fourteen miles of lanes, also drains and water supply "at such time and in such manner as they saw fit." They disposed of their interests to an Indian businessman, Mr. Allidina Visram [one of the wealthy Indians who also owned major portions in the bazaar area], before they "saw fit" to do any of these things . . . Lord Cranworth . . . recouped £5,000 on the sale of the depot plot in Nairobi which he had previously bought for almost nothing.[6]

The Indian bazaar became more congested than ever, and new African villages sprung up around town. Outbreaks of plague occurred in 1911, 1912, and 1913.[7] In his book *Kenya*, published in 1924, Norman Leys drew attention to the fact that around 1912, the 2,235 Europeans of Nairobi occupied some 2,700 acres, while in the bazaar area some 4,300 persons – the majority of them Indians – had only seven acres for habitation.[8] Without control, the subdivision and development of plots had contributed to generating a situation where persons and companies with capital for investing could strongly influence the conditions of habitation of the different cultural groups living in Nairobi. Furthermore, the practices of the local administration, where sale and occupation of plots was allowed only within each ethnic group, supported ethnic segregation during the processes of the growth and expansion of Nairobi in the first decades.[9]

---

5   Hake 1977, 255. Muthaiga and Eastleigh were then situated outside the municipal boundary.
6   Hake 1977, 38.
7   Hake 1977, 38.
8   Leys 1973, 286, refers to "official medical reports twelve years old." Leys was employed as a medical officer in Nyasaland and Eastern Africa from 1902 to 1918, of which 1908-13 in the East Africa Protectorate (Kenya). He was - as the editor of his correspondence with Oldham (Cell 1976, 7) has noted - "possessed by Kenya." Nb. Leys' population figures do not correspond to those of 1912 given above.
9   Barnow 1990, 60, did not give the source of his claim that sales between races were forbidden, but the example of Eastleigh from 1912 (quoted above from Hake) would seem to contradict it. However, other researchers have also commented on the adopted practices - unsupported by law - which rejected Asian expansion within the central business area

The appearance of plague resulted first in the setting up of a local commission, and in 1913 an outside expert, Professor W.J. Simpson, was invited to give advice on sanitary matters. His analysis of the conditions of Nairobi was harsh:

> The present temporary Government offices are for the greater part the most decrepit looking structures it is possible to imagine. The Sub-Commissioner of Ukamba Province, the Collector and the Sub-Collector of Nairobi district, the Chief Veterinary Officer, the Commissioner of Lands, the Director of Survey, the Land Officer, the Transport Officer, and the Government Bacteriologist, with the whole staff of clerks and subordinates, carry on their work in these corrugated iron sheds, which appear to be overcrowded and as inconveniently arranged as possible. The sanitary arrangements are very defective. At the time of my visit of inspection one closet served for the officials in the whole of the offices, about 30 in number, one for 40 or 50 clerks, and one for a large number of native orderlies, porters, police, etc . . .
> [In the Civil Native Hospital] the ward in which I was informed plague patients had been treated is only thinly partitioned from the receiving room. The rain water from the roof and the effluent from the latrines is conveyed by a cement channel to a point at the back where it discharges into the open about 30 yards from the irrigation channel, which at this place runs parallel to Government Road. Into this channel the drainage finally soaks. The post-mortem room has no drainage of any kind. The Hospital was constructed some three or four years ago, and was condemned from the outset by the medical authorities as being hopelessly insanitary.[10]

Simpson also commented on the slow completion of the drainage scheme suggested by Bransby-Williams and the fact that despite the proposals, the Indian Bazaar had not yet been moved:

> These, together with the haphazard growth of the town which is being permitted, have brought about such a condition of insanitation that Nairobi, although scarcely 14 years old, and aspiring to be a European town, is in its commercial area one of the most insanitary I have seen.[11]

---

outside the bazaar; see e.g. Kimani 1972, 394; Seidenberg 1983, 12. Kimani also referred to Mary Parker's unpublished thesis (1949, 33-75) and to the East African Royal Commission Report of 1953-1955 (200-50).

10 Simpson's *Report on Sanitary Matters in the East Africa Protectorate, Uganda and Zanzibar* has been quoted from and referred to in the *Master Plan* of 1948 (pp.13-16); Hake 1977, 39, 129, 176. In the Master Plan, the report was dated at 1913, in Hake at 1914. Tiwari (1981, 129) also referred to Simpson's report, but his source was titled "Nairobi Sanitary Commission, Report and Evidence" (1913). In 1903, Simpson had given similar advice on plague remedy in Hongkong in his *Report on the Causes and Continuance of Plague in Hongkong and suggestions as to remedial measures*; the report is included under Colonial Office in the *British Library Catalogue of Printed Books II*, 1975.

11 Simpson 1913, 5, quoted in MP 1948, 16.

Simpson's proposals included the removal of the Indian Bazaar from its present location, the establishment of a new, non-residential bazaar further away from the commercial area, and the erection of a native location near the place where it had been suggested earlier.[12] Simpson recommended the separation both of different races and of different functions, a plan based on complete segregation. To support the recommendations, he elaborated:

> In towns where the nationality is the same, town planning resolves itself into arranging for residential, commercial and manufacturing areas, which are further governed in character by rental and class, and in such a way as to secure convenience, good transit, pleasing amenities, and permanent healthiness for all. Something more than this is required in towns, such as those in East Africa, where the nationalities are diverse and their customs and habits different from one another. Though the same objects have to be aimed at, it has to be recognised that the standard and mode of life of the Asiatic, except in the highest class, do not consort with those of the European, and that, on the other hand, many European habits are not acceptable to Asiatics, and that the customs of the primitive African, unfamiliar with and not adapted to the new conditions of town life, will not blend in with either. In the interest of each community and of the healthiness of the locality and country, it is absolutely essential that in every town and trade center the town planning should provide well-defined and separate quarters for European, Asiatic and African, with easy and good communication between them, as well as those divisions which are necessary in a town of one nationality and race.[13]

Simpson's ostensibly practical arguments were in reality not only ethnocentric and blind to the particular contents of the non-European cultures, but also illustrated a belief in the preordainedly higher civilization of the Europeans and in their superior capacity to organize the ways all the other cultural groups of Nairobi lived. Thus ethnic segregation was to secure, for the Europeans of Nairobi, the advantageous positions they had by then managed to gather for themselves; the interests of the other groups were referred to only as deviating from those of the Europeans – "except in the highest class" of Asiatics. Functional segregation, on the other hand, was seen as the universal and self-evident purpose of town planning in general; the notion that integration was typical to non-European – as well as some European – urban traditions was not noticed nor accepted as a viable alternative.

In this context, a town plan of 1913 illuminates the problematic of segregation from a slightly different direction. The plan, titled "Nairobi: Sketch-map of Segregation Proposals", is signed by A.M. Jeevanjee, one of the two Asian members of the Municipal Committee (*Fig. 10.1*).[14] Two

---

12 According to the *Master Plan* of 1948, the bazaar was to be located north of the river, and according to Hake, south of it.
13 Simpson 1913, 53, quoted in Thornton White et al 1948, 15.
14 Barnow 1990, 61; the original was a hand-colored card attached to Mary Parker's unpublished Ph.D.thesis (1949).

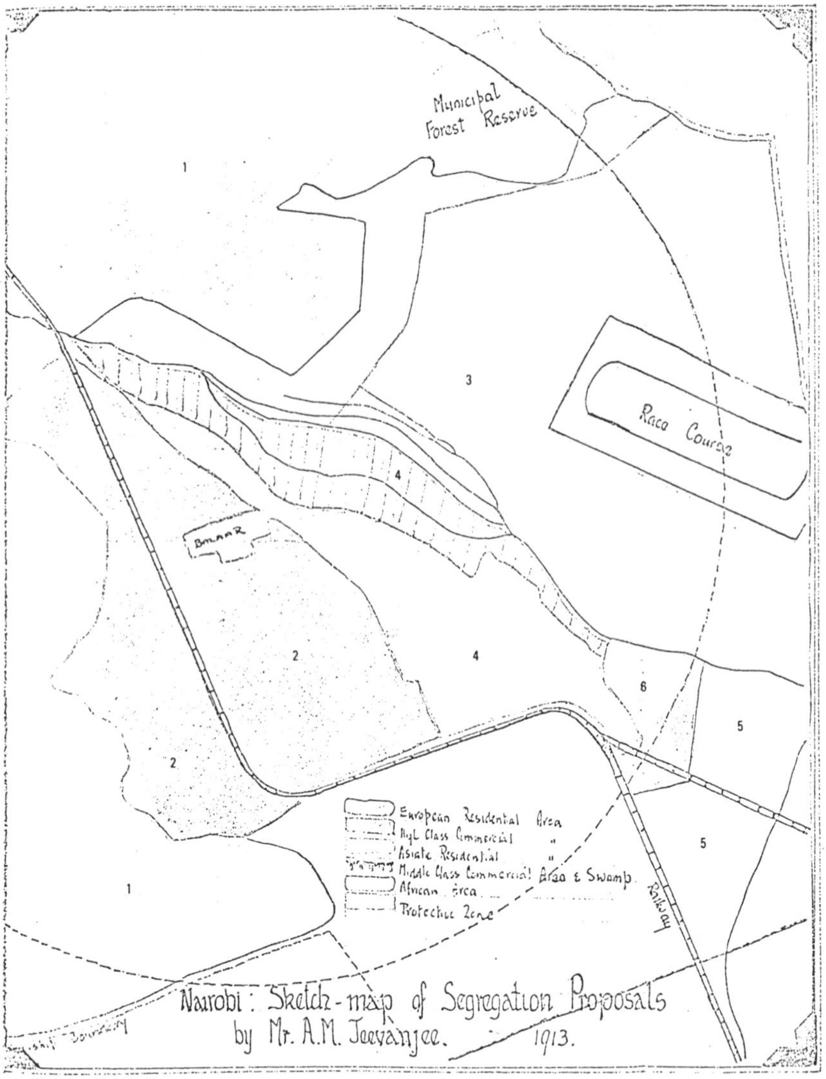

Fig. 10.1 Map: Segregation Proposals, 1913

municipal boundaries are indicated on the plan: the circular boundary at "1½ miles from the Protectorate Offices" of 1900, and another one, marked as "[Tow]nship Boundary" but shown only partially to the south and the northeast of the center, which seems to correspond roughly with the position of the boundary extension which Halliman and Morgan in 1967 dated as seven years later, that is, as 1920, in their map of the boundary changes in Nairobi.[15] Jeevanjee's "Sketch-map" was a pure land-use plan, identifying neither existing nor planned roads or buildings.

In Jeevanjee's plan, six different kinds of areas are distinguished:

---

15 Halliman and Morgan 1967, 99.

120 ■ PART III   HISTORIES OF URBAN FORM IN NAIROBI

1. the "European Residential Area," located on the Hill to the west of the center and in Parklands to the north;
2. the "High Class Commercial Area," west of the Station Road-Government Road, including both the existing commercial area (but excluding the bazaar enclave), the existing railway subordinate residential area, and the mostly unbuilt area between the railway line and the foot of the Hill;
3. the "Asiatic Residential Area" to the northeast on the other side of the Nairobi River, surrounding the "Race Course";
4. the "Middle Class Commercial Area and Swamp," east of the Station Street-Government Road from the railway line on the southeast to the tip of the triangle in the northwest, and including the existing "Bazaar";
5. the "African Area" southeast of the center, between the Nairobi River and the railway line; and
6. the "Protective Zone" between the "African Area" and the "Middle Class Commercial Area."

Jeevanjee's plan indicated consent with the notion of segregation, both ethnic and functional. Whether his reasons coincided with those of the Europeans involved, invited experts such as Simpson or locals, is open to question. In the plan, for example, the residential areas allocated to Europeans are noticeably larger than those allocated to Asians, despite the reverse proportions of the population groups; furthermore, the European residential areas are situated more advantageously than the Asian ones in terms of buildability and microclimate. In these respects, the plan advocated an urban policy in favor of the interests of the Europeans. This may seem puzzling, if the plan is perceived as the work of an Asian whose role in the Municipal Committee was supposedly to guard the interests of his own cultural group. However, the two Asian members of the Committee were defined as "Indian traders" and were selected by the (European) Commissioner. In addition to speaking for only one section of the Asians – for example, the Asians employed by the Railways or the military forces were excluded – Jeevanjee was no ordinary trader but one of the most prominent members of the Asian community in Nairobi. He owned land in the town center, including a large portion of the bazaar and of the River Road area closer to the Nairobi River, and presented a marble statue of Queen Victoria to the town.[16]

From this perspective, the weight of Jeevanjee's plan is not in the ethnic segregation of its residential areas, but in the zoning of the level land in and around the town center into a commercial area. This functionally segregated zone was further divided into two parts, one for "High Class" and the other for "Middle Class" commercial functions. Although the "High Class" area

---

16 Hake 1977, 175; see also Barnow 1990, 60. Born in India, Alibhoy Mulla Jeevanjee made a fortune as a railway contractor who transported from India and fed the 25,000 workers building all the stations and hospitals on the main railway line from Mombasa to Lake Victoria; later he became Nairobi's leading builder (Rosberg and Nottingham 1966, 20).

could be read as a development of the existing European bazaar and the "Middle Class" area as that of the existing Indian bazaar, Jeevanjee's plan did not utilize the ethnic distinctions. It may even be argued that the plan was used to promote distinctions not based on ethnicity but on a hierarchy of classes, within which the position of the Asians in Nairobi would be legitimated as a self-evident, therefore permanent element of urban life. This would support the establishment of the right of the Asian community to fully participate in the building of the society. In the plan, the center of the city was proposed as an area reserved exclusively for commercial purposes, devoid of the existing railway subordinates' housing, the administrative functions conveniently not mentioned. The proposal's acceptance would not only have improved opportunities to gain profits on centrally-located land, but also, in effect, established, for the Asian commercial activities, access to a considerably larger part of the town center than they then had. In this respect, the plan furthered the interests of the Asian community, albeit mostly of its wealthier section.

Fig. 10.2 Government Road to the north, 1913

Jeevanjee's proposal to extend the commercial center into the existing Railways housing area was not an isolated idea. After some years of economic depression, Nairobi was again growing, and centrally-located plots were in great demand. Initially, the structures of the railways had been built as temporary ones, and suggestions were made to transfer the staff quarters to allow business premises to be built in their place. In his annual report for the year ending on 31 March, 1913, the General Manager of the Railway, Major H.B. Taylor, wrote of the problems arising from the development of town from a railway depot into an administrative and commercial center:

> The town is not well located as the railway runs right through it, or rather the town has been built around the railway, and unless the railway track can be sunk (which is possible at considerable expense), there must be numerous level crossings in the centre of the town, which will in the future be very inconvenient to both road and rail traffic. A siding also runs right through the town to several mills and factories, and it will be necessary to sink this track at some future date.[17]

Two photographs of the main street provide windows on urban life in Nairobi in the second decade. The first shows Government Road in 1913: one-story shops, some with arcades in the front, lining both sides of an earth road which extends for several hundred meters (*Fig. 10.2*). The only trees visible in the photograph are in the distance, at the other end of the street. Except for a bicycle, there are no vehicles, but the form of building – shops immediately adjacent to each other at the edge of the street – suggests a street with a character both intense and urban. The other photograph shows, according to

---

17 Quoted in Hill 1949, 333. On the temporary character of the Railways' structures, see Hill ibid., 304f. This report may be the "Taylor Report" referred to by the authors of the Master Plan of 1948 (p.84), see above.

the caption, the same road further north, leading to the Norfolk Hotel, in April 1914: the road is flanked with full-grown trees and, on one side, a river. No buildings can be seen; in this sense, the photograph could have been taken anywhere. In the photograph, three persons, one ankle-deep in water, pose for the photographer, their car parked on the side of the flooded road. The view and the pose do not carry any of the urban character of the other photograph, even if the distance between the two places is at most a few kilometers.[18]

The character of Nairobi around this time may also be illustrated by a description by Karen Blixen, member of the Danish upper class, part owner of a coffee farm, and later writer, who lived near Nairobi from 1914 to 1931. In her book *Out of Africa*, published in 1937, she wrote of the town:

> Nairobi was our town, twelve miles away, down on a flat bit of land amongst hills. Here was the Government House and the big central offices; from here the country was ruled . . . When I first came to Africa, there were no cars in the country, and we rode in to Nairobi, or drove in a cart with six mules to it, and stabled our animals in the stables of The Highland Transport. During all my time, Nairobi was a medley place, with some fine stone buildings, and whole quarters of old corrugated iron shops, offices, and bungalows, laid out with long rows of eucalyptus trees along the bare dusty streets. The offices of the High Court, The Native Affairs Department, and the Veterinary Department were lousily housed . . . All the same Nairobi was a town; here you could buy things, hear news, lunch or dine at the hotels and dance at the Club. And it was a live place, in movement like running water, and in growth like a young thing, it changed from year to year, and while you were away on a shooting safari. The new Government House was built, a stately cool house with a fine ballroom and a pretty garden, big hotels grew up, great impressive agricultural shows and fine flower shows were held . . . at one time I drove through the town

---

18   These two photographs were published in "Motoring Echos", an article on the "informal history of motoring in Kenya, chapter 2: 1907-1920" (*Autonews*, November 1983). The depictions identified the places.

and thought: There is no world without Nairobi's streets.

The quarters of the Natives and of the coloured immigrants were very extensive compared to the European town.

The Swaheli town, on the road to the Muthaiga Club, had not a good name in any way, but was a lively, dirty and gaudy place, with, at any hour, a number of things going on in it. It was built mostly out of old paraffin tins hammered flat, in various states of rust, like the coral rock, the fossilized structure, from which the spirit of the advancing civilization was steadily fleeing.

The Somali town was farther away from Nairobi . . . [It] lay exposed to all winds and was shadeless and dusty, it must have recalled to the Somali their native deserts . . . The Somalis' houses were irregularly strewn on the bare ground, and looked as if they had been nailed together with a bushel of four-inch nails, to last for a week. It was a surprising thing, when you entered one of them, to find it inside so neat and fresh, scented with Arab incenses, with fine carpets and hangings, vessels of brass and silver, and swords with ivory hilts and noble blades . . . The Indians of Nairobi dominated the big native business quarter of the Bazaar, and the great Indian merchants had their little Villas just outside the town: Jeevanjee, Suleiman Virjee, Allidina Visram. They had a taste for stonework stairs, balusters, and vases, rather badly cut out of the soft stone of the country – like the structures which children build of pink ornamental bricks. They gave tea-parties in their garden, with Indian pastry in the style of the Villas, and were clever, travelled, highly polite people.[19]

In the first and second decades of the century, the segregation of spaces by ethnicity was becoming an established practice among European colonialists, although in strictly legal terms it was not confirmed. Legislation concerning land acquisition and alienation succeeded practices adopted earlier, and both the laws and their application strongly supported the interests of the European settlers and restricted those of Africans and Asians. As Norman Leys wrote in an extensive letter to the Secretary of State for the Colonies in 1918, after returning from a service of sixteen years in Eastern Africa,

> In British East Africa, by the influence of European members of the Legislative Council, a large mass of legislation has been enacted with the object of regulating the conduct of natives when they live or travel outside the purely native areas. Sanitary byelaws, regulations to prevent movement of stock, regulations forbidding natives being out at night, forbidding them to travel across land in European occupation, unfenced and uncultivated although most of it is, forbidding them to travel outside the reserves except to and from work for Europeans, are examples of a rapidly increasing body of law under which the younger generation of natives finds itself. Most local ordinances in fact prescribe different duties from, and give a different status to, Europeans and natives. The law itself is thus increasingly partial.[20]

---

19 Blixen 1954, 19-22. Karen Blixen also wrote under the name Isak Dinesen.
20 Leys on 7 February 1918 (Cell 1976, 127).

Within Nairobi, both ownership of land and its use were controlled by practices and regulations which had been based on European conventions and which, in many respects, mostly supported the interests of Nairobi's European community. In the first two decades, Nairobi grew from a railway town into a commercial and administrative center. Initially planned in practical response to the requirements of the Railway, its urban form soon became an instrument for private economic profit and – especially for the Europeans – for public ethnic control. Thus the urban form of Nairobi emerged not only as a result of various urban practices, but as a practice itself. As a practice, the urban form assisted in the establishment of a power structure in Nairobi. Within this structure, the European colonial power was absolute legislatively, militaristically, and technologically, and very dominant politically; economically, individual members of the Asian community had some influence. In terms of democratic practices, however, the Africans held the majority and the Asians also by far outnumbered the European minority. In this context, the Europeans counteracted their subordinate position with an urban form where access to land was utilized for the benefit of the Europeans by allocating them the prime locations in the center for commercial and administrative purposes and on the hills for residential purposes, and to the disadvantage of the other groups by spatial restrictions. Through the urban form, the legislative, military, technological, political, and economic dominance of the Europeans was also strengthened and maintained. In this sense, the urban form of Nairobi in the first two decades had been developed into an instrument for the production and re-production of the systems of colonial power.

11 The municipality takes form, 1919–1940

The First World War altered Nairobi. During the war, not only was the town crowded with troops recruited locally and from other countries, especially India, but the military operations connected to the conquest of German East Africa (today's Tanzania) increased the importance of the railway.[1] The war had changed the outlook of the town center. In a photograph of 1913, traffic on the main street included a bicycle and an ox;[2] in a photograph taken six years later, in 1919 in the "post-war boom," cars have begun to dominate the view (*Fig. 11.1*). In this photograph, Government Road is also lined with trees, seemingly newly planted, but not discernible in later photographs.[3] For example, neither the two postcards nor Hjalmar Frisell's photograph show any trees on the same stretch of road (*Figs. 11.3, 11.4*).[4] Nairobi's "first traffic jam" occurred at the junction of the two major streets of the town, Government Road and Sixth Avenue, on Armistice Day when the soldiers went on parade (*Fig. 11.2*).[5]

The social consequences of the war were irrevocable. Participation in war time activities gave the European settlers, the Asians, and, to some extent, also the Africans grounds to expect to gain more influence in social matters. The European settlers had long pursued some level of self-government, the Asians hoped to establish their position as equal members of a colonial society, while some of the Africans had become aware of the necessity of African politics to achieve the recognition and protection of their traditional relation to the land. Of the three groups, the Europeans were by far the most successful in reaching their goals. The impositions on the settlers, made by

---

1 Hill 1949, 352-374.
2 See above, chapter 10.
3 *Autonews*, November 1983, 21. On the basis of the dominant mosque in the background, the view may be identified as that of Government Road (now Moi Avenue) north of Sixth Avenue (now Kenyatta Avenue), today without trees.
4 One of the postcards was marked "Government Road 1927" and was taken from almost an identical place to the photograph of 1919. Frisell 1939, 40a; Frisell first came to Kenya in 1920. Errol Trzebinski has noted that in the "rutted track known as Station Road (which later became part of Government Road)...in 1902, in an attempt to improve its unremitting ugliness, Ainsworth had planted eucalyptus saplings right up to the bazaar at regular intervals during the heavy rains; they grew to over fifty feet but many were felled to make way for power and telegraph lines as Nairobi developed" (Trzebinski 1985, 72). The electric poles and transformers were erected during 1907 and 1908 (p.148). The 1919 photograph indicated both electric poles and trees.
5 The journalist's caption attached to a photograph taken in 1918 (*Autonews*, November 1983, 25).

the government because of the war, provoked demands for representation; it was not only an issue of "no taxation without representation" but of offering lives for one's country.[6] In 1916, the European settlers were granted electoral representation in the Legislative Council of the Protectorate.[7] The first elections were held in January 1920. Of the thirty-one members of the Legislative Council, just over half were senior officials, with the rest comprised eleven members elected by the Europeans, five members elected by the Asians and nominated by the Governor, and an Arab representative of the "former slave-owning aristocracy of the coast."[8] The change in the country's status from the East Africa Protectorate to the Kenya Crown Colony in 1920 further reinforced the position of the settlers. Responses to the expectations of the Africans and the Asians – who also had participated in the war-time effort – were minimal, if not mostly negative, which contributed to the evolution of both African politics and the "Indian question" in the 1920s.[9] These also became critical in the development of Nairobi.

For the Africans, the issues arising in the aftermath of the First World War concerned their rights to continue their traditional ways of living, set against the colonizers' intentions and resources. The almost immediate effects of the settlers' input in the Legislative Council, particularly on the Africans, may be identified in the amendments to and enforcement of earlier legislation weakly carried out so far. Among these was the Master and Servants Ordinance, passed in 1910 and amended in 1919, containing rules on the minimum conditions the employers had to provide their employees in terms of housing and food. In his study on colonial capitalism and labor in Kenya in the interwar period, R.M.A. van Zwanenberg has argued that since the legal obligations of the employees were defined vaguely in the ordinance, labor inspectors checked and ameliorated the conditions on the basis of individual persuasion (rather than regulations) and the Medical Department pursued definite standards mostly on its own.[10] The Native Registration Ordinance of 1915, amended in 1920 and only then put into effect, required all male Africans working outside native reserves to produce upon request a certificate of identification – the *kipande* – containing the person's fingerprints, carried in a metal case on a string around the neck. The main purpose of the ordinance was to catch employees who deserted their employer, but it

---

6 Huxley 1968b, 35. For a more detailed description of the views advanced by the settlers in the various phases, see also 21ff., 53.
7 Rosberg and Nottingham 1966, 32f.
8 Leys 1973, 170.
9 For example, Leys referred to the American representative's figures presented at the Paris Peace Conference that 350,000 unarmed porters, of whom 150,000 were from Kenya, were recruited by Britain, with 14,000 Kenyan natives among the armed forces (quoted in Rosberg and Nottingham 1966, 30). Huxley 1968b, 39, has noted that about 200,000 Africans were estimated to have served in the Carrier Corps and of whom about 46,000 of them died on duty. According to Hill 1949, 355, over 52,300 troops – of which 5,400 white British troops – came from India.
10 Zwanenberg 1975, 60ff; for the role of the labor inspectors, see 113ff. See also Huxley 1968b, 61.

*Fig. 11.1
Government Road,
eastern side, 1919*

violated the personal freedom of all the Africans.[11] The Railway historian formulated the problem as a practical one:

> The Native Registration Ordinance has often been criticized as discriminatory legislation, but it provided the sole means of identifying backward and illiterate Africans.[12]

For the Africans, however, the *kipande* system was a thoroughly ideological practice: one more way for the European colonists to undermine the Africans' morale and underestimate their intelligence, making them more comparable to domestic animals.[13] The Native Authority Ordinance of 1912, amended in 1920, permitted the native chiefs on government request to recruit labor, male and female, adults and children, for public works on a fixed low wage, for up to sixty days in any one year, unless the person could produce evidence of having worked outside the reserve for three out of the previous twelve months. Work for one's own food, without wages, was not an acceptable excuse for the compulsory labor. The recruitment of labor on low wages was seen by the settler farmers as a means of alleviating labor shortages; by the Africans, however, it was perceived as forced labor, obtained through coercion against the will of the persons recruited.[14] Norman Leys, one of the ardent critics of colonial practices in Kenya, pointed out that the profits of the settlers' farms depended on getting cheap African labor, most of the time available only through force.[15]

Thus after the First World War, the control of the Africans multiplied and became more elaborated, affecting life both in the rural areas and in Nairobi.

---

11 Ogot 1974, 267f.
12 Hill 1949, 391.
13 For example, C. Ojwando Abuor, an anti-colonial politician in the 1950's and later a journalist, does not hide the bitterness towards the methods of the foreign oppressors (Abuor 1973, 21f.; for the language attached to the colonial practices, see also his Appendix 1). Ogot (1974, 267f.) refers to the kipande system, abolished only after the Second World War, as "one of the major grievances of the Africans."
14 Zwanenberg 1975, chapter 4; see also Ogot 1974, 267f. Zwanenberg reminds us that the enlistment of Carrier Corps during the war was based on similar coercion (p.104). For the settlers' views, see Huxley 1968b, 57-70.
15 Leys to Oldham, 10 June 1921 (Cell 1976, 183); see also Leys to Borden Turner, 3 May 1921 (Cell ibid., 170ff.).

Fig. 11.2 Traffic jam, Sixth Avenue and Government Road, 1918

The Native Pass Law of 1918 and the Vagrancy Ordinance of 1920 restricted residence in Nairobi only to those employed, thus excluding, for example, not only vagrants and the unemployed, but also self-employed Africans.[16] This caused Karen Blixen to remark, in a letter to her mother in 1918, on the "unfair treatment" of the Somalis who also had to submit to the pass laws, even though they considered themselves as separate from the "local natives."[17] Earlier practices of segregation in Nairobi had concerned more the ownership of land and habitation on it. The new regulations not only limited sale and residence, it also restricted spatial movement: some areas were inaccessible to some groups of people. The colonial administration issued a special urban pass system to control the influx of people into towns, policing major roads of entry and punishing offenders with strict sentences. R.M.A. van Zwanenberg and Anne King have noted that such a system must have been difficult and expensive to administer, and that in Nairobi, it never seems to have worked for more than a year at a time in the 1920s and 30s because the area was too large to control.[18] Whether access was also restricted within different parts of Nairobi does not appear in the sources consulted, but this seems possible; for example, the journalist C. Ojwando Abuor mentions in his description of the apartheid practices in Kenya that in Nairobi, Africans could not go beyond River Road into the area on the other side of Government Road, which was reserved for the "whites."[19]

For the Asians, the issues culminating after the First World War centered on land and on electoral representation. The Crown Lands Ordinance of 1915 had established the Highlands as an area reserved only for Europeans and gave the Governor a veto on all sales or leases between members of different races, legalizing the earlier practice expressed by Lord Elgin in 1908 that "as a matter of administrative convenience grants in the upland areas should not be made to Indians."[20] This practice and the ordinance in effect restricted the

---

16 Ogot 1974, 267ff; see also Elkan and Zwanenberg 1975, 665f.
17 Blixen to Dinesen, 30 July 1918 (Dinesen 1983, 77).
18 Zwanenberg and King 1975, 270; see also Elkan and Zwanenberg 1975, 663.
19 Abuor 1973, 22; however, he did not identify the time of this practice.
20 Quoted in Hill 1949, 380.

Fig. 11.3 Government Road, western side, 1920s

economic activities of the Asians to urban areas. In 1915, the Government also announced that segregation of Europeans, Asians, and Africans would gradually be implemented in the commercial and residential areas of major urban centers.[21] Electoral representation, granted to the European settlers and, at least superficially, also to Asians, nevertheless distinguished the two groups in a manner foreign to democratic principles: in 1921, for example, the some 9,650 Europeans of Kenya had eleven representatives against the five representatives of the 23,000 Asians.[22] It was also unequal in the sense that the elected Asians had to be nominated by the Governor.

In terms of the different cultural groups living in Kenya, the position of the European colonialists shifted in the five years following the First World War. The Asians' demands for equal representation and for no segregation in townships and in the highlands were met with arguments pertaining to the negative economic and moral effects of the Asians on the Africans. Politically, the administrators confirmed their support of the Europeans against the Asians; in official letters of 1919, this was expressed directly:

> Universal suffrage for the Asiatics in this Protectorate on equality with the whites is out of the question.[23]

and

> This country is primarily for European development, and whereas the interest of the Indian will not be lost sight of, in all respects the European must predominate.[24]

---

21 Seidenberg 1983, 17.
22 The population figures for Kenya in 1921 are from the *Census of the Non-Native Population*, quoted in Zwanenberg and King 1975, 14.
23 Chief Secretary to Convention of Associations in 1919, quoted in Huxley 1968b, 114.
24 Governor Northey to the Indian Association in 1919, quoted in Huxley 1968b, 115.

Fig. 11.4 Government Road, eastern side, 1927

The "Indian question" – as Elspeth Huxley formulated it in her biography of Lord Delamere – was fundamentally the question of the equality of persons originating from India with those originating from Britain within the various parts of the British Empire. The British saw it as attached to the nationalist politics arising in India after the First World War, with its effects sprouting in other British dominions and colonies. In 1923, however, the Indian question of Kenya became part of the discussion of colonialism in Britain: Kenya was used as an example to judge and question British colonial policies and practices in general. Both the European settlers, led by Lord Delamere, and the Asians of Kenya sent deputations to plead their cause. In a letter to *The Times*, the Bishop of Uganda supported the Europeans' views, maintaining that racial segregation was both natural and convenient:

> The confining of Europeans to their own quarters in Chinese towns, the exclusion of Europeans from certain towns in Nigeria, the exclusion of European settlers from native reserves in Kenya itself in no case carries with it any stigma of inferiority.
> When two races differ widely in language, habit and tradition it is better, from the point of view of either, that they should occupy separate areas . . . Indians not only observe rigidly the principles of segregation in their own caste system in India, but themselves demand in East Africa that Africans should be segregated from the Indian community. Segregation between European and Indians, is, however, condemned as being inconsistent with the status of complete equality.[25]

Within the context of the discussion of British colonial policies, the British Government in 1923 announced the Devonshire White Paper – Command

---

25 Bishop of Uganda in a letter to The Times, 1923, quoted in Huxley 1968b, 144f.

Paper No.1922, "Indians in Kenya" – where the colonial policies to be followed in Kenya were defined in a way deviating, for example, from the views of the Governor just four years earlier. Instead of declarations on the priority of the European interests, the White Paper pursued the importance of safeguarding the rights of the African natives:

> Primarily, Kenya is an African territory, and His Majesty's Government think it necessary definitely to record their considered opinion that the interests of the African natives must be paramount, and that if, and when, those interests and the interests of the immigrant races should conflict, the former should prevail . . . His Majesty's Government regard themselves as exercising a trust on behalf of the African population, and they are unable to delegate or share this trust, the object of which may be defined as the protection and advancement of the native races.[26]

The paper also contained specific decisions on issues which had caused much controversy in Kenya. These included the confirmation of the composition of the Legislative Council and of its communal basis. The Highlands were to be reserved for European settlement, "not by law, but by the established practice of the Governor-in-Council refusing to approve an initial grant, or a transfer, of rural land in the Highlands to an Asian."[27] In towns, racial segregation between Europeans and Asians was explicitly abolished:

> Following upon Professor Simpson's report [of 1913], a policy of segregation was adopted in principle, and it was proposed by Lord Milner to retain this policy both on sanitary and social grounds. So far as commercial segregation is concerned, it has already been generally agreed that this should be discontinued. But in regard to residential segregation, matters have been in suspense for some time, and all sales of township plots have been held up pending a final decision on the question of the principle involved. It is now the view of the competent medical authorities that, as a sanitation measure, segregation of Europeans and Asiatics is not absolutely essential for the preservation of the health of the community; the rigid enforcement of sanitary, police and building regulations, without any racial discrimination, by the Colonial and municipal authorities will suffice. It may well prove that in practice the different races will, by a natural affinity, keep together in separate quarters, but to effect such separation by legislative enactment except of the strongest sanitary grounds would not, in the opinion of His Majesty's Government, be justifiable. They have therefore decided that the policy of segregation as between Europeans and Asiatics in the townships must be abandoned.[28]

---

26 *Command Paper* no.1922, 1923, quoted in Hill 1949, 399f.
27 Hill 1949, 400.
28 *Command Paper* no.1922, 1923, quoted in MP 1948, 15f.

Walter Elkan and Roger M.A. van Zwanenberg have suggested that the Command Paper was largely irrelevant, because segregation occurs even without legislative support when the distribution of income levels corresponds with racial distinctions.[29] Thus the distribution of land prices would result in racial segregation in a situation where the racial group with the lowest income level cannot afford to purchase or lease land in the expensive parts of the town, as was the case in Nairobi then.

In the development of Nairobi in the 1920s, the Municipal Council was in a central position. During the first two decades of Nairobi's history, municipal power had been derived directly from the Protectorate Commissioner (later Governor) who selected the members of the Municipal Committee for an advisory role in the affairs of the township. Governor Northey granted Nairobi Municipal status with a Municipal Corporation on 15 July 1919. The new Municipal Council was based on elected representatives and held, on some issues, a decisive role. Initially in 1920, the Governor fixed the number of Councillors to sixteen, with twelve European and four Indian elected members;[30] the Africans were not represented on the Council. The Asian community was not satisfied with this form of representation and, in protest of the racial discrimination, boycotted the Council for much of the period from 1919 to 1933.[31] In 1924, the Town Council constitution was revised to include a Council of twelve members, comprised of five elected Europeans, four elected Indians, one nominated Goan, one Government official and one additional member chosen by the Council, usually a Government official. However, although the Indian councillors were elected by the Indian community, the Europeans were

> only prepared to agree to the members proposed in view of the Indian representation being based on nomination by the Governor, not on election, and on condition that the two officials should be Europeans thereby securing a European majority.[32]

In other words, the European community insisted on having not only the majority but also the possibility of rejecting any councillor elected by the Indian community. Although the Governor was in principle not dependent on the European community in his decisions, in practice the influence of the settlers in Kenyan policies had increased after the war so that their opinion carried weight.[33] With the Asians boycotting participation on the Municipal

---

29 Elkan and Zwanenberg 1975, 664.
30 MP 1948, 17.
31 Hake 1977, 40ff., has identified 1925 to 1928 as the years of Indian participation. See also Seidenberg 1983, 18. According to the description of the history of local government in Nairobi, presented in the Master Plan of 1948 (p.17), there were no Indians on the Municipal Council from 1918 to 1924.
32 Quoted in MP 1948, 17.
33 MP 1948, 17. The composition of the Municipal Council was altered several times. In 1928 because of the Feetham Report (see below), the Council was again reorganized: the nineteen-member Council was to include nine European elected councillors, seven Indian elected councillors (still nominated by the Governor), two members representing the

Council and the Africans left out of it, the European settlers continued to have the dominant role in the affairs of the township, a role they had also held earlier, only now it was legally more established. Compared to the Legislative Council with its majority of (European) officials, the Municipal Council with its majority elected by the European settlers reflected more directly the interests of the local Europeans, irrespective of Imperial politics.

In the first two decades, the township authorities had carried out public services like the removal and disposal of sewage, meat inspection, and the control of scavenging, with the Railways providing the water, and the plot owners being responsible for the construction and the maintenance of the roads.[34] After the establishment of the municipality, the activities of the municipality increased. According to Halliman and Morgan, around the same time the town boundary was also extended to include areas surrounding the earlier town boundary "1½ miles around the Protectorate offices," determined in 1900; among the annexed parts were residential areas like Parklands but not, for example, the "autonomous township" of Muthaiga. The boundary of 1920 shown in Halliman's and Morgan's map seems to coincide with that of Jeevanjee's "Sketch-map" of 1913.[35] From 1920, the Municipal Council had the power to acquire land compulsorily within and without the Municipality and was allowed to

> lay out native locations and to erect dwelling houses, or make loans for buildings, to erect hospitals, acquire and maintain omnibus services, erect aerodromes, laundries, broadcasting stations, child welfare institutions, run its own water and electricity, cleaning, sewage and drainage services, and to make by-laws as to licencing and in matters relating to safety, health and the well-being of inhabitants.[36]

In 1922, the Council discussed matters like curfews, pass-laws, the repatriation of vagrants, the prevention and demolition of illegal huts, and the stricter control of the natives, particularly at night. Rates were introduced, to be paid on plots within the town regardless of whether they were developed or not.[37]

By 1921, the population of Nairobi had reached over 24,000, with some 2,900 Europeans, some 9,400 Asians, and an estimated 12,000 Africans.[38]

Government (nominated by it) and one administrative officer of the Nairobi District to represent the interests of the natives. Africans were not allowed to elect their own representatives to the Municipal Council until 1946.

34 On public services, MP 1948, 17; the supply of water, Hill 1949, 305; roads, e.g. Hake 1977, 38.
35 Halliman and Morgan 1967, 104. The time is identified as 1919 in the text but as 1920 in the map on boundary changes (p.99). Jeevanjee's map of 1913 preceded the extension of 1919/1920 by 6 or 7 years. One possible explanation for the discrepancy in dates could be that the boundary of 1900 was in practice expanded in 1913 or even earlier, but that it was formally acknowledged only in 1919/1920 in conjunction with the change to municipality status.
36 MP 1948, 17.
37 Hake 1977, 41.
38 The population figures for the Europeans and Asians are from the Non-Native Census of 1921, and those for the Africans from the Feetham Report of 1927, both quoted in the *Master Plan* of 1948 (p.84).

Compared to the population figures of 1912, the number of Europeans had increased by 1,700, that of Asians by 5,700, and that of Africans had decreased by 3,000 persons. Thus in 1921, the Europeans comprised some 11%, the Asians some 39% and the Africans around half of the population of Nairobi. Nevertheless, in the Municipal Council the interests of the Europeans dominated. Issues important for their well-being – like the construction and maintenance of public facilities and services including roads, street lighting, water, electricity, sewage and drainage, especially for the city center and the European residential areas – were generally placed high on the municipal priorities. Issues which more profited the other groups – like the provision of facilities or services for the Asian and African areas – were seen as less important. Discussing the economy of Nairobi around 1920, Norman Leys indicated the uneven disposal of resources within the municipality because of the low densities of the European areas and the overcrowding of the Asian areas. Thus the cost of supplying the European inhabitants with roads, water, street lights and sanitary services was extremely high, with the Asians – because of the practiced segregation – forced to live in restricted areas in unhealthy and squalid conditions. The European areas covered 2700 acres and had 33 miles of roads and 510 public street lamps, while the Asian community occupied 300 acres and shared 5 miles of road and 30 public street lamps; at the same time, the Europeans paid £4700 and the Asians £5900 in rates.[39] Most of the costs of the municipality – including, for example, those of the police and partly of the schools – were paid by the Government and were based on national revenue, that is, on taxes paid mainly by Africans. According to Leys, the rates carried in Nairobi were exceptionally low, but higher rates were opposed by the Europeans of the Municipal Council of Nairobi because they would have benefited more the Africans and the poorer Asians.[40] The Asians and the Africans were not completely excluded from the municipal issues. The Ngara area on the other side of the Nairobi River was opened for Asian habitation, and an official native location east of the center for the Africans.

By European standards, the housing conditions of the Africans had long been unacceptable. In his 1922 Annual Report, the Medical Officer of Health for Nairobi registered the demolition of 218 native huts as an "anti-plague measure," noting that:

> In the Commercial Area, in the majority of cases, natives cannot reasonably be stated to be housed at all, odd corners, kitchens, passages, verandas, bathrooms and even latrines being used by them, or in other words, any odd place which provides some sort of a roof.[41]

---

39 Statistics presented at a meeting of the Nairobi Town Council in 1920, quoted in Leys (1973, 287f.) who characterized the figures as "not challenged at the time and may be taken as substantially accurate, both for 1920 and for 1924."
40 Leys 1973, 288.
41 Quoted in Hake 1977, 42.

Similarly, Norman Leys, a retired Medical Officer, in his critical discussion of Kenya described the conditions of the Africans' lives:

> The African population of Nairobi is about 12,000, most of them temporary residents. All but a few live in shelters that are inferior to village huts and are quite unfit for human habitation. The fact is widely recognised and bewailed in the colony. For many years the accepted remedy has been the wholesome removal of the African population from the frequently unauthorised sheds and hovels at present use, to a municipally managed location.[42]

Leys referred to the Health Officer's Report of 1923 where the death rate among the Nairobi Europeans was given as 8.4, among the Asians as 16.5, and among the Africans as 33.5 per thousand: "These are crude facts."[43] In Nairobi, the attitudes of the Europeans towards African villages had been negative, not only because of their sanitation problems but also because of their uncontrollability in general, being temporary huts built illegally on land without roads and services. Within the first two decades of the founding of the town, several unplanned villages had grown, some of the first ones soon being destroyed, others existing longer, so that by 1921, around seven of these villages had become established. These included Masikini, Kaburini, Kariokor, Mombasa, and Pangani to the north and northeast of the town center, Kibera to the southwest, and Kileleshwa to the west.[44] Some of the villages were small: Kaburini, for example, was referred to in a contemporary newspaper article as a "collection of unauthorised huts";[45] others were large: in Kileleshwa on 728 acres of Crown land on the periphery of the town lived a thousand Africans from various tribes.[46] Kibera with its Sudanese and two Somali settlements, had developed from 1912 onwards outside the town boundary on land set aside by the Governor as a military reserve and for houses and small farm plots for Sudanese soldiers recruited for the King's African Rifles, later veterans of the First World War.[47] These unofficial villages contained a large part – if not most – of Nairobi's African population, in 1921 estimated to be some 12,000.[48]

Pumwani was different: it was the first area in Nairobi planned for Africans. Pumwani had been discussed as the site of a "native location" in the early

---

42　Leys 1973, 288f.
43　Leys 1973, 289.
44　Parker (1949, 2, 80) referred to in Rosberg and Nottingham 1966, 24. Masikini means "poor," Kaburini "beside the cemetery," Kariokor refers to the Carrier Corps camp, and Mombasa and Pangani relate to the coastal connections of the swahili inhabitants (Hake 1977, 24, 112, 131).
45　*East African Standard*, 1922, quoted in Hake 1977, 113.
46　Native Affairs Department Annual Report of 1925 (p.34f.) quoted in Rosberg and Nottingham 1966, 24.
47　Dorothy Halliman, *Kibera: A Plan for Suburban Renewal*, unpublished thesis, 1952, referred to in Hake 1977, 96. Kibera was handed over to the civil administration in 1928 (Rosberg and Nottingham 1965, 357n49).
48　Feetham Report, *Report of the Local Government Commission*, 1927, vol.I, Nairobi and its Environs, quoted in MP 1948, 84.

years of the township and again in 1911, but the plans had been postponed.[49] With the growth of the African population during and after the war, the matter was reintroduced around 1919, the exact site fixed and the principles of habitation decided. The Municipal Council leased the land from the Government, built communal ablutions and latrines, and laid out the roads and the "stands," plots for the construction of huts. In the "1920 Pumwani Scheme," the stands were allocated for the construction of temporary structures between 100 and 750 sq.ft., to be inhabited only by the allottee and his family with no subletting, at a maximum of 15 persons per stand.[50] The plans were based on South African models.[51] Pumwani was to be the official native location, sufficient to contain all the Africans of Nairobi, not only at the time of construction, but also in the foreseeable future.[52] For the European authorities, Pumwani was an area planned and built to replace the unauthorized villages which would have to be demolished because of their insalubrity. In Pumwani, the Africans could live in conditions which would be controlled and healthy; and if an allottee would not subscribe to the set norms, eviction could be administered within a month's notice. In this sense, Pumwani was also to become a model area where the ways of life acceptable to the European colonizers could be pursued. Although Masikini, Kaburini, and Mombasa were demolished in 1923 and their inhabitants moved to the new location,[53] Pumwani grew only slowly, with only 317 houses and a population just under 4,000 in 1931, ten years after its establishment.[54]

In the maps identified as Nairobi in 1920 compiled by Barnow and others, indicating the physical and social structure of the town around 1920, some six African villages may be distinguished to the north-northeast of the city center.[55] Of these, four appear on locations where an African village also existed earlier, shown in the maps marked as Nairobi in 1900 in the same publication.[56] This seems to indicate that although the African villages were not only seen by the Europeans of the municipality as temporary, illegal, and hazardous to health, and were also demolished occasionally, they nevertheless existed for longer periods of time and therefore offered their inhabitants

---

49 See above, chapter 10. Pumwani colloquially means "take it easy"; the area is also known as Majengo, referring to the house type.
50 Farnworth 1964, 3f. For the history of Pumwani until 1970, see Hake 1977, chapter 9. For the plans and realizations of the buildings, see below, chapter 16.
51 Hake 1977, 26; see also Zwanenberg and King 1975, 267.
52 Parker 1949, 80, quoted in Rosberg and Nottingham 1966, 24.
53 MP 1948, 36. Zwanenberg and King (1975, 267) included Kileleshwa among the demolished villages and specified that they were burned down.
54 Parker 1949, 80, quoted in Rosberg and Nottingham 1966, 24.
55 Barnow et al 1983, 26, 30. The source is given as "Map 22/10/1919, Key Plan of Nairobi Township, scale 1:10.000 or 6,33 inches to 1 Mile, showing: European Residential Area, High Class Asiatic Residential Area, Asiatic Commercial & Residential Area, African Area etc." and its quality assessed as approximate.
56 Barnow et al 1983, 16, 20. The source was identified as "Map 16/5/1906, Nairobi Township, Plan Showing the Present Locations of Various Nationalities of the Inhabitants, scale 1:10.560 or 6 inches = 1 mile, signed E.L.Waring, Survey Department, Nairobi" and its quality estimated as accurate.

something that was not available elsewhere. Materially, the huts of the villages were rudimentary, but this coincided with the inhabitants' incomes: with the low wages paid to Africans in colonial Kenya at that time, they could not have afforded more expensive forms of habitation. Socially, however, the villages provided for their African inhabitants a community with both continuity and budding urban traditions. Life in one of these villages was described in a newspaper article of 1921:

> Out Pangani Village way the natives are very busy these days holding meetings of the mass kind. Every Sunday thousands of Jeroges and Kamaus may be seen listening raptly to others of their kind holding forth on, presumably, the question of the hour. It is fairly apparent that these meetings have a savour of politics about them and that the natives are discussing matters connected with, say, registration, taxation and so on. For the most part, of course, the addresses are in Swahili.[57]

The role of the African villages in Nairobi must therefore be conceived as not only to house Africans, but, more importantly, to establish a basis from which African ways of life and interests could be discussed and promoted, eventually generating political movements. In this sense, to demolish the villages was also to disturb a social entity, to attempt to destroy a form of urban life, a cultural community.

Why the establishment of a native location? For the municipality with its European majority, to provide a site for African housing was a new expense; why was it seen as profitable? One of the reasons may have been the problem of sanitation posed by the unauthorized African settlements; in the native location, the terms of allocation – including the allowed maximum densities of construction and of habitation – had been determined to further more salubrious building practices. But sanitation was not something new to Nairobi; it had been a problem from the very foundation of the town. Furthermore, the improvement of African housing conditions around 1920 was not exclusive to the areas managed by the municipality: similar policies were also initiated for the Railways Native housing, according to Zwanenberg for reasons which have never been fully ascertained.[58] Thus it may be argued that the improvement of the conditions of the Africans was the result of changes in the attitudes of the Europeans – both of the British colonial administration and of the settlers – towards the Asians and the Africans. In the development of the country, the role of the Asians had been and around 1920 continued to be essential: most of the subordinate positions requiring clerical or professional skills, a large number of various vital independent professions, and a major portion of the small-scale trade were based on the

---

57 The leader of *British East Africa*, Nairobi, September 3, 1921, quoted in Rosberg and Nottingham 1966, 25.
58 Zwanenberg 1975, 67.

input of the Asians. Their demands after the war for equal representation were based partly on the understanding of their own central role, partly on their population increase; at the same time, the demands were seen as a real threat to the domination of the Europeans:

> Full equality of citizenship for Indians was a noble and a just sentiment, well in keeping with England's post-war mood. But . . . [c]arried to its conclusion in East Africa it would ultimately mean domination, not equality . . . The admission of Indians to equal rights would mean the end of British colonisation and the ruin of the settlers.[59]

After being elected in 1920 as a representative to the Legislative Council, Lord Delamere summarized as his policy that all minor government and other posts be kept for educated Africans instead of being given to Asiatics, and that the Africans must be educated as quickly as possible to fill such posts.[60] To replace the Asians with Africans was not immediately possible, because the Africans lacked the necessary skills and the incentive to settle in an urban area. To improve the conditions of the urban Africans, then, may be seen as one step in a process where the dependence of the Kenyan colonial society – more particularly, of the Europeans – on the Asians was beginning to be reduced.

Pumwani was followed by other housing estates planned for Africans, but the principle of providing plots for the dwellers to construct their own huts, which had been applied in Pumwani, was replaced by constructions built with public funds. The first municipal housing estate, built in 1929, was Kariokor on the old Carrier Corps camp northeast of the town center on the other side of Nairobi River. Initially, the structures were dormitories, but after they proved unsuccessful they were converted into rooms in the early 1930s. Around the same time, the Government built for its African employees the first phase of Starehe estate, located between Pumwani and Kariokor. Between 1924 and 1938, the Railways constructed, in Muthurwa next to the railway yard, for its African employees, altogether a hundred housing blocks, each with twenty rooms ten by ten feet, with shared kitchen, toilet, and shower facilities, as accomodation for bachelors.[61]

In 1926, the population figure of Nairobi was nearing 30,000. Since 1921, the European community had grown by some 700 persons to about 3,700, the Asian community by 1,100 to about 10,600, and the African community had increased by some 4-6,000 to an estimated 16-18,000.[62] By 1930, the

---

59   Huxley 1968b, 142f.
60   Huxley 1968b, 84.
61   Hake 1977, 256n15. For the dwellings, see chapter 15.
62   In the Master Plan of 1948 (p.84), several figures for 1926 were quoted: the non-native census, the Feetham Report and the Williams Report. In these, the number of Europeans ranged between 2,665 (Feetham) and 4,600 (Williams), and of Asians between 7,400 (Williams) and 10,551 (census); for both, the non-native census was used here. In the Williams Report, the number of Africans was estimated at 16,000, in the Feetham Report, at 18,000.

population had increased to 49,000, with around 28,000 Africans, 16,000 Asians, and 5,000 Europeans.[63] Economically, the years between 1924 and 1929 were promising. With the rapid population increase, the problems within the municipality were mounting, but the economic situation provided resources to prepare for their management. For the development of Nairobi, two events of 1926 proved important: one was the Governor's appointment of a Local Government Commission, chaired by Justice R. Feetham of Johannesburg, South Africa, to look into the organization and planning of the municipality, the other was the invitation of F. Walton Jameson of Kimberley, South Africa, as a consultant to prepare a new town plan for the city.

The Feetham Commission examined the relations of the Municipality to the Government and the Railway, the Municipal Council, the financial provisions, public health administration, native affairs, and questions relating to staff and procedures, but the most important issue was its recommendation to extend the town boundary.[64] For the residential areas outside the existing town boundary, the inclusion signified the obligation to pay municipal rates for roads, services, and the like. The strongest objections came from the autonomous garden city north of the center of Nairobi, Muthaiga, which had been declared a township in 1922. However, in 1928 the town boundary was extended and, despite their resistance, Nairobi absorbed more of the residential areas including Eastleigh to the northeast of the center, Upper Parklands and Westlands to the north, parts of the Hill and Kilimani and the Thompson Estate to the west, and Muthaiga.[65] Even after the extension of the town boundary, new peri-urban areas continued to develop, without the disadvantages of municipal regulations and rates, and on lower land prices. These included not only residential areas like Karen and Langata to the south and Spring Valley to the north, with five, ten, and twenty-acre plots, for European habitation, but also industrial enterprises which mainly served the needs of the urban population.[66] In the *Master Plan* of 1948, the Local Government (Municipalities) Ordinance of 1928 which incorporated many of the suggestions of the Feetham Commission, was described as the "real charter of independence to the town."[67]

F. Walton Jameson worked on the town plan with Herbert Baker, an architect who had established his fame in the British colonies.[68] Jameson's

---

63 Medical Officer's Annual Report of 1931, quoted in MP 1948, 84.
64 Local Government Commission Report (London, 1927) quoted in MP 1948, 18; Hake 1977, 44.
65 Hake 256. For the boundary changes in Nairobi, see the map in Halliman and Morgan 1967, 99. The year is identified as 1928 in the text (p.104) and as 1927 on the map.
66 Halliman and Morgan 1967, 104f; see also MP 1948, 44. An example of an industrial enterprise was the Karen Coffee Company, partly owned by Karen Blixen, who lived from 1917 to 1931 south of Nairobi in the area renamed Karen after her in the 1930's.
67 MP 1948, 18.
68 Baker (1862-1945) had been trained in London but worked in South Africa from the late 1890's. At the time he became involved with the planning of Nairobi, he had designed the symbolically important Union Buildings (1910-12) in Pretoria, South Africa, the twin Secretariat Buildings of Edwin Lutyens' New Delhi administrative center (1913-30) in India,

plan included the realignment of the railway line and the construction of a wide avenue on the land which was to be released from the railway, the suggestion of a grand Appian Way to connect the railway station and the Government House, and the embellishment of the town with a civic center. For the implementation of Jameson's plans, a joint Government and Municipal Town Planning Authority was appointed. Although it seems to have been short-lived, it facilitated the rapid development of Nairobi in the next few years.[69] An explanatory memorandum of 1927 of the town planning authority – which Sören Emig and Zahir Ismael have called the "Plan for a Settler Capital" – described the establishment of zoning to regulate the land use in different parts of Nairobi as one the primary functions of the authority.[70] In the memorandum, the grounds for zoning were explained:

> Zoning is the application of common sense and fairness to the public regulations governing the use of private real estate. It is a painstaking effort to provide each district or neighbourhood, as nearly as practicable, with just such protection and just such freedom as are reasonable and consistent in that particular district. It avoids the wrong of trying to apply exactly the same building regulations to every part of a city or town regardless of whether it is a suburban residence, section, or a factory district, or a business and financial centre. Zoning gives every one who lives or does business in a community a chance for the reasonable enjoyment of his rights. At the same time, it protects him from unreasonable injury from neighbours who would seek private gain at his expense.[71]

By the Town Planning Authority, then, zoning was seen as a device to control land use and protect the public from the unwanted effects of land speculation. At the same time, however, zoning also improved the possibility of controlling the occupation of land indirectly. The direct means of control had included the restriction of entry into town and habitation within the town without a proper pass (for Africans), the restriction of ownership of land in areas allocated for a different ethnic group (for Asians and Africans), and the demolition of illegal or unsanitary houses by the municipality (for both Asians and Africans, at different times). The indirect systems of control included the

---

the Cathedral (1913-30) in Salisbury, Rhodesia (now Harare, Zimbabwe), and the "rebuilding" (1921) - as it has been critically defined - of John Soane's Bank of England in London, in addition to numerous less-known residential, commercial, and public buildings (Fletcher 1987, 1202-05, 1274, 1337).
69 MP 1948, 18; Hake 1977, 43f.
70 *Nairobi Area Town Planning Authority, Explanatory Memorandum* (1927), quoted and described in Emig and Ismael (1980, 18-33), on which this discussion is based. Emig and Ismael reconstructed the plan of the proposed road system on the basis of the descriptions in the text, because, as they put it, "the [original] maps have been destroyed" (p.24). The usefulness of the source was somewhat limited because of the purpose of Emig and Ismael's study, "to seek to understand the plans as instruments of a total political strategy, that makes use of special tools (zoning, etc.) to carry out the interests of the ruling class factions as regards the safeguarding of certain social divisions, a specific use of urban space as a part of the total political control"(p.3).
71 *Nairobi Area Town Planning Memorandum* 1927, 50, quoted in Emig and Ismael 1980, 19.

adoption of building by-laws which the Town Council introduced in 1926[72] and the implementation of the system of zoning. Through zoning, the issue of segregation by ethnicity was transformed into an issue of distinction by standards of construction, therefore, a technical and unpolitical issue. That the standards imposed were those of the Europeans, who in Nairobi were the group with the highest incomes, was not questioned, nor was the cultural bias in favor of the Europeans inherent in the standards.

In the plan, the town was divided into areas identified as containing a particular function, and, in the residential areas, also a particular ethnic group, despite the policies of the British Government expressed, for example, in the White Paper of 1923. The areas included the administrative center, the commercial and manufacturing area, and separate residential areas for Europeans, Asians, and Africans, in addition to sites allocated for the three hospitals and for recreation.

The main administrative buildings were to be located between the existing commercial center (around the junction of Government Road and Sixth Avenue) and the railway yard, the same area which had been used to house Railways employees from the founding of the town and which Jeevanjee had in his "Sketch-map" of 1913 identified as suitable for the extension of the commercial center.[73] In the plan, the administrative buildings were perceived as a totality to be designed to generate symbolic meanings for the community: "The Town Hall, the Municipal Offices, the Law Courts and other public buildings can all be arranged to provide a combined effect"[74] where the architecture of imposing buildings would serve the ideas of political progress and of making the colony a new home of the settlers. Baker, who designed three prominent public buildings in Nairobi - the Law Courts and Railway Headquarters in 1929 in the center of Nairobi, and later in 1934 the Government House on the Hill - believed in the relationship between colonial rule and architecture; he saw as the architect's mission "to give outward expression to the colonist's national ideals."[75] Emig and Ismael noted that in relation to the administrative center, the purpose of the plan was clearly, with architecture, to relay "a message to [the controlled] classes . . . of who has control over them and moreover [to encourage] the settlers and the administrators in their new second 'home-making.'"[76] In other words, the administrative center was beginning to be perceived not only as the practical arrangement of facilities for administrative functions but also as the presentation of the image of a colony or, at least, of a municipality in its own right.

---

72 Soni 1983, 1f. Building by-laws for other urban areas were prepared in the Local Government (Municipalities) Ordinance of 1928. These regulations were complemented by the Town Planning Act in 1931.
73 See above, chapter 10.
74 *Nairobi Area Town Planning Memorandum* 1927, 59, quoted in Emig and Ismael 1980, 22.
75 Fletcher 1987, 1384f. In addition to the public buildings designed by Baker, the Jamia Mosque was constructed in the commercial area just south of the Asian bazaar in 1925-33 (Fletcher 1987, 1386).
76 Emig and Ismael 1980, 22.

The plan indicated different densities for each residential area. For the European residential areas on the Hill, the minimum size of plots was to be one acre, and further to the west, a half acre. Two different kinds of residential areas for Asians were proposed. Parklands, an area earlier restricted to Europeans, was to be opened for Asian occupation of "a better type of development" with the size of plots for dwellings a minimum of half an acre. Pangani, which contained some African villages, and Lower Parklands were to be designated for Asians with smaller incomes: "a pressing need . . . is the provision, within such easy reach of the centre of the town that motor transport is unnecessary, of small houses of an unexpensive type of construction which can be rented or purchased on easy terms by the clerk or shop assistant on a low salary."[77] The densities were to be a maximum of 12 houses per acre. African developments were not permitted to the west of Racecourse Road. This demarcation line which started towards the north-northeast of the railway station, left to its east two areas earlier developed by the Europeans for Africans: Muthurwa Landhies, the Railways housing area, and Pumwani, the "native location" established by the municipality. However, the realization of the plan implied the demolition of several existing villages developed by the Africans, including Pangani and Kileleshwa, which in 1925 had a thousand inhabitants[78] but which was, according to the plan, "destined to become one of the finest residential suburbs"[79] – for the Europeans.

In addition to zoning, one of the main issues in the plan was the organization of vehicular traffic within the municipality. In the memorandum, the present connections between the different parts of the town were analyzed, with the conclusion that there was in Nairobi "a general lack of direct communication between such suburbs as Parklands, Kilimani, Kabete Road, Muthaiga; or indeed any external linking up of the main roads converging on Nairobi town for the purposes of through traffic."[80] In the plan, roads were given the highest priority in terms of economic investment since the scheme involved an expenditure of £252,266 on the construction of roads, representing about 72% of the total cost of the plan.[81] At the same time, the number of cars in the whole of Kenya was just 5,000.[82] The plan included the construction of some fifty new roads, their average length approximately 5,000 feet. The shortest ones were around 1,500 feet and the longest ones included the 10,000 foot road connecting Eastleigh with the Prison area located in the manufacturing area south of the railway yard, the 12,300 foot

---

77 The quotations are from the *Nairobi Area Town Planning Memorandum* 1927, 51f., quoted in Emig and Ismael 1980, 20f. Lower Parklands obviously refers to the area later identified as Ngara.
78 See above.
79 *Nairobi Area Town Planning Memorandum* 1927, 51, quoted in Emig and Ismael 1980, 21.
80 *Nairobi Area Town Planning Memorandum* 1927, 5, quoted in Emig and Ismael 1980, 24.
81 Emig and Ismael 1980, 24.
82 Hake 1977, 27.

road connecting Kabete Road in Westlands with Ngong Road at the edge of Upper Hill Estate, and the 17,000 foot road connecting Kabete with Muthaiga. The maximum gradients were 6½% (*Figs. 11.5, 11.6*).[83]

Fig. 11.5 Map: Roads, 1927

Based on an analysis of the plan, Emig and Ismael have suggested that "the plan, to all purposes and intents, seemed to serve the objective interests [of the hegemonic settler class of Nairobi] in an authoritative manner," designating the "residential areas of the different classes/races in complete agreement with the interests of the settler class," and proposing a "road system in conformity with the requirements of the only ones who would be using automobiles when travelling in and out of Nairobi - the settlers."[84] According to Emig and Ismael, the purpose of the construction of the roads was to "ease the travelling activity by automobile of the upper class,"[85] that is, the Europeans. However, many of the proposed roads also "eased the travelling activity" of the other groups, providing shorter walking paths from residential areas to the town center and to the manufacturing area and improving the quality of some existing paths. It may be argued that these proposals, while

Fig. 11.6 Map: Planned roads

---

83 The description of the proposed road system (*Nairobi Area Town Planning Memorandum*, 1927) quoted in full in Emig and Ismael 1980, 24-27, with a map reconstruction (p.30f.) based on the text.
84 Emig and Ismael 1980, 32. See also Barnow 1990, 148.
85 Emig and Ismael 1980, 24.

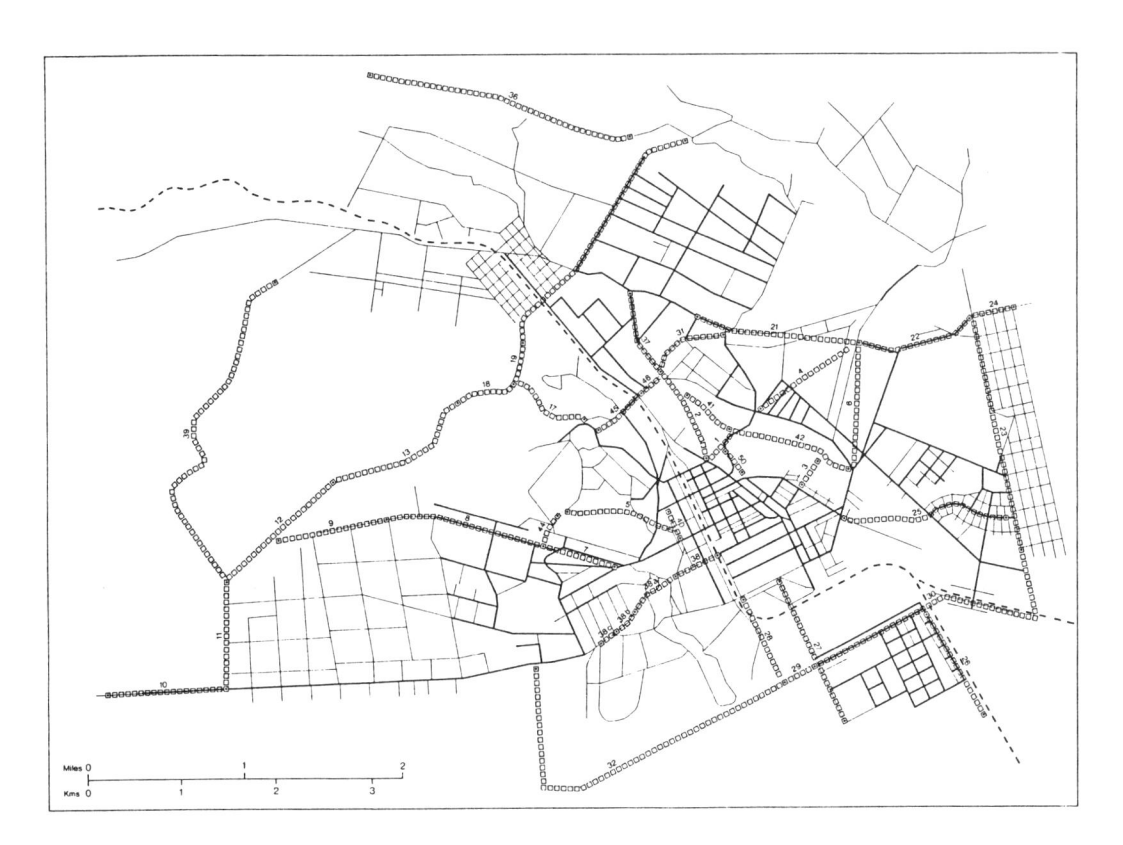

improving the traffic conditions of all groups nevertheless also served other intentions of the Europeans. For example, judging from the reconstructed plan of Emig and Ismael, the new roads established movement patterns which effectively separated areas inhabited by different groups. Thus the construction of the roads which would shorten distances between the town center and the African housing areas, would also change the movement paths of the Africans away from the roads leading to the European residential areas. Similarly, the new roads providing connections between two suburbs would also provide a connection which would not pass through parts of town inhabited or used by the other groups. In effect, the road network proposed in the plan was based on ideas similar to those used in zoning: in both, indirect systems of control were introduced to complement the already existing direct systems of control.

Thus the activities of the Town Planning Authority could be described as one of the first phases in a process of transformation where the blatantly perceptible forms of segregation practiced towards the "other" groups by the (European) colonial administrators in general and the settlers' representatives in particular were being replaced by more subtle and hidden forms of segregation, domination, and discrimination. In this process, urban space was an essential instrument. As an institution with elected members, therefore formally more democratic than rule by a single administrator, the Municipal Council was used to convert the spatial norms of the Europeans of Nairobi into spatial norms represented as universal and justified with reasons pertaining to sanitation and practical convenience. The realities of the different ethnic groups living in Nairobi were excluded from the argumentation. These included the general racial discrimination, both with the numerous regulations and in addition to them, socially.[86] These also included the discrepancies in land prices within the European, Asian, and African areas, where Europeans had access to the cheapest land while the Asians and Africans had to pay much more.[87] The spatial standards were presented as strictly pragmatic requirements for ensuring an acceptable minimum. Through a seemingly technical control over the location of areas in relation to each other and over the kinds of building allowed, the actions of the Asians and Africans were disciplined and controlled by the Europeans. By structuring the city, Europeans structured the fields of action available for the others, not only on a concrete and practical level, but also on a more abstract cultural and ideological level. In this sense, the 1927 Memorandum of the Nairobi Area Town Planning Authority determined some of the cultural boundaries of town planning in Nairobi for a long time, maybe permanently.

In effect, the Memorandum established for Nairobi a spatial structure which corresponded with the colonial and municipal policies and practices in terms of segregation: in both, the idea of ethnically separate development dominated. In the colony, political rights and social and urban services were distributed on a racial basis, with separate provisions for Europeans, Asians, and Africans. Lord Delamere supported the policy of separate development, since it was

> based on a perfectly rational desire to protect a civilised standard of living from an economic competitor on a lower grade of life.[88]

The policy was applied widely from economic issues to education, medical services, housing, and sports, with the amount of public funds and other resources unevenly distributed between the different ethnic groups. For example in the early thirties, the Legislative Council allocated £40,000 for housing African Government employees, and over £586,000 for housing expatriate officials.[89] In 1932, Lord Moyne drew attention to the imbalances in the financial situation of Kenya:

> On examining the general structure of these Colonial services and the proportion of cost due to the provision of such convenience as motor

---

86 The social discrimination was practiced in a manner self-evident to the settlers, as Henry Seaton described it: "Segregation was observed without question. That hated phrase 'the colour bar' was not in currency. The racial distinction was obvious and accepted as a natural order. No one bothered to think about it"(*Lion in the Morning*, 1963, quoted in Miller 1971, 538). Furedi (1979, 226) mentions examples like denial of access to hotels, restaurants, and other private establishments, pay differentials, inequality of educational opportunities etc.
87 For example, Leys (1973, 287ff.) compared the prices of plots in the early twenties: in the European suburbs, land cost £100 an acre or less, in the unsanitary Asian area next to the swamp, land owned mostly by Europeans, a twelfth of an acre plot cost £65, while African villages were located on land valued at £200 to £500 an acre.
88 Quoted in Ogot 1974, 275.
89 Hake 1977, 45.

roads, municipal services, comparing also the services in settled areas with those provided in neighboring areas where European interests are less dominant, I have formed the opinion that in the development of the undivided or colonial services in Kenya the prevailing bias has been towards the convenience of a civilisation in which the native so far shares little of direct advantages.[90]

In Nairobi, most of the resources were spent for the benefit of the European community. Between 1932 and 1947, for which figures are available, the share of the services for the African population of Nairobi was around 1 to 2 per cent of the total revenue of the municipality.[91] During the same period, the Africans represented between 55 and 70 per cent of the total population of the town.[92] The Europeans had both higher demands in terms of roads, water, sanitation, public lighting, education, and medical services, and the majority in the Municipal Council. Their residential areas were widely spread in the municipality which raised the costs of the municipal services per European to an extremely high level. In consequence, the African areas continued to have insufficient basic urban services like sewage and clean water, while the areas where Europeans lived increased their services in the forms of an extensive network of macamadized roads, well-equipped secondary schools and similar European-style provisions.

During the 1930s, the social, political, and spatial structure which had been introduced to the municipality during the 1920s, was strengthened and institutionalized. Within the colony, some of the earlier unofficial practices were endorsed. For example, the exclusion of the Africans and the Asians from the so-called White Highlands was confirmed by the Land Commission, chaired by W. Morris Carter, in a Report of 1934, which declared that the prime land would be reserved exclusively and permanently for European settlement, with the boundaries legalized in 1939.[93] Thus a policy practiced for 40 years was finally made formal. In Nairobi, demolitions of African villages continued on sanitary grounds with demolition orders by the Medical Officer of Health without a formal slums act.[94] After having been an object of destruction plans from the early 1920s, the African village Pangani was finally demolished in the late 1930s, to be developed as an Asian residential area after the Second World War. For the inhabitants of Pangani, the municipality started construction on a new housing estate consisting of 170 houses, each four to six rooms and a central corridor, at Shauri Moyo, across the river from Pumwani.

The population of Nairobi had stayed around 49,000 from 1931 to 1936,

---

90 Quoted in Ogot 1974, 278.
91 Zwanenberg and King 1975, 268.
92 Population figures between 1932 and 1944 from the *Master Plan* of 1948 (p.84), based on the Annual Reports of the Medical Officer of Health between 1933 and 1939 and of the Town Clerk between 1940 and 1945.
93 *Kenya Land Commission Report*, Cmd.4580, 1934, referred in Ogot 1974, 273f.
94 MP 1948, 32.

Fig. 11.7 Nairobi railway station

possibly because of the depression in the world economy, but between 1936 and 1937, the population suddenly increased by over 10,000, mostly Africans.[95] With the improvement of the economic situation, social provisions were again perceived as affordable, and in 1937, the Municipal Council appointed a Five Years' Programme Committee to examine the priorities. Although the report of the Committee was later rejected by the Council, the municipality started various public works, including the Ruiru Dam Project to increase the water supply and more "native housing" projects. Medical services were also improved, and finally the possibility of plague seemed to have been overcome.[96]

Views of Nairobi

During the period between the two world wars, the character of Nairobi as an urban built form changed from what was described as its "wild west" appearance into a more urban and organized entity.[97] This was due to several new elements. Partly, it was due to the erection of the larger public buildings in the center, not only the Law Courts containing the Secretariat and the

---

95 According to the reports of the Medical Officer of Health (quoted in MP 1948, 84), between 1931 and 1936 the number of Europeans varied between 5,200 and 6,000, of Asians between 14,700 and 16,000, and of Africans between 26,800 and 28,000; in 1937, there were 6,000 Europeans, 17,300 Asians, and 38,000 Africans in Nairobi.
96 Hake 1977, 50f.
97 The metaphor referring to the wild west in connection with Nairobi was used by both Kirsti Gallen-Kallela (1982, 49) who lived in Nairobi in 1909-1910 as a teenager and by Dorothy M.Halliman and W.T.W. Morgan (1967, 104) in their historical background of the development of the town. Elspeth Huxley (1968a, 256) described early Nairobi as a place which at times had "something of an eighteenth-century spirit."

Fig. 11.8 Norfolk Hotel, 1928

Railway Headquarters designed by Baker in the "City Square," the new administrative area between the commercial center and the railway yard, but also other public buildings, including the Cathedral of the Holy Family and the Municipal offices in the City Square, and the Jamia Mosque, the City Market, and the McMillan Memorial Library within the commercial area. Important older buildings, including the Railway Station and the Norfolk Hotel, still represented the earlier history of Nairobi (*Figs. 11.7, 11.8*). The change towards a more urban appearance was also partly due to the replacement of the wood and iron constructions of the initial decades with structures made of local stone. In this sense, the modernization – as it was called in the *Master Plan* of 1948 – of the Indian bazaar by a large-scale rebuilding assisted, as did the new facades on some of the commercial buildings on the main street. Although stone buildings of three or more stories, like the Khoja Mosque at the corner of Government Road and River Road, and the hotel on Sixth Avenue, had also been constructed earlier, they had been individual buildings which did not suffice to alter the overall appearance of the street, and even less of the town center. The third element contributing to the change in how Nairobi appeared was the conversion of the murram roads, which were muddy and sometimes impassable during the rainy season and dusty in the dry season, into tarmac roads within the extensive road works program commenced in 1926.[98] In addition to the town center, the garden suburbs extended to the north and west of the center, also participating in the newly acquired appearance of the town originally founded as a railway center.

Four photographs, taken in the center of Nairobi in the late twenties and early thirties, illuminate the processes of conversion. Two of them show one

---

[98] Descriptions of new constructions in MP 1948, 18f.; Halliman and Morgan 1967, 104; Hake 1977, 45-50. Cf. the photographs discussed earlier.

*Fig. 11.9
Government Road,
western side, 1920s*

of the main streets, Government Road and Sixth Avenue; these two seem to have been taken in the late twenties. The two others are aerial photographs of the town center, taken some years later than the previous ones. All four photographs were published as postcards in the 1980s.

The photograph of Government Road has been taken at the junction of Sixth Avenue towards the north, partly showing the same section of the street, to the west, as the photograph of 1913 referred to earlier (*Fig. 11.9*).[99] In relation to the earlier view, some changes may be observed. In general, there are more two-story buildings along the street than earlier. The arcades at the edges have been retained but the edge is more defined because of the construction of sidewalks and the paving of the street. A four-story stone building – Nairobi House – has been erected at the corner of Sixth Avenue, articulating the junction; the same building, from the Sixth Avenue side, was also visible in the photograph taken of the Armistice Day parade. The plot at the end of Sixth Avenue appears undeveloped. Signs on one of the buildings indicate the shops of "Husein & Co" and "Peter & Son, Photographers." The photograph also shows a traffic police on a stand about a foot above the ground in the middle of the junction, with a number of cars, a motorcycle, a bicycle, and pedestrians.

The other photograph, of Sixth Avenue, has been taken slightly west of the previous one, at the junction of Hardinge Street, towards the west with the Hill in the background (*Fig. 11.10*).[100] Sixth Avenue continues across the

---

99 Postcard.
100 Postcard. Sixth Avenue was later Delamere Avenue, now Kenyatta Avenue. Hardinge Street is now Kimathi Street. Arthur Hardinge was Her Majesty's Agent and Consul-General at Zanzibar from 1894, and Commissioner from 1895 after the declaration of the British East Africa Protectorate, until 1900 (Hill 1949, 125, 128, 248). Dedan Kimathi (1920-1957) was the commander - "Field Marshal" - of the forest fighters during the Mau Mau movement

150 ■ PART III HISTORIES OF URBAN FORM IN NAIROBI

Fig. 11.10 Sixth Avenue, northern side, at Hardinge Street, 1920s

railway line up to the Hill. The character of Sixth Avenue differs from that of Government Road: Sixth Avenue is considerably wider, the central part with its two lanes in both directions flanked by feeder streets between the buildings and the through lanes. Cars are parked at the edges of the feeder streets. The photograph shows the northern side of Sixth Avenue. Most of the buildings have one or two stories. However, a fine six-story building – Torr's Hotel – is located at the corner of Hardinge Street and another, also a hotel, further down the street near the railway crossing, at the corner of Sadler Street.[101] In front of Torr's Hotel is a taxi stand. Two statues can be distinguished further down the street, marked in the map of 1961 as "War Memorial" (on the northern side) and "Memorial" (on the southern side). Rows of trees framing the central part of the street start still further down. In the middle of the junction at Hardinge Street, a traffic police conducts traffic.

One of the two aerial photographs has been taken from a position somewhat northwest above the railway station towards the north (*Fig. 11.11*). The view is dominated by the town center located on flat land, with only the beginnings of the more hilly parts shown to the north. Several urban layers are visible. The oldest layer, in the postcard in the front, consists of the Railways housing units which were among the first structures to be built in Nairobi. Despite the age of this area, the "avenues" within the area have been feebly developed,

---

in the fifties and one of the leading "freedom fighters" for the independence of Kenya (Abuor 1973, 141ff.).
101 Torr's Hotel was shown in a photograph in the *Master Plan* of 1948 (p.20a, ill.10). Trzebinski (1985, 170) noted that Torr's Hotel rivalled the New Stanley Hotel for popularity for years after the Second World War. In the Nairobi and District Topographic Map 1:2500 of 1961, sheet NE 13/B, the first one is marked as a bank and the latter as a hotel. Sadler Street is now Koinange Street.

Fig. 11.11 Aerial view: Nairobi city center to the north, 1930s

Fig. 11.12 Aerial view: Nairobi city center to the southwest, 1930s

Fig. 11.13 Map: Railways area and Law Courts, 1940s

152 ■ PART III HISTORIES OF URBAN FORM IN NAIROBI

the footpaths appearing more pronounced than the planned streets. Government Road, Nairobi's first road and later main street, connecting the railway station (not shown) with the administrative offices which are barely visible in the upper left hand corner, dissects the urban fabric on the right. Victoria Street parallel to it on the east can only just be distinguished on the photograph. The compact Indian bazaar with its smaller plots and high densities is clearly discernible on the upper left hand corner, west of Government Road and the conspicuous three-story mosque at its farther end. The more open land beyond the center to the right is adjacent to the swamp area.[102]

On the upper right hand corner of the photograph, starting from the Khoja Mosque at the corner of Government Road, we can identify consecutive layers, including the low structures along River Road to the east between the Nairobi River and the town center, mostly built from the 1910s onward. Around the same time, the one and two-story buildings were erected along Sixth Avenue, the other major street; these can be seen on the photograph crossing horizontally from the middle left hand edge to Government Road on the right, with the prominent six-story building in the middle of the photograph. The four-story building of the Government Road photograph described above and of the Armistice Day photograph mentioned earlier, is

---

102 Postcard.

also visible in this photograph at the junction of Government Road and Sixth Avenue. Between the two higher buildings on Sixth Avenue, the two-story structure with a higher roof portion in the middle is Woolworth's shop. The large plot at the end of Sixth Avenue seems to be undeveloped as it was in the Government Road photograph. A traffic island with some planting can be seen in the middle of the crossing of Sixth Avenue and Hardinge Street; this seems to date the photograph somewhat later than the two photographs described previously. The arcades at Government Road and Hardinge Street appear as a more coherent built edge in this photograph than in the earlier ones, even though it was already a common practice in commercial structures in Nairobi at an early stage.

The newest layers include several public buildings of which only two can be seen in the photograph: the Jamia Mosque with its two minarets and the McMillan Memorial Library following a classical style with an entrance portico and columns, next to each other in the upper left hand corner. One of the buildings just outside the view was the City Market to the left of the mosque and library. The road leading from the center to the suburbs, in the upper right hand corner, gives an impression of being newly constructed. The buildings on the other side of the River, in the Ngara area, are just visible. The small plots with buildings located next to each other at the edge of the road differ totally in character from those of, for example, the Railways units in the center: the Ngara ones appear very urban even though they are located outside the center, in the suburban fringe.

In general, the photograph shows a well-organized town center where the plots are in effective use, building is controlled, and plot sizes and functions vary in different parts of the center. Although the general building height is only two stories, stone buildings of several stories are beginning to dominate the views on some streets. The core of the center is still quite small, with plots being fully developed only around the three main commercial streets, Government Road, Sixth Avenue and Bazaar Street. A whole block on Hardinge Street is undeveloped right in the middle of the town, one block off from all of these three main streets, next to the Library. Judging from the photograph, the Railway area with its housing seems to be part of a different town, with the streets of the commercial center discontinued at the edge of the residential area, and the residential parts of the center just waiting for conversion into a more densely developed part of the town.

The other aerial photograph complements the view shown in the previous one: taken from a position above River Road area towards the southwest, it shows the middle part of Government Road, most of Sixth Avenue, and a large part of the section between the railway yard and the commercial center, later to be identified as the "City Block" and developed as an administrative center (*Fig. 11.12*). In the photograph, Sixth Avenue appears as an almost extravagant avenue, with double lines of planted trees on both sides of the central part of the street, reaching until the crossing at Hardinge Street with a large planted traffic island and a statue in the middle. A smaller traffic island with plants is also visible at the end of the avenue at the junction of Government Road. The plot which was unbuilt in two of the earlier photographs has now been developed and contains a large two-story structure filling the whole block. At Hardinge Street a modern four-story office building can be seen on the corner of the undeveloped area of the earlier photograph.[103]

The railway subordinates quarters, visible in the other aerial photograph, have been demolished to enable the full development of a new administrative center, which had commenced in 1929 with the construction of the Law Courts (*Fig. 11.13*).[104] The change may also be perceived in the map of around 1940 showing the railways area and the surroundings of the Law Courts.[105] The aerial photograph indicates that new buildings have been constructed on Sixth Avenue, the most conspicuous one being a four or five-story stone building on the southern side of the avenue at the corner of Eliot Street;[106] on the 1961 map, this building is marked as a bank. Standard Street, south of and parallel to Sixth Avenue, now contains higher structures. In the photograph, the Town Hall and the Cathedral of the Holy Family, both with large unbuilt areas surrounding them, are clearly visible, with the front of the Law Courts building partially showing but in shadow, at the edge of the photograph. Adjacent to the three buildings, Sergeant Ellis Avenue has been constructed parallel to Sixth Avenue.[107] Next to the Law Courts is a large planted garden, and beyond it, some small structures of the Railways. On the other side of the railway line closer to the Hill, the Railway sports ground may be discerned and, on the Sixth Avenue, All Saints Cathedral with its towering form. On the basis of this photograph, all the plots at the edges of the two main streets seem to be developed, mostly with two stories, although higher structures can be seen at the corners of Government Road, Sixth Avenue, Hardinge Street and Eliot Street. However, large areas of undeveloped land still remain within a block or two of the main streets, indicating the level of concentration in the development of the urban structure.

In the interwar years, Nairobi had grown from a small railway town into a proud European-style city. The town center had been transformed from a collection of a few streets with odd one-story structures for shops, workshops, warehouses, and dwellings into a commercial center with many stone buildings several stories high, housing banks, hotels, and various commercial enterprises, and a group of impressive public buildings like the Law Courts, the Town Hall, the Railway Headquarters, the Market, the Library, and edifices for the different religious communities. The scattered clusters of

---

103 Postcard printed in a mirror image of reality; for the study, a reversed version was developed from a negative of the postcard.
104 According to Tiwari (1981, 129), the railway subordinates housing area located in the City Square was demolished in 1941.
105 Barnow et al 1983, 45, based on Kenya and Uganda Railways and Harbors, Nairobi City Square, scale 1:1250, File 111 F9-1-1, Drawing No.3997/1.
106 Eliot Street is now Wabera Street.
107 Sergeant Ellis Avenue is now City Hall Way.

houses, connected earlier to the center by narrow murram roads, had given way to well-organized garden suburbs and to more tightly-built Asian residential areas, efficiently and comfortably reached via the macadamized road network. The population had almost tripled from the some 23,000 of 1921 to the over 65,000 of 1940. In the development of Nairobi, the role of the municipal administration had been central, not only because of the initiatives taken by the Municipal Council dominated by the European settlers, but also because of the wide-ranging technical – both local and external – expertise utilized in the planning and execution of the urban improvements.

The urban form of Nairobi during the interwar years was, in most respects, culturally European. For its European community, Nairobi was a western town, built for the transportation of goods to and from the Highlands and Uganda, and for the service of the Europeans. In this context, the Europeans regarded both the Africans and the Asians as temporary phenomena in Nairobi. The Africans they saw as basically rural dwellers, allowed to enter and stay in Nairobi only while needed by the European community. The Asians they perceived as a transitory group, useful in the initial converting of a jungle into civilized territory, but eventually potential competitors in the government of the country, not settlers but transients. The Europeans conceived of themselves as civilizers and the colony as an extension of their own country and its culture (which for many ultimately referred to the British Empire). At best, Kenya was regarded as a refuge where one could continue to pursue a way of life which was getting increasingly scarce in Europe: a life of comfort, idleness, plenty of cheap servants, and exotic means of recreation in a continuously pleasant climate. Many of the European settlers of the early decades in the history of Nairobi were members of the upper and middle classes. Those who were not nevertheless felt elevated to blue-blooded aristocracy on arrival. Something of the attitudes of the Europeans of Nairobi at this time is conveyed in Margery Perham's diaries of 1929-30:

> We drove past the last scattered houses of suburban Nairobi, houses very much like their opposite numbers in England. But here ordinary people can live in sunlight; get their golf and their tennis more easily and cheaply than at home; keep three or four black servants; revel in social freedom that often turns, by all accounts, into licence, and have the intoxicating sense of belonging to a small ruling aristocracy . . . certainly, on the surface, life is very charming in Nairobi, and very sociable with unlimited entertaining; all the shooting, games and bridge anyone could want. And in many houses a table loaded with drinks, upon which you can begin at any hour from 10:00 am onwards, and with real concentration from 6:00.[108]

---

108 Perham, *East African Journey: Kenya and Tanganyika, 1929-30*, London, 1976, quoted in Ngugi 1981, 30. Dame Margery Perham was a historian; she wrote the biography of F.D. Lugard, the "architect of the British Empire on the African continent and the man more responsible than any other single individual for Uganda's incorporation into that realm" (Miller 1971, 227).

■ 12 Establishing the colonial capital, 1940–1963

In terms of economic growth, Kenya experienced a dramatic leap immediately after the war had ended. Investors got interested in Kenya, not only new settlers, but also companies: both saw the country as a ground for profitable investments, for the generation of capital. In the colonies, this global phenomenon was the beginning of industrialization. Land values in the Nairobi city center rose, and office buildings became economic investments.[1] In the 1920s and 30s, the colonial government had discouraged the industrial development of the colonies to protect the British economy; the colonies were seen as mineral and food resources, and as markets for goods and capital, providing Britain with, among other things, revenues from import duties. The settlers' interest in furthering industrial development was overlooked. After 1940, the policy of the colonial government changed and economic development of various kinds, particularly in industries, began to be encouraged. One of the reasons were the difficulties in obtaining commodities which during the war had forced the East African countries to increase their self-reliance in manufactured goods, essentially forcing industrialization.[2] Asian enterprises contributed to the process, with profits invested into the creation of a more diversified economic base, expanding fields like food manufacturing and service industries such as hotels, catering, transportation and insurance; in the 1950s, the building boom attracted small and medium scale Asian companies into the construction sector. The economic activities were matched with investments in education, providing professionals and technicians with local knowledge for the developing industries.[3]

In many ways, the Second World War formed a division between the old and the new character of Nairobi. During the war, the population of Nairobi jumped from 65,000 in 1940 to 109,000 in 1944.[4] The settlers' town of the 1920s and 30s, located in a British colony in Africa, acquired an international role in the war: it became the headquarters of the East African Command and the base of East African troops active in Abyssinia (Ethiopia), Middle East, and Asia.[5] After the war, the social changes in Europe and the crumbling

---

1   Hake 1977, 56. For a discussion of the inflow of foreign capital into Kenya after 1945, see Swainson 1980, chapter 3.
2   Zwanenberg and King 1975, 125ff.
3   D.Ghai 1970, 102f.
4   Town Clerk's Reports of 1941 and 1945, quoted in MP 1948, 84.
5   MP 1948, 19; see also Obudho 1981, 17-21.

of the British Empire also affected Nairobi. Migrants from Britain flooded to Nairobi where the abundance of food was unseen in Britain during and after the war. A reporter for National Geographic Magazine, visiting Kenya in 1950, described them:

> "People coming here," one official later told me, "are of two types - those who want to escape the 20th century, and those who want to find it."[6]

Middle-class European ways of life were introduced, and the aristocratic practices of earlier years ceased to be uncontradicted. Because of the war, Africans were more urgently needed to participate in the urbanization of Nairobi. Already in the beginning of the 1940s, there was a permanent even if limited demand for labor for industrial purposes. In 1941, the Municipal Native Affairs Officer was of the opinion that

> In Nairobi labour has passed from the migrant stage to that of temporary or permanent urbanisation. It is becoming less mobile and more stable and in fact the growing amount of industrial work proper, which much increased with the war, offers a field of employment where that desirable figure, the stable skilled or semi-skilled African worker, can emerge.[7]

Africans moved to town to become wage-earners, because the rural areas lacked the economic opportunities that towns were able to offer.

Nairobi Master Plan for a Colonial Capital

Thus both economically and socially, Nairobi not only had changed during the war but was facing new kinds of challenges. It had, according to the Mayor of Nairobi,

> reached the stage where a new purpose and directive was imperative, to fit it for the mature rôle of a Colonial Capital.[8]

To realize the new direction, a team was invited in 1945 to develop a town plan for Nairobi. The team consisted of three experts from South Africa: Professor L.W. Thornton White, practicing architect and Head of the Department of Architecture at the University of Cape Town, Mr. P.R. Anderson, Senior Town Planning Engineer of the Van der Byl Park Estate Company, of Johannesburg, and Mr. L. Silberman, sociologist and Lecturer in the Department of Social Studies at the University of the Witwaterstrand,

---

6   Moore 1950, 313f; according to the article, many residents sent food packages to relatives in Britain, in 1949 more than 200,000 parcels, 90 per cent containing food, were dispatched there only from Nairobi.
7   Municipal Native Affairs Officer's Annual Report of 1941, quoted in Stichter 1975, 35.
8   F.G.R. Woodley, Mayor of Nairobi, in his foreword to the *Master Plan* of 1948 (p.iii).

Johannesburg. As the experts noted, to include a sociologist on a team of town planners was "still somewhat of an innovation,"[9] particularly in relation to Britain, but it was based on the notion that social organization and development are integrated; they perceived that by experimenting with a team of three planners, Kenya had made town planning history.

The experts visited Nairobi three times: in July 1945, in December 1945-January 1946, and in July 1946. Their work included a study of the physical layout of the town, an analysis of its social structure as well as a civic survey, an aerial photograph, separate observations by each team member concerning their specific fields, and interviews; they also collected maps and previous documents, reports, minutes, and declarations of policy. In 1946, the team submitted an initial map of the master plan and a 50-page interim report to the Town Council and senior members of the government, and, after clarifications made during the third visit, presented the final *Nairobi Master Plan for a Colonial Capital*, published in 1948. The report contained almost 90 pages of text with several tables and drawings, eight pages with 47 photographs, and fourteen maps, plans or perspective illustrations in color, including the main master plan.[10] The material may be described as covering three main topics: existing conditions in Nairobi, principles for planning, and the actual plan, all involving both texts and drawings. About half of the texts and drawings were descriptions of existing conditions; of the other half, the planning principles and the actual plan were given approximately the same amount of text, but out of the seven drawings, two indicated planning principles and five presented the actual plan.

In the report, the description of the conditions existing in Nairobi formed the basis for the plan. The experts discussed the history of the town, its peoples, climate, geology, physiography, engineering services, social services, economy, and the size of the city, both in terms of area and population (*Figs. 12.1, 12.2, 12.3*). The analyses of the economy and the size of the city and its inhabitants also included a discussion of future prospects and the determination of the projected population on which the plan would be based. The team estimated a population growth pattern which at a three per cent annual increase would be somewhat reduced from the pre-war rate. Maintaining the existing proportions between the three races, that is, roughly one European to three Asians to six Africans, the population increase from 1948 to 1975 was expected to be two and a half times the figure then existing, to reach 270,000 inhabitants, with 25,000 Europeans, 85,000 Asians, and 160,000 Africans. The conclusion of the team was that for 1975, the envisaged – "both likely and desirable" – population of Nairobi would be roughly 250,000.[11] The size of the Nairobi area the team evaluated as sufficient, and

---

9   MP 1948, 1.
10   MP 1948. Of the attached drawings, the master plan was about 34cm by 60cm, three were A3, eight A4 and two half of A4 in size, all in color.
11   MP 1948, 42ff.

Fig. 12.1 Aerial photograph: City center, 1940s

the *Master Plan* was based on confining further growth within the existing boundaries, determined in 1926.[12]

The principles for planning were derived from various sources. These included not only South African examples with which the planners were the most familiar, several referred to in the report, but also the latest developments in British planning as well as historical and contemporary parallels from different countries. The specific problems of towns in "new" countries and of town planning in Africa were identified. The team saw the result of their work less as a meticulous plan and more as a program for statutory planning, concentrating on the major planning issues of Nairobi which would affect the town as an interrelated whole. The *Master Plan* was

> conceived as a key plan to the general physical, economic and social development of Nairobi over the next 25 years."[13]

In other words, it was seen as a frame within which the local detailed plans could be made and executed. For the team, the master plan was a vehicle to address the major issues of Nairobi and to propose responses to them. In their formulation, the "Nairobi problem" involved several aspects of similar importance: the relationship of the city to the railway, industrialization, population growth, regional development, the multiracial populace, the aesthetic characteristics of the city center, the industrial area, and the road network. The team also identified issues which would not pose difficulties often met in towns in Europe: there was no intricate slum clearance problem, there were adequate open spaces, public authorities had access to sufficient land, and the beautiful spots of the city had not been spoiled.[14]

The actual plan prepared by the team involved some twenty pages of text and five drawings. The plan was based on the notion of preserving the existing urban structure, primarily for practical and economic reasons. The objective of the planners was

> to merge any development into existing so that the values of existing sites and buildings are not suddenly and seriously disturbed, particularly in the business area. That is to say, we do not want a plan which will disrupt the gradual evolution of Nairobi, but rather a plan which will develop naturally out of the present land usage and particularly the present land values.[15]

In the plan, the total area of the town was divided into distinct functional zones, each with its specific land use, fourteen different uses in all:

---

12 MP 1948, 44f. R.C. Tiwari (1981, 129, map p.131) has claimed that after 1900, the municipal boundary was extended in 1926, 1941 and 1964. To my knowledge, Tiwari's claim of an extension in 1941 is not supported by other sources. According to Halliman and Morgan (1967), the post-1900 extensions date from 1919, 1926/28 and 1963 (p.104), marked on their map (p.99) as 1920, 1927 and 1963.
13 MP 1948, 1.
14 MP 1948, 2-4.
15 MP 1948, 57.

THE POPULATION OF NAIROBI

1906
EUROPEAN		559
ASIATIC		3,582
AFRICAN		7,371
	TOTAL	11,512

1926
EUROPEAN		2,665
ASIATIC		9,199
AFRICAN		18,000
	TOTAL	29,864

1936
EUROPEAN		5,600
ASIATIC		16,000
AFRICAN		28,000
	TOTAL	49,600

1944
EUROPEAN		10,400
ASIATIC		34,300
AFRICAN		64,200
	TOTAL	108,900

Fig. 12.2 Population of Nairobi, 1906, 1926, 1936 and 1944

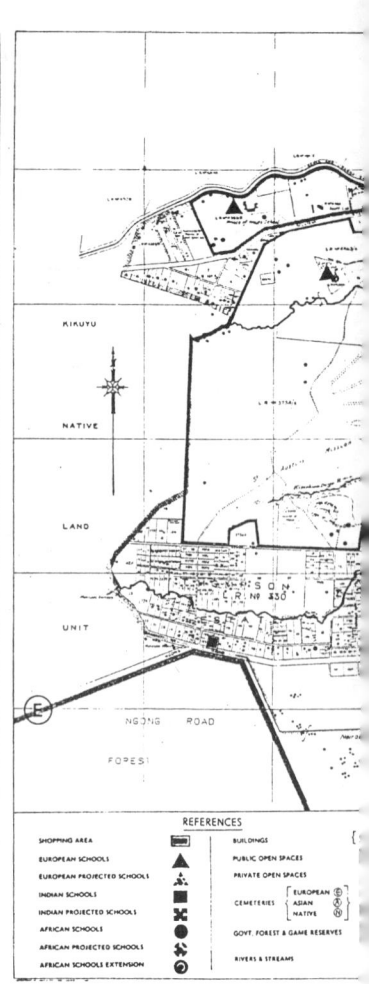

	Use	% of total
(a)	Kenya and Civic Centre Buildings	0.27
(b)	Kenya and Civic Centre: Open Spaces	0.54
(c)	Business or Commerce	1.07
(d)	Reserve for Business or Light Industry	0.13
(e)	Light Industry	0.58
(f)	K.U.R.& H. Yards (existing and new)	0.59
(g)	Existing Heavy Industry	1.25
(h)	New Heavy Industry	3.39
(i)	Noxious Industry (excluding open space)	0.33
(j)	Residential (excluding open space)	38.37
(k)	Official Housing	16.73
(l)	Reserves for Official Housing Extension	3.33
(m)	Open Spaces of all kinds excluding (b)	28.71
(n)	Major Roads: trunk and circulatory	4.71
	Total	100.00% [16]

---

16 MP 1948, 57. The acreages given have not been included in the table here.

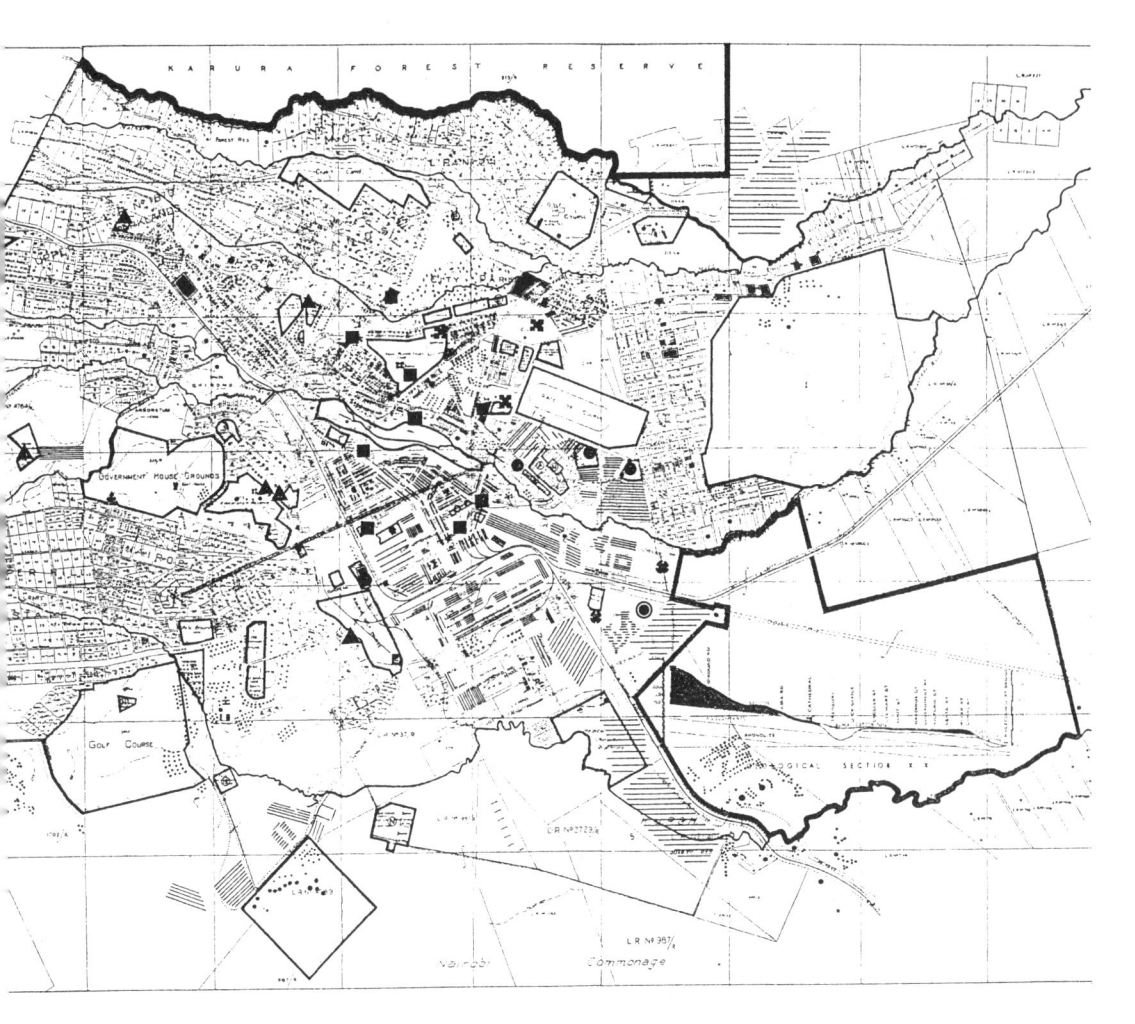

Fig. 12.3 Map: Buildings and open spaces distribution

The drawn master plan was presented in roughly a scale of 1:30,000, the different areas distinguished according to land use. Within the municipal boundary, these included the ones mentioned above, although in the drawn plan, the reserves were not identified. Only the official buildings – mostly in the civic center – and the proposed blocks of flats were separately indicated on the plan.

The areas surrounding the municipality comprised green belt areas, the game reserve, the forest reserve, and the Kikuyu land unit. The road network presented on the plan included the national (trunk) roads, the main parkway roads, and the main local distribution roads. Of the natural conditions, only the rivers were shown. The existing conditions and the planned changes were not distinguished on the plan; the drawn plan thus presented an envisaged future Nairobi. (*Fig. 12.4*)[17]

---

17   MP 1948, inside front cover.

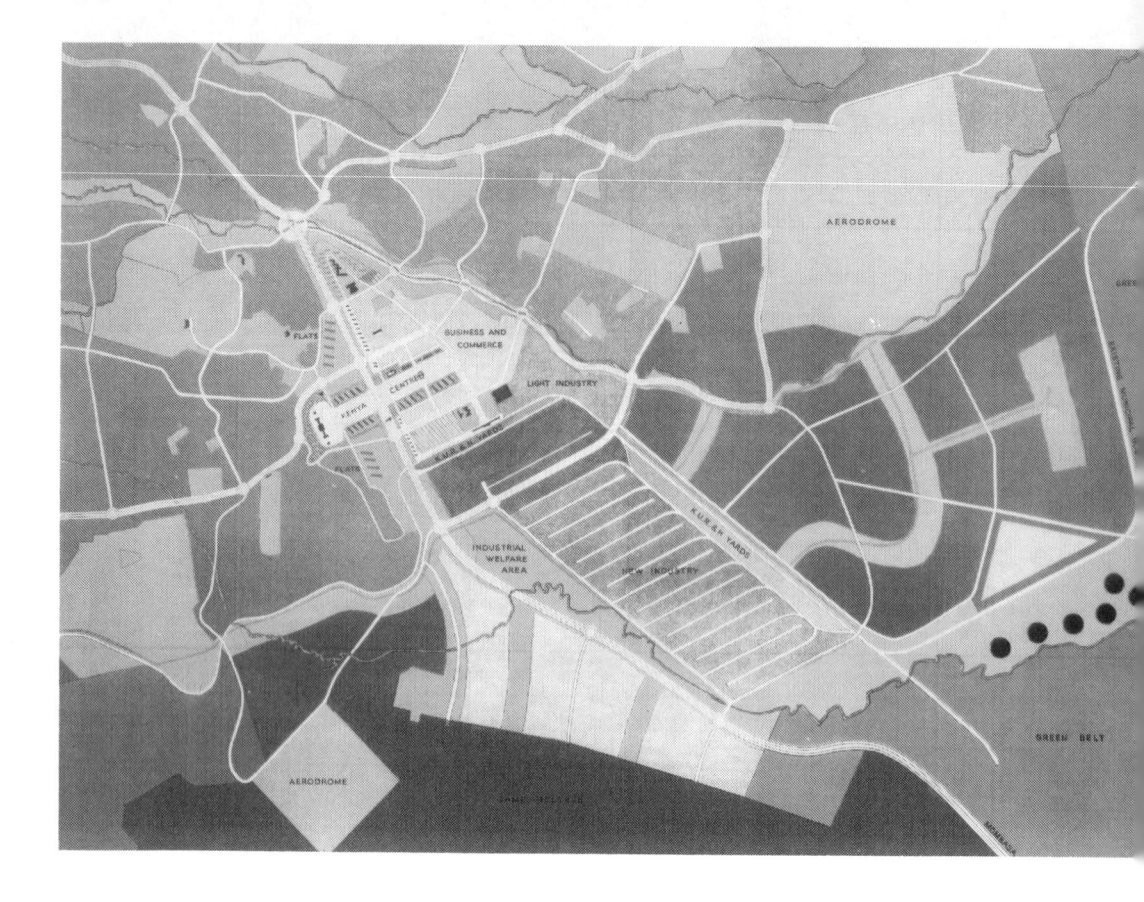

The most important issues of the *Master Plan for a Colonial Capital* were attached to the urban structure, Kenya Center as the new administrative "capitol," and the development of the commercial center, the industrial areas, and the residential areas as well as the orientation and architectural control of buildings.

The urban structure. In the plan, the organization of the road system was the instrument to generate the urban structure of Nairobi. Clearly distinguished systems of roads of different kinds were used to serve different traffic needs and to define the relations between the parts of the city: the parkways would separate the commercial and industrial areas from the residential areas and discourage through-traffic in the residential areas, while the local main distribution roads would determine the neighborhoods and the service roads lead to individual buildings.[18] The network of green areas and open spaces was employed to support the structuring of the city. One of the major changes involving the prevailing conditions was the proposal to realign the railway. The tracks passing the city center on the west and continuing up to the hills on the north, originating from the very beginning of Nairobi, were seen as a

---

18 MP 1948, 53f, 57, 67-70.

Fig. 12.4 Master Plan, 1948

barrier to the city's natural growth. The railway line was to be realigned to make a detour around the residential areas on Upper Parklands and the Hill, towards the south after leaving the station for Uganda, then to the west through Kibera, along the southern boundary of the municipality. *(Fig. 12.5)*[19]

In the city center, the realignment of the railway line made the planning of a new parkway possible, or, as the team formulated it, the

> removal of the railway line . . . provides a heaven-sent opportunity to plan a new East African Highway.[20]

This new road would combine several functions: it would connect Nairobi with other cities (forming part of the trunk road between Mombasa and Lake Victoria), enable traffic between different parts of the city to pass the city center, and distribute traffic to the city center through a limited number of main streets. At the time, through-traffic traversed the city center on Government Road and Delamere Avenue. In the plan, the new main road was called the East African Highway or Kenya Parkway.[21] It was planned as a parkway with two sections (for slow and fast traffic) in both directions and a wide reserved strip for planting in the middle. In the plan, three roundabout junctions connected the parkway with the city center, and a major "traffic circus," located at Ainsworth Bridge north of the center, served to connect the parkway with the main road to the northeast (Thika and Kiambu) and to a new "Swamp Parkway," planned to be built on both sides of the Nairobi River, northeast of the center. The plan of the road system also included bicycle paths, the team describing the estimated 11,000 cyclists of Nairobi (in 1944) as "predominantly the man living in the official housing zones and working in the industrial or commercial centre of the city,"[22] that is, mostly Africans.

The administrative center. The *Master Plan* also introduced the idea of establishing a land reserve for the future civic center to be constructed around the area already containing the Law Courts and Secretariat. This was a mostly unbuilt site, much of the land publicly owned.[23] They saw the congregation of government offices as a natural neighbor to the commercial area, since

---

19 MP 1948, 63. To enable the realignment in Kibera, the planners proposed a slight extension of the municipal boundary.
20 MP 1948, 69.
21 The proposed road was identified as the East African Highway in the list of maps and charts (p.v) and in the text (p.69f.) and as the Kenya Parkway in the depiction attached to the illustration (facing p.60). After construction, it was called the Princess Elizabeth Way (see e.g. Nairobi and District Map 1:2500, sheet NE13/B, second edition 9/1961). Now it is called the Uhuru ("Freedom") Highway.
22 MP 1948, 67-70, "Nairobi Master Plan: Roads," inside back cover. On the plan, the bicycle paths were identified only within the official housing zones, around the new industrial area with a section branching off towards Kibera, and north of the Swamp Parkway. Emig and Ismael (1980, 46) failed to recognize the bicycle paths in the drawn Master Plan.
23 Maps "Land Controlled by Kenya-Uganda Railways & Harbours" and "Land Owned by Public Authorities," MP 1948, between pages 56 and 57.

Fig. 12.5 Master Plan: Roads, 1948

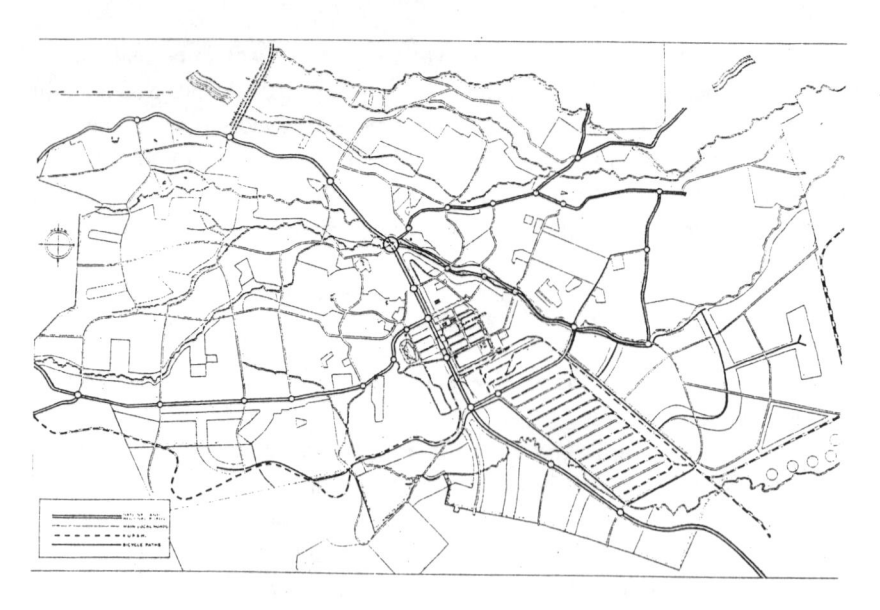

> Government in our modern Development Empire has too many links and points of contact with trade, industry and banking to be pushed away from the Commercial Centre, as some people have proposed.[24]

In the plan, the new civic center was alternately called the Kenya or East Africa Centre, referring to its future position as the legislative and central administrative offices of either Kenya only or the possible union of the East African territories. The civic center was to be integrated within the center of an existing city, avoiding the "social, cultural and economic disadvantages of creating a separate capital such as at Canberra and New Delhi."[25] It was to be located on an area which combined the flat land of the city center with the topographical prominence of the Hill, immediately adjacent to, but visually separate from, the existing commercial and railway areas of the city center and the government residential areas on the Hill (*Fig. 12.6*). Its outlook was to be grand:

> The general conception is of a ceremonial open space in the centre, commanded by new Government buildings at one end and with the present Law Courts against a background of architecturally controlled commercial offices or entertainment buildings at the other end.[26]

A perspective drawing of the Kenya Center showed a diagrammatic interpretation of the planned civic center: a prominent building of neo-Classical style on top of the Hill overlooking an extensive open space with trees and a large fountain in the middle, surrounded at the edges with two existing buildings, the Town Hall and the Cathedral, and with some twelve office buildings of three stories, all designed in a uniform and nondescript

---

24 MP 1948, 50.
25 MP 1948, 58.
26 MP 1948, 58.

style. The green area was traversed in the middle by the highway. *(Fig. 12.7)*[27] Another drawing of the central area, marked "Air View – Proposed Central Area," indicated not only the buildings at the edge of the open space of the Kenya Center but also the blocks of flats proposed for the edge of the hill to the west and north of the city center. In the "Air View," the existing built blocks and street network were not indicated, the areas between the proposed main streets marked with brown-colored hatching. For the Hill, the existing road network was shown in a sketchy format. *(Fig. 12.8)*[28]

The team assessed the site reserved for the Kenya Center – approximately 1900m long and 450m wide – as adequate, avoiding both the insufficient size of the Union Buildings area of Pretoria and the extravangance and inhuman scale of capital centers like Washington [D.C.], New Delhi, or Canberra. The size of the site was similar to the Louvre and Tuileries Gardens of Paris, "well-known as a world example of human monumental scale." This was also illustrated by comparative plans drawn in the same scale *(Fig. 12.9)*.[29] The proposed East African Highway was to cross the Kenya Center, dividing it into two parts, the easterly half developed for local administration and civic activities and the westerly half for governmental (Kenya and East Africa) functions. The team emphasized the importance of vegetation in the creation of the capital center, not merely for aesthetic reasons, but because of the equatorial location with the need of shade to provide efficient and comfortable working conditions. Finn Barnow has suggested that the Kenya Center was in reality an architectural celebration of the initiators of the plan, the colonial administration, the ideological goal of the plan being a tribute to the liberal elite, particularly the bureaucracy.[30]

The commercial center. In the *Master Plan*, the development of business and commercial activities was restricted to the zone comprising the existing European commercial center and the functionally integrated Indian Bazaar and River Road areas adjacent to it. The team assessed the existing commercial area as adequate also for the near future, if its incongruous uses, such as industries, warehouses, and assembly shops could be forced to move out and the area developed exclusively for commerce, and if the height zoning was generous enough to allow vertical expansion.[31] They noted that in the city center, height restrictions based on actual widths of streets had been unsuccessful in other cities, resulting in disrupted site values, unbalanced development of adjacent sites, and "a very jagged picture of population capacity achieved." They also discouraged a uniform maximum height limit because it would allow for a commercial floor area which the population would "never need or use". Therefore, to "ensure a proper, economical

---

27   MP 1948, facing p.60.
28   MP 1948, between pages 56 and 57. In the list of contents, this drawing was called "Aerial Perspective of Central Area."
29   MP 1948, 59.
30   Barnow 1990, 150.
31   MP 1948, 49f.

Fig. 12.6 Master Plan: Central area

development of the central area and to avoid the confusion and difficulties which would follow an uncontrolled scattering of tall buildings, with their haphazard concentration of workers,"[32] the team proposed that two height zones be established. A maximum building height of 100 feet would be adopted for the area bounded by Sadler Street, Portal Street, Victoria Street, and Whitehouse Road,[33] that is, the blocks on both sides of Delamere Avenue and on the southern part of Government Road – the two main streets, the few built blocks south of Delamere Avenue, and the mostly unbuilt area between these and the railway line, including the proposed Kenya Center. A maximum building height of 50 feet was proposed for the remaining commercial center, that is, the areas around the Indian Bazaar and River Road,

---

32   MP 1948, 60.
33   Sadler Street is now Koinange Street, Portal Street is Banda Street, Victoria Street is Tom Mboya Street, and Whitehouse Road is Haile Selassie Avenue.

Fig. 12.7 Master Plan: Kenya Center

Fig. 12.8 Master Plan: Kenya Parkway

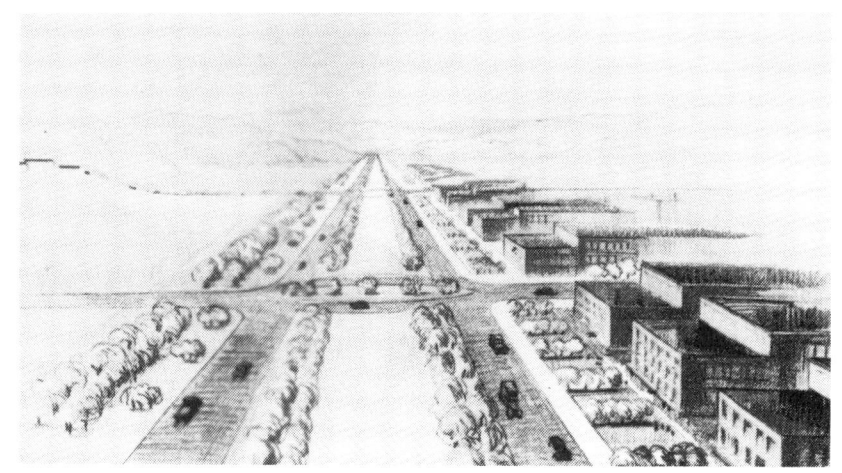

mostly owned by Asians; for this area, the planners presupposed the reduction of residential functions in the future.[34] They also suggested that an increase of the 100 feet height could be authorized in exceptional cases, as for the new government building on the Hill, as part of the Kenya Center. The area adjoining the business center on the north, near the proposed major traffic circus at Ainsworth Bridge, in the corner of the triangle formed by the city center, was suggested to be reserved for buildings for higher education, cultural activities, hotels, and blocks of flats.[35] The team also proposed the use of the reserve for the East African Highway for car parking, and strongly advised against a centrally located bus station.[36]

The industrial areas. The provision of adequate land for industrial purposes

---

34 MP 1948, 62.
35 MP 1948, 60f.
36 MP 1948, 71f.

Fig. 12.9
Comparative plans

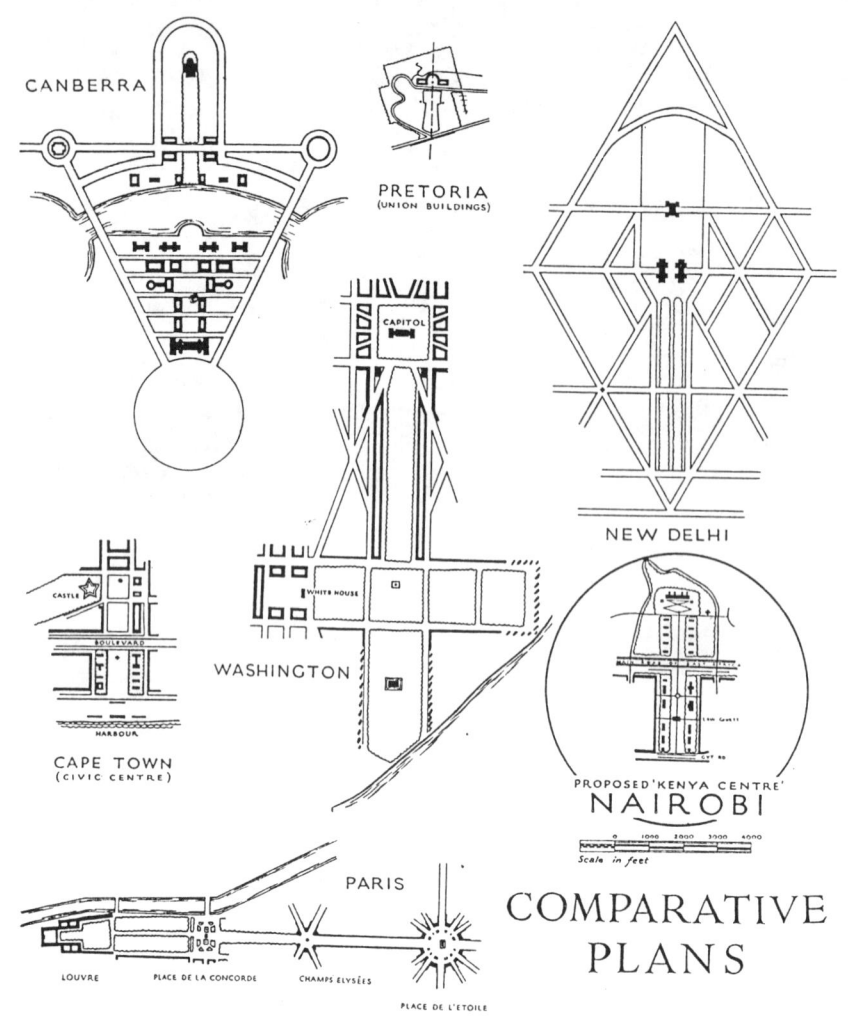

and railway yards was one of the prime points of interest in the *Master Plan*, with altogether six different kinds of land use areas indicated for them. The industrial areas were to be distinguished from other functions and based on the idea of the factory or trading estate, similar to the neighborhood unit in the residential areas. In general, the team said that "The *Master Plan* must contribute towards a reduction of the cost of industrial production."[37] The new heavy industry area was planned close to the railway line, immediately south of the railway yard and station area and the existing industrial area, and east of the planned national trunk road. The proposed area contained government facilities such as the prison, the isolation hospital, the medical quarantine area, military facilities as well as a cement factory, a considerable number of buildings of "obsolescent or temporary character" and two housing areas. Of these, located closer to the city center, was Kaloleni, a housing

---

37 MP 1948, 50-53, quotation from p.50.

project described as a "model neighborhood unit," initiated by the government, constructed in 1944-45 and taken over by the municipality in 1945. The scheme was intended to house 3,000 people. The other, further southeast, was Makongeni, built by the Railways for its employees, its 1,700 rooms in 170 blocks completed in 1944.[38] According to the *Master Plan*, these very recently built housing areas were eventually to be demolished, even if they would be

> not likely to be required for at least 20 years, after which a decision can be taken as to the future of these housing schemes, balancing the then residual value of the housing against the requirements of the industry and the full development of the marshalling yards.[39]

In other words, these African housing areas were seen as temporary, to be replaced if and when the needs of the expanding industrial activities would require the land. Attached to the *Master Plan* was also a specific industrial estate model plan from South Africa;[40] however, the South African example was not directly discussed in the text nor did the adopted plan for the Nairobi industrial area follow the model. In the planned industrial area, plots had individual rail sidings and access to an adjoining industrial welfare area with "amenities and lunch hour recreation facilities."[41]

The residential areas. According to the team, Nairobi had first developed, like other cities which had grown without formulating town planning principles, on speculative interests, with the municipality later taking refuge in gridiron layouts. The planners argued that the gridiron system which municipalities had used in flat areas was not only unpleasing in its monotony but also impractical and uneconomic, wasteful of roads and space, encouraging ribbon development and too low densities, offering few public or commercial services, and lacking focal points. The garden city idea which had been developed as an alternative for the residential areas to overcome what they called the "deadening effect of the gridiron layout," they critized for its limitation on urban form only, town planning seen primarily as landscape gardening and residential areas providing plenty of private open space. According to the planners, the garden city idea had failed to promote the development of a community. The neighborhood unit proposed by the team was therefore not only a plan to organize the built urban forms but a social plan to initiate a community where the physical forms and the social services supported the development of social bonds between the inhabitants. The social policy inherent in the plan was perceived by the planners as one of prime importance. According to their analysis, when rural Africans move into towns, they tend to look for tribal associations; however, the friction

---

38 Hake 1977, 56, 257. Kaloleni (in coastal language referring to a look-out post) was built with support from a grant from the Colonial Development and Welfare Fund covering half its cost.
39 MP 1948, 63.
40 MP 1948, facing page 52.
41 MP 1948, 63.

between the different tribes had proven to be unsatisfactory. In a modern city, they saw that the real base of community life was the

> community spirit born from a multiplicity of contacts and common experiences. Such a community life cannot be generated under migratory conditions of African labour. Stabilisation of the labour force and the creation of units which have the opportunity and the freedom to build up a collective experience must be the objective of all those who admire the smooth operation of the social business in the African tribe.
>
> A stable community will know how to manage its misfits. It will create public opinion which will keep the individual better disciplined than any coercive machinery from above will do . . . From early childhood the ways of modern, regular, timebound, life can be instilled, and need not be acquired arduously in later life. All along the undesirable features of the "déraciné" are obviated by the social sanctions of the community and the strong integrations forged in social co-operation. It is this translation of the values of tribal life into modern terms which is most clearly realised in "Neighborhood Planning."[42]

In other words, the neighborhood was to be the means of injecting modern social values and practices into newly urbanized citizens whose earlier experiences were limited to tribal associations.

The experts also indicated the economic superiority of the neighborhood unit, comparing the land use of 500 acres on the basis on the "average gridiron speculative layout," the "garden city type of development" and the "T.W. neighborhood unit." In the comparison, using the same density figure of eight houses per acre, the road system in the gridiron required 25 per cent of the land, in the garden city 40 per cent, and in the neighborhood unit only 10 per cent, leaving more land for open spaces and public buildings. If the amount of land for open spaces and public buildings was kept constant, the same 500 acres would accomodate more people within the same density in the neighborhood unit plan than in the speculative or the garden city developments.[43] Thus the planners' proposal of the neighborhood unit was not only socially desirable but also rationally the most effective.

The team described the objectives of neighborhood planning extensively, not only in terms of planning principles developed by Patrick Abercrombie in his Greater London Plan of 1944,[44] and in terms of "desiderata" evolved by Thornton White for Nairobi,[45] but also in terms of a model plan of the adapted principles on what the planner called "a definite site."[46] In the model plan – the "T.W. Neighborhood Unit" – the neighborhood contained around

---

42   MP 1948, 7f.
43   MP 1948, 47. In the latter comparison, the land available for houses was calculated as 277 acres in the speculative development, as 217 in the garden city development, and as 357 acres in the T.W. neighborhood unit.
44   MP 1948, 46.
45   MP 1948, 46f.
46   MP 1948, 73; the site was unidentified.

Fig. 12.10 Master Plan: TW neighborhood unit

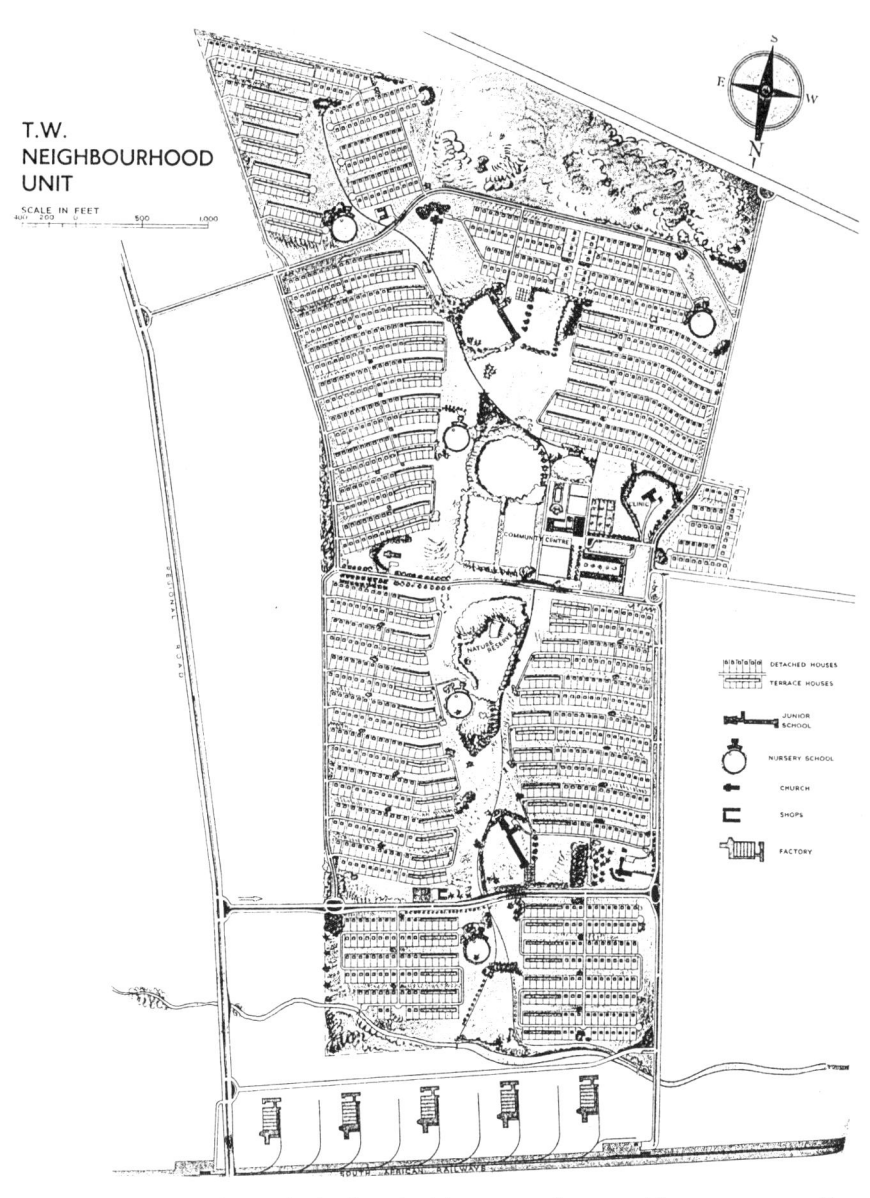

a thousand housing units in detached houses and terraced houses surrounding a central green area with five nursery schools, two junior schools, three churches, several shops and a community center. Factories were located to one side of the area. (*Fig. 12.10*)[47] As the planners noted in the report,

> This example was worked out for a non-European population and its house plots are therefore small (8 to an acre).[48]

---

47 MP 1948, facing page 72. The scale was approximately 1:1050.
48 MP 1948, 73.

CHAPTER 12 ESTABLISHING THE COLONIAL CAPITAL, 1940–1963 ■ 173

A green area separated each row of plots from the neighboring ones, and the collective roads were at the periphery of the area, enabling footpaths in the central green to provide the shortest paths to the services which was one of the planners' goals. According to the report, the neighborhood unit system of planning had become standard practice in planning schemes, largely because of its financial and social advantages over older systems; immediate results and immediate savings, however, could have been achieved only in the entirely new units, because completely built up areas would have required re-planning to form a complete unit.

In the *Master Plan*, two different types of housing zones were distinguished: residential zones and official housing zones. With the concept of official housing, the planners referred to

> housing schemes, erected by the Municipality, the Government, the K.U.R. & H. [Kenya and Uganda Railways and Harbours], and any similar schemes which may be erected in the future by the private enterprise of commercial or industrial firms to accommodate their own workers.[49]

Thus the "official housing zones" contained housing provided by the public sector and private companies for their employees, and the "residential zones" (or "economic residential zones") housing funded by private individuals. For the "residential zones," the planners proposed an average figure of 15 persons per acre, including the household and any servants living on the premises; at this density, the residential zones would have a population of about 123,000 persons. For the "official housing zones," the planners recommended an average of 30 persons per acre, including service roads, but not including open spaces, allotment gardens, and community buildings generally; at this density, the official housing zones and their reserves would accomodate some 130,000 persons.[50]

The density of the residential zones was calcuted to be less than European urban standards which sometimes exceeded 100 persons per acre – "obviously undesirable" – but to be more than the standards existing in some parts of Nairobi of more than one acre per person – which "cannot possibly persist if the target population is to be reached" within the existing municipal boundary.[51] According to the map "Existing Residential Density Zoning,"[52] the different density zones existing in Nairobi in 1945 were:

> Twelve houses per acre in the areas marked as no.1 (Lower Parklands) and no.2 (parts of Ngara and Pangani), immediately to the north and

---

49   MP 1948, 64.
50   MP 1948, 65. Two-thirds of the area for residential use was allocated for "residential zones" (excluding open spaces) and one-third for "official housing zones," with roughly equal populations (see above).
51   MP 1948, 64.
52   MP 1948, between pages 56 and 57.

northeast of the city center; these areas were mostly identified as "lower class" Asian.

Two houses per acre in the areas marked as no.2A (part of Pangani), no.3 (small section on Nairobi Hill between the Government House grounds and Ngong Road), no.4 (the part of Upper Parklands now known as Westlands), and no.5 (Parklands), further north and west from the city center; of which Parklands was identified as "upper class" Asian.

One house per acre in the areas marked as no.6 (Muthaiga and most of Upper Parklands) and no.7 (Upper Hill, Kilimani Estate, Thompson Estate, Chiromo, most of Nairobi Hill, and the area now known as Lavington at St. Austin's Mission), to the north and west of the city center; these areas were usually identified as European. (*Fig. 12.11*)

Although the existing residential zoning generally corresponded with particular ethnic groups, there were exceptions. These included the areas marked as no.3 (part of Nairobi Hill) and no.4 (Westlands),[53] zoned as the upper class Asian areas at a density of 2 houses per acre but located within the part of the city restricted to Europeans only.[54] In the map "Existing Population Distribution" only the officially accepted housing areas were acknowledged, leaving out the unofficial squatter housing which had been part of the Nairobi reality from its very beginning. Thus the existing African population, estimated in 1944 as over 64,000 or almost 60 per cent of the total,[55] was shown on the map to inhabit only a small portion of the land used for residential purposes in the municipality: the Pumwani Native Location established by the municipality, the Makongeni housing area built by the Railways, and the area between the two marked as a general industrial and factory area, including the Railway Muthurwa Landhies area and Kaloleni municipal housing. In the map "Existing Residential Density Zoning," neither the African areas nor Eastleigh (identified in the 1930s as an Asian area) were included among the zoned areas.

In the *Master Plan*, the residential zones were planned for a population "irrespective of race, colour, or creed."[56] The planners rejected outright the racial identification of different areas:

> We do not suggest the allocation of units to different racial groups, even if such allocation were legally possible.[57]

---

53 In the map "Buildings and Open Spaces Distribution" (MP 1948, facing p.56), part of Westlands was identified as a shopping area.
54 The restrictions were imposed by the private estates like Muthaiga (Map "Existing Population Distribution" attached to MP 1948, between pages 56 and 57). A similar smaller enclave marked as restricted for Europeans was shown within Lower Parklands, a "lower class" Asian area.
55 Town Clerk's Report of 1945, quoted in MP 1948, 84.
56 MP 1948, 64.
57 MP 1948, 64.

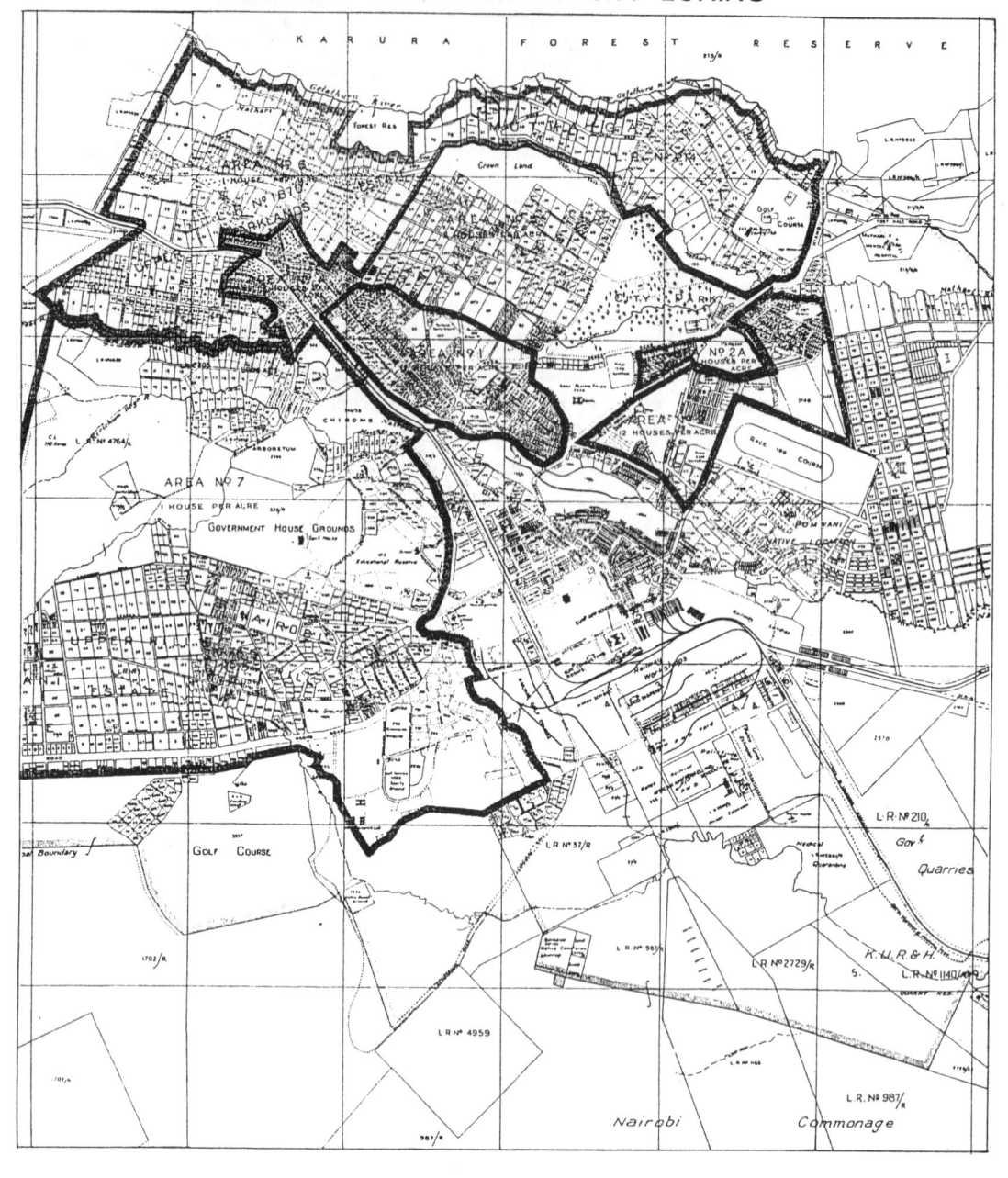

EXISTING RESIDENTIAL DENSITY ZONING

Fig. 12.11 Map: Existing residential density zoning

But the reasons may not have been disagreement with the notion of segregation; the planners seemed to see racial distinction as unnecessary because, as they continued,

> With some working out of densities in the details of the statutory scheme, however, it is inevitable that each unit will in practice house

a particular economic group and develop a particular racial character, as indeed such units do in other parts of the world.[58]

For the official housing zones, the situation was less clear. In the *Master Plan*, the official housing zones were mostly proposed for the east of the city center, near the industrial areas, with reserves for extension further east and southeast. Some small official housing areas were also suggested at the municipal boundary near the residential zones, to provide accommodation for persons employed in domestic service. Both groups were described as predominantly non-European.[59] In principle, the distinction between the residential zones and the official housing zones was one of ownership where official housing referred to housing provided by the employer. In the context of Nairobi in the 1940s, ownership of houses in the officially accepted residential areas was almost totally exclusive to the European and Asian communities; the Africans lived in housing provided by their employers. But Europeans and Asians also inhabited employer housing, for example the Railways housing units. For both groups, these were located outside the "official housing zones" in the "residential zones," that is, in contradiction with the expressed definitions. In effect, then, the "official housing zones" referred to areas built and controlled by the public authorities and intended for Africans, while the "residential zones" referred to areas built by the private sector, and in some cases, the public sector, and intended for Asians (the more dense parts) and Europeans (the less dense parts).

The orientation and architectural control of buildings. Finally, the team of planners recommended the orientation of buildings according to the solar conditions of tropical areas, emphasizing not only the advantages to comfort and economy but also to architectural quality:

> better conditions can be obtained and an interesting architectural character created if the new buildings in the Kenya and Civic Centres and along the new frontage to the East African Highway, are set at an angle to the roadways, as near as possible in building blocks running East and West.[60]

Architectural control over the appearance of the city was seen as essential, both in the "enlightened housing estate" and in the "formal dignity of the tropical civic center." However, the team acknowledged the difficulties of architectural control:

> The old ideal of complete architectural regularity in our streets and particularly in housing estates, is now very frequently abandoned, because it so often achieves nothing but a dull monotony – the dignity of a dead city rather than the vigorous character and beauty of a young and constantly rejuvenated one.[61]

---

58 MP 1948, 64.
59 MP 1948, 65.
60 MP 1948, 74.
61 MP 1948, 75.

Thus the built forms of Nairobi were perceived as a means of achieving a particular aesthetic purpose, the expression of the newness of the town.

In many respects, the *Master Plan* of 1948 repeated proposals already made in Jameson's plan and the explanatory memorandum of 1927 of the joint Government and Municipal Town Planning Authority. These included the realignment of the railway, the organization of the roads, the establishment of the civic center, the utilization of zoning, and the inclusion of different kinds of residential areas for different inhabitant groups. The novel issues of the *Master Plan* were related to the industrial areas, the official housing zones, the general increase of densities, and the regional aspects in planning, all ingredients in the changed role of Nairobi within the postwar British Empire. The reluctance of Britain to encourage the growth of industries in the interwar years was replaced by policies of industrial development during and after the Second World War. The planners saw the position of Nairobi as crucial to the economic prospects of the country. With slender natural resources and an agricultural sector vulnerable to international price fluctuations, manufacturing industries and the secondary sectors they stimulated were perceived as the means to stabilize the economy and increase national income. In this, urbanization was essential.[62]

The *Master Plan* of 1948 was used to promote these policies. The planning of various kinds of industrial areas was extensively discussed. Housing for the industrial workers in the official housing zones was recognized as a necessary prerequisite in the process of industrial development and urbanization, and was allocated one third of the areas reserved for residential purposes. To ensure the planned land usage, both the industrial areas and the official housing zones were located on land mostly publicly owned. The improvement of the road system and the general increase of densities were seen as ways to make land use more effective and therefore more economical. Regional considerations supported the rational location of urban functions for their later extension outside the existing municipal boundary. New regulations were also developed: in 1948, the building by-laws introduced in 1926 were replaced by the Nairobi City Council By-Laws which included town planning requirements.[63]

In the *Master Plan*, the role of the Africans – and of areas, facilities, and services provided for their use – was perceived as important for the processes of industrial development and urbanization. In this sense, Peter Hall's assessment of the *Master Plan* of 1948 was grossly misleading. In the context of describing plans made for British colonial cities, Hall maintained that the planners of Nairobi did not acknowledge the existence of the Africans:

---

62   MP 1948, 38ff.
63   The City Council of Nairobi (Building) By-Laws, 1948, ("Planning") were still in force in 1983. See also Soni 1983, 1f.

Africans were dismissed on the ground that though they were the most numerous they were also the most transitory; the plan did not even show African housing areas.[64]

Obviously Hall failed to notive the numerous references in the report to the official housing zones. Although the planners did not directly refer to "African" housing areas, the official housing areas were planned for persons working in the industrial area and commercial center, identified as predominantly non-Europeans;[65] in this sense, Hall's concept of "African" housing seems to contain more racist connotations than the *Master Plan* itself. His view, however, does not seem to have been exceptional. Several researchers have assessed the *Master Plan* of 1948 as having been based on racial segregation, presenting this – in passing – as a fact, without explanation or argument.[66] Andrew Hake's description of the plan was more indirect. Discussing the historical development of Nairobi, Hake suggested that the *Master Plan* prepared by Thornton White and the others was "inevitably influenced by the racial assumptions of its period and was planning in the imperial tradition for a colonial capital."[67] He did not not define what the "racial assumptions" or the "imperial tradition" were; according to Hake, the planners applied the principles of town planning of their time, incorporating the notions of zoning, traffic segregation, and neighborhood unit into the *Master Plan*.

However, instead of containing a dismissal of the Africans or racial assumptions, the *Master Plan* of 1948 represented a change in how planners perceived the different ethnic groups inhabiting the city. Finn Barnow has suggested this in his study on colonial cities, maintaining that unlike the previous plan of 1927, the *Nairobi Master Plan* of 1948 was not racist:

> To summarize, the plan appears as liberal and elitist but not racist. The double role of functionalism as a progressive professional program and a legitimating ideology means, together with the wish of the colonial power to establish the architectural monument . . . that the plan is presented as an at once rational and aesthetic product."[68]

Barnow stressed the role of ideology in planning, conveyed in the report in the technical parts, with proposals concerning the establishment of industrial areas and the introduction of an administrative center. Comparing the town plans of Nairobi and Lusaka of around 1950, Barnow denounced claims that

---

64 Hall 1988, 190.
65 MP 1948, 65.
66 For example, Gattoni and Patel 1973, 5; Memon 1982, 150.
67 Hake 1977, 57.
68 "Sammenfattende fremtraeder planen som liberal og elitaer men ikke racistisk. Funktionalismens dubbelrolle som progressivt fagligt program og legitimerande ideologi betyder, sammen med kolonimagtens önske om at saette sig det arkitektoniske monument... at planen fremstår som et på samme tid rationelt og aestetisk produkt" (Barnow 1990, 150; my translation). On the plan of 1927, see p.148, 154.

there existed a particular, typical or common mode of planning practiced by the colonial power; instead, they could be seen as plans made by Europeans, inspired by European town planning.[69]

Sören Emig and Zahir Ismael's assessment was more emphatic: they perceived the *Master Plan* of 1948 as politically biased. Using Nairobi as a typical example of "large cities in the periphery" within a general frame of countries characterized by "accelerating urbanization," Emig and Ismael analyzed the most important official town plans of Nairobi from 1900 to 1980 and evaluated them

> on the basis of their declared intentions as well as on the nature of the class interests that they represent,

seeking to

> understand the plans as instruments of a total political strategy, that makes use of special tools (zoning, etc.) to carry out the interests of the ruling class factions as regards the safeguarding of certain social divisions, a specific use of urban space as a part of the total political control.[70]

Thus Emig and Ismael assessed the *Master Plan* of 1948 as a plan which

> more than anything else expresses the objective interests of the emerging industrial bourgoisie . . . The *Master Plan* is part of the total state intervention expressing a modern bourgoise strategy in favour of the dominating fraction in the city with everything that industrial capitalism contains, economically (factory work, skilled labour, etc.), politically (concessions to the industrial bourgoisie, the establishing of trade unions, etc.), ideologically ('alienation', economism, the spread of reformism, etc.) and in the urban context (the laying out of industrial areas, the infrastructure, workers housing areas, etc.).[71]

In other words, they perceived the *Master Plan* as a political instrument based on liberal ideology and on the notion of class, and used by the ruling classes for their own benefit and against the interests of the urban proletariat. At the same time, however, Emig and Ismael noted that the political character of the plan was hidden, its appearance being that of a purely technical document:

> The liberal functionalistic ideology of the plan covers a class position which – in its wider perspective – points to the maintenance of bourgeois order. The form may seem liberal, but the contents are conservative . . . The basic common authoritarian outlook is preserved – albeit concealed – behind the liberal facade of the plan.[72]

---

69 Barnow 1990, 154f.
70 Emig and Ismael 1980, 3.
71 Emig and Ismael 1980, 54.
72 Emig and Ismael 1980, 55.

While the character of the *Master Plan* of 1948 has been defined as dismissive towards the Africans (Hall), as racist (e.g. Memon) and imperialistic (Hake), as liberal and elitist (Barnow), and as part of the bourgeoise strategy for maintaining the status quo (Emig and Ismael), the planners saw their own work as unbiased. In terms of segregation, for example, the team acknowledged that segregation between Europeans and Asians had been declared illegal by Government policy,[73] but that many Nairobi citizens nevertheless had expressed their desire of it;[74] on the matter, they claimed impartiality:

> The *Master Plan*, however, is able to be completely neutral on the subject of racial segregation by being confined to the principles of planning which take their measure on the human and technical needs. It is concerned with the satisfaction of wants which all men require such as privacy, open space, education, protection form through-traffic, water supplies, etc. The more attention that can be devoted to what is common to man the more likely are we to concentrate on what can to-day be planned in the light of reason while leaving to political and educational action and to the individual to sort out the rest. If the Plan has a bias it is this humanistic one.[75]

Thus the team not only perceived the plan as "completely neutral," that is, as detached from any ideological presuppositions or goals, it also defined the different social groups of Nairobi as similar in terms of human needs which were to be satisfied as efficiently and economically as possible. The satisfaction of needs through the urban plan was seen as a purely technical operation without any political content or cultural favoritism. In fact, what the team saw as technicalities were based on European conceptions. This was also reflected in the sources of information the planners used. For example, the team interviewed, as they put it, both "local personalities" representing various institutions and "excellent persons with ideas" who were in "no particular sense 'leading' or 'authoritative'";[76] but of the 92 names listed under "Acknowledgements," only seven appeared non-European.[77] From this aspect, the expressed wishes of "many Nairobi citizens" for segregation seem to have been largely – if not totally – those of European origin. In terms of needs, the team perceived the peoples of Nairobi to all share the universal notion of development, of progress towards a more and more civilized society. Inherent in the presupposition was the idea that the models of progress, of developed societies, were European – more precisely, British – cultural practices.

---

73 The White Paper of 1923, see above, chapter 11.
74 MP 1948, 49.
75 MP 1948, 49.
76 MP 1948, 2.
77 One was an Alderman, five were Councillors, and one was attached to the Secretariat (MP 1948, vi-vii).

A universalization similar to the one attached to the different social groups was also evident in how the past and future development of the town were seen. The team noted that "towns in 'new' countries all over the world have passed through similar phases of development"[78] and that this was not only to be seen in the past history of Nairobi, but also to be expected in its future.[79] Their view encompassed Nairobi as a socially integrated town:

> Nairobi is being kept a "new" town by the welter of influences rushing in from the world outside, and it is this "openness" of social structure which has prevented discontent from turning destructive. On the other hand, it has prevented the emergence of a social pattern, and it is only now that some of the grand lines are looming into sight. Nairobi will be more strongly assimilationist than any other East African town.[80]

From the colonial English point of view, Nairobi with its large non-European population may indeed have been experienced as an "open" society. At the same time, however, what the planners saw as an "openness" of social structure was for the non-European groups in practice something quite different. For the Asians, the experience of Nairobi included their under-representation in the elected bodies – both legislative and municipal – and the enforcement of restrictions on immigration from India. For the Africans, Nairobi was a place where one needed special passes even to enter and to live in. Neither group could hardly perceive Nairobi as an "open" town. Nor was life in the town "open" in a social sense: the colonial administration and the local European community had strict control over most of the activities occurring within the town.

The planners expected the means of making the different groups of people into one society to be assimilation. However, assimilation did not refer to, for example, the assimilation of the European settlers into the African indigenous people, but to the assimilation of the non-European communities into the European community: to the conversion of the practices of the non-European peoples into European practices defined as universal. The assimilationist policies included the political progress towards a class society modeled on European principles:

> A multi-racial society throws many difficulties in the path of democratic planning ... As soon as there are rich and poor, intellectual and lowbrow, professionally trained and unskilled, as recognisable types in every race, with inter-racial organisations, each pressing for bigger slices of the cake, multiracial society is normalised.[81]

In essence, then, assimilation was used by the planners to suggest the cultural subordination of the already colonially subordinated groups.

---

78 MP 1948, 5.
79 MP 1948, 2-6.
80 MP 1948, 23.
81 MP 1948, 9f.

This included not only the general scope of the plan, but also specific elements which were considered fundamental. For example, for the team of experts, Nairobi was a town with a national appearance attached to the colonial power responsible for its administration, the British, describing it as one which "will excel in delightful suburbs and ample space for sport".[82] In the town plan, adequate open spaces were to be maintained, not only to protect them from the spread of house building or industries, but also to promote sport, the "supreme means of bringing people of all classes and races together."[83] Sport was essential because the

> common rules that are imposed in games, the sense of fairness and good sportsmanship, of leadership and subordination, of effort and restraint, are the rules upon which civilisation is built.[84]

Thus town planning in general and the planning of open spaces in particular were instrumental in the furthering of civilization in Nairobi. With the notion of civilization, the planners referred to its British interpretation.

The European idea of civilization and its practices was conveyed through the corresponding outward expression in the architecture of the city:

> In outward appeareance the town is fixed in its western atmosphere, to which some variety will be given by Indian Bazaars, a very English suburban belt, and a garden city tendency in the African townships . . . It will go ahead as a European type town, that is, European in architecture, a little frigid, but efficient, tidy and progressive. In this it mirrors its economic function . . . With all the want of and need for common meeting places and common institutions for the interchange of ideas the three races exhibit the same progressive spirit. Their lives, so different in the outward forms of dress, language and manner, are also bounded by the same social interests – the family, work and sport. It is not idle to expect that civic pride and social endeavour will form a common basis of increasing importance.[85]

In terms of built and urban spaces, then, the European colonialist notions were also presented as universal. The policies promoted in the *Master Plan* also included the symbolic aspect. The planners noted that while "planning is the conscious application of intelligence to national and local evolution,"[86] the *Nairobi Master Plan* will only be executed when it has become the "Plan of the Citizen of Nairobi":

> Neighborhood principles, parkways, the East African Centre, the reduction of sprawl, should become the symbols of desirable advance, a real investment in a good and prosperous future of the Colonial Capital.[87]

---

82 MP 1948, 5.
83 MP 1948, 55.
84 MP 1948, 55.
85 MP 1948, 23.
86 MP 1948, 76.
87 MP 1948, 77.

It was not only a question of assimilating the non-European groups politically into the European community, but of the conversion of their symbols into those of the dominant colonial society.

The photographs included in the report also reflected these attitudes. There were eight pages with 47 photographs showing Nairobi people, buildings and housing areas, urban activities and rural landscapes. Eleven of the photographs contained one or more Africans, two included Asians, and two Europeans. While the Asian and European activities were limited to managing a clinic (a European woman), working by a machine (an Asian man), and attending school (Asian and European children in separate illustrations), the Africans were presented in a large variety of functions from household work, coming "to town," going to the market, washing clothes, doing craftwork or living in a village on the outskirts of Nairobi at the beginning of the photographic section, to repairing a typewriter, being involved in sport, attending a Child Welfare Clinic, participating in Native Tribunal hearings, and working in a factory at the end.[88] In the photographs, the Africans were presented as colorful but uneducated natives with potential for improvement, the Asians as skilled, and the Europeans as the mostly invisible but unquestionably dominant layer of the society. The colonial European presence was transmitted indirectly, through the solid buildings and orderly residential areas which carried western symbols, and the modern institutions which the buildings and areas represented (*Fig. 12.12*). In the *Nairobi Master Plan*, the Africans were seen as objects of development, to be transformed to adopt western models and practices. The suitability of the European conceptions to the African practices was not once questioned.

The frame within which the planners observed Nairobi, defined its problems, outlined possible solutions and made their plans was not explicitly described in the *Master Plan*. Although the team classified Nairobi historically as a town in a "new" country, functionally as a town owing its existence to transport, culturally as mixed like most African towns, and geographically as

Fig. 12.12 Buildings of Nairobi, 1940s: Law Courts and Secretariat, Railways Headquarters, East African Lighting Company offices, and an African family housing area.

---

88 MP 1948, between pages 20 and 21.

a town with specific "African" town planning problems, applicable to towns all over the continent,[89] these aspects did not evoke a town planning approach which would have differed from the one adopted in the "old" countries of western Europe and particularly Britain. Neither the notions of social organization and development nor their integration – which were seen as the reason behind involving a team of experts from different fields to prepare the plan – were discussed but were employed as self-evident and widely accepted basic concepts. In this sense, the European cultural frame with its inherent presuppositions, then, permeated all the levels of the plan from the initial surveys, interviews, and setting of objectives to the planning principles and proposed plans.

How did the *Master Plan* of 1948 influence the changes in Nairobi? According to Ramesh C. Tiwari, its most important effects may not have been related to its content but to its administration. Using the realization of the plan to realign the railway line as an example, Tiwari maintained that the *Master Plan* altered the established power structure by removing the right of veto from the Railways and bestowing the authority of change on the Municipality.[90] Whether the changes of the urban form of Nairobi after 1948 can be attributed to the *Master Plan* or whether they occurred in spite of it, may, of course, be argued. As the comparison to the plans of the 1920s indicated, several of the proposals forwarded in the *Master Plan* of 1948 had already been made earlier. Since the plan was based on an extensive survey, including both various kinds of background material and interviews of leading individuals in the major institutions like the Government and the Municipality, there are grounds to assume that many ideas, suggestions, and plans made within these instutions prior to the *Master Plan* and regardless of it, may nevertheless also have been integrated into the *Master Plan*.

An examination of more recent maps of the city of Nairobi – from 1960, 1970, and 1981[91] – seems to indicate that several major changes proposed in

---

89 MP 1948, 4f.
90 Tiwari 1981, 121.
91 Maps of the physical structure (built-up areas) of Nairobi in 1960 and 1970 in Barnow et

the *Master Plan*[92] which were not visible in the maps showing the conditions existing in Nairobi around 1945-48,[93] have taken place in the city. In addition to the realignment of the railway, these included:

- the new combined trunk road and main north-south parkway (Princess Elizabeth Highway, now Uhuru Highway) located west of the city center;
- the regional road (Fort Hall Road, now Thika Road) from the "traffic circus" north of the city center towards the northeast, passing the City Park on its southern side;
- the administrative buildings around an open space, its eastern end next to the commercial area in the city center and its western end on the Hill,
- the industrial area south of the railway station and yard (although not exactly with the same boundaries);
- the extension of the privately owned residential areas to the west and northwest of the city center;
- the extension of the official housing areas on the publicly owned land southeast of the city center, next to the industrial area; and
- the preservation of the open space between the Hill and the city center.

Among the unrealized parts of the *Master Plan* were

- the "Swamp Parkway," intended to connect the main north-south parkway to the areas northeast of the city center;
- the governmental office buildings on the flat open green space between the north-south parkway and the main administrative buildings on the Hill;
- the blocks of flats at the edge of the open space between the city center and the hills to its west and north.

In a geographical study of Nairobi, Dorothy M. Halliman and W.T.W. Morgan described the historical development of the city and the region, but only mentioned the *Master Plan* of 1948 in connection with its recommendations to establish an industrial area and the Kenya Center.[94] They approached the development of Nairobi not so much in relation to its planning history – as

---

al (1990, 56, 66). The map of 1960 was based on the "City of Nairobi, Map and Guide" (SK 1962); the map of 1970 on "City of Nairobi, Map 1:20,000", published in July 1972, and on aerial photographs from December 1971 and January 1972; for both, the information was assessed as "accurate" (Barnow et al 1990, 86f.). The map of 1981 was marked "City of Nairobi, Map and Guide, 1:20,000" (SK), revised from aerial photography (August 1970, January 1971, 1976, and 1978) and the Schedule of New Street Names for the City Area (1974), reprinted 9/1981. The maps of 1940 and 1950 (in Barnow et al 1990, 36, 46) were partly based on the Master Plan of 1948 and therefore could not be used for for comparison. None of the city maps in Barnow et al show the road network of the time.

92 See particularly the drawings "Master Plan" (MP 1948, inside front cover) and "Nairobi Master Plan: Roads" (inside back cover).
93 See particularly the drawings "Transport Services" and "Municipal Services" for the road system (MP 1948, both between pp.56-57) and "Buildings and Open Spaces Distribution" (facing p.56).
94 Halliman and Morgan 1967, 109f.

in the historical parts of Thornton White's report – but in relation to the changes in functions and their urban and built forms. From this aspect, in-depth references to the *Master Plan* may have, indeed, been seen as marginal. The contents of Halliman's and Morgan's study seem to imply that the proposals included in the *Master Plan* had been accepted as self-evident by 1967 by the various institutions involved, without disagreement or discussion. In other words, the Nairobi envisaged in the *Master Plan* conformed with the conceptions held within the leading institutions in the city in general.

Post-war boom town

From the point of view of the European colonists and the local European community, the post-war years can be assessed as phenomenally successful. Between 1946 and 1956, the flow of investments into the country led to an "undreamt-of prosperity," as Hake expressed it.[95] Compared to the 1930s, foreign trade and government revenues multiplied after the Second World War: exports from Kenya rose from over two million pounds in 1931 to over five million in 1945, ten million in 1949, 24 million in 1951, and over 35 million in 1961. Imports to the country increased from over four million pounds in 1931 to over 62 million in 1961, and government revenues from three million pounds in 1931 to over 46 million in 1961. Manufacturing and distribution expanded rapidly in the 1950s, accounting for over twenty per cent of national income.[96] As the capital and major industrial center of the country, changes in Nairobi reflected these developments. The Municipal Council had raised in loans less than 600,000 pounds by 1940, but by 1945, the total had grown to nearly 900,000, by 1949 to over 2.6 million pounds, and by 1957, to over 9 million.[97] The loans were used for the improvement of municipal services; social provision was also increased. Hake has mentioned the improvement of the supply of water from the Ruiru Dam and Chania Sasumua Dam, the building of a hospital with beds for 650 Africans and 42 Asians, and the expansion of schools for African children from the 1,000 pupils in 1942 to more than treble by 1946.[98] The municipality built over 12,000 housing units in the period between 1945 to 1952,[99] mostly on estates like Bahati, Gorofani and Mbotela in the Eastlands area on land owned publicly; in the same area, the government completed Starehe and the Railways enlarged the Makongeni housing area built during the war.[100]

---

95 Hake 1977, 62; see also D.Ghai 1974, 372.
96 Ehrlich 1974, 341f.; Hake 1977, 56.
97 Hake 1977, 58.
98 Hake 1977, 57.
99 *Legislative Council Debates*, 23 October 1953 (vol.LVIII, cols.95-96) quoted in Stren 1972, 71.
100 Hake 1977, 57; maps of the physical structure (built-up areas) of Nairobi in 1950 and 1960

The population of Nairobi which in 1944 had been estimated as 108,900, comprised of 64,200 Africans, 34,300 Asians, and 10,400 Europeans,[101] was growing, albeit still slowly immediately after the war. According to the first full census of Nairobi's whole population in 1948, there were some 65,000 Africans, 44,000 Asians, and 11,000 Europeans, totalling almost 120,000 inhabitants.[102] In the following 14 years, however, the population more than doubled, by 1962 reaching the figure of around 267,000 inhabitants, with 160,000 Africans, 86,000 Asians, and 21,000 Europeans.[103] Although Nairobi was experiencing a boom, the increased prosperity seemed to be directed only to a few; as Hake formulated it,

> Nairobi was an island of wealth, attempting to defend its shores against intruders.[104]

It would have maybe been more precise to refer to the European community in Nairobi as the island of wealth and power.

During and particularly after the Second World War, the colonial administration had started to promote policies which recognized Africans as members (or potential members) of a modern society. A stabilized urban African population was seen as essential in developing Kenya into an industrial country. In the process, urban forms had an instrumental role: they were both conceived and used as instruments in the social transformation. Permanent urban residences would enable more efficient working conditions, neighborhood facilities would support the creation of an urban non-tribal community, and the civic center would generate a public spirit.

Cultural institutions may be used as an example of this. British theater was instituted in Kenya, in Nairobi first by starting a theater club, the Donovan Maule Theatre, in 1949, and the British National Theatre in 1952. Ngugi wa Thiong'o has argued that this occurred in response to the resurgence of popular dance and theater after the war, and that the purpose was to maintain the British positions through an "imperialist cultural program." He quotes Richard Frost, former head of the Empire Information Service and the first representative of the British Council in East Africa:

---

in Barnow et al 1990, 46, 56. The map of 1950 was based on MP 1948 and on aerial photographs of 1948; the map of 1960 was based on "City of Nairobi, Map and Guide", (SK 1962). Bahati means "luck," Gorofani "two stories," and Mbotela was named after an African leader killed in 1952.

101 Town Clerk's Report of 1945, quoted in MP 1948, 84.
102 *Geographical and Tribal Studies* (East African Population Census, 1948, 7), The East African Statistical Department, Nairobi (1950), *Report on the Census of the Non-Native Population of Kenya Colony and Protectorate* (Taken on the Night of the 25th of February, 1948, Table VI, 14), quoted in Barnow et al 1983, 47.
103 Urban Population Analysis based on the Kenya Population Census of 1962, quoted in Barnow et al 1983, 57. The average annual growth of the African population in Nairobi was estimated as 6.5% (Kenya Population Census 1969, quoted in Memon 1981, 84).
104 Hake 1977, 59.

> The National Theatre was built where it was because those who planned the scheme, including Thornly Dyer, the architect who designed the Parliament Building and conceived the master plan for Nairobi, wanted to build the National Theatre in the "snob" centre of Nairobi. The instruction given by the Secretary of State to the British Council representative was to build a National Theatre and Cultural Centre where people of culture and position could meet. At that time no Africans were able to live anywhere near the site which was selected, but that site was chosen because it was hoped that is due time the residential *apartheid* would be brought to an end and Muthaiga, Westlands, the Hill and other areas, which were then open only to Europeans, would become districts where leading people of all races would live.[105]

The National Theater was constructed on a site opposite the Norfolk Hotel, close to the initial office of the Protectorate. In the *Master Plan* of 1948, this "arrowhead" area had been suggested to be reserved for cultural activities like the National Theater.[106] The location had strong historical connotations not only for the settlers but also for their particular European way of life, in the Nairobi context distinct from the African and Asian practices.

Before the Second World War, the colonialists commonly perceived the Africans as temporary town-dwellers, to be provided only temporary housing arrangements in shared bachelor units.[107] Well into the 1950s (and possibly even later), the typical pattern of wage employment in East Africa was attached to what Walter Elkan called circular migration where the head of a rural household sought temporary wage employment in town, to return later to the homestead.[108] With the changed policies of industrialization, the role of Africans in towns was beginning to be seen in a new light. In the influential Colonial Office pamphlet, *Labour Conditions in East Africa*, published in 1946, the views of the British Government were clearly presented:

> There appears to be little doubt that there must gradually be a readjustment of population to bring the workers nearer their place of employment, and thus to eradicate the existing constant waste of time and energy represented by the journey to and from the industrial centres.[109]

In Kenya, the Labour Department presented similar views, emphasizing the interdependence of housing, stabilization, and efficiency; in its bulletin of 1950, it pointed out that lack of family housing was "a powerful contributing factor to the lag of the African's social progress behind social changes."[110] These views were not unanimously accepted. For example, memoranda from

---

105 Richard Frost, *Race Against Time*, s.a., quoted in Ngugi 1981, 68. Dyer's involvement in the conception of the "master plan" has not been clarified in other sources.
106 MP 1948, 61.
107 Elkan and Zwanenberg 1975, 666.
108 Elkan 1973.
109 Major G.St.J. Orde Browne, *Labour Conditions in East Africa*, Colonial No.193, H.M.S.O., London, 1946, 22, quoted in Stren 1972, 67.
110 *Labour Department Bulletin*, Vol.IV, No.1, 1950, 2, quoted in Stren 1972, 67.

the same year by the Commissioner of Lands were still based on the notion that "the African is not a town dweller" and that therefore, housing for urban workers would have to be provided by the public sector and subsidized.[111] Similarly, in the report of the East African Royal Commission 1953-55, the urban Africans were seen with paternalism:

> They are still, however, regarded socially and financially as liabilities for whose housing and welfare the urban authorities are responsible.[112]

Ernest Vasey's recommendations in his 1950 report on African housing policy changed official thinking in Kenya and became the basis of the country's housing policy in the fifties.[113] Until then, the wages paid to the Africans were so low that they could not afford rents without subsidies; at the same time, with the increase in the need of housing for Africans, most European councillors rejected the notion of continuously subsidized housing. Instead, Vasey proposed that the government encourage African-owned housing on a large scale, arguing that it would both "open the door to a stable urban population" and enhance the ability of the Africans to compete economically with other races.[114] The relation between wages and housing was analyzed definitively by the Carpenter Committee on African Wages whose report was submitted in 1954. The economic disadvantages of the migrant system were used in support of higher wages; as it was formulated by the Carpenter Committee:

> We cannot *hope* to produce an effective African labour force until we have first removed the African from the enervating and retarding influences of his economic and cultural background.[115]

In addition to proposals for sufficient minimum wages, the committee suggested other means of stabilizing the urban workers: one of the objectives was to provide, by 1965, the majority of the working population with family dwellings which were seen as vehicles for stabilization. The committee also recommended the adoption of the neighborhood unit as the basis of housing schemes; this had been introduced in the *Master Plan* of 1948.[116] In its official reply to the report, the government accepted the principles of ownership and of the neighborhood unit as the basis of planning. Richard Stren has suggested

---

111 Quoted in Ernest Vasey, *Report on Housing of Africans in Townships and Trading Centres*, 1950, Appendix A, quoted in Stren 1972, 68.
112 The *East African Royal Commission Report*, Cmd.9475, Her Majesty's Stationery Office, London, 1955, 201, quoted in Werlin 1981, 196.
113 Ernest Vasey, *Report on Housing of Africans in Townships and Trading Centres*, unpublished report, 1950, and *Legislative Council Debates*, vol.LV, 6 May 1953, col.46, quoted in Stren 1972, 68ff.
114 Vasey, *Report on Housing of Africans in Townships and Trading Centres*, 1950, 9, quoted in Stren 1972, 69.
115 *Report of the Committee on African Wages* (Carpenter Committee), Nairobi, Government Printer, 1954, quoted in Stren 1972, 75ff. See also Elkan and Zwanenberg 1975, 666ff.
116 See above.

that the official recognition of the concept of neighborhood was that the urban planning

> would now be as concerned with making living conditions pleasant and orderly for Africans as it had in the past for Europeans.[117]

The admission of the Africans into the sphere of a society progressing towards well-being was not as uncomplicated as Stren presented it. The time after the Second World War until Independence in 1963 was, indeed, a period of fundamental changes in the history of the country and of Nairobi. For the Europeans, the economic progress and the social improvements indicated development towards a modern society. Politically, the colonial administration also offered the Africans a place in society, more prominent than earlier. The first direct African representative was nominated to the Legislative Council in 1944,[118] and two African nominated councillors were added to the Municipal Council in 1946.[119] The official policy of urban segregation was discontinued after 1945.[120] Kenya and Nairobi were to become places for a multi-racial society. However, the settlers' views of the country and its capital stressed their European characteristics: they saw the African nationalists as emotional and uneducated, and themselves as the only true Kenyans, possessing

> a nationalism with its own distinct symbols and legends rooted in the history of pioneering endeavor of each district in the Highlands.[121]

The settlers of Kenya distrusted the British colonial administration and particularly the post-war Labour government, because its objectives contradicted those of the local Europeans. One example of this, for Tanganyika, was the proposal for equality of representation of Africans, Asians, and Europeans in the Legislative Council. When Nairobi was granted a Royal Charter for the status of city in 1950, the European dominated Municipal Council regarded it as a symbolic landmark towards the permanent dominance of Europeans in the country.[122]

The improvement of the position of the Africans in Kenya was further emphasized by the weakening of the role of the Asians. During the war, the Kenyan government had issued new regulations to increase control of immigration into Kenya, Tanganyika, Uganda, and Zanzibar, stipulating that

---

117 Stren 1972, 77.
118 Rosberg and Nottingham 1966, 212; the first representative was Eliud Mathu. In 1947, a second African, B. Apolo Ohanga, was included. In 1948, the number of African representatives was raised to four nominated members, and in 1952 to six, with Mathu appointed to the Executive Council. The first direct African elections, on a limited franchise, were held in 1957 (Ogot 1974, 284f., 291).
119 MP 1948, 17.
120 Zwanenberg and King 1975, 267.
121 Rosberg and Nottingham 1966, 226.
122 Rosberg and Nottingham 1966, 226f.

entry permits would be granted to applicants whose occupations were deemed as

> necessary or expedient for securing the public safety, the defence of the Colony, the maintenance of public order or in the efficient prosecution of the war, or for maintaining supplies and services essential to the life of the community.[123]

Dana April Seidenberg has noted in her study of the role of Indians in Kenya politics that although the regulations did not directly refer to Indians, they were nevertheless interpreted by them to have been issued, by the government but under pressure from the local settlers, with the intent of preventing Indian immigration.[124] Two years later, the colonial government passed a draft bill, the Immigration (Control) Ordinance of 1946, which Seidenberg assessed as "nonracial in language and form . . . [but] discriminatory in conception and effect,"[125] because it proposed moderate monetary criteria for activities in which potential European immigrants would be involved (agriculture, animal husbandry, mining) and disproportionately high monetary criteria for activities in which potential Indian immigrants would be involved (trade and industry). In 1948, it was passed into law; Seidenberg described it as the "closure of the colony to future Indian immigration."[126]

From the African point of view, the development also carried negative elements. Although Africans in general were perceived as essential for the process of industrialization, some of them were nevertheless seen as useless or even harmful to the development of the country. Towards the Africans "not usefully employed" the colonial administration employed strict measures of control. The new Vagrancy (Amendment) Bill, passed by the Legislative Council in 1949, gave the police the power to repatriate "vagrants" – anyone walking on the street who could not prove employment in the city – to a house of detention and to the tribal reserve. It was supported by other legislation, for example by the Voluntary Unemployed Persons (Provision of Employment) Ordinance of 1949.[127] Despite official policy, the Africans of Nairobi included, in addition to employees, also those seeking employment,

---

123 Defence (Admission of Male Persons) Regulations (Government Printer, Nairobi, 1944) quoted in Seidenberg 1983, 27.
124 Seidenberg (1983, 27) also referred to the Meeting Report of the Executive Committee of the East African Indian National Congress, 25 February 1944 (Kenya National Archives' microfilms, EAINC Records, reel 9). Seidenberg has discussed the legislative process at length (chapter 2).
125 Seidenberg 1983, 34.
126 Seidenberg 1983, 34.
127 Hake 1977, 59. Vagrancy laws had been used in the control of Nairobi from 1920, see above, chapter 11; see also Zwanenberg and King 1975, 270. The "kipande" or identity card ordinance, which had been applied only to Africans, was replaced by a new National Registration Ordinance entailing fingerprinting for all the inhabitants regardless of race; the Europeans bitterly opposed it and a commission recommended that persons who could fill in the form in English and provide two photographs of themselves would be exempt from fingerprinting, providing to the Africans further evidence of the European bias (Rosberg and Nottingham 1966, 228f.).

self-employed persons, and various kinds of vagrants. Nairobi had attracted people from the rural areas from the 1920s. Roger van Zwanenberg and Anne King have suggested that this occurred because the potential wages for employees in the city were higher than those offered on the farms.[128] But employment was not the only reason to come to the city. Nairobi, like any developing town, offered also a variety of unofficial opportunities to earn a living:

> to sell food, to brew and distil liquor, to carry water from the nearest standpipe, to cook meals, to supply charcoal, to collect and sell old clothes and bottles, to draw handcarts or rickshaws and to sell sex.[129]

Walter Elkan and Roger van Zwanenberg have indicated that the colonial administration did not perceive the vital role of the people involved in the informal sector (as it has later been named) in the economy. They were seen as hindrances in developing the city, the administration continuously attempting to restrict their entry, limit their numbers, and prevent their activities.[130] The number of Africans the new vagrancy legislation involved was high. Herbert Werlin has described the situation:

> Since a surplus of labour was to the advantage of employers in Nairobi, the pass system was not really enforced until 1950, when the Voluntarily Unemployed Persons Ordinance came into force, under which unemployed men could live in Nairobi only seven days. Nevertheless, despite strong police action in Nairobi in the two or three years prior to the Emergency, the number of homeless transient Africans in Nairobi was estimated to have been 10,000 by the Member for Law and Order in 1952, because as fast as they returned them as vagrants to the reserves, the faster they flocked back in again.[131]

There were also intermediate forms of employment which could be described as somewhere between employees and the self-employed of the informal sector. They lacked a fixed place of work, being employed by the job, involving occupations like taxi drivers, barbers, and artisans such as masons, carpenters, and stone-dressers. From the wartime period onwards, these groups were faced with various kinds of actions from the government and the City Council to license and otherwise regulate their work; to protest against these forms of control, the occupational groups formed trade organizations. Sharon Stichter has shown that the trade organizations were not only economic but also political.[132]

---

128 Zwanenberg and King 1975, 269.
129 Elkan and Zwanenberg 1975, 665. On self-employed Africans in colonial Nairobi, see also Werlin 1981, 195-198.
130 Elkan and Zwanenberg 1975, 665f.
131 Herbert Werlin, "The History of Race Relations in Nairobi," unpublished paper, quoted in Hake 1977, 60.
132 Stichter 1975, 38-41.

In both the informal sector and among the "intermediate" occupations, employment may have been irregular and incomes subsequently varied. Many of these persons could only afford to live in the unofficial housing areas – "squatters" or "slums." In the late 1940s and early 50s, unofficial settlements grew in places like Mathare Valley north of Eastleigh, along Mathare River.[133] The demolition of the unofficial settlements – part of the history of Nairobi from its very beginning – was also continued after the war, but in addition to sanitary, disciplinary, and legal reasons, in the early 1950s there were also current motives. In the politically tense climate of the 1940s and 1950s, the colonial administration perceived these kinds of areas as centers of aggression, managed by subversive elements for disruptive purposes. When the State of Emergency was declared in 1952, the government used the demolition operations as a method to screen possible subversive persons;[134] for example, the some 150 huts in Mathare Valley were destroyed and many of the inhabitants detained.[135]

Richard Stren has indicated that inadequate urban housing was seen – both officially and semi-officially – as one of the major reasons (if not the prime cause) of the outbreaks of the Mau Mau violence which led the colonial administration to declare the State of Emergency, although, as Stren noted, the evaluation of the validity of these claims is difficult.[136] The notion of "stability," or "social unrest" as its opposite, was presented as the main issue in the different reports. By the Europeans of Kenya, Mau Mau was perceived

> primarily as a barbarous, atavistic, and anti-European tribal cult whose leaders planned to turn Kenya into a land of "darkness and death." Mau Mau was looked upon as a dangerous hypnotic obsession based not on intellect but on primitive emotions.[137]

In later research, it has been described as a nationalist movement[138] and as several simultaneous revolutions forming a united front.[139]

The consequences of the State of Emergency on Nairobi were dramatic. Kikuyu, Embu and Meru residents were forced to move from Kaloleni and Ziwani housing estates to Bahati, Bondeni and Kariokor housing areas.[140] The

---

133 Hake 1977, 147. Mathare Valley, which started to grow only in the 1960's, is the best known and most studied of the unofficial settlements of Nairobi, see e.g. Etherton 1971; Caminos and Goethert 1980, 94f., 215; Oliver 1987, 219ff.
134 Stren 1974, 7.
135 Hake 1977, 147f.
136 Stren (1972, 74) notes that this view was given credence even in the Corfield Report, *Historical Survey of the Origins and Growth of Mau Mau*, Government Printer, Nairobi, 1960, 24.
137 Rosberg and Nottingham 1966, xvi. "Mau Mau" is an anagram of the Kikuyu word "Uma, uma" which means "Go, go" (Ojwando Abuor 1973, 77; see also Rosberg and Nottingham 1966, 332.).
138 Rosberg and Nottingham 1966.
139 Ogot 1974, 288f.
140 Annual Report of 1953 of the African Affairs Department (Nairobi City Council, 1953, 86) quoted in Ross 1975, 20.

effects of the forced removals were still visible some fifteen years later when Marc Howard Ross observed that these areas had retained an ethnically homogeneous character atypical of African residential areas in contemporary Nairobi.[141] During "Operation Anvil" in April 1954, the "surplus" population of the city – some 27,000 persons, almost all Kikuyu, Embu and Meru people, members of other tribes allowed to take their place – was removed to camps and to the countryside;[142] as Zwanenberg and King described the operation:

> The Emergency from 1952 provided the Nairobi authorities with the opportunity to do what they had always wanted to do . . . At a stroke, massive measures of urban population control had been enforced and the policy of preserving the city for Europeans had been reaffirmed. The standards and provisions for European services could only be maintained if welfare resources did not have to be expended on "unemployed" Africans.[143]

By the end of 1954, partly due to Operation Anvil, there were altogether some 17,000 convicts and 50,000 imprisoned detainees.[144] African housing areas were fenced with barbed wire, an elaborate pass system was adopted, and a nightly curfew imposed.[145]

Nairobi described

In the *Master Plan*, Nairobi was described as a rapidly growing town on the path of developing into a modern European-type city. As a symbol of modern Nairobi, contemporary photographs both in the *Master Plan* and in other connections presented Delamere Avenue – the more European of the two main streets – with its elaborate traffic arrangements, modern cars and buses, planted lines of trees, and the wide variety of businesses. (*Figs. 12.13, 12.14, 12.16*)[146] In the *Master Plan*, Nairobi was seen in a frame of its history as a town established in the middle of nothingness to fulfill a practical function; now, it would spread western civilization to the wilderness. The same approach may be observed in how the National Geographic reported on Nairobi in 1950. In a context of topics mostly centering on "natives," wild animals, and

---

141 Ross 1975, 21.
142 Hake 1977, 61.
143 Zwanenberg and King 1975, 270f.
144 Department of Community Development and Rehabilitation (Annual Report of 1954, 21) quoted in Rosberg and Nottingham 1966, 335. By February 1959, more than 77,000 persons had been "rehabilitated" and released, leaving some 1,100 in detention camps (Rosberg and Nottingham ibid., 342, quoting The Report of the Committee on Emergency Detention Camps, Nairobi, 1959, 10). According to death statistics, over 10,000 Africans were killed during the seven years of Emergency, as opposed to less than 100 Asians and 100 Europeans (Anthony Clayton, *Counter-Insurgency in Kenya 1952-60*, Transafrica Historical Papers No.4, Nairobi, 1976, 54, quoted in Seidenberg 1983, 111).
145 Zwanenberg and King 1975, 271.
146 Thornton White et al 1948; postcard; Blair 1980, 19.

Fig. 12.13 Delamere Avenue to the east, 1940s

the use of science and technology to overcome natural obstacles in East Africa, Nairobi was only briefly discussed; of the thirty-eight photographs, only one was of Nairobi (*Fig. 12.15*). In its caption, Nairobi was described as a town with a bleak history but a promising future, a town in progress:

> Fifty Years Ago, Nairobi, Capital of Kenya Colony, Was Only a Railway Camp. To celebrate its golden anniversary on March 30, this year, H.M. King George VI will raise the town of 120,000 persons to the status of a city.[147]

A short section titled "Nairobi Now a Boom City" presented the town:

> Today Nairobi is popping at the seams with these newcomers. Hotels are packed, housing shortage is acute, and building costs are high.[148]

A more illustrative description of how Nairobi appeared in the early 1950s may be found in *Something of Value*, an adventure novel, set in 1952, by Robert Ruark:

> The drive from the Eastleigh Airport to the Norfolk Hotel is shocking to a newcomer. As you drive along Race Course Road you are past the better Indian residences and come upon the native quarter, the squirming bazaars. In the bazaars most of the shops, duccas, are still Indian, but they are smaller and dirtier and more flyblown and more higgledy-piggledy than the ones closer in toward town, with cheaper prices and inferior goods . . . Straggling between are a few shops, shabbier, smaller, and less well stocked, which bear names like Karioki was Muchiri or Njuguna wa Kamau, indicating that a native has come to commerce. These are shops enclosed by crazy-slanting walls of dented tin from hammered petrol drums, or walls of mud and thatch, or old packing boxes, and they have lumpy earthen floors and dark

---

147 Moore 1950, 312.
148 Moore 1950, 313.

Fig. 12.14 Delamere Avenue to the west, 1950s

smoke-crusted interiors . . .

Traffic on Delamere Avenue and Government Road thins out past islands on which plum-black native police swing their batons with military precision and savage grace . . . The streets ferment with a fantastic assortment of races and colors . . . The shops of Nairobi are mainly Asian, and the names reveal that the followers of Allah, Buddha, and of the Agha Khan have mostly collared the commerce . . .

The native parade on Nairobi's streets, especially its side streets and back streets, is motley . . . There is always a tremendous squawk of auto horns and bicycle bells in Nairobi, always a great bustle on the main streets and a jabber of a hundred different languages and dialects. The city's appearance is as polyglot as its people.

It is rather an ugly, largely treeless city, except for the scabby eucalypti which line its dusty streets, but out toward the edges there is a sudden upthrust of damp green of fir and fig and acacia, of jacaranda and flame, of cedar and palm. The private homes are almost obscenely riotous with flowers.

The city's architecture is fantastic, square white buildings of several stories, slashed by sunlight and shade, and mostly all ugly; here the delicate minaret of a mosque, here a sprawling Indian school of a violent yellow, there a house of pierced plaster in the Arab mood, and on the edges, long, ugly, crumbly-molding green wooden barracks. The suburbs towards Muthaiga and Limuru are rolling and wet-green and lush-forested, as in any good suburb. The better-class white dwellings are snugged by trees and flowers, and the best boast their swimming pools and clipped tennis courts. The richer Indians have their fine homes, too, on the dusty plains on the road to Thika. They sit starkly like yellow boxes, plastered in the front for show, but revealing ugly gray cement block, unstuccoed, behind, and with their plastered porticos carven in Indian scrollwork.[149]

---

149 Ruark 1955, 184-188.

Fig. 12.15 Portal Street with MacMillan Library, Jamia Mosque and the City Market, 1950

In Ruark's novel, Nairobi is presented as a town with many appearances. The ugliness of the town is its disharmony, each different element shrieking its own truth. At the same time, Ruark seems to perceive the differences as romantic, emphasizing the whiteness of the modern office buildings, the "higgledy-piggledyness" of the slums, the stark colors of the Asian houses, and the "obscenely riotous" flowers of the European suburbs. Ruark's Nairobi appears as an exotic place, the setting of dangerous events evoked by the untamed nature of the natives.

In another adventure novel, set in 1960, Ruark described the changes which had taken place in Nairobi during the 1950s:

> [Earlier] everything about the town was romantic, the eddying crowds on Delamere Avenue and Government Road, the seething bazaars by the old mosque, the black traffic policemen in neat starched khaki and high blue puttees, the brown-kneed settlers in shorts and floppy double teral hats, the busy drinkers in the bars at the Stanley and the Norfolk [hotels], the waiters and room boys in the white nightdresses called kanzus, padding silently barefoot across the tiles. Now most of the help wore pants and tennis shoes as a badge of emancipation . . .
> How it all has changed . . . The slums and the old bazaar quarters have been razed – burned down, during the Emergency . . .

Fig. 12.16 Government Road to the north

> Nairobi had come on tremendously in the last five years. Even now in the late afternoon he could see the Sikh fundis fly-crawling on their scaffoldings as new buildings shot up everywhere like mushrooms after rain; new mosques, new schools, new office buildings, new stores, new arcades - they said the money was tight and so it was . . . One of the reasons it was tight was that the Indians had sunk millions into building schemes, vast housing projects.[150]

In Ruark's description, Nairobi changed during the Emergency towards the more modern society envisaged in the *Master Plan*. It seems that at least in this respect, Ruark's novel illustrates something essential – even if strongly biased in favor of the colonizers' views – of the changes which occurred in Nairobi in the 1950s.

The African points of view, rejected by the colonialists then, have been presented later. Of Nairobi, the description of the fire at the Burma Market in 1952 may be used as an example. The Burma Market, located near the Nairobi African Stadium, had been started by African soldiers who fought in Burma during the Second World War. It comprised some 750 stalls and shops, or, as the journalist describing the events later formulated it,

> to use the colonial language employed at the time, "a ramshackle collection of dilapidated huts and stores," which the Nairobi City Council regarded as "illegal" structures.[151]

On the night of November 27, that is, one month after the declaration of the Emergency, the police carried out a raid, arresting the 425 male persons normally living at the market and taking them to be interrogated at the Kingsway Camp. During the operation, the market started on fire and burned

---

150 Ruark 1962, 97f, 416.
151 Abuor 1973, 203; the quotation within is from the *East African Standard*, 28 November 1952.

down, the occupants losing not only all their valuables and other property, but with the shops, their meager means of making a living. The Burma traders were not compensated. In the colonialists' reports quoted by Abuor, the emphasis was on the technical description of the police procedures and the flimsiness of the building materials:

> Due to the fact that the whole of the market was made of material of a most inflammable nature, i.e., tarred hessian, bamboo and dried wood and aided by a fresh wind, it took immediate hold and spread throughout the whole market. The Fire Brigade was powerless to stop the extremely rapid progress of the flames and by 1.10 a.m. the whole of the Burma Market was completely burnt out.[152]

The Africans alleged that the police started the fire, because the residents had resisted the demolition of the old stalls and their replacement with more expensive ones. The imminent demolition coincided with the finding of the body of an African councillor, Tom Mbotela, near the Burma Market the same morning and with the suspicions that the market was the meeting point of criminals.[153] Regardless of whether the fire was intentionally started or whether it began due to a careless putting out of fires during the arresting of the residents, Abuor's description indicated the conflict of the interests of the European colonialists and the African inhabitants, at issue in the Burma Market.

More generally, for its part it confirmed that with the exceptional regulations enforced during the Emergency, the colonial administration had the means to control both the influx of Africans into Nairobi and how they lived within the city. In this sense, a photograph and its caption in Abuor's book are illuminative. The photograph showed a Nairobi street with two and three-storied stone buildings in the background and some people in the front: five African men with their bicycles and two European men, armed and in military attire; attached to the photograph was the caption:

> One of the sudden security checks on African workers in the streets of Nairobi during the Emergency.[154]

A more dramatic illustration of how the Emergency affected the daily life of the Nairobi inhabitants was a photograph in a travel guide, showing some tens of African men collected in an urban open space surrounded by barbed wire and guarded from the roof by a military official with a machine gun, ordinary activities continuing – "as usual" – on the adjacent streets (Fig. *12.17*). The caption informed the reader:

---

152 Quoted in Abuor 1973, 203f.
153 Abuor 1973, 200-204; see also the photograph of the fire, Appendix.
154 Abuor 1973, Appendix.

Fig. 12.17 Nairobi street view during the Emergency, 1950s

British soldier guards Mau Mau freedom fighters after mass arrests in Nairobi.[155]

For the Africans, then, Nairobi during the Emergency was a city not only dominated by the European colonizers, but one where their practices and models could be and were imposed on the non-Europeans by force; in that context, the economic prosperity and the industrial development in the 1950s carried only marginal meanings for the colonized groups.

During the Emergency, the population continued to grow. According to a sample census taken in 1957, the total had reached over 220,000 persons, indicating an average yearly growth of almost 10,000 from the 119,000 of the 1948 census.[156] The year 1957 also marked the change in housing policy from building shared rooms for bachelors; the last of these was the Ofafa stage I scheme following the model typical to the 1940s and 1950s public housing in Nairobi.[157] The new policy promoted family dwellings for African workers, conforming to suggestions already made in the *Master Plan* of 1948 and by several later committees and reports. The first scheme based on the family concept, with 136 flats, was erected in Ngara in 1958, but most were built in the Eastlands area where the "official housing zones" were proposed in the *Master Plan* of 1948. The new City Council schemes included Ofafa Maringo with 1,400 flats completed in 1959, Jerusalem with 500 flats in 1960, and Jericho with 3,000 flats constructed by 1962 and 1963.[158] The ending of the seven-year official State of Emergency in January 1960 meant the release of the restrictions of movement, and people started to move into Nairobi. The

---

155 *Kenya Insight Guide* 1985, 53.
156 Hake 1977, 62.
157 Hake 1977, 64.
158 Hake 1977, 80. Maringo means "posh."

housing available could not possibly suffice to accomodate all the inhabitants, and uncontrolled settlements – largely demolished during the Emergency – began to mushroom in various parts of the city, some, like Kaburini, in the same places as earlier. Mathare was reborn and grew rapidly into a village with maybe a thousand inhabitants by 1963. A large illegal settlement was established near the Nairobi River between Muthurwa Landhies area and Pumwani, in the area now known as the Country Bus Station.[159]

The number of persons involved in the informal sector also increased after 1960. As Hake described the situation of the hawkers operating on the streets, at street corners, and other strategic points of the city:

> Such markets were frequently raided by the police; goods were confiscated or destroyed, hawkers arrested, and the site cleared. Next day the market would be in operation again, selling bowls, cups, ballpoint pens, cheap textiles, meat, dried fish and vegetables, including the "sukuma wiki" (stretch out the week) made of the outer leaves of cabbages gathered and tied together to make an artificial cabbage, sold for ten cents (one penny), and popular with the poorest. The authorities would argue that it was a threat to health, safety, law and order, and the established trades but for the people it was a chance to earn a few honest shillings.[160]

In the history of Nairobi, the years following the ending of the Second World War in 1945 and preceding Independence in 1963 were in many ways significant. The changed colonial policies of Britain meant the promotion of industrialization; for this, the *Master Plan* of 1948 was essential. It was an instrument to direct and control the development of land use and the location of activities in the capital in ways which would benefit the industries in particular and the economy in general. Although all the changes which occurred in the city after the plan may not have taken place because of the plan, some nevertheless conformed to and were articulated through it. During the Emergency, the control of the urban forms and of the practices they helped maintain was used by the colonial administration as a means of restricting and regulating the inhabitants. Also, the enforcement of the principles presented in the *Master Plan* of 1948 was more efficient during the Emergency than at any time before or after it. But the changes in Nairobi during the two decades were not only – and maybe not even primarily – due to planning. Despite stricter regulations which controlled influx, vagrancy, and illegal settlement, the population of Nairobi increased, the informal employment sector became a more important part of the economy, and unofficial housing accounted for a larger portion of the needs of accomodation. While the planned changes of Nairobi were attached to the values, models, and practices of mostly the European community and, to some

---

159 Hake 1977, 81, 113, 148.
160 Hake 1977, 179. "Hawkers" refers to persons selling goods without a permanent shop, on the street.

extent, supported by the Asians, the informal, unofficial and – according to the administrators – illegal sector developed on the initiative and resources of the Africans. In this sense, Nairobi at the threshold of the independence of Kenya was a product of all three cultures.

This was not, however, how it was experienced then. While the colonialists perceived it as fundamentally a city progressing towards the urbanism typical of western Europe, for the Africans it was primarily a colonial city: a city built for non-Africans. In his novel *A Grain of Wheat*, set on the verge of independence, the author Ngugi wa Thiong'o made the main character, Gikonyo, reflect on Nairobi:

> The Uhuru Highway (formerly Princess Elizabeth), was lined on either side with columns of the new black, green and red Kenya flags, and flags from other African countries. For a time Gikonyo forgot his mission to the city as his heart fluttered with the flags. He got out of the bus and walked down Kenyatta Avenue feeling for the moment as if the city really belonged to him. The statue of Lord Delamere that proudly dominated the Avenue (the Avenue previously bore his name) had been replaced by a fountain around which African men and women crowded, spilling into the grounds of the New Stanley Hotel, all pointing at, and talking about, the rotating jets of water . . . To Gikonyo, Nairobi seemed ready for Independence . . .
>
> He crossed Government Road to Victoria Street and his business mind started to work again. He started wondering, he often did when crossing the two streets, why there was not a single African shop in the whole of the central and business areas of Nairobi. In fact, Nairobi, unlike Kampala . . . was never an African city. The Indians and Europeans controlled the commercial and the social life of the city. The African only came there to sweep the streets, drive the buses, shop and then go home to the outskirts before nightfall.[161]

---

161 Ngugi 1982, 54.

■ 13 Modernizing the African metropolis, 1963–1983

Kenya became independent on December 12, 1963. From the colonialists, the new nation inherited some resources and many problems. In Nairobi, one of the problems demanding immediate action was a population growing at an explosive rate. The census of 1962 revealed a total of some 267,000 inhabitants inside the city boundary.[1] Just before independence, the colonialists had allowed unlimited influx to the city, but the consequences of this were not recognized in advance. Two parallel elements contributed to the processes of urbanization: industrialization particularly after the Second World War and the change of the colonial economy from food crops to exportable cash crops, the first attracting people to the city, the second reducing their number in the rural areas.[2]

One of the administrative changes made in Nairobi to facilitate independence was the extension of the city boundary retained, with only minor changes, from 1928. This boundary encompassed 35 square miles and included Nairobi South in the south, Thompson Estate and Bernhard Estate in the west, Parklands and Muthaiga in the north, and Eastleigh and Makadara in the east.[3] It was surrounded in the south, east, and north by the Nairobi Extra-Provincial District, which had been established in 1918 and which was administered by the central government, and in the west and north by the Kiambu District, traditionally a part of the Kikuyu tribal territory.[4] The arguments presented to the Regional Boundaries Commission of 1962 emphasized the inclusion, within the boundary of the city, of adequate land for future residential and commercial development, of the peri-urban

---

[1] The figure on Nairobi is based on the 1962 Kenya Population Census (Vol.I, Government Printer, Nairobi, 1964), quoted in Blacker 1965, 61. In another table in the same source (p.63), the population figure quoted as "226,794" seems to be a misprint, because the average yearly population growth from 1948 estimated as 5.9% corresponds with the higher figure; also Halliman and Morgan (1967, 107) and Barnow et al (1983, 57) quote the 1962 census for Nairobi as 266,795. These figures refer to the boundaries of 1962. For the extended boundaries of 1963 - which included also the peri-urban area - the 1962 population was estimated as around 344,000 in Blacker (ibid., 63) and Halliman and Morgan (1967, 100), and as 315,000 in Gugler (1972, 5).

[2] Elkan 1973; Elkan and Zwanenberg 1975, 667ff.; Davidson 1978, 212.

[3] Halliman and Morgan 1967, 100, 105. The boundary of 1962 equals about 91 sq.km. For the boundary changes in Nairobi, see map above, based on Halliman and Morgan 1967, 99.

[4] On Nairobi Extra-Provincial District, Halliman and Morgan 1967, 98; on the peri-urban zone of western Nairobi, in Kiambu District, Memon 1982, 146, 148.

dormitory areas inhabited by people depending on the city for their livelihood, and of strategic assets, without encroaching good agricultural land, located to the north of the city; as Dorothy M. Halliman and W.T.W. Morgan noted, the extensions of the boundary appeared to take account of these arguments. Thus the boundary was extended to include the Nairobi Game Park (later renamed the Nairobi National Park) to the southwest, some peri-urban residential suburbs like Karen and Langata to the southwest, Dagoretti to the west, and Spring Valley to the north, and a large extent of farmland suitable for future development to the east.[5] With the extension, the area of the city grew to 266 square miles, with some 344,000 inhabitants. In some sixty years, Nairobi had grown from a town of seven square miles (1901) and 11,500 inhabitants (1906) to a metropolis with thirty-eight times its area and almost thirty times its population.[6]

From the colonialists, Nairobi also inherited a multicultural society in which privileges had been unevenly divided. For the census and the land use survey of 1962, Nairobi was divided into six areas:

- the Central area comprising the city center,
- the Industrial area south of it,
  and four primarily residential parts of the city:
- Nairobi South,
- Upper Nairobi which included all the areas to the west of the city center, north of the new alignment of the railway on the southwest, and areas like Upper Parklands and Muthaiga to the north,
- Parklands and Eastleigh, and
- Eastlands.

Comparing the residential areas in Nairobi on the basis of the census and the land use survey of 1962, that is, before the extension of the city boundary, Halliman and Morgan indicated the discrepancies in residential densities and population densities between different parts of the city. The number of dwellings per acre varied considerably: from 26.00 in Eastlands to 8.46 in Nairobi South, 4.47 in Parklands and Eastleigh, and 1.15 in Upper Nairobi. Similar variations could be observed in densities of population per acre: from 125.9 persons per acre in Eastlands to around 47 in Nairobi South and in Parklands and Eastleigh, and to 6.0 in Upper Nairobi.[7]

In terms of racial composition, the parts of the city differed from each other. In Eastlands, most of the residents were Africans, over 110,000 compared to the total of 500 of all other groups. Parklands and Eastleigh with its around 59,000 Indians, Pakistani and Goans, had a mostly Asian population (74%), but nearly 16,000 Africans (20%) also lived there. Nairobi South was

---

5   Halliman and Morgan 1967, 98; Nairobi Area Map, 1:50.000, Sheet A, 1979.
6   Halliman and Morgan 1967, 100. The boundary of 1963 equalled 689 sq.km.
7   Halliman and Morgan 1967, 105-112. The land use survey was carried out in 1960-61 (ibid., 115). The land divisions of the census and the land use survey did not completely coincide (cf. maps, ibid., 105).

similar: some 6,300 Asians comprising 57% and 2,700 Africans comprising 25% of the population lived there. The Asian population dominated the Central area (76%), while Africans were most populous in the Industrial area (69%). In Upper Nairobi, the number of Africans (18,500, 49%) was higher than that of Europeans (17,700, 47%). Somewhat corresponding observations may be made on the basis of where the majority of each population group lived. Of the 155,400 Africans living in Nairobi in 1962, the majority (71%) lived in Eastlands. Of the 86,500 Asians, the majority (68%) lived in Parklands and Eastleigh; this part of the city also contained the majority of the less than thousand Arabs and of the some 900 Somalis. Of the 21,500 Europeans, the majority (82%) lived in Upper Nairobi.[8]

The density figures may, therefore, conceal even more extreme divergencies. For example, comparing the densities of Eastlands to those of Upper Nairobi, the density of dwellings per acre in Eastlands was some twenty-five times that of Upper Nairobi, and the density of population per acre some twentyfold. But if we also take into account the assumption that in Upper Nairobi to a large extent, the Africans were in domestic employment[9] and that they were usually housed in conditions with less space and more inhabitants than those of their employees, the extremely low density figures concerning the European occupants of Upper Nairobi are buried in the average of the area.

Halliman and Morgan also described the different areas. According to them, Upper Nairobi lying on higher ground over 5,500 feet was the

> best residential area . . . The typical dwelling is a one-family detached house of one storey built of stone under a tile roof with separate servant's quarters on a plot of a quarter of an acre or more.[10]

Parklands-Eastleigh was evaluated as an area where

> the cultural differences with the primarily European areas of Upper Nairobi are quite striking. The flat topped houses are distinctive and the different family structure results in three times the number of persons per dwelling . . . A notable feature of the Parklands-Eastleigh area is the range of prosperity from the poorest at Eastleigh in the east to the richest in Parklands in the west.[11]

Nairobi South was

> not a particularly attractive area, being flat and on black cotton soil but the buildings are modern and also convenient for employment in the industrial area.[12]

---

8   Halliman and Morgan 1967, 107.
9   Halliman and Morgan 1967, 106.
10 Halliman and Morgan 1967, 106.
11 Halliman and Morgan 1967, 106.
12 Halliman and Morgan 1967, 106.

Eastlands contained

> the working class estates principally constructed by the City Council or by large employers . . . The flat site on black cotton is not as attractive as parts of Upper Nairobi, diversified by its wooded valleys[,] and amenity must be planned for rather than allowed to occur naturally.[13]

The Industrial Area was

> officially zoned for that purpose in 1947 . . . Although officially zoned for industry, only 309 acres (44 per cent) are used for manufacturing and well over half the land is undeveloped. The remainder is occupied by a variety of uses: government, railway, commerce and residential, some of which are appropriate to the area and some are not . . . It is level land and unattractive for residential development but adequate for factories and workshops.[14]

The Central Area

> where the town began . . . the city is still well defined on the western side by a barrier consisting of the highway and the steep rise on to "the Hill" . . . The central functions will not want to be separated from the centre of the city and will therefore be unwilling to locate outside these barriers. At present the land available is adequate but any considerable growth in Nairobi is liable to lead to severe competition for land within this restricted central area. A comparison might be made with the history of the central "Loop" area of Chicago . . . [where] the restricted site led to building upward in the form of some of the earliest skyscrapers . . . [I]n listing the principal functions of the area, it will be seen that each tends to be grouped together in a distinct quarter of the town.[15]

In a map of the central area, Halliman and Morgan indicated the functional differentiation which they had observed (*Fig. 13.1*). The "Railway" area and the "Railway Housing" area adjacent to it were located south of the central area. Immediately north of them was the area marked as "Public" – of public services – also called "City Square" on the map, roughly stretching from the Uhuru Highway on the west to Government Road on the east and from Haile Selassie Avenue on the south to Kenyatta Avenue on the north, and including the Railway Headquarters next to the Railway area. A small additional public services area was located at the northern end of Government Road. In the map, the "1st Shopping Area" contained the plots on both sides of Government Road from Haile Selassie Avenue on the south to the junction of Bazaar Street and River Road in the north; it also included areas on both sides of

---

13 Halliman and Morgan 1967, 108f.
14 Halliman and Morgan 1967, 116.
15 Halliman and Morgan 1967, 109.

Fig. 13.1 Map: Central area

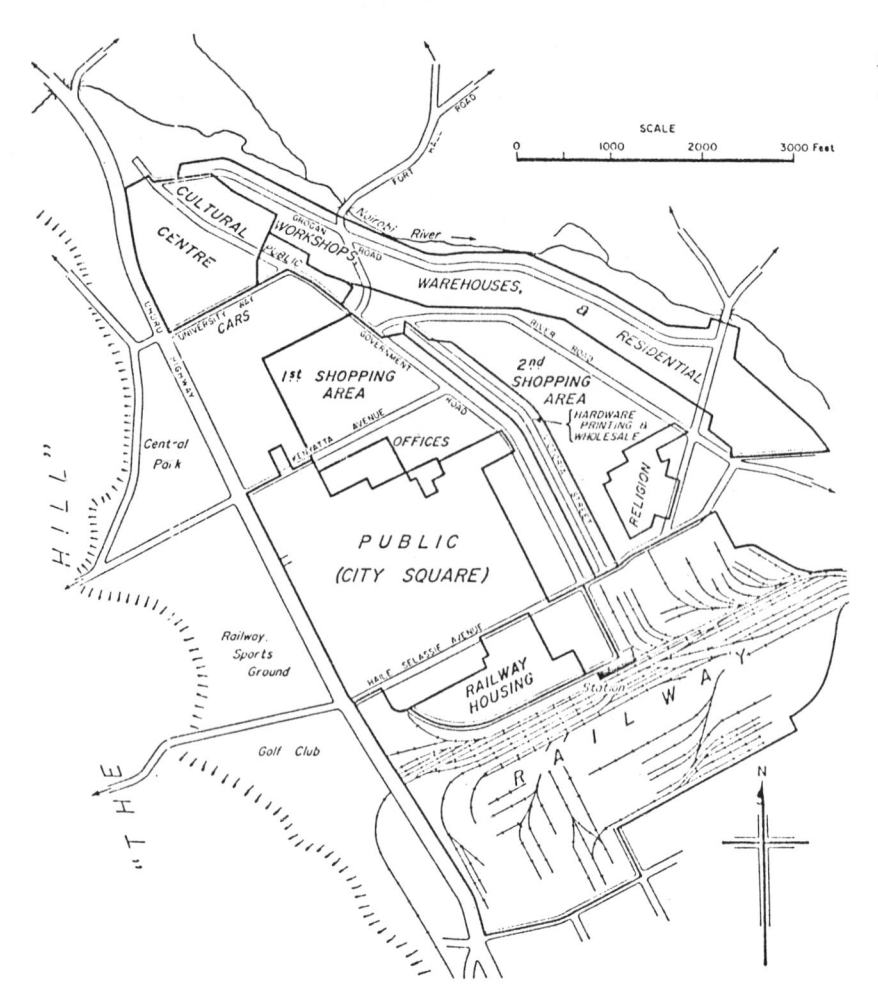

Kenyatta Avenue up to Bazaar Street, with "Offices" marked in the part next to the City Square. The "2nd Shopping Area" extended on both sides of River Road, with the plots on Victoria Street marked as "Hardware, Printing & Wholesale," and the plots next to Nairobi River, on Grogan Road, as "Workshops, Warehouses & Residential." Within the "2nd Shopping Area" was a small functional island for "Religion." The area for the "Cultural Centre" was located on the northern edge of the city center, in the triangle formed by the Uhuru Highway, University Way, and Nairobi River.[16] Halliman and Morgan also noted that

> despite the public and commercial land use predominant in the central area, many people continue to live there . . . The majority of the residents in the central area live in multiple purpose buildings above

---

16 Halliman and Morgan 1967, 111. Haile Selassie Avenue was formerly First Avenue, later Whitehouse Road; University Way was formerly Kingsway. Today, Victoria Street is Tom Mboya Street and the eastern part of Grogan Road is Kirinyaga Road, the western part Kijabe Road.

or behind shops, warehouses or even workshops. These range in style from luxury penthouses to the backs of dukas.[17]

Halliman's and Morgan's study of the central area may be compared to Ramesh C. Tiwari's analyses of the same area.[18] Generally the two descriptions corresponded. Tiwari used the dominant functions of buildings as the basis of his description, distinguishing between administration, educational, community or religious, commercial, combined commercial and residential, and residential functions. In his map, the administrative zone was located south of (and including) the City Hall, bounded by Uhuru Highway on the west, the railway line on the south, and Nkrumah Lane (one block west of Government Road) on the east, with smaller zone fragments dispersed in other parts of the center. The commercial zone extended north and east of the administrative zone, bounded by City Hall Way on the south, Loita Street (one block east of Uhuru Highway) on the west, University Way on the north, and to the east, reaching approximately two or three blocks east of Government Road and Tom Mboya Street. A smaller commercial zone was located at the southwest corner of the central area, next to the crossing of Uhuru Highway and Haile Selassie Avenue. The area between the commercial zone and the Nairobi River was identified as a combined commercial-residential area. The educational zone was located in the northern corner of the "triangle," north of University Way.

Tiwari also analyzed the center using two methods for locating the central business district (CBD): the Murphy-Vance method based on floor space used for central business activities, modified for the Nairobi study to include wholesale and certain light industries, and the de Blij method based on retail frontage on the ground floor. According to the Murphy-Vance method, the CBD of Nairobi almost exactly corresponded with the commercial zone of Tiwari's functional description. According to the de Blij method, the CBD also included the zone with combined commercial-residential activities. In both, the peak land value intersection was located at the crossing of Kenyatta Avenue and Kimathi Street.[19] Tiwari identified the CBD defined by the Murphy-Vance method as the Occidental Central Business District and the additional area incorporated with the de Blij method as the Oriental Central Business District, indicating that already in 1918, the European commercial zone of Nairobi coincided with the Occidental CBD and the Asian commercial zone with the Oriental CBD.[20] Thus also historically, the Nairobi city center contained two commercial areas. Tiwari showed that the differences of the

---

17 Halliman and Morgan 1967, 112. "Dukas" refers to small shops.
18 Tiwari 1981; in the article, Tiwari does not specify the date of his data, but refers to his earlier study, *Nairobi: A Study in Urban Geography* of 1964, University of Reading, Ph.D.thesis, where he analyzed the CBD with the methods referred to here.
19 Next to, for example, the Stanley Hotel; see above, chapter 12.
20 Tiwari, *Nairobi: A Study in Urban Geography*, University of Reading, Ph.D.thesis, 1964, quoted in Tiwari 1981, 138.

two CBD's were not only related to the use of space – the Occidental CBD representing a concentration of single-function commercial spaces, the Oriental CBD containing an integration of functions – but also to the types of establishments, the kinds of goods and services offered, and the variation of commercial practices. Cultural differences, then, were seen as fundamental in the study of the spatial formation and growth of multiple central business districts in Nairobi.[21]

Halliman and Morgan perceived the character of Nairobi as the result of the interaction of several factors, from the physical characteristics of the site of the city to practices and ideas imported from different cultures. They noted that lack of control in the early years and confusion due to parallel administrative bodies had contributed to the emergence of land use patterns where future development was not considered. Since all the major population groups seemed to have "two homes" – the Africans with their "shambas" in the countryside, the Europeans with permanent homes outside the country, and the Asians with strong ties to their places of origin – there did not seem to be inhabitants who saw the city as their permanent home:

> Nairobi, therefore, does not enjoy the benefits of a stable urban population whose total creative, social and economic effort is concentrated exclusively on the city.[22]

Halliman and Morgan estimated that with the growth rates of that time, the city would be faced with a population of around a million in twenty years, which they saw could constitute either an asset or a liability, employment and housing provision presenting the major problems. For the middle income groups, tenant purchase schemes on a high density basis could be expected to result in assisting the indigenous population to move to former European suburbs and in forming a "stable middle class urban population."[23] For the future of the lower income groups, they proposed realistic programs:

> It would be unrealistic to think in terms of palaces for which they cannot pay or of establishing them in already developed areas whose value and amenity would be severely damaged. Cheap land, easily serviced will be required.[24]

Inherent in Halliman's and Morgan's study was the notion that areas for lower income groups, most in need of involvement from public authorities, would have to be located on undeveloped land publicly owned and planned so that the minimum technical requirements would be fulfilled. Within an existing urban structure, land which is at once cheap and does not threaten to damage the value or amenity of already developed areas is land which is located at

---

21   Tiwari 1981, 138-146.
22   Halliman and Morgan 1967, 118.
23   Halliman and Morgan 1967, 119.
24   Halliman and Morgan 1967, 119.

the outskirts and which lacks services. This kind of land differs from land occupied by "illegal" or "unofficial slums" mushrooming in locations either adjacent to or with good connections to places offering opportunities for "unauthorized" employment, that is, near the city center and imbedded within the urban structure. For the inhabitants, the advantages of the location surpass the "unacceptability" of the lack or low standard of technical services. In Halliman's and Morgan's analysis, neither the existing housing situation regarding the "slums" nor policies for dealing with them was discussed: in their Nairobi, these areas did not seem to exist.

Around the same time, Richard Cox, a journalist, described a very different Nairobi, as he put it, "the alien city":

> One trouble about Nairobi is its very opulence. It is a luxurious, polyglot city, completely unrelated to the simple life of the bush around it. Squalor and splendour exist side by side in a South American profusion. It was created by Europeans, by the adventurers and the speculators, and latterly by more solid citizens, some simply the gamblers grown older, plus many industrious Asians. The only truly African parts of it are the slums and shanty towns that the City Council is systematically destroying . . .
> [W]ooden one-storey verandahed offices gave way to three-storey stone ones, then to semi-skyscraper concrete blocks that soar white and dazzling as a mirage out of the surrounding African plains. So fast has been the change that you can see all three incongruously alongside each other. The avenues are now adorned with statues and planted with blue flowering jacaranda tress or great sweeping stretches of bougainvillea. In the suburbs, growing now eight and more miles from the centre, and still occasionally visited by the lions whose home it was before, the traditional Cotswold house and the white stuccoed Spanish villa replace the old corrugated-roof bungalows. Occasionally, as in the new cathedral, massive beside the diminutive spire of a pioneer church, or in the oriental inspiration of the Ministry of Justice offices, there is a bloom of exciting modern architecture, as though the British designers had been liberated from their inhibitions by the Equatorial sun.[25]

What for Halliman and Morgan had appeared as a city with potential for development and prosperity, if proper measures were taken, was seen by Cox as a mixture of mostly imported influences, its colonial past continuing to distort the African present. The illegally constructed settlements also evoked opposite responses: from Halliman and Morgan, the absence of comments and the emphasis on future policies for low income groups in general, exhibiting a reluctance to acknowledge the existence of slums; from Cox, the denigration of the European models applied in the built forms and the identification of the slums and shanty towns as the only truly African parts of the city. Thus the two aspects relevant to Nairobi's newly-acquired position

---

25 Cox 1965, 148ff.

as the capital of an African country which had recently gained its independence emerged in the descriptions. The first was the notion of progress towards a modern city which would hold the means of providing for all its inhabitants, in essence, of modernization as the vehicle for well-being. The second was the notion of Kenyan and African practices and built forms as distinct from European (or Asian) ones, in essence, of new values attached to practices and forms seen as indigenous. Of these, modernization had been included in the goals of the colonial government of Kenya after the Second World War; in independent Kenya, modernization was related to the processes of nation building and to the acceptance of the country, on an equal basis, among other nation-states in the international community.[26] In terms of value attributed to indigenous practices and forms, however, independence meant a reversal from the dominant values of the colonial state.

Within Kenya, Nairobi at independence was not only the capital in an administrative and historical sense, it was also the core area of the nation, its most modernized, most urbanized, and most industrialized center. Halliman and Morgan indicated that within the private sector, for example, about half of the employees in commerce and in building and construction were in Nairobi, and that the City of Nairobi was the principal industrial center of the country, accounting for 41 per cent of the industrial employment and 44 per cent of the value added by manufacture.[27] In addition to being the "largest single concentrated market in East Africa" at the time, as Halliman and Morgan evaluated it, Nairobi also functioned as a distribution center both within the region, in Kenya, and in East Africa as a totality.[28] Analyzing the geography of modernization of Kenya, Edward W. Soja has shown that Nairobi not only dominated the network of communications and transport as well as the social, economic, and political organization of the country, it also

> became the primary generator and distributor of the forces of change [in modernization] for all of Kenya.[29]

Thus for other countries, Nairobi became the gate to the rest of Kenya and of East Africa, both in practice and in image. At issue, then, was not only how Nairobi could fulfill practical needs but also how its physical forms represented its functions. In this, the urban practices and forms exhibited in the city center were perceived as particularly crucial.

Hawking was seen by the authorities as one of the more undesirable urban

---

26 On modernization and nation building in Kenya, see Soja 1968, 1f.
27 Reported employment in Nairobi and the whole of Kenya (Ministry of Economic Planning and Development, 1963) and Industries in Kenya and the city of Nairobi (Kenya Census of Manufacturing, 1961), quoted in Halliman and Morgan 1967, 112-115.
28 Halliman and Morgan 1967, 114. Its role was further strengthened with the plans to form an East African Community of Kenya, Uganda, and Tanzania; the community was formed in 1967 but was later dissolved.
29 Soja 1968, 114; see also p.107. Soja's fieldwork in East Africa was done around 1964 (p. v). For a reappraisal of the approach, see Soja 1979.

practices. The population flow into Nairobi in 1960, following the relief of the restrictions of the Emergency, brought with it many persons with little choice for making a living. For those who did not find employment, the alternatives were hawking or, if that was prevented, crime. In his study of the hawkers of Nairobi, Herbert H. Werlin noted that just before independence, it was no longer possible for the European-dominated City Council to ban hawking completely. The sudden increase of hawkers made it difficult for the ones established earlier, because of reduced incomes, to pay the required fees to the City Council and for the police to supervise the enforcement of regulations, particularly on the sale of food and drink.[30] In 1961, the Medical Officer of Health of Nairobi warned of the dangers of the situation:

> The hygienic standards of many of these stalls are deplorable, and could cause serious illness to the people who buy food from them. People with shops nearby have complained that they attract filth and disease. They are also used as an excuse by loiterers, who hang about the stalls to steal from parked cars.[31]

In 1962, the newly-elected African mayor, Charles Rubia, was first unwilling to increase control of the hawkers. A City Council spokesman justified the prevailing laissez-faire policy by referring to the difficult socio-economic conditions:

> If there is little the Council can do to remove the large number of unemployed and destitute from the city, we have to live with the problem until there is work and provision for them outside the urban areas.
> What we try to do is strike a humane balance between demands of established traders who regard widespread hawking as a threat to their livelihood, and the claims of hungry people who seek to earn some food through petty trading.[32]

A Hawkers Sub-Committee tried in November 1963 to establish a set of resolutions to curb illegal hawking, but this did not seem to have brought conclusive results.[33]

In terms of City Council policies, then, the slums with their illegal settlements and the hawkers involved in illegal selling were both related to the issues of unlimited influx and overcrowding of the city. As urban practices which were perceived as undesirable, they also generated similar responses from the authorities. In May 1964, warned of the possibility of plague by its Chief Medical Officer, the City Council decided to "clear," with force, one of the areas located in the city center and infested by hawkers and squatters.

---

30 Werlin 1981, 200f.
31 *East African Standard* (February 20, 1961) quoted in Werlin 1981, 201.
32 *East African Standard* (October 18, 1963) quoted in Werlin 1981, 202.
33 Werlin 1981, 203.

"Operation Clean-Up" thus became, after independence, the first in a long succession of campaigns enforced by the City Council to remove "undesirable elements" from conspicuous sites in Nairobi.[34]

These "slum" areas commonly consisted of shacks and huts built of temporary materials like plastic sheeting, cardboard, cloth, scrap metal, and used timber. Within the housing systems of Nairobi, the squatter type dwellings have been identified within the popular sector (distinct from private and public sectors) and described as "unapproved housing on land which the developers do not have the legal right to occupy,"[35] with an estimated population of 97,000 or 18% in 1970. In Hunter Morrison's summary of low-income, privately built house types in Nairobi in the early 1970s, the three most elementary popular house types were covered beds, tents, and cardboard houses, the first two usually found in areas without any security of tenure (that is, illegally occupied) and with a consistent threat of demolition. In contrast, traditional mud and wattle structures, although the most popular housing form, were not found in these areas, but in the outskirts of the city or in villages nearer the city center on locations with more secure tenure.[36] David Etherton has indicated that a third of the population in Nairobi around 1970 lived in unauthorized and illegal settlements, with some 143,000 in "central" Nairobi (in the areas within the pre-1963 boundary) and some 66,000 in the outer areas (within the extended 1963 boundary). Of these, the temporary urban settlements most eligible for demolition contained over 10,000 inhabitants. Etherton identified several of these areas, all located along the Nairobi River valley within a three-mile radius from the city center (*Fig. 13.2*). Kirinyaga was immediately adjacent to the city center, north of the River Road area. Kaburini, "Box Estate," and "Banana" were near the area now known as the Country Bus Station. Kitui Village, Muthuri, "Carton City," and Kinyango were close to the housing areas of Eastlands.[37] Photographs of Kirinyaga in 1971, published in Horacio Caminos' and Reinhard Goethert's *Urbanization Primer*, display "primeval squatter dwelling[s]" and temporary shanties made of frames covered with cloth, of cardboard constructions, of abandoned vehicle bodies, and of wooden packing boxes.[38]

The clean-up campaigns continued through the 1960s, evidently with more unyielding measures taken towards those unofficial settlements which were located closer to the center of Nairobi.[39] Usually the settlements were just

---

34 Werlin 1981, 203.
35 *Appraisal of a Sites and Services Project in Kenya*, Report No.607a KE, April 14, 1975, quoted in Soni 1980, 48.
36 Morrison 1972, 55f.; see also Morrison 1974, 279. Cox (1965, 156) mentioned huts roofed by flattened *jembes* (petrol cans).
37 Etherton 1971, 4f. Etherton's figures seem also to include the unapproved housing on land which the developers had the legal right to occupy (e.g. the "company housing" of Mathare Valley); in the Appraisal... quoted in Soni (1980, 48), this type accounted for some 103,000 inhabitants (19%), the popular sector, including the squatters, totalling some 200,000 people and accounting for 37% of Nairobi housing in 1970.
38 Caminos and Goethert 1980, 210f.

demolished without providing the inhabitants any other places to build on. One of the exceptions was a housing redevelopment program initiated by the Nairobi City Council and the Kenyan government in 1964 "to aid squatters living just a few hundred yards from the modern central areas of Nairobi,"[40] as Thomas S. Weisner has described it. It involved

> "tearing down the squatters' illegal shacks and thus improving what was felt to be an unhealthy, dangerous, and unsightly blight on the capital of newly independent Kenya. Every squatter household was to be given a plot of land, fully prepared with essential services, on which to build a new home."[41]

Kariobangi, at the periphery, northeast of the city center, was planned as the new location, providing "site and services" for the former squatters. Kariobangi was to be developed with houses built of mud and wattle by the occupants. Weisner has noted that later Kariobangi was judged by many as a failure, since it did not function as a squatter rehousing scheme, but as a housing area for newly-arrived migrants, with absentee landlord-investors collecting the rents.[42] A slightly different resettlement area, for Kaburini squatters, was established in Karura Forest north of the city center in 1970, as a temporary shelter; photographs show structures made of carton and canvas (*13.3, 13.4*).[43]

Some settlements were "cleared" more than once. For example, for the period between 1968 and 1971, Etherton listed the demolition of the temporary urban settlements in Kaburini near the city center three times by Nairobi City Council askaris (officials), affecting altogether 6,100 people, and in the Nairobi River/Grogan Road area (possibly referring to the Kirinyaga settlement) also three times, the number of persons affected not indicated; moreover, in both settlements, shacks were rebuilt on the site after the first demolitions.[44] In 1970, a massive "City Cl[e]an-Up Campaign" was put in effect in all major squatter areas excluding Kibera, Mathare Valley, and Dagoretti.[45] Andrew Hake has estimated that the systematic demolition of the unauthorized settlements between 1970 and November 1971 destroyed almost 9,000 dwelling units and left some 48,000 persons homeless, without replacement.[46] Both the City Council and the Government seem to have agreed on the policy of demolishing the unauthorized settlements: the City Council continued the campaigns despite public criticism, and the Cabinet supported it.[47] Richard E. Stren also referred to President Kenyatta's later comment to

---

39 Hake 1977, 99.
40 Weisner 1976, 77.
41 Weisner 1976, 77f.
42 Weisner 1976, 78. On Kariobangi, see also Hake 1977, passim.; Caminos and Goethert 1980, 58f., 103, 216f. (including photographs).
43 Hake 1977, 127f.; Caminos and Goethert 1980, 212f.
44 Etherton 1971, 84f.
45 Stren 1974, 7f.
46 Hake 1977, 99.

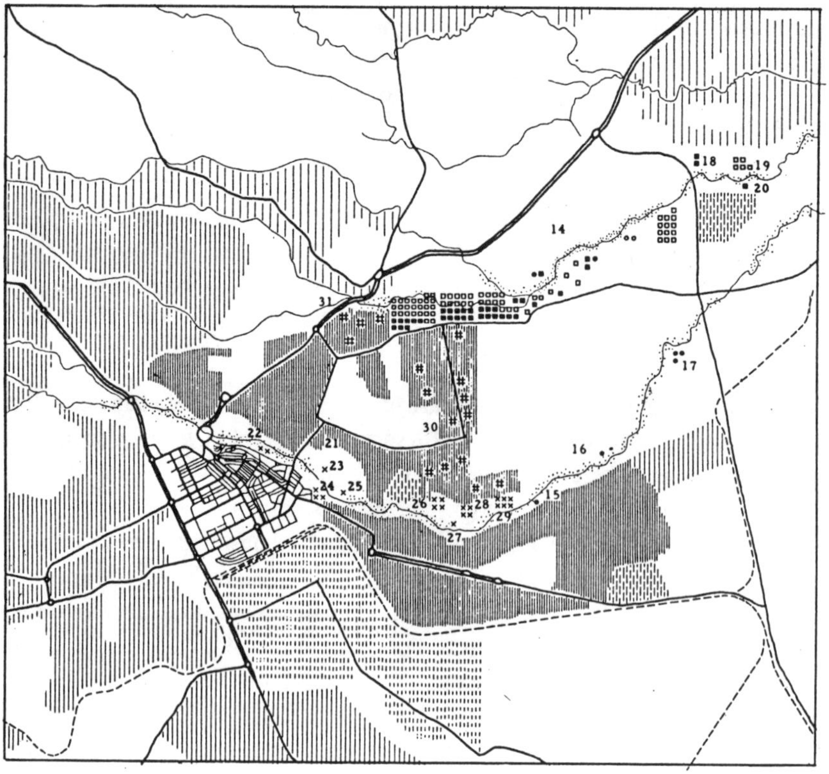

Fig. 13.2 Map: Uncontrolled settlements in central Nairobi

a City Council delegation of not wanting Nairobi to turn into a "shanty-town."[48]

References to the methods used in the campaigns varied from the general "demolished" or "total demolition," and the disguised "slum clearance" or "ridding the central city of squatters" to the more precise "burned down" intentionally all or most of the structures; some were destroyed by accidental fire, the City Council preventing the rebuilding of the structures.[49] It seems that other forms of demolition were also employed: for example, in a newspaper article of 1971, settlements in Mathare Valley area were described as a "target of the City Council for a long time. The shanties have been razed to their foundation several time[s]."[50] In other words, the shanties were bulldozed.[51]

---

47 *East African Standard*, November 21, 1970, quoted in Stren 1974, 8.
48 *Nairobi City Council Minutes*, 1970-71, p.2497-98, quoted in Stren 1974, 8.
49 See e.g. *Nairobi City Council Minutes* of the working party on illegal squatting in Nairobi held on the 15th January, 1964, quoted in Weisner 1976, 80; Stren 1974, 7; Zwanenberg and King 1975, 271; Hake 1977, 114-127 and passim. Ambjörnsson (1971, 169f.) even specified that the officials poured kerosene on the structures before lighting the fire. Journalist Philip Ochieng called the Council's actions "legalized arson" (*Sunday Nation*, January 25, 1970, quoted in Hake 1977, 122f.). Cf. the description of the process of "slum clearance" of central Lagos (Marris 1962, 84ff).
50 "The Slum Dwellers Talking, Dam Manyatta Reports from Mathare Valley," *Sunday Nation*, April 18, 1971.
51 See also *East African Standard*, 20, 21, and 23 January 1970, quoted in Obbo 1980, 25.

Fig. 13.3 Karura Forest uncontrolled settlement

Fig. 13.4 Dwellings, Karura Forest

The "clean-up" campaigns evoked strong opposition from the people without other alternatives for living. Dwellers in the unauthorized settlements were disconcerted because of the continuous threat of demolition. In an interview of "slum-dwellers" in Mathare Valley, Dam Manyatta quoted their reactions:

> We thought that after Uhuru . . . we would be no longer molested. We have been hoping against hope. It is only the stranger in Nairobi

---

During the Emergency, the Burma market was bulldozed after it had burned down, see above.

who does not know us. Now and then it is either Mathare or Majengo that makes headlines in papers. We are an enemy of the City Council for ever. But where to go? . . . If they were replacing them with houses of their taste and allowed us to live in them . . . but you know what they do. They are simply chasing us. They do not want us. We are an eye-sore. But where shall we go?[52]

In a satirical article, Hilary Ng'weno, another journalist, gave "free advice" to the other party of the communication, the spokesmen of the City Council, on issues like the demolition of unauthorized settlements and control of illegal hawking, which had turned out to be controversial:

> Take the shanty demolition decision, for instance. How about the following as an ideal press release to take care of the cries and protestations of hundreds of people made homeless by bulldozers and demolition squads:
> "The shanties are an eyesore to our numerous visitors from abroad. I know their demolition will cause hardships to hundreds, even thousands of our people. But let us think of the comforts of our foreign visitors and particularly of their glorious dollars. Yes, friends and fellow citizens, let us not think of ourselves, let us think of the foreigner and his dollar."
> And on the occasion of the closure of food kiosks:
> "Some of you, friends and fellow citizens, have protested against our closure of food kiosks and canteens on the grounds that the move will cause untold hardship to many thousands of workers who have nowhere else to eat. But, we say unto you, your protests are misguided.
> "You should not worry about hunger, but you should worry about cholera, not so much on account of the fact that it might kill you, but because if some of you should die of cholera the city will lose its tourism. Yes fellow citizens, let us not think of your hunger, let us not think of the harm that cholera will do to you, but let us think of the harm that it will do to this beautiful "City in the Sun."[53]

Ng'weno captured in his satire some of the contradictions inherent in the situation. In the clean-up campaigns, the City Council, in principle representing the citizens for the purpose of furthering their common interests, seemed to operate in ways which in practice were harmful to large groups of these same citizens. For the affected groups, the demolition of temporary settlements had no more than a decade earlier represented one of the unjust and biased practices of the colonial European administration; now, the same unjust policies were pursued by the Kenyanized administration. Furthermore, it was not even an issue of losses now against advantages in the long run; as Ng'weno so poignantly illustrated, not even ultimately was the objective of the clean-up campaigns to improve the living conditions of the inhabitants

---

52 "The Slum Dwellers Talking, Dam Manyatta Reports from Mathare Valley," *Sunday Nation*, April 18, 1971.
53 Ng'weno 1982, 75, originally published under the title "How to Open Your Mouth and Keep Your Foot Out" in *Daily Nation*, April 26, 1971.

of Nairobi, but to present a more attractive image to "our foreign visitors." Within the changes made in the urban forms of Nairobi the demolitions were, however, only part of the story. Serious attempts were being made to map the extent of the housing needs and to plan for viable strategies. In the 1960s, two operations were particularly illuminating for the development of Nairobi: the United Nations Mission to Kenya on Housing and the redevelopment projects for Pumwani.

In 1964, the Government of Kenya invited Lawrence N. Bloomberg and Charles Abrams, under the United Nations Program for Technical Assistance, to

> conduct a study of short- and long-term housing needs and to make recommendations . . . on housing policies within the framework of social and economic development planning.[54]

As background data on Nairobi, the team evaluated that there was no shortage of land for urban development and housing, the extended boundaries sufficing "comfortably [to] absorb at least five times its present population" of some 340,000 persons, that much of the land was publicly owned, the sewage system extensive, and the water supply adequate, and that the local agencies functioned well. Comparing Kenya with other countries, the experts indicated that the urban population of 7.8% in Kenya was considerably lower than in countries like Ghana (23.1%), Congo (22.3%), and Brazil (45.1%) but higher than in the rest of East Africa: Tanganyika (4.1%) and Uganda (2.4%).[55] Of the African population of Kenya, only 5.3% lived in cities, compared to 84.8% of the non-Africans. 93.4% of the Asians and 62.5% of the Europeans were urban.[56] The experts also assessed that the housing of the urban African population was of comparatively low quality, over a third made of temporary materials like mud and wattle or corrugated iron. On average, African dwellings were small, 95% consisting of three rooms or less, one-room dwellings predominating; in comparison, 75% of the Asian dwellings and 38% of the European ones had three rooms or less. Inside the dwellings, only 49% of the urban Africans had access to water closets, generally shared with other households, and separate kitchens were virtually non-existent.[57]

In Nairobi, 8.0% of all dwellings were owned by the occupant, 56.0% were rented, and 32.7% supplied by the employer. Of the Africans and Somalis, 2.3% owned their dwellings, 50.0% lived in rented dwellings and 43.8% in employer housing; of the Asians, 19.5% owned their dwellings, 69.6% rented, and 9.1% had employer housing; of the Europeans, 13.2% owned their dwellings, 43.6% rented, and 26.6% lived in dwellings supplied by their employer.[58] Among the Africans and Somalis of Nairobi, overcrowding was

---

54 Bloomberg and Abrams 1965, 1.
55 Bloomberg and Abrams 1965, 2f.
56 Blacker 1965, 62.
57 Bloomberg and Abrams 1965, 4f.

estimated by the group to be immense. One-room dwellings accounted for 76.4%, two-room dwellings for 13.8%, and three-room dwellings for 2.8% of the total 37,145 African dwellings, with only 1% having four or more rooms (6% were not stated).[59] Even using the high ratio of three persons per rooms as an acceptable level, 52% of the African households lived in overcrowded conditions with more than three persons per room.[60] For Nairobi, the team estimated that between 1962 and 1970, a minimum of about 3,400 additional housing units would be required each year -a total of 27,000 units - to cater to the population increase through migration and changes in household structure; the projection did not take into account loss of housing units through demolition or fire, the replacement of substandard housing, or the relief of overcrowding in the existing housing stock.[61] The Mission recommended that, for the most part, the "use of Government funds be directed toward serving the lower income groups,"[62] that is, groups earning between Ksh.300 and 700 a month, because these groups did not earn enough to have access to privately constructed housing, they lived in conditions with most overcrowding, and "social pressures as well as health requirements demand[ed] it." Site and service projects were seen as able to reach the income group with a Ksh.150 monthly income.[63]

In relation to Nairobi, the work of the experts was focused on the increase in housing demand from the increase of population. It conveniently avoided the difficult issues attached, for example, the low quality of the existing dwellings - one of the motives for the massive demolitions and slum clearance operations during the long history of colonialism in Nairobi and after independence. The experts did distinguish between housing needs, expressed in terms of a housing standard, and housing demands, indicated through the "prices at which housing is or may become available, the ability of families to pay and the proportion of their income they are willing to devote for shelter,"[64] concluding that "if housing cannot be provided for less than Sh.60 a month," which Stren,[65] commenting on the report of the mission, described as a very low rent, "the gap between need and demand in Nairobi is 21,600 units [over the period 1962-1970] . . . or at Sh.90 the gap is 24,200 units."[66] That is, the group of people with the lowest incomes would also in the future be left outside any housing programs which would require the occupant of the dwelling to pay even a very low rent. In reality, these people would have

---

58   Blacker 1965, Appendix B (64); source: Kenya Population Census 1962. Of the total, 4.9%, of the Africans and Somali, 3.8%, of the Asians, 1.8%, and of the Europeans, 16.6% [sic] were not reported.
59   Bloomberg and Abrams 1965, Appendix F (72); source: Kenya Population Census 1962.
60   Bloomberg and Abrams 1965, 15, 23.
61   Bloomberg and Abrams 1965, 13ff, 69.
62   Bloomberg and Abrams 1965, 38.
63   Bloomberg and Abrams 1965, 38.
64   Bloomberg and Abrams 1965, 12.
65   Stren 1972, 84.
66   Bloomberg and Abrams 1965, 23.

only the alternative of living in a minimal shelter nearly or totally without rent: for example, under constant threat of demolition in temporary shelters in the squatter settlements, like the ones described earlier.

The first housing policy of the government, based on Bloomberg's and Abrams' study, was published as Sessional Paper No.5 in 1966.[67] Joyce Malombe has noted that although the most critical issue of the time was the need to increase dwellings for the low income groups, the paper specified no policies on this. On other issues, the policies were more articulate. For example, slum clearance was one of the prime methods of promoting a healthy society:

> If towns are not to develop into slums, and centres of ill-health and of evil social conditions, low income urban housing and slum clearance must continue to form the major part of the nation's housing programme.[68]

In a historical review of the evaluation report on site and service projects, T.S. Chana and others noted that in the Sessional Paper, aided self-help schemes were "identified as the panacea for the housing problems"[69] for the low-income groups. Investments from the private sector were invited for low cost housing, but Malombe assessed that the expectations put on the private sector had not materialized: not only did it remain out of low income housing, it also could not meet demands from higher income groups.[70]

Despite these efforts, the number of dwelling units built in Nairobi remained lower than the need. During 1964, only 240 units were completed,[71] against the need estimated by Bloomberg and Abrams as about 3,400 units annually.[72] Between 1966 and 1970, the City Council built 3,800 on estates mostly in the Eastlands, including Uhuru, Kimathi, Harambee, and Madaraka, as well as California in Pumwani and Jamhuri near Kibera to the west of the city center. The National Housing Corporation built some 1,300 units a year (1970), while the private sector produced some 300 to 350 units annually.[73] The growing housing shortage, due to the gap between the population increase and housing production, was further exacerbated by a policy change within housing provided by employers. In 1962, a large portion (43.8%) of Africans in Nairobi had been housed by their employers.[74] In 1970, the Federation of Kenya Employers decided to discontinue the practice of providing housing for their employees,[75] according to Malombe, to the disadvantage of the lower

---

67 Sessional Paper No.5 of 1966/67 (Housing Policy for Kenya, Republic of Kenya, Government Printer, Nairobi, 1966) quoted in Malombe 1992, 31f.
68 Sessional Paper No.5, 1966, quoted in Malombe 1992, 32.
69 Chana et al 1979, 19.
70 Malombe 1992, 32.
71 Hake 1977, 85.
72 Bloomberg and Abrams 1965, 14.
73 Hake 1977, 85.
74 Bloomberg and Abrams 1965, 64.
75 M.A. Tribe, *Some Aspects of Urban Housing Development in Kenya, Developmental Trends in Kenya*, Edinburgh, 1972, quoted in Malombe 1992, 32.

income group.[76] Andrew Hake has criticized the public policy for its emphasis on the building of conventionally designed and more expensive housing units; with these public resources, more housing units could have been produced by focusing on low-cost housing programs like site and services with houses built mostly by the people themselves.[77]

Fig. 13.5 Pumwani residential area

In a sense, the idea of site and services housing had already been experimented with in Nairobi earlier. Pumwani had been established around 1920 as a "native location" where the municipality provided the roads, communal ablutions and latrines, and plots for the allottee to construct a house according to requirements defined by the municipality.[78] The description of the founding conditions corresponds with those defining site and service areas in the 1970s. For example, according to the Ministry of Housing and Social Services of Kenya, site and services are

> projects in which residential plots of land are provided with basic services, i.e. water and sanitation, roads, surface water drainage, electricity, etc. and allocated to eligible applicants so that they can, through self-help, construct permanent houses. These can initially be constructed to various standards in such a manner as to match the paying ability of low-income households.[79]

At the International Bank for Reconstruction and Development (IRBD), the concept of site and services is used to refer to

> the preparation and subdivision of land for residential buildings and the provision of various combinations of public utilities and community facilities.[80]

Immediately after the Second World War, plans were prepared to demolish Pumwani and to rebuild the site;[81] although they did not materialize, the expectation of demolition seemed to prevent improvements for a long time.[82] During the Emergency, Pumwani had a reputation of being a center of nationalist political activity; it was also identified as one of the "vice-ridden" areas of the city, typically literal dens of thieves, pimps, prostitutes, illicit liquor-stills, and terrorists.[83] Redevelopment plans for Pumwani were discussed in 1960, 1961, 1962, and 1963, but no decisions were made until September 1963 when the new Council was elected, appointing a Sub-

---

76 Malombe 1992, 32.
77 Hake 1977, 85f.
78 On the history of Pumwani (also called Majengo), see above, chapter 11; on the dwellings, see below, chapter 15.
79 Ministry of Housing and Social Services definition quoted in Chana et al 1979, 22.
80 Roberts Merville and William Grindley, *Sites and Services: The Experience and Potential*, unpublished, IBRD, 1973, 1, quoted in Soni 1980, 2.
81 Municipal Council of Nairobi Minutes, 1946-47 (Native Affairs Committee, December 9, 1946; Town Planning Committee, January 7, 1947) quoted in Hake 1977, 132.
82 Hake 1977, 132f., referred e.g. to a 1959 proposal to improve roads rejected on these grounds.
83 Cox 1965, 156f.

Committee to consider the redevelopment of the area.[84] E.T. Farnworth, Chief Valuer, submitted a report

> to present sufficient information in a logical order, to enable the Council to establish [the] principles [of the type of scheme required].[85]

Farnworth saw the issue of redevelopment as a problem of reconciling three conflicting interest areas: the demands of the present residents, finance, and the "Council's duty to the City as a whole." On the demands of the residents, Farnworth summarized that no scheme would satisfy everyone and that social problems would be created. His view was that finances could not be allowed to dictate the broad principles of the redevelopment scheme. From the City's point of view, as he formulated it in brief, the existing Pumwani Estate not only constituted a health risk and a fire hazard to the City generally and to the residents in particular, its location was so close to the center (*Fig. 13.5*) that

> visitors to the City are likely to see this area.[86]

Moreover, the potential value of the land was estimated to be so high that redevelopment was necessary for full utilization of the value.[87] According to

---

84 Hake 1977, 133.
85 Address to the Chairman of the Pumwani Redevelopment Sub-Committee, Farnworth 1964.
86 Farnworth 1964, 2.
87 Farnworth 1964, 1ff.

the Police Report attached to the survey, Pumwani had higher crime rates than other Eastlands estates, "providing" between half and three-fourths of the more serious crimes of the Penal Code and some 80 to 90% of the lesser offences under the Liquor Acts; the police, however, did not perceive this as grounds for demolition, but saw the

> localisation of the criminal element [as] useful.[88]

Of the arguments supporting redevelopment, the ones relating to sanitation could have been responded to, at least to an extent, with improvements but not a total demolition. Even the issue of the image the area presented to visitors could have been countered with arguments on its actual non-visibility from the center. But the argument of the incomplete use of the potential value of the land was presented by Farnworth as conclusive in favor of demolition and rebuilding, or, as it was expressed throughout the report, of the "redevelopment" of Pumwani.

Farnworth proposed that the redevelopment scheme consist of

- blocks of flats with single room dwellings, grouped in four or six rooms with a shared toilet and bathroom, for letting by the Council;
- two-story semi-detached houses (and where the site necessitated, some "terraces," row houses) with one or two rooms planned for subletting, and
- a very limited number of three-story terraces with eight to ten rooms in each, both the two-story and the three-story house types for tenant purchase.[89]

Farnworth recommended that the density in the redevelopment scheme would be an absolute maximum of 200 persons per acre, against the existing density of 250 persons per acre; to provide housing for all the present inhabitants, extra land was available to the east of Pumwani.[90] In general, how the potential value of the site was seen to be better used in the new scheme was not explained. The report did, however, contain an in-depth analysis of the relevant bylaws and recommendations on the procedures to be adopted in the demolition of the present constructions and compensation to standholders.[91] Throughout, Farnworth emphasized legal aspects, however biased (like the 1920 terms of allocation defining the houses as property movable within a month's notice), and disputed the long-standing practices of the residents. These practices included the "illegal" extension of buildings over the allowed 750 sq.ft., subletting without permission, and the use of the buildings for other than residential purposes.[92] In effect, Farnworth's recommendations were based on the notion that the value of the area was strictly a legal and

---

88 Farnworth 1964, 9.
89 Farnworth 1964, 9-12.
90 Farnworth 1964, 8f.
91 Farnworth 1964, 13ff.
92 In 1963, just 2 of the 343 "stands" were occupied only by the standholder and his/her family, and 138 rooms were used for shops (Farnworth 1964, 4ff).

financial issue, in no way attached to how the people living in the area had developed it, shaping it – albeit illegally and without formal consent from the City Council, but nevertheless with its implicit approval – into a neighborhood with its own urban forms and practices. Farnworth expected the new scheme to face opposition because some of the present standholders could profit more from the present conditions; in contrast, the redeveloped area would

> demand better standards of hygiene . . . make illegal brewing of beer more difficult to conceal . . . [and] make the operation of prostitution less acceptable.[93]

From the official point of view, Pumwani seemed to be perceived as an eyesore, all the more suitable for demolition and rebuilding because of its proximity to the city center, its legal status as publicly owned land, and the terms of allocation allowing the City Council to remove undesirable elements relatively easily. Discussion of the redevelopment scheme continued all through the 1960s, with more detailed studies of the area.[94] Hake reported that by 1970, part of the area had been demolished and new blocks of flats built in their place, Phase I (later called California) catering to only about a quarter of the displaced households, the rest being dispersed to other uncontrolled settlements in different parts of the city, with rent within their reach.[95] In 1983, a large portion of the old Pumwani, earlier earmarked for destruction, nevertheless still remained intact.[96]

During the 1960s, then, the population influx generated changes to which the City Council responded, partly by continuing pre-independence practices such as the demolition of unauthorized settlements and the eviction of unregistered hawkers, partly by developing new policies like the housing program to cater to the migrants and the redevelopment schemes to house inhabitants of areas to be demolished. In 1968, new building legislation more compatible with the needs of the country was enforced, with two requirement levels in the "Grade 1" and "Grade 2" Building Order, the latter tailored for peri-urban areas within the extended municipal boundaries and involving low cost or high density residential areas.[97]

The 1969 population census indicated that Nairobi had grown into a

---

93 Farnworth 1964, 15.
94 Reports by the Director of Social Services and Housing (J.P.Mbogua: *Pumwani Estate Social Survey: Analytical Examination of the Demographic and other relevant Social Trends in relation to the Re-Development of Pumwani*, Nairobi City Council, 1965, quoted in Hake 1977, 135ff.) and by a Working Party at St.John's Church and Community Center (National Christian Council of Kenya: *Pumwani Redevelopment, 1968-69*, unpublished, quoted in Harris 1972, 48ff.; see also Hake ibid.). On Pumwani "slum clearance" in more detail, see Hake 1977, chapter 9.
95 Hake 1977, 143f.
96 Field study in 1983. For a description of dwellings and dwelling practices in Pumwani, see below, Part IV. For a photograph of Pumwani, see photographic section in Hutton 1972.
97 For details, see Soja 1983; Etherton 1971, Appendix F2.

Fig. 13.6 Map: Existing roads, 1972

Fig. 13.7 Metropolitan Growth Strategy for 2000

metropolis of some 509,000 inhabitants, representing an average annual growth rate of 9.7% from 1962.[98] Compared to the period between the previous censuses of 1948 and 1962, with a high average annual growth of over 5.9%, after independence the population growth of Nairobi had accelerated. With the influx of rural migrants, the proportion of (Kenyan) Africans had increased and that of Asians and Europeans decreased. In 1962, the census had shown the population of Nairobi to contain 59.4% Africans, 32.4% Asians, and 8.0% Europeans;[99] in 1969, 80% were Africans, 13.2% Asians, and 3.8% Europeans. Despite the influx, Nairobi was home to many fewer (Kenyan) Africans than Asians or Europeans: of the country's African population, only about 3.8% lived in Nairobi, while about a third (32.1%) of the Asians and nearly every other (47.3%) European of Kenya were inhabitants of the capital.[100]

By 1970, Nairobi had expanded both in area and in population from the figures projected for 1975 in the *Master Plan*. In 1948, the team of experts had envisaged a city of 35 square miles (that is, within the boundaries determined in 1926) and with a population of some 250-270,000 to be reached by 1975.[101] By 1970, the boundaries had been extended to 266 square miles

---

98 Barnow et al (1983, 81) based on Kenya Population Censuses of 1962 and 1969.
99 Calculation of the proportions on the basis of Kenya Population Census of 1962, quoted in Barnow et al 1983, 57.
100 Kenya Population Census of 1969 (Vol.I, Statistics Division, Ministry of Finance and Economic Planning, Nairobi, 1970) quoted in Ross 1975, 22.

and the population had increased to 509,000, of whom about a third were estimated to be living in unauthorized settlements. Realities had surpassed the projections of the *Master Plan* of 1948. In 1970, the Nairobi City Council set up the Urban Study Group – local staff backed up by consultants, the British planner Colin Buchanan and Partners – to examine, as Hake formulated it, the strategies for the development of the city, both short-term and long-term (up to the year 2001); essentially, to prepare a new master plan.[102] In 1973, the results of their work were published under the title *Metropolitan Growth Strategy*, funded by the Nairobi City Council, the Kenya Government, the World Bank, and the United Nations.[103] The publication included two volumes, the first volume discussing demographic and social issues, the city's potential for physical growth, strategy recommendations, and implementation, and the second volume containing background material, including appendices on population projections, employment trends, regional land use patterns, housing, and finances.[104] Some of the background studies had been published

---

101 See above, chapter 12.
102 Hake 1977, 86; both Kimani (1981, 160) and Tiwari (1981, 147n24) referred to it as a master plan. Peter Hall (1988, 316; see also Hall 1984, 30) has described Colin Buchanan as the planner-engineer and director of the group which produced a report, *Traffic in Towns*, published by the Minister of Transport of Britain in 1963, converting the then unknown Buchanan into a public figure overnight. Buchanan advocated an approach that within an existing environment and defined environmental standards, the amount of traffic on a particular street would be automatically determined; given the existing road network and standards, traffic could be increased only by comprehensive reconstruction.
103 Emig and Ismael 1980, 59.

earlier as research papers, interim reports, or technical papers.[105] (*Figs. 13.6, 13.7*)

The purpose of the *Metropolitan Growth Strategy* was seen much in the same way as that of the *Master Plan* in 1948, a general frame within which local plans could be executed:

> [The *Metropolitan Growth Strategy*] is distinguished from other plans in being comprehensive rather than piecemeal, so that its proposals . . . fit in a logical whole. The purpose of a strategic plan of this scope is not to present the various sectorial parts in detail, but to fit them into an overall structure over time.[106]

The Nairobi Urban Study Group also identified the intended users of the report:

> We commend the report to the citizens of Nairobi and friends overseas who may invest in our city and assist our development with technical assistance or loans.[107]

The *Master Plan* of 1948 had been conceived as a vehicle to collect the varied views of how Nairobi should be developed and combine the interests of the different groups - albeit seriously restricted to mostly the colonial European views, both those of institutions and of individual citizens. In this sense, the *Master Plan* also was a presentation of the city's potential and plans to the core of the Colonial Empire, the British Government. The *Metropolitan Growth Strategy* seems to have carried largely the same kinds of intent: to provide potential funders, both local and international, with analyses of Nairobi showing its possibilities for profitable investments.

What was different compared to the *Master Plan* were the alternatives presented, not only on growth patterns in the region but also on the distribution of the projected populations into different parts of the city. For the year 2000, the group projected a total population of 3 million or 4.2 million. In the alternatives, the planned population of, for example, the area defined as the "Old City" in the *Metropolitan Growth Strategy* - its boundaries roughly corresponding those of pre-1963 Nairobi - varied between 556,000 and 850,000. The population projections for the "Eastern" area which consisted of the large undeveloped land to the east of the "Old City" outside the Outer Ring Road, a part of the 1963 extension, varied between 240,000 and 670,000.[108]

---

104 *Metropolitan Growth Strategy* quoted in Emig and Ismael 1980, 59f.
105 For example, Kimani 1972; Kimani 1981; A. Vukovich and A. Rozental, *Economic Outlook*, Interim Progress Report, 1972, quoted in Tiwari 1981, 146; T. Hussell, "Preliminary Study of Requirements for Provision of Housing for Present and Future Low-Income Population," Technical paper H3, 1972, R.W. Marshal, "Estimate of Nairobi Housing Stock," Technical Paper H8, 1972), A.A. Rozental, "Nairobi Urban Study and the Housing Problem," Technical Paper H2, 1972), all three quoted in Blair 1980, 18ff.
106 *Metropolitan Growth Strategy*, vol.I, quoted in Emig and Ismael 1980, 59.
107 *Metropolitan Growth Strategy*, quoted in Emig and Ismael 1980, 59f.
108 Maps presenting "Strategy 1.1, 1.2, and 2.1" of the *Metropolitan Growth Strategy*, in Emig and Ismael 1980, 60.

Fig. 13.8 Map: Central area land use, 1972

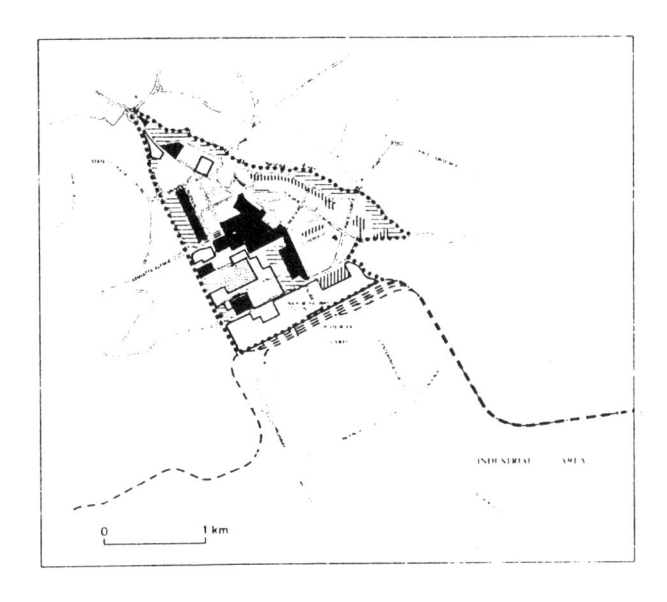

The map of the land use of the central area in 1972, attached to the *Metropolitan Growth Strategy*, indicated a slightly different land use pattern in comparison to the functional areas distinguished some years earlier by Halliman and Morgan.[109] In 1972, two kinds of commercial areas were identified. One included "prestige shops, offices, hotels and entertainments" and was located roughly a block on both sides of Kenyatta Avenue and Government Road south of Biashara Street; smaller fragments – not presented by Halliman and Morgan – included Koinange Street between Kenyatta Avenue and University Way, the southwestern corner of the city center between Haile Selassie Avenue and Harambee Avenue, and two international hotels. The other commercial area contained "secondary shops, offices etc." – Halliman and Morgan's "2nd shopping area" – and was located north and northeast of the prestigious commercial area; this area extended partly into the area which Halliman and Morgan had identified as the "1st shopping area." Government functions mostly surrounded the open space between the Law Courts and Uhuru Highway and extended along Harambee Avenue. Large portions of undeveloped land (not included in Halliman's and Morgan's study) were located in three areas: on the eastern side of Uhuru Highway between Kenyatta Avenue and University Way, immediately adjacent to and southwest of the prestigious commercial area approximately between the Law Courts and Government Road/Nkrumah Lane, and the northeastern banks of the Nairobi River next to Ngara. (*Fig. 13.8*)

In the *Metropolitan Growth Strategy*, the capital was perceived within a regional context, extending beyond the city boundaries. The recommended strategies included the decentralization of industrial development from the existing industrial area, established in the *Master Plan* of 1948 southeast of

---

109 For the map by Halliman and Morgan, see above.

the railway station, to several industrial areas dispersed in the urban structure:

> restrictions [should] be placed upon the growth of the present . . . industrial area, linked with a policy for the development of . . . additional industrial employment centers at Dagoretti, Karen/Langata, Wilson Airport, Dandora, Ruaraka and Kassarani . . . [In the existing industrial area] additional development should be limited to industries that are capital intensive and with consequent low levels of employment, and to those that are directly related to central area functions.[110]

A similar decentralization was proposed for the commercial functions, with restrictions on the growth of the existing city center, the new commercial centers receiving the increase of commercial activities.[111] In an analysis of the plans for Nairobi between 1900 and 1980, Sören Emig and Zahir Ismael criticized the arguments presented in support of the decentralization proposals, pointing out that in the *Metropolitan Growth Strategy*, the hazards of the industrial areas would surround the workers' housing areas located next to them. The advantages of the reduction of the need of mechanical transport for the workers and consequently of municipal investments in roads and public transport was, according to Emig and Ismael, actually a transfer of the benefits to the investors, since the City would be expected to provide access by road and rail to the new industrial areas. The decentralization of the commercial center, including the administrative functions, international agencies, tourist services, and the like, Emig and Ismael dismissed as a "far fetched one that will not materialize."[112]

In the *Metropolitan Growth Strategy*, the planning of the road network (*Fig. 13.9*) received even more attention than it had in the *Master Plan* of 1948. For each population distribution alternative, there were corresponding plans for long term transportation requirements and public transportation networks. The proposed traffic system was based on English models[113] – as the *Master Plan* of 1948 had been – using highways of ten, twelve, or even twenty lanes organized into a hierarchy of importance, the roads leading to the city center and to the industrial area highest on the hierarchy. Thus not only Uhuru Highway but also major roads like Fort Hall Road and Ngong Road, old roads passing through existing residential areas, were proposed to be reconstructed into roads with ten or eighteen lanes.[114] If implemented, this would have effectively destroyed those parts of the residential areas located

---

110 *Metropolitan Growth Strategy*, vol.I, Summary of findings and recommendations, p.101, quoted in Emig and Ismael 1980, 63.
111 *Metropolitan Growth Strategy*, quoted in Emig and Ismael 1980, 65.
112 Emig and Ismael 1980, 63ff.
113 Among the models, Emig and Ismael (1980, 66) identified the transportation plan for Manchester and another for South Hampshire by Colin Buchanan. (In the text, the Manchester plan was mistakenly dated as "1984".)
114 *Metropolitan Growth Strategy*, Appendix II: Figs. 4.29, 4.30 and 4.31, quoted in Emig and Ismael 1980, 67f.

Fig. 13.9 Map: Proposed transport network in the central area

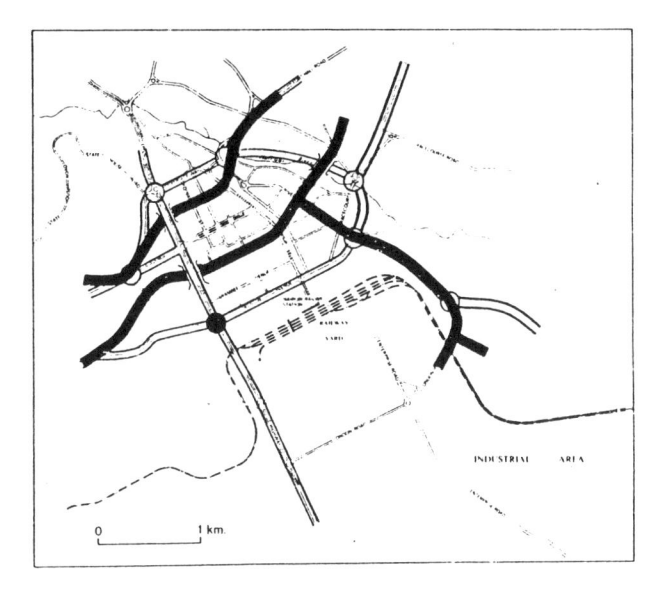

closest to the roads and affected the more distant parts.

For the central area, the *Metropolitan Growth Strategy* included a transport network proposal with major changes to the existing road network. It was suggested that a new 6-lane road system pass the center on the north, connecting the roads leading to the western and the eastern parts of the city by widening existing streets and constructing new ones, including a highway along the Nairobi River. The proposal also contained mass transit routes, to be established as totally new links through the center: one from Valley Road through the Uhuru Park and under Uhuru Highway, via Moktar Daddah Street to Fort Hall Road, the other from the Hill through Uhuru Park and under Uhuru Highway, via City Hall Way and Accra Road, through the River Road area on a new street opened into the existing urban structure, across the Nairobi River to Park Road. In the central area, then, the transport network proposal would require new roads to be built both along and across the Nairobi River valley, through two large parks, under the main Uhuru Highway at two points, and through a partial demolition of an existing urban area.

In describing the *Metropolitan Growth Strategy*, Emig and Ismael indicated that the main task of the team of experts was to

> secure the safety of the upper class by strengthening its hold on the existing upper class residential areas and make only minor expansions near to the existing upper class residential areas, so that there occurs no infiltration, human or industrial, close by which will threaten their spacious surroundings.[115]

Thus the old segregationist traditions based on class were to be retained in the proposal:

---

115 Emig and Ismael 1980, 60.

(a) "areas north of the old city" – between the existing upper class residential areas of Kabete and Muthaiga, around the "coffee plantations and the Spring Valley and Ridgeway Estates" be developed "as at present, of low densities for high income households."

(b) "areas south of the old city" – "which includes Kibera, Wilson Airport and land south of the Industrial Area be developed primarily for low and middle income housing."[116]

For Emig and Ismael, then, the *Metropolitan Growth Strategy* was both an instrument to establish and present the development possibilities of Nairobi to potential investors, and a means of protecting the interests of the existing upper class; the first to attract international businesses, the second to preserve the status quo within the city. This the master plan was geared to do, not as an openly political statement, but as a statistically and technically founded report, that is, as politically neutral, as Emig and Ismael formulated it:

> The *Metropolitan Growth Strategy*, as part of the total state intervention, continues the liberal ideology that dominated the *Master Plan* [of 1948]. The politicians assign technicians to plan, so that the plan can be characterized as politically neutral.[117]

The *Metropolitan Growth Strategy*, according to Emig and Ismael, concealed the thoroughly political character of planning in Nairobi. They implied that the planning technique used – they called it "diluted functionalism" – was employed for the division of the working class and the increasing unification of the ruling class by means of decentralization, both of residential areas and industrial areas, the spatial interventions concealing political intentions:

> The *Metropolitan Growth Strategy* seems to be a distinguished representative of the trend towards the transformation of physical planning into a political strategy – or rather, the politicizing of urban planning through the use of spatial intervention as a means of political control.[118]

Similarly, Finn Barnow has described the *Metropolitan Growth Strategy* as a means to

> create the best possible services for the most advanced functions of the neocolonial society, namely to further the multinational companies' freedom and opportunities to invest in Nairobi. In this sense, the plan proposal is elitist and liberal.[119]

---

116 Emig and Ismael 1980, 60; the quotations within are from the *Metropolitan Growth Strategy*, paragraphs 102 and 103.
117 Emig and Ismael 1980, 80.
118 Emig and Ismael 1980, 82.
119 "Sammenfattende fremtraeder planen som et redskab til at skabe de bedst mulige betingelser for det ny-koloniale samfunds mest avancerede funktioner, nemlig at fremme de multinationale selskabers investeringsfrihed og -muligheter i Nairobi. Planforslaget er i denne forstand *elitaert* og *liberalt*." Barnow 1990, 152. N.b. Finn Barnow was an advisor to Emig and Ismael 1980.

Barnow also identified the *Metropolitan Growth Strategy* as a combination of European decentralization plans in the 1960s.[120]

Although the *Metropolitan Growth Strategy* can be perceived as an adaptation of European decentralization plans fashionable at the time, connecting the development of Nairobi with its regional surroundings, it also contained strong standpoints in terms of the existing and expanding core. In many respects, the approaches employed in the *Metropolitan Growth Strategy* repeated ones already presented in the *Master Plan* of 1948. In both, functional segregation and zoning were adopted as self-evident without argumentation. Also in both, the development of the urban structure of the city as a totality was based on the road network. In the *Master Plan*, the most significant road proposal had been connected to the building of a north-south highway in place of the realigned railway line, with the distribution of traffic to and from the city center as the governing idea behind the proposals on the road network. In the *Metropolitan Growth Strategy*, the organization of east-west traffic past the city center was presented as the main principle, emphasizing the separation of mass transit routes (i.e. public transportation) from other kinds of roads. The "Swamp Parkway" starting from the major "traffic circus" at Ainsworth Bridge, proposed in 1948, was in the 1972 plan converted into an unnamed stretch of a 6-lane road connected further south to University Way. The new residential areas were mostly proposed for publicly-owned land.

In both plans, it was suggested that residential areas for workers (i.e. potential areas for public housing projects) be located next to the industrial area for economic reasons. Because the industrial areas were decentralized in the *Metropolitan Growth Strategy*, this also supported the dispersal of the workers' residential areas – not advocated in the plan of 1948. The main differences between the *Master Plan* of 1948 and the *Metropolitan Growth Strategy* of 1972 were attached to the urban forms of the city center. The plans for the "Kenya Center" as the core of the colonial capital had been an essential part of the *Master Plan*; nothing like it was included in the *Metropolitan Growth Strategy*. In 1972, the city center was perceived as a combination of existing commercial and administrative buildings next to open spaces and "undeveloped" areas. The *Master Plan* had been criticized as technical and unpolitical, but these criteria fit the *Metropolitan Growth Strategy* even better. Both in the presentation of the plans and in the background material, simplified schematic drawings off-scale, figures on map bases, and mathematic calculations – that is, abstractions of the planned city – dominated, while the three-dimensional, physical aspects of the planned city were largely excluded. The consequences of the plan to the urban forms of Nairobi, as the planners perceived them, seemed to have been more important in the conception of the *Master Plan* of 1948 than in the

---

120 Barnow 1990, 155.

Metropolitan Growth Strategy of 1972.

An examination of a more recent map of Nairobi showed that by 1981, few of the proposals of the *Metropolitan Growth Strategy* had been implemented.[121] The clearest changes had been executed in the construction of residential areas, particularly of the Dandora Estate northeast of the city center, outside the Outer Ring Road. Another residential development had been begun along Langata Road near the Nairobi Dam, to the southwest of the city center. None of the major new roads had been constructed: neither the new road proposed along the Nairobi River, the roads from the Hill to the city center to pass through the parks and under Uhuru Highway, nor the street which was to cut through the River Road area. Improvements had been made to the road to Thika northeast of Nairobi, the *Metropolitan Growth Strategy*'s selected direction of expansion.

Of the background reports of the Urban Study Group, one of the most referred to studies was Samson M. Kimani's analysis of the structure of land ownership in 1970 in Nairobi within its pre-1963 boundaries. Kimani's data was from the Valuation Rolls of the City Council and accounted for over half of the built-up area and over three-fourths of the rateable value of land in the city.[122] Because large portions of land owned by the City Council or the Kenya Government were exempt from taxes and thus not assessed for rating,[123] it must be emphasized that the figures Kimani showed did not present a comprehensive view of land ownership patterns in Nairobi in 1970. Kimani estimated that in 1970, over 60% of the plots studied, both in terms of number of plots and acreage and in terms of value, were owned by Asians, Europeans, and businesses, and that

> taking into account the fact that most of the businesses are Asian-owned, there is no doubt that the Asian community has the lion's share of the City's land. [Individually,] Europeans own as much land as Asians.[124]

The European-owned land was mainly composed of large residential plots and the Asian-owned land of plots usually small but high-valued. Africans owned barely 3.9% of the acreage studied, representing 2.7% of the value gathered. In relation to the population, Kimani calculated that there was 1 acre of African-owned land for every 800 Africans, 1 acre of Asian-owned land for every 32 Asians, and 1 acre of European-owned land for every 7

---

121 City of Nairobi, Map and Guide, 1:20,000, SK, revised from aerial photography (August 1970, January 1971, 1976, and 1978) and the Schedule of New Street Names for the City Area (1974), reprinted 9/1981.
122 Kimani 1972, 379f. See also Kimani, "Spatial Structure of Land Values in Nairobi, Kenya", *Tijdschrift voor Economische en Sociale Geografie*, 1972, vol.63:2, 105-114, quoted in Soja 1979.
123 Kimani 1972, 382f.
124 Kimani 1972, 382. The source of the statement that most businesses were Asian-owned was not given.

Europeans.[125]

The distribution of ownership varied in different parts of the city. Kimani noted that individually owned plots predominated in western and northern Nairobi, while the southern and eastern parts contained relatively little privately owned land. Judging from the figure presented by Kimani, this generalization may be questioned in relation to some areas.[126] On the west, which Kimani identified as mostly privately owned, in several areas less than half of the plots were privately owned: for example, only about a third in Nairobi Hill, less than a quarter in the Delamere division (south of Nairobi Hill), very little in the Hospital division, some two fifths in Woodley, and about a third in Kileleshwa seemed to have been privately owned. On the east, which Kimani described as having very little individually owned land, some areas nevertheless included considerable portions of such land: for example, the three divisions comprising Mathare and Eastleigh seemed to have contained from around three to four fifths of individually owned land, while even in the Industrial area (the division identified as "London") and Nairobi South, individual ownership represented around a quarter or a third of the total.

Kimani also indicated that in relation to racial groups,

> most of the privately owned land in the northern and western areas (except Parklands) is held by Europeans, and much smaller amounts by Asians and Africans. In Parklands, Ngara, Juja, Eastleigh and Mathare, the Asians dominate by owning more than 50% of the acreage collected. In these same divisions and also in the so-called "traditional African locations," little land is owned by indigenous Africans, except in Bahati and Eastleigh South where substantial amounts (about 25% and over) of highly fragmented land is in their hands.[127]

He noted that over half of the land owned by Africans was not located in areas "traditionally reserved for Africans" but in the areas formerly identified for European or Asian occupation, mentioning that

> penetration of Africans into the European domain is rather recent and most likely occurred during the post-independence period (1963-1970).[128]

As the European colonialists expressly restricted African ownership of land in the areas attributed to Europeans, this is not surprising; for the Africans, this land was accessible not "most likely" but definitely only after independ-

---

125 Kimani 1972, 383. The population figures were based on the 1969 census, excluding the 1963 boundary extension.
126 Fig.2: Nairobi area: Collected acreage and ownership by enumeration divisions (Kimani 1972, 384). Kimani identified ownership between African, Asian, and European individuals, and by the Kenya Government, Nairobi City Council, Foreign Governments, Businesses, the East African Community, and others such as religious bodies, clubs etc.
127 Kimani 1972, 385.
128 Kimani 1972, 385.

ence. That the Africans owned more land in the western and northern parts of the city may also have been due to the availability of land. In the traditional African areas like Pumwani – Kimani even included Kaloleni, Mbotela, Makadara, Jerusalem, Doonholm, Maringo, and Jericho, that is, areas built during or after the Second World War, in the "traditional [sic] African areas"[129] – land was publicly owned both before independence and after it; it was only leased to individuals and thus not available for purchase. After independence, the land previously owned by European or Asian individuals became available for Africans as well.

The land rated highest in value was mainly located in the city center, in Ngara north of it, and in the industrial area east of it, these divisions comprising almost two-thirds of the total values.[130] As Edward W. Soja has indicated, Kimani also noted that land in the European sector seemed to be consistently undervalued in relation to its location and density, while land in the African sector seemed to be as consistently overvalued, even though the infrastructure in these areas was less developed than in the European areas.[131] Soja attributed this to the colonial history of land ownership:

> This pattern almost surely evolved early in the colonial period and worked effectively over time to subsidize European and to some extent Asian urban settlement in much the same way that the White Highlands were subsidized through the underdevelopment of the African rural economy. Here is further evidence of the depth to which colonial and postcolonial underdevelopment has tightly structured the spatial organization of East Africa.[132]

Kimani indicated that with the restrictions on occupation and ownership of residential land, imposed by the colonialists, the land accessible to non-Europeans was in low supply and in high demand, resulting in an elevated price level.[133]

It does not seem possible to explain conclusively the continuation of the value pattern where plots in the former European residential areas were undervalued and those in former African areas overvalued after independence by referring to colonial restrictions which had been discontinued. The amount of publicly owned land may also have affected the valuation in the different parts of the city. For example, in Eastlands, the concentration of public land essentially repeated the colonial situation of low supply and high demand, and may have increased the value of rateable land. In the northern and western parts where land was mostly privately owned, numerous plots were available and the relative demand for them was probably lower than in the eastern parts of Nairobi. The reliability of the Valuation Rolls as indicators of land values

---

129 Kimani 1972, 388.
130 Kimani 1972, 389f.
131 Kimani, "Spatial Structure of Land Values in Nairobi," 1972, quoted in Soja 1979, 43.
132 Soja 1979, 43.
133 Kimani 1972, 395n21.

may also be questioned. For example, Etherton noted that the official figures on which the Valuation Department based its estimates of land values were misleading for land sales in Mathare Valley because the buyers and sellers seemed to declare much lower sums than the real prices in their official documents to reduce their stamp duty.[134] According to Kimani,

> The study . . . demonstrated that a blatant disparity exists between Africans and others in the amount of land acquired . . . The African has suffered deprivation for a long time; yet, most of the current land transactions are going on among the wealthy non-Africans and businesses and mainly for speculative purposes. There can be no doubt that if this trend continues, it can only mean a further guarantee that most of the urban land (especially residential) will remain in [the] possession of non-Africans for a long time to come.[135]

It may be argued that although the study indicated disparities among individual land-owners – at least partially due to biased colonial policies – conclusions on how both privately or publicly owned land was occupied and used, for instance, among different racial or other groups, cannot be drawn on the basis of them.

The residential areas built by public funds may be used as an example. Elkan and Zwanenberg argued in 1975 that since independence,

> overwhelmingly the greater part of official house-building in Nairobi . . . has been for middle-income earners and above.[136]

One of the reasons may have been the processes of Africanization attached to the end of colonialism in Kenya, of which the one directly affecting housing involved the replacement of expatriate civil servants with local ones. Among the higher grade civil servants, the proportion of Africans changed from around 3% in 1957 to 87% by 1971.[137] Of the lower executive and technical staff, at independence less than half were citizens of Kenya, but by 1966, on average three quarters had been Africanized.[138] In the early years of the independent country, public housing was necessary to attract the emerging middle-class comprised of the newly established civil servants, particularly since housing provided by the employer had historically been rooted in Nairobi and colonial Kenya. By the early 1970s, the emphasis on middle-income housing was becoming an object of criticism, with increased discussion of the advantages of housing policies catering to lower income groups. This meant a change in policies. Housing programs favoring the construction of conventional complete dwelling units conforming to accepted

---

134 Etherton 1971, 50.
135 Kimani 1972, 398f.
136 Elkan and Zwanenberg 1975, 670. For similar later comments on public housing in the 1960's and 70's, see Chana 1984, 18.
137 Hake 1977, 245.
138 Ghai 1974, 375.

standards and the demolition of unacceptable shanty developments were discontinued. In their place came policies advocating site and service schemes providing basic services and the upgrading of unauthorized settlements.[139] In an evaluation of the site and services programs in Kenya, T.S. Chana and others showed that site and services schemes had been recommended in the official development plans from independence, the first plan presented for 1964-70.[140] From around 1970, they were complemented with policies intended to improve the basic infrastructure of squatter areas and the houses.

The case of Mathare Valley illuminates how policies towards squatters changed. After independence, the unauthorized settlements in Mathare Valley grew rapidly, as David Etherton observed in his study of the area from aerial photographs taken at two-year intervals. By September 1969, the population was nearly 20,000, living in nine squatter villages built illegally on mostly privately owned land.[141] These villages failed to win the acceptance of the officials both in the Nairobi City Council and in Government, and were under constant threat of demolition.[142] To shield themselves and their homes against harassments the villagers started to form co-operative associations – "companies" in local terminology – for securing land tenure by buying land from the Asian owners. Initially intended as a more protected form of residence for the members (shareholders) and their families, the co-operatives (with the exception of 2 out of 21) gradually transformed into speculators engaged in the building of tenements, that is, into landlords. Between September 1969 and January 1971, the population of Mathare Valley dramatically increased by at least 33,500 inhabitants moving into the 7,628 one-room dwelling units built by the housing companies. *(Fig.13.10)* According to Etherton's study, of the inhabitants, only 7% were company members and 93% were tenants. Most of the companies approached the City Council with demands to remove the squatters.[143] Around 1969, discussions on the improvability of Mathare Valley began. The proposed and partly executed operations included the security of land tenure, the maintenance of a clear water supply, the replacement of the worst pit latrines, the establishment of effective garbage collection and street lighting, and the

Fig. 13.10 Company housing in Mathare Valley

---

139 For a description of the concept of site and services, see above. World Bank loans for Nairobi housing in the mid-1970's included a condition against the demolition of substandard unauthorized settlements (Senga et al, *Monitoring and Evaluation Study of Dandora Community Development Project*, MEDIS report 3, Nairobi, 1977, 25, quoted in Andreasen 1987, 36). On Nairobi as center for high-income staff in the 1960's and 70's, see also Obudho 1979, 253.
140 Chana et al 1979, 20.
141 Etherton 1971, 10f., 16, 25.
142 See above.
143 Etherton 1971, 46ff. The population increase between 1969 and 1971 in the squatter villages was not studied, but Etherton noted that any increase must have occurred within the existing villages, since no new land was occupied by squatters by 1971. In the census of 1969, the population of Mathare was given as 21,375, and in the census of 1979, as 68,456 (Kenya Population Census, [1969], Ministry of Finance and Economic Planning, Nairobi, 1970, 2-3; Kenya Population Census, 1979, Ministry of Finance and Economic Planning, Nairobi, June 1981; quoted in Barnow et al 1983, 67, 82).

improvement of the vehicle access road.[144] Jörgen Andreasen noted laconically that after demolitions ceased in Mathare Valley in 1971, "plans for upgrading brought new hope (to the landlords)."[145]

Towards the end of the 1970s, the site and services strategy for catering to the needs of the low-income groups had become "the overriding official policy which is no longer open to negotiation."[146] In the *Development Plan for 1979-83*, the urban housing program included both site and services schemes and squatter upgrading.[147] The first site and services project to be initiated on the basis of the Nairobi *Metropolitan Growth Strategy* was Dandora, located some 10 km to the northeast of the city center, outside the Outer Ring Road. The Nairobi City Council made available 350 hectares of land for the development of 6,000 serviced plots for low-income families. The first phase of Dandora was a pilot project, conceived as a model and basis of evaluation for future low-income residential development projects in Kenya. Involved in the planning, funding and management were the Nairobi City Council, the Government of Kenya, the World Bank, the International Bank for Reconstruction and Development, and the International Development Agency. Construction started in 1975.[148] (*Figs. 13.11, 13.12*)

---

144 Hake 1977, chapter 10, esp.168ff; Etherton 1971, section E, 65-69.
145 Andreasen 1987, 36.
146 Chana et al 1979, 21.
147 Development Plan 1979-1983, vol.I, 172f.
148 Soni 1980, 4; Chana 1984, 20ff.; see also Malombe 1992, 34f.

Fig. 13.11 Layout plan: Dandora area, phase I

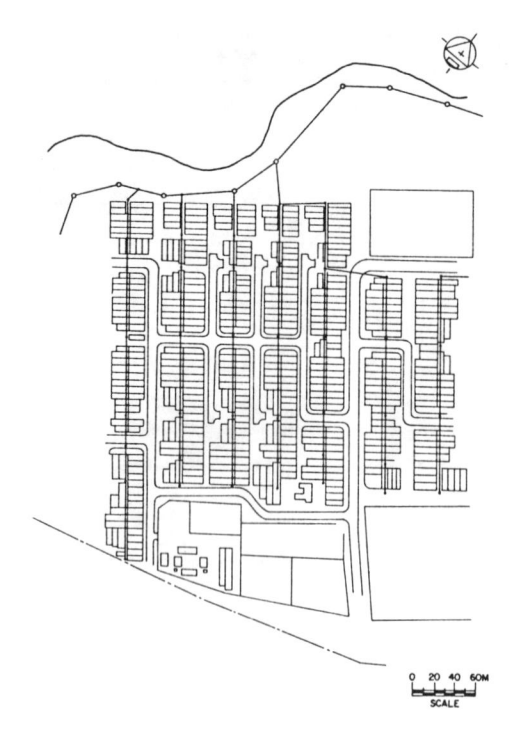

Fig. 13.12 Dandora area

In the urban development of Nairobi in the 1970s and early 80s, the input of international agencies had considerably increased from colonial times.[149] Agencies such as the United Nations Development Program, the World Bank, the International Development Association as well as national agencies such as the United States Agency for International Development, and the Overseas Development Administration (of Britain), have been involved not only in giving aid and technical assistance in terms of funding or loans, but also in participating in the planning and construction of both residential areas and infrastructure. Many of the publicly funded housing projects – including, for example, Umoja and Buru Buru – have contained input from international agencies.[150]

By 1979, the population of Nairobi had increased to nearly 830,000.[151] The number of non-Africans had continued to decrease, both absolutely and proportionately. In 1962, the population of some 267,000 had included 159,000 Africans (about 60%), 86,000 Asians (32%), and 21,000 Europeans (8%). Seventeen years later in 1979, there were 770,000 Africans (93%), 39,000 Asians (5%), and 19,000 Europeans (2%).[152] Comparing the ethnic

---

149 On the increased role of international agencies in East Africa, see Ghai 1974, 379.
150 For a description of the Buru Buru and Umoja residential areas and examples of dwellings, see below, chapter 18.
151 Kenya Population Census, 1979 (Ministry of Economic Planning and Development, Nairobi, June 1981) quoted in Barnow et al 1983, 82.
152 Kenya Population Census 1962, quoted in Barnow et al 1983, 57; Kenya Population Census 1979, quoted in O'Connor 1983, 116. The percentages have not been adopted from O'Connor's table but calculated on the basis of his figures (in his table, Asians in 1979

240 ■ PART III HISTORIES OF URBAN FORM IN NAIROBI

developments from colonial times to post-independence in different countries of tropical Africa, Anthony O'Connor noted that the greatest changes occurred in Zambia and Kenya which many Europeans perceived as their country until independence.[153] The correspondence between race and income (or class, as some would define it) according to which generally in colonial Nairobi, the Europeans formed the high-income group, the Asians the middle-income group, and the Africans the low-income group had, after independence, disintegrated, Africans now dominating all three groups. Spatially, however, the urban patterns which were established during colonialism seem to have persisted. In the city center and some residential areas, the non-African influences continued to exist, not only because of historical reasons, but because the large international community and expanding tourism supported the European – and, to an extent, the Asian – urban forms and practices. In describing the morphology of Nairobi, O'Connor noted that the administrative, commercial, and industrial zones could be clearly distinguished. He also indicated that the residential areas differed not only in terms of some having been planned and others having developed spontaneously, but also in their

---

accounted for 4% of the total). All the figures quoted include both Kenya nationals and other nationalities. E.g. of the Europeans in 1979, 2,000 were Kenyan Europeans and 17,000 other Europeans. (O'Connor's figures for 1979 are not exactly the same as in his tables on p.103.) For comparison, in 1969, the population of 509,000 included 421,000 Africans (83%), 67,000 Asians (13%), and 20,000 Europeans (4%) (Kenya Population Census 1969, quoted in O'Connor op.cit.).

153 O'Connor 1983, 104.

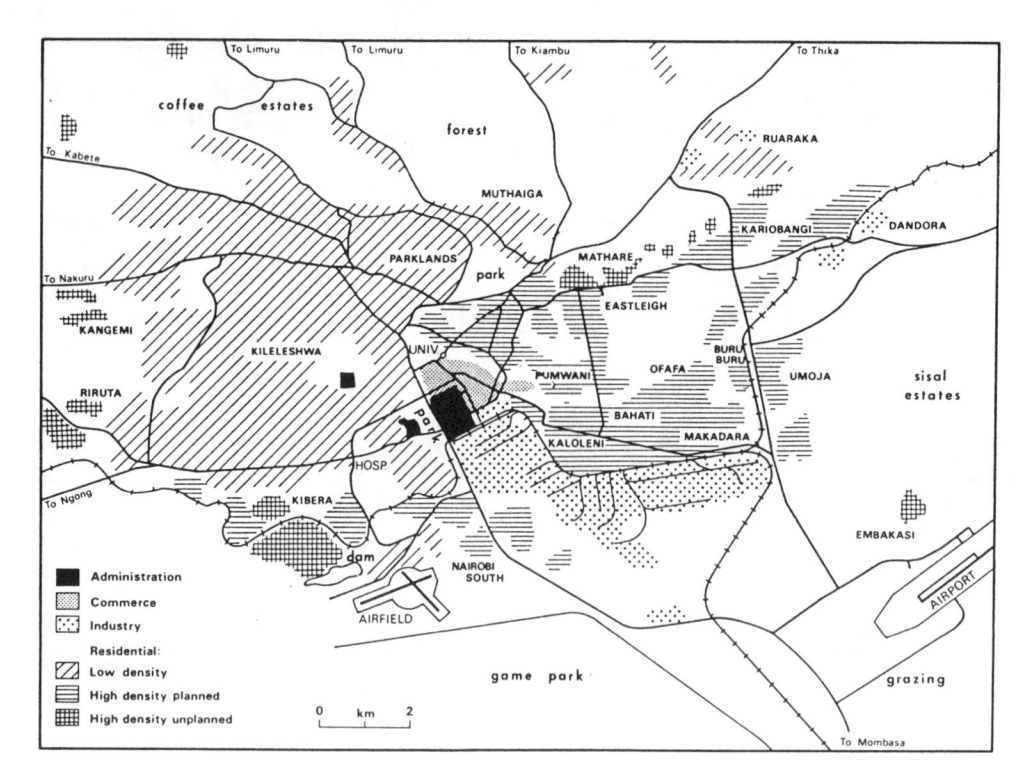

appearance and functioning, some resembling European high-class suburbs, others African rural areas. In the map showing the physical structure of Nairobi, the administrative area filled the "City Block" bounded by Uhuru Highway, Kenyatta Avenue, Moi Avenue, and the railway line (*Fig. 13.13*).[154] Thus the demarcation of the administrative area by O'Connor was considerably larger than that shown in the land use map of the central area in the *Metropolitan Growth Strategy* where the government and the open space next to it accounted for only about a third of O'Connor's area. According to O'Connor, the contrasts of residential densities in Nairobi, existing from its foundation, still remained in 1983, maybe even more extremely (*Fig. 13.14*). In the western sector, during colonial times restricted to Europeans, the 1962 census recorded a density of three dwellings and fifteen persons per hectare; in 1983, the density was still under nineteen persons per hectare. In the Parklands-Eastleigh area, earlier identified as Asian, in 1962 there were eleven dwellings and 120 persons per hectare; in 1983, the density was between 79 and 199 persons per hectare. In the eastern sector, colonially defined as African, in 1962 the density was 65 dwellings and 320 persons per hectare; in 1983, O'Connor estimated it as over 200 persons per hectare.[155]

---

154 O'Connor 1983, 198; neither the source nor its date was given. Moi Avenue was formerly Government Road.
155 O'Connor 1983, 214.

Fig. 13.13 Map:
Physical structure

Fig. 13.14 Map:
Residential densities

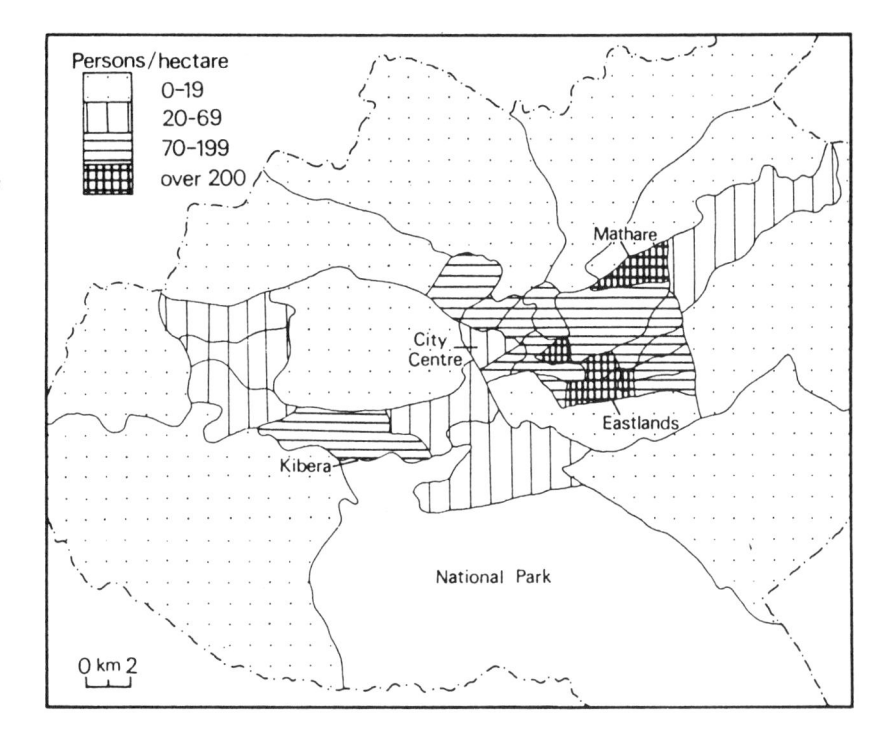

A comparison of maps of 1960 and 1970 indicated that most of the large-scale building of this period had taken place at the edge of the built urban structure. The more extensive new areas were built along Thika Road to the northeast, near the Outer Ring Road to the east, near Dagoretti Corner south of Ngong Road, in Kileleshwa and Lavington to the west, and in Spring Valley to the northeast, all located more or less at the edges of the existing town. Concentrations of smaller infill areas were built in the Hill to the west of the city center, Chiromo north of it, the industrial area, Eastleigh, and Parklands.[156] Changes in the city center may be observed from maps of 1973[157] and 1978,[158] and an aerial photograph of 1980.[159] In the map of 1973, two alterations can already be perceived in the road network compared to earlier maps. One of these was the construction of an enormous roundabout with a diameter of over 200 meters on the Nairobi River between the city center

---

156 Barnow et al 1983, 56, 66. The map marked 1960 was based on City of Nairobi, Map and Guide (SK 1962); the one marked 1970 on City of Nairobi, Map 1:20,000 (February 1968), City of Nairobi, Map and Guide 1:20,000 (July 1972) and aerial photographs (SK, December 1971-January 1972). Both maps were evaluated by Barnow et al (1983, 86f.) as accurate; however, for example Kibera southwest of the city center was excluded from the 1960 map, although the area was established already in the 1910's and had some 3,000 inhabitants in 1958 (see e.g. Hake 1977, 96). In the 1970 map, Kibera was identified as a completely newly built area, although large sections existed before 1960.
157 Map 1:14,000, Barnow 1990, 207.
158 City of Nairobi, Map and Guide, 1:20,000, 1978, revised from aerial photography in 1970, 1971, and 1976, and the Schedule of New Street Names for City Area, 1974.
159 SK, aerial photograph, sheet 2210, 1:6000.

and Ngara, connecting Moi Avenue and University Way on its south and west to Muranga Road on its northeast, and providing a parking area in the middle. The other was the redirection of northbound traffic on Nairobi's oldest road – Government Road, initially linking the railway station with the government offices, later renamed Moi Avenue: the connection to Uhuru Highway at Chiromo (Ainsworth Bridge) was cut off, the traffic lead via University Way, the junction at Government Road (its northern part renamed Harry Thuku Road) moved westward and a new building (the central police station) erected on the land left from the redirection, that is, in the middle of the former Government Road. (*Fig. 13.15*)

The maps and aerial photograph also indicated that building in the city center had been concentrated on the area immediately adjacent to the open space of the administrative center which the experts of the *Master Plan* of 1948 had called Kenya Center. Public buildings had been constructed to its south along Harambee Avenue and Haile Selassie Avenue, including institutions such as the President's Office, the Vice-President's Office, the

Fig. 13.15 Map: Nairobi city center in 1973

Fig. 13.16 Nairobi city center from the Hill, 1973

Treasury, the Central Bank of Kenya, the State Law Office, the Lands Department, and the Map Office. At the other end of the open space west of Uhuru Highway and Uhuru Park, additional administrative buildings on the Hill included the Ministries of Agriculture, Health, and Community Affairs. The compound for the Forestry Department was located in Uhuru Park and adjacent to Kenyatta Avenue. Two international hotels were also constructed at the northern edge of the open space, one east of Uhuru Highway, the other west of it, on the northern side of Kenyatta Avenue. The core of the central open space was surrounded on three sides with major landmarks: the Law Courts to the east, the City Hall to the north, and Kenyatta Conference Center to the south. Kenyatta Conference Center was designed as a crown to the administrative core, its distinct forms highly visible from different parts of the city, marking the point of orientation. The two-part construction was designed by K.H. Nostvik of Norway in 1973. In an overview of post-independence architecture in Africa, David Aradeon described the building as

> an attempt to adapt an African architectural form, a Musenge house, to a large-scale contemporary programme; the two main elements, a thirty-two storey office tower and an amphitheatre conference hall, are set on a podium which houses the reception area, lecture theatre, banks and a post office.[160]

A second urban focus thus had begun to emerge around the southern part of Government Road and on Harambee Avenue. In the older commercial center, high-rise office buildings were being constructed along the middle part of

---

160 David Aradeon in Fletcher 1987, 1393.

Fig. 13.17 Moi Avenue, southern part, 1980s

Fig. 13.18 Kenyatta Avenue with Stanley Hotel and the ICEA skyscraper, 1983

Government Road (between City Hall Way and Kenyatta Avenue) and on Kenyatta Avenue. Another commercial concentration had begun to develop in the northwestern section of the city center, on the western side of Koinange Street. In the "triangle" to the north – in the *Master Plan* of 1948 proposed as the location for cultural institutions – were the main buildings of the University encircling the central green. To its west, at the northwestern point of entry to the city center, was a collection of religious buildings such as the Synagogue, the Lutheran Church, and St.Paul's Church, and a little farther, St.Andrew's Church.

With few exceptions – Kenyatta Conference Center being the most visible of them – the new administrative and commercial buildings in the city center

Fig. 13.19 Biashara Street and City Market, with Koinange Street to the right, 1980s

Fig. 13.20 Law Courts and the Kenyatta Conference Center, 1987

conformed to the modernistic standards of the "International Style." Photographs of the city center in the 1970s and early 1980s illustrated this.[161] One of the most popular views showed the administrative center, with the Law Courts and the Kenyatta Conference Center in the middle, framed by the modern ornamented boxes floating in the open space, most of the unbuilt ground area used for parking cars. In these views, the point of observation was located on – or, in the case of aerial photographs, above – the Hill, the

---

161 For example, photographs in the City of Nairobi Map and Guide, 1978; the cover in Barnow 1990; postcards; *Kenya Insight Guide* 1985.

exact position which in the *Master Plan* of 1948 had been conceived as the location of the prime governmental buildings. In these photographs, the expanse of open space and the low-density areas around the center were left outside the picture. (*Fig. 13.16*) Other popular views included street views of the southern more modern part of Government Road (Moi Avenue) and pictures of individual buildings such as the Parliament Building, the Kenyatta Conference Center, and the Hilton Hotel, a conspicuous landmark at the corner of Government Road and City Hall Way marking the end of Kimathi Street. All of these photographs illustrated the modernistic character – of the 1960s and after style – of the city center. Much rarer were photographs of Kenyatta Avenue with its mixture of buildings from different decades of the history of the city. The oldest parts of the city center, parts of streets like Government Road between Biashara Street (earlier Bazaar Street) and Kenyatta Avenue or River Road were not popular objects in the published contemporary photographs of central Nairobi. (*Fig. 13.17 - 13.20*)

Views of Nairobi were also articulated in writing, but the impressions differed from those expressed in photographs. For example, around 1970, the Swedish writer Ronny Ambjörnsson described Nairobi:

> The temporary European visitor in Nairobi does not meet any stagnation and underdevelopment. On the contrary, he walks into a city which could be anywhere in Europe. Everywhere buildings are being torn down and built, streets are being widened and new buildings grow like skyscrapers from the earth. A casino, hotels, bank palaces, government buildings, police buildings, parking houses, palaces of oil and insurance companies with texts in Latin: Caltex House, Agip House, New Jogoo House, Prudential Assurance Building (Fortis qui prudens), Development House, Silo Park House, all in a nice and illustrious mixture. Highest of all rises, as it should, the twenty-story high Hilton Hotel, from whose top floors one can barely feel the shanty towns far away at the edges; one is too high up be able to distinguish any details.
>
> If one takes the trouble to go out eastward, the houses change after each block. They continue to shrink until one finds oneself on the other side of the Nairobi River, a sewage ditch which separates the town itself from the African housing areas. Along the Nairobi River the Africans have pitched their huts of made of sacks and pieces of wood. They are waiting for a job. Some have waited two years, others longer. Some have a piece of land on the reserves where the family is waiting, others have no land at all. They live with their family behind the sacks. These sack-towns do not make any pleasant view, they are hardly even picturesque. They may not even be hygienic ... In Kenya, demolitions are organized so that tourists will get air and light. But people continue to live in the same place now under canvases and boxes.[162]

---

162 Ambjörnsson 1971, 169f, my translation. For the original text in Swedish, see Appendix 4.

In a sense, Ambjörnsson's view of Nairobi as a dual city was a combination of the two earlier conceptions: Halliman's and Morgan's view in 1967 of a capital of a recently independent African country progressing towards a modern European-type metropolis and Cox' concept, around the same time, of an urban conglomeration growing without control, the poorer inhabitants making their own urban forms and practices.[163] In Ambjörnsson's description, the polarities seem more pronounced: business palaces and tourists are seen against sack-towns and the urban poor. Judging from the recurring descriptions, these kinds of dramatizations seem to have appealed to the Euro-American readership. For example, in February 1983, the journal *African Business* started its special issue on Kenya with an overview article carrying a very similar dramatization:

> Despite the events of 1 August 1982, the casual visitor to Nairobi is unlikely to detect much change. Kenya's capital city, with its European ambience, its modern skylines and its plenteous Mercedes and Volvos, still exudes the air of prosperity. Council workers can be seen regularly pruning the brilliant displays of bougainvillea that bedeck the city's main thoroughfare, Uhuru Highway. Old Africa hands still pull into Nairobi and sigh with relief as they relax with their cold beers at such favourite haunts as the Norfolk bar. To many, Nairobi is the place where things still work. The phone service, for example, has been improved tremendously in the past year, and in 1983 Kenyans will be able to dial direct abroad. Even if one edges out of Nairobi on the right roads one will come across a string of comfortable suburbs.
>
> But only if one scratches at this glossy surface and starts to stray into some of the downtown slum areas such as Mathare Valley, which shelter the majority of Nairobi's population, or into the incredibly densely populated and agriculturally rich Kiambu district adjacent to Nairobi, does one begin to see that the realities now facing Kenya are not so comfortable. In some cases they are frightening.[164]

In both descriptions, the view of Nairobi as a dual city offering the latest modern technology and comforts side by side with primitive living conditions and insalubrity is emphasized by excluding the whole range of ways of life between the two; could it be that for reasons of drama, the play has to be put in a setting with only the starkest contrasts?

The series of maps compiled by Finn Barnow and others in 1983 illuminates the changes in the built structure of Nairobi between 1900 and 1970. (*Fig. 13.21*) The modest beginnings around a railway depot in no way heralded the realities of the metropolis of over half a million inhabitants some seventy or eighty years later. During the first decades, the core of the town barely extended beyond short stretches of a handful of roads, with the dwelling groups dispersed in the surrounding landscape. By the Second World War,

---

163 For Halliman and Morgan's and Cox' views, see above.
164 Robert Shaw, "Harsh realities and hard options" in *African Business*, February 1983, 23.

1900

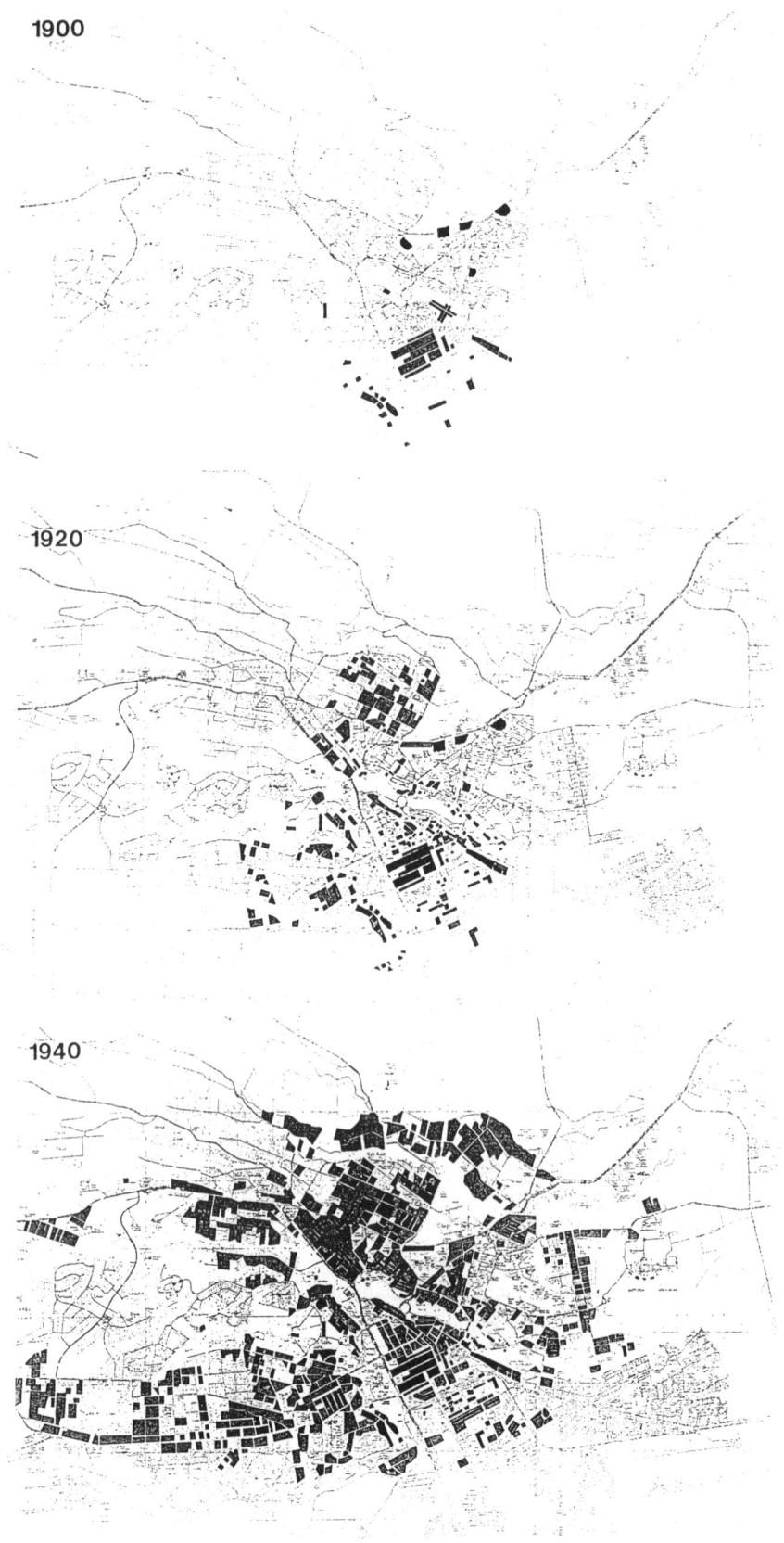

1920

1940

Fig. 13.21 Maps: The built structure of Nairobi, 1900, 1920, 1940, 1950, 1960, and 1970

1950

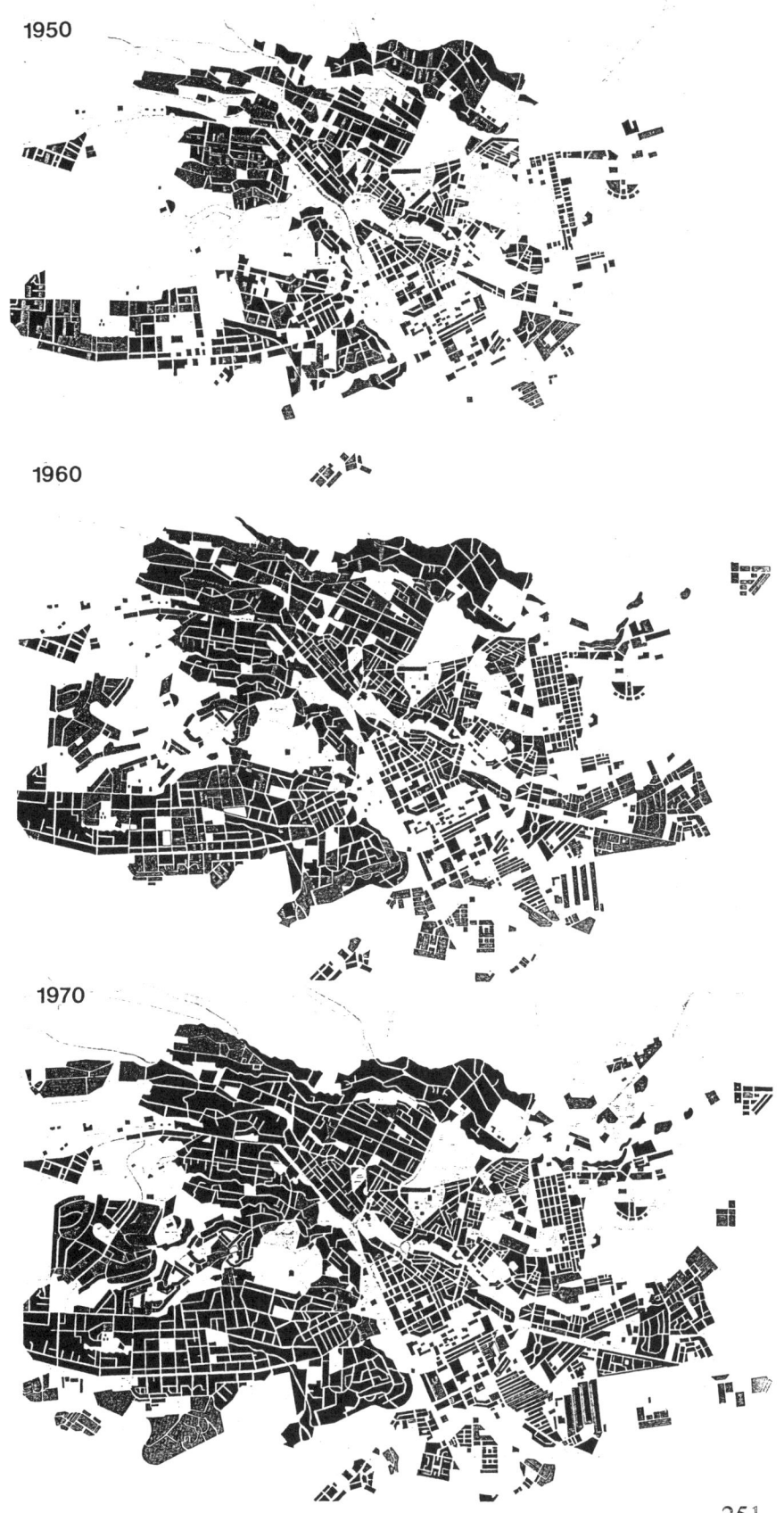

1960

1970

CHAPTER 13 MODERNIZING THE AFRICAN METROPOLIS, 1963–1983 ■ 251

Nairobi had gradually grown into a town with characteristics which could be described as culturally European, such as a commercial center, lushy suburbs, and a system of public services, but also those displaying the cultures of Asian – and to some extent African – communities, particularly in the functionally integrated and densely built areas in and near the center. By the 1960s, much of the present urban structure of Nairobi had already been established with the beginning of the industrial area to the south of the core and the erection of the publicly funded residential areas on the level land to its east. The map of 1970 indicates some of the tendencies of development realized later: the intensification of land especially in and around the center, the outward extension of the urban structure particularly along the main thoroughfares, and the establishment of the new dwelling areas to the east of the city center.[165]

By 1983, compared to Nairobi at independence, both the urban conglomeration as a whole and its center had changed. The primacy of the city center, so evident in the early 1960s, had been replaced by a chain of sub-centers in the residential areas, with the largest one at Westlands attracting not only commercial services but also companies and hotels. Residential areas were spreading further into the surroundings, also outside the city boundary, indicating that the regional emphasis of the *Metropolitan Growth Strategy* of 1972 was becoming materialized. Within the city, Eastlands had become a major focus of public housing. The residential areas formerly restricted to Europeans and Asians had started to be transformed with African families moving into all parts of the city, subdivisions providing plots for development with more densities, and Asian joint family dwellings converted into tenements or lodging houses. Whole parts of the city were going through changes in character: while some neighborhoods ceased to carry a European or an Asian spirit, others became distinctly African.

In the city center, the former commercial focus along Kenyatta Avenue, Biashara Street, and that part of Government Road adjacent to them was being challenged by a second focus developing to its south. The expanding administrative center next to it also attracted activities like restaurants and shops. Buildings serving functions conventionally attached to the commercial center were also being constructed outside the core, on the Hill and in Ngara. The former Asian combined commercial and residential area around River Road still retained its integrated functional character, but fewer families lived in the same house where their shop was. Nairobi city center was still changing, as it had all through its history.

The aerial view from the northwest towards the city center in the early 1980s shows a modern city which could almost be located anywhere in the world, judging by appearance (*Fig. 13.22*).[166] For those initiated into the

---

165 Barnow et al 1983.
166 Postcard.

Fig. 13.22 The city center, 1980s

histories of urban forms of Nairobi, the view is illuminating. On the left, the oldest road of the city – Station Road, Government Road, now Moi Avenue – initially connecting the railway station to the government offices, can clearly be discerned from its surroundings; it passes the largest mid-town park, Jeevanjee Gardens, in the front. The positioning of the new police station on a site demarcated in the middle of the old Government Road (just visible at the lower left corner of the photograph) severed one of the movement spines of the center of Nairobi. At the edges of the old main street, the two-storied structures, some including dwellings on the upper floor, are being replaced by office buildings. On the right, Uhuru Highway – initially Princess Elizabeth Highway – connects the core to the suburbs and to the industrial area and feeds the main streets of the center with a continuous flow of vehicles. Until the early 1980s, demand for sites along its eastern side was low, but the aerial view of only a few years later indicated how several skyscrapers have been completed there, with others under construction. In the middle right edge of the photograph, the tower of the municipality marks the point of entry to Kenyatta Avenue. On the old commercial streets between Moi Avenue and Uhuru Highway, historical buildings are being replaced by high-rise office blocks. Further south, a whole legion of towers of glass give a new prominence to streets earlier considered peripheral, near the railway station. Around the center, the former natural landscape is receding: the built landscape will soon touch the horizon.

PART FOUR

DWELLING FORMS IN NAIROBI

14 Colonial European dwelling forms

From the establishment of Nairobi until the independence of Kenya, the planning of dwellings was mostly in the hands of the Europeans. The major input of the Europeans on dwelling plans was channelled through the housing built by the employers – companies and European families employing domestic staff – and this was maintained all through the colonial phase. Even today, employer-housing continues to be an important part of the housing sector. The earlier housing plans were type plans of detached, semi-detached or row houses, and after World War II, also of blocks of flats. The houses were located in different parts of Nairobi, depending on the intended dwellers. Houses for Europeans were built in clusters of just a few units, while houses for Asians and Africans were grouped into larger housing areas of sometimes over a hundred units and with common services. Six employer-built dwellings were selected for the study: four dwellings in various house types, planned for Railways employees, and two post-war flats. In addition to employer-built dwellings, the Europeans also built housing privately for themselves. These were usually individual houses built on relatively substantial garden plots in the suburbs. Two privately built dwelling units were selected for the study, one in a detached house and the other in a row house.

Employer-built dwellings: Railways staff quarters

In the early decades of the century, the most important employer was the Kenya and Uganda Railways and Harbours which had provided housing for its employees from the beginning.[1] For the Railways, housing was a means to recruit new employees in a situation where they were badly needed. As B. Eastwood, the Chief Accountant, noted in the early years of the town:

> It is a very difficult matter to obtain competent staff in this country . . . In a country like East Africa, where there is practically no housing accommodation beyond what we provide, the importance of housing our staff cannot be considered other than a matter of the greatest importance, not only for the comfort of the staff and its well-being, but also for its absolute necessity to enable us to employ the staff necessary to meet the demands of the increased traffic.[2]

---

1 Later East African Railways and Harbours, now Kenya Railways. Hereafter Railways.
2 A report of around 1913, quoted in Hill 1949, 336, 339.

In the colony, proper housing was seen as a question of staff recruitment and as a moral obligation of the Europeans who had taken the mission of civilizing the native. This involved not only the employer but the colonial government in general. The Governor of the newly established Crown Colony, Sir Edward Northey, wrote:

> Having got the native out to work, we must see that he is properly looked after by initial medical attention and subsequent medical care, by proper feeding and housing and by provision of reasonable comfort when travelling by road or rail.[3]

All the early buildings of the Railways had been constructed of wood and corrugated iron. In the report by Lt.Col. F.D. Hammond, who had been appointed in 1920 by the Secretary of State of Britain as Special Commissioner for the Railways in Eastern Africa, wood and iron as semi-permanent materials were estimated to last for some twenty years in the local conditions. Hammond noted that undoubtedly the semi-permanent materials were used in the original construction to keep the capital investment low. However, with the annual cost of maintaining them at about five per cent of the original cost (compared with permanent buildings, for which the cost of maintenance was estimated at one per cent) and with the necessity of increased yearly repairs, the economic consequences were seen as one of the most serious problems of the Railways. Hammond therefore suggested that new buildings should be of permanent materials. This included office buildings, workshops, and staff quarters.[4]

During colonialism, the housing policy of the railways was based on a 7-tiered hierarchy of grades according to the employee's position and ethnic group.[5] In building staff quarters, the Railways used type plans developed in their own Architects' Office. Type plans enabled the Railways to build suitable housing in large numbers within a short time. The same type plans were sometimes used in different parts of town, even in different towns. For this study, four early Railways type plans were selected, all one-story buildings: a detached house for a European manager, a semi-detached house for an Asian employee in a senior position, a row house for Asian clerical staff, and a shared room for African bachelors. The house type for European managers contained two bedrooms and was constructed on at least twelve plots in different parts of town both in the city center, in the inner suburban belt near the city center, and in the suburbs. The house type for senior Asian employees contained two bedrooms and the house type for Asian clerical staff contained one bedroom, both built in several tens of units in a Railways housing area near the city center. The dwelling type for Africans consisted

---

3   One of Northey's later circulars (of which the first was in 1919), quoted in Hill 1949, 391.
4   Lt.Col. F.D. Hammond's report of October 1921, quoted in Hill 1949, 424f.
5   Communication from the Housing Secretary of the Railways in 1983. Today, the company uses a grading based on the person's position at work.

of shared rooms for four to six persons with common kitchen, shower, and toilet facilities, of which several hundred were built next to the station yard in the city center.

Detached houses for Europeans. The Railways offered their European management detached houses on large individual garden plots. The dwelling selected for the study was located on the Hill, on the inner suburban belt around the city center, near the crossing of the then Chamberlain Road and Kilimanjaro Avenue. With its slightly higher elevation than the center of the town, the Hill had a more pleasant climate. The location plan indicates five houses constructed according to the same house type plan. In the plan, three of the houses are arranged in a crescent as an end to Kilimanjaro Avenue, with the crescent form repeated in the driveway in the front of all five houses: the view of the house behind the front lawn is framed by the two gates. The garages, the boys' quarters, and the native latrines are located at the back of the plot, with separate entries from the back lane.[6] (*Fig. 14.1*)

The plan of the "Nairobi-type European house No.2," as it is identified in the drawings, shows a detached house with walls of brick and concrete or stone block, and a mangalore tile roof. The house had a front veranda, a sitting room with a bay, a fireplace and built-in cupboards, a dining recess, two bedrooms connected through a lobby to a bathroom and a toilet, as well as a kitchen with a built-in sink, a pantry, and a storage room around a back veranda. The area of the dwelling was about 120 m, with the verandas adding an additional 30 m. Built-in cupboards for china in the dining recess, for linen in the lobby and one in the main bedroom were also shown on the plan. The drawing indicated the alternative for building a door to the lavatory; initially, a separate toilet was to be built away from the building, with the corridor and door to be replaced by the toilet inside "when water bourne sewage is laid by Nairobi Corporation."[7] The plan of the dwelling studied was reversed from the described drawing. Later, the toilet was added but with the connection to the exterior retained. Other changes have included the boarding of both verandas and the construction of a separate guest house behind the main building.[8] (*Figs. 14.2, 14.3*)

In the plan, the resulting environment recalled the English garden city concept: the houses were clustered in an informal fashion, yet discernibly according to a formal plan, the road – grandiosely named avenue – ending in a crescent form. Located on the top of the hill, the houses commanded views of both the private gardens, and, further off, of the center of the town. Aesthetically, the buildings announced individuality, despite the identical plans of the five houses; variation was generated by the reversed plans and by the diversity of frontage angles in relation to the observer. The gardens

---

6   KR/PA Drawing No.3863, dated 12.3.30; Nairobi and District Topographic Map 1:2500, sheet NE 13/D, 1955. Now, Chamberlain Road is Mara Road.
7   KR/PA Drawing No.3311/1, dated 11.4.28 and August 1928. Re-traced 27.1.42.
8   Field study in October 1983.

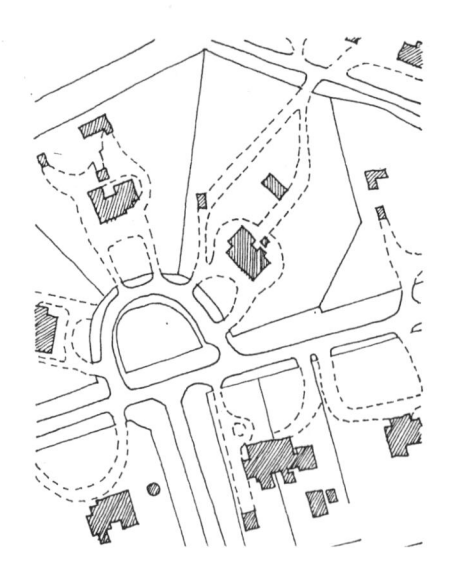

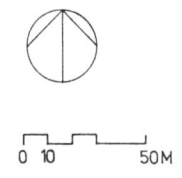

Fig. 14.1 Railways housing for Europeans, the Hill, site plan

Fig. 14.2 Railways housing: detached house for Europeans, the Hill, dwelling plan

Fig. 14.3 Railways housing: detached house for Europeans, the Hill

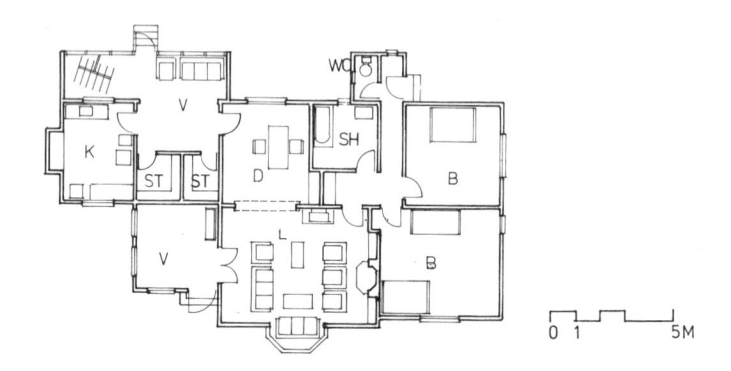

260 ■ PART IV DWELLING FORMS IN NAIROBI

provided additional opportunities for enhancing identity. The houses were smaller than their counterparts in an English garden suburb, but the design of the exteriors contributed to the visual association with "back home." Within the house, the reminders were even stronger. Not only did the arrangement of the rooms follow English models, including distinctions between the front and the back or between the public and the private spaces, but the house also encompassed elements like the veranda, the fireplace, and the bathroom which functioned almost as signals of Englishness. Although the group of houses was just a minute fragment of the garden suburb, and even then in reduced scale, it nevertheless succeeded in confirming its role as being part of England.[9]

Row houses and semi-detached houses for Asians. Asian employees were provided with dwellings in an area for Railways staff housing located in the inner suburban belt in Ngara, close to the city center, in the triangle formed by the then Park Road, Desai Road and Fort Hall Road, dissected by Delhi Road. The plan contained over 230 dwelling units in semi-detached houses and row houses, both of more than one type. The area was not subdivided into plots, but a clearly demarcated, walled back yard was attached to each dwelling, with secondary access from the back lane, the "sanitary lanes." The inhabitants were also provided with an Asian dispensary, playgrounds, and a "Goan hockey field."[10] (*Fig. 14.4*)

The location of the area in the suburbs and the plan of the area appear very English, but not in the same sense as the fragment of the garden suburb reflected in the cluster of detached houses discussed earlier. In this area, the house types were more mixed, with the majority of the units in houses with four dwellings. The density was also higher, but a certain level of privacy and individuality could still be attained in the back yards. Spaces left over from houses were allocated for recreational purposes, encouraging community formation in the immediate vicinity of the dwelling, different from the European suburbs with their separately located sports clubs.

The two-roomed row house dwelling, the "Type 3/2 unit Asian barrack," was planned for the Asian clerical staff members and was made of concrete blocks and a galvanized corrugated iron roof. The plans show a front veranda, a living room, a bedroom, and a back veranda with access to a bathroom with a shower basin and to a store room. The main living area was a little over 40 m. The two rooms, the living room and the bedroom, were the same size. At the other side of the walled murrum yard was a kitchen, a room for

---

9 For the ideals and practices of English middle class housing in the 19th Century and early 20th century, and the connections with the English country house, see Burnett 1986, Chapter 4; H.Muthesius 1979, 79-81, 181; S.Muthesius 1982, 42, 144. On English country houses, Girouard 1980; Franklin 1981. For similar examples in colonial India, e.g. King 1976, Chapter 6; Moorhouse 1983, 120ff.

10 KR/PA Drawing No. 4519/1, "Fort Hall Rd.-Layout of Asiatic Staff Quarters," dated 10.11.37. Marked: retraced as original tracing deteriorated, on 8.8.52. Now, Desai Road is Ngara Road, Fort Hall Road is Muranga Road, and Delhi Road is Park Road. Within the area, 16 roads have later been named.

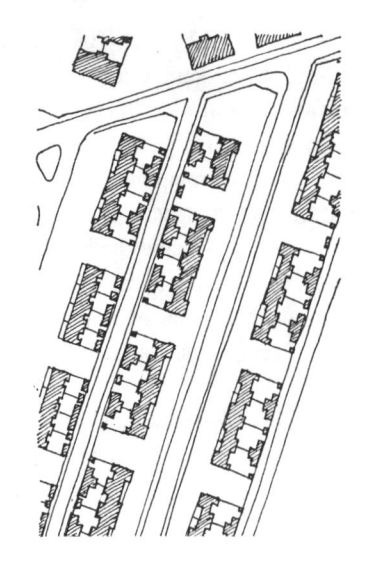

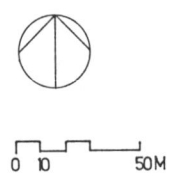

Fig. 14.4 Railways housing for Asians, Ngara, site plan

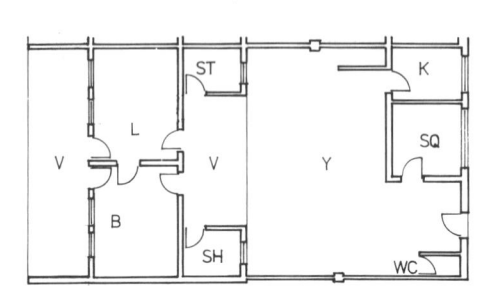

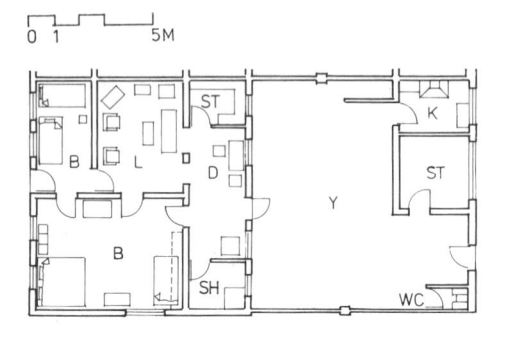

Fig. 14.5 Railways housing: row house for Asians, Ngara, dwelling plan

Fig. 14.6 Railways housing: row house for Asians, Ngara

262 ■ PART IV DWELLING FORMS IN NAIROBI

Fig. 14.7 Railways housing: semi-detached house for Asians, Ngara, dwelling plan

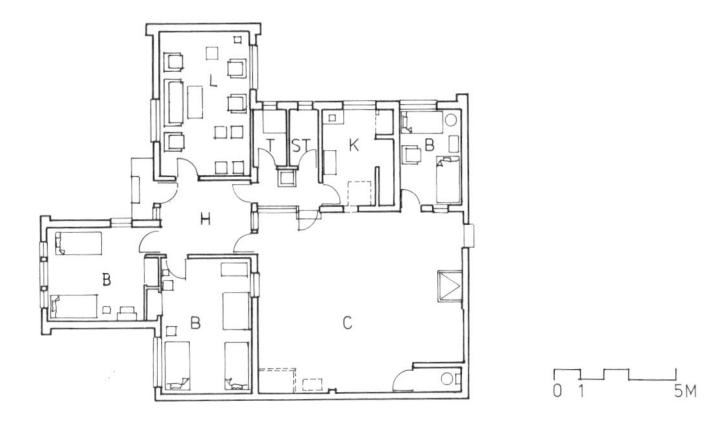

the domestic staff – in the plan, a "boys' room," and a latrine.[11] Later, the front and back verandas have been converted into habitable space. In the dwelling studied, part of the front veranda was used as an extension of the bedroom, part as the creation of a second bedroom at the entrance, closing off the living room window. The back veranda has been converted into a dining space. The store room is now the kitchen, and the kitchen and the boys' room in the separate building at the back of the yard are now store rooms.[12] (*Figs. 14.5, 14,6*)

The low density and the one-storied structures made the area into something of a blend between a working class area and a middle class suburb in England. The lack of private grounds and the repetition of the same house types, typical of working class areas, were complemented with generous dwelling widths, cool verandas, and the possibility of distinguishing between the more formal appearances of the front and the more familial communications of the back, typical of middle class dwelling environments. The walled back yards also enabled the inhabitants to engage in activities conceived by the colonialists as "Asian" (i.e. non-European); in this sense, the back yard with its stone floor and high walls provided the dwellers with an extension to the interior spaces, in addition to having the advantage of being restricted from outside view.

For senior Asian staff members, the Railways provided semi-detached houses of concrete block walls and mangalore tile roofs with a walled back yard. These were larger houses, with areas around 100 m. The plan of "Type 1-3 unit and 2-3 unit senior Asian staff quarters" depicts a living room and two bedrooms with built-in cupboards opening to a hall with an ironing table, and, connected with a separate corridor, a bathroom with a shower slab, a

---

11 KR/PA Drawing No.3630, dated 29.1.28. The plan of another two-room row house dwelling (dated 11.4.28) within the same area was presented in Barnow et al. 1983, 33.
12 Field study in October 1983.

store room with tier shelves, and a kitchen with a fireplace and a built-in sink. The back yard included a toilet, a boys' room, a fuel store and a washing slab. The plan represented improvements, such as the possibility of cross-ventilation through two windows located on opposite walls in the living room, the bedrooms, the kitchen, and the boys' room. A bucket opening from the back of the toilet had also been provided on to the "sanitary lane" for emptying the toilet.[13] Later, the boys' room has been converted into a bedroom.[14] (*Fig. 14.7*) With the semi-detached house type, the resemblance of the area to an English middle class suburb increased.

Ngara, with its row houses and semi-detached houses planned for the Asians, resembled in some respects English working-class areas. Recommendations made in England in the 1910s on housing in general and working class housing in particular may well have also produced effects on this kind of housing in the colonies. The recommendations included, among other things, a 70-foot minimum between opposite houses to enable proper sunlight penetration in the winter, the maximum length of a house as eight dwelling units, a preference for wider frontages, the use of spare backland as common recreational space, and the undesirability of areas with only one house type and tenants of all the same social class.[15] All these were also fulfilled in the Ngara Railways area in Nairobi.

Landhies for Africans. For their African workers, the Railways built "landhies": bachelor housing with shared rooms and common kitchen, toilet, and shower rooms. The Muthurwa Landhies area, located immediately adjacent to the railway station area, was developed from 1900 onwards in several phases. Andrew Hake has identified that some 55 blocks were built during the years 1924-29, eleven during 1930-31, and 34 blocks during 1936-38, replacing most of the blocks built in 1900.[16] A plan of the Muthurwa Landhies shows more than 60 twenty unit buildings, with approximately 4 common kitchens to each building, 1 latrine to two buildings, and 1 bath to six buildings. In addition to this, the plan includes some thirty 4-unit row houses with apparently larger dwellings, two mosques, eight shops in two clusters, two overseers' offices, a police station, the railway welfare office, a charcoal dump, a lime store, and a playground with a bathing tank, all fenced within the compound by a steel pale fence. The two dwellings selected for the study were located in the middle of the area.[17] (*Figs. 14.8, 14.10*)

---

13 KR/PA Drawing No.6158, dated 4.12.43.
14 Field study in October 1983.
15 One of the most influential on the development of twentieth century urban Britain was the Tudor-Walters Report of 1918, presented by a committee on housing, and based on experiences from the garden city movement and various earlier recommendations, among them Raymond Unwin's pamphlet "Nothing Gained from Overcrowding!" of 1912; on the Tudor-Walters Report, Burnett 1986, 222ff; Hall 1988, 66-74. Unwin was member of the committee.
16 Hake 1977, 256. In 1983, the Railways had prepared plans for the replacement of the landhies with multi-storied blocks of flats. Muthurwa has also been referred to as Muthurwa Landhies, Landhi Mawe, and Landhies.

The plan resembles a military area with its barracks in regimental lines, its common washing and cooking facilities, and its controlled points of entry. Although the densities are relatively low, with ample space between buildings, the plan is far from the garden city. Everything in it portrays the idea of temporary habitation, a place for shorter or longer visits but not for permanent dwelling. The plan does not allow expressions of individuality: external spaces are shared, public, and unarticulated in either function or form.

The "Type 2 to 20 unit landies for native location" were built in concrete blocks with galvanized corrugated iron roofing, each unit comprised of a five-foot deep veranda and a ten-by-ten-foot (about 9 m) room. The drawing depicted 6-inch thick walls, concrete floor, and two small fixed windows – "fixed lights" in the drawing – close to the roof. Each room had only a small outlet for ventilation.[18] (*Fig. 14.9*) Later, the verandas have been converted into habitable space. Of the two dwellings studied, in one it was a bedroom and in the other a kitchen.[19] (*Fig. 14.9*) The idea of temporary and controlled habitation is continued in the dwelling plan. The rooms are simple boxes for sleeping. In the Nairobi climate, the lack of a ceiling and of windows which could be opened imply unpleasant, at times even unbearable living conditions: the room offers little shelter from the climatic extremes. The windows high up have not been planned for visual contact, they only provide minimal light; and the front of the building lacks windows altogether. With the minimal space, no functional distinctions can be made within the dwelling.

The dwellings the Railways built for Africans resembled the labor lines of South African mining towns. Already in the 1880s in Kimberley, South Africa, an industrial diamond mining company devised and implemented a formal strategy of racial segregation. The earlier haphazard settlement of the tent town was replaced by a segregated pattern of housing within which the black and white workers were disunited and the blacks were housed in all-male barrack-like compounds, thus allowing the company to limit labor unrest and to maintain tighter discipline. The system of residential segregation established in Kimberley became the example followed in other mining towns in Africa. The urban practices of racial segregation executed in South Africa influenced those of other British colonies; Andrew Hake has maintained that between 1903 and the 1950s, "Nairobi looked towards South Africa."[20]

---

17 KR/PA Drawings Nos. 5427/1 and 5427/2; Nairobi and District Topographic Map 1:2500, sheet 14/A, 1955. No dates were visible in the Railways drawings.
18 KR/PA Drawing No.3296/1, dated May 1928.
19 Field study in October 1983.
20 Mabin, "Labour, Capital, Class Struggle and the Origins of Residential Segregation in Kimberley, 1880-1920," *Journal of Historical Geography*, Vol.12, No.1, 1986) quoted in Lemon 1991, 3, and Pirie 1991, 120. According to Hake 1977, before 1903, Nairobi looked to Bombay, and from the 1950's, to London (p.26).

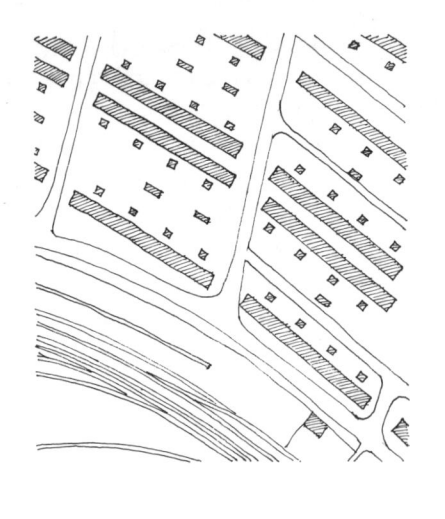

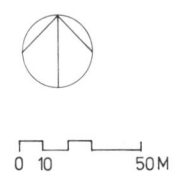

Fig. 14.8 Railways housing for Africans, Muthurwa, site plan

Fig. 14.9 Railways housing: landhies for Africans, Muthurwa, dwelling plan

Fig. 14.10 Railways housing: landhies for Africans, Muthurwa

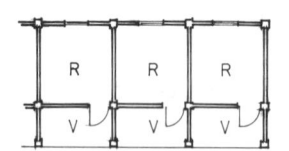

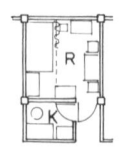

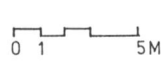

266 ■ PART IV   DWELLING FORMS IN NAIROBI

Other employer-built dwellings: post-war flats

In the post-war years, the European middle classes of Nairobi expanded: the newcomers included government officials, army officers, professionals involved in higher education, as well as executives and professionals for the industrial sector. Flats were introduced as the new types of dwellings in employer-built housing. Many of the blocks of flats were located close to the city center, in the inner suburban belt near the newly established institutions. These included the Royal Technical College of East Africa which had received the Royal Charter in 1951, and eventually developed into the University of Nairobi. Some blocks of flats were also built further off in the suburbs. Both of the dwellings selected for the study now house University staff, but the suburban one was part of a compound initially planned and built for army personnel.[21]

The older of the flats was located in Spring Valley, a former coffee farm area converted after the Second World War into plots reserved for Europeans. At this time, the plots in Parklands which had been a European residential area, were being further subdivided and inhabited by Asians, and the Europeans moved west of it, to Upper Parklands, later extended to Spring Valley.[22] It is located on the red soil, considered to be favorable both for building and for growing plants; the topography combines ridges and river valleys, and provides a climate cooler than the one on the plain in the center of the city and to the east of it. Compared to the other areas in the municipal area, the plots in Spring Valley were initially among the largest, comparable to those of the suburban Muthaiga and Karen. The predominant house type was the detached house on a large garden plot.[23] In the area, flats – even of the modified type that the dwelling studied represents – have been and still are extremely rare; to my knowledge, within the core of Spring Valley, the compound studied is the only one.

The Spring Valley flat was situated on a compound with two older blocks of flats, two more recent buildings of maisonettes (row houses with two-story dwellings) and, for domestic staff, a separate building with rooms and common showers and toilets. The dwelling studied was situated in the one of the older blocks of flats, built of stone blocks and with a tile roof. There were four dwellings in the block, two on each floor, each with a floor area of about 85 m. All dwellings were directly accessible from the outside, the ones on the lower level via an external staircase leading down from the ground level, and the ones on the upper level via one leading up. The dwellers on the lower level could utilize the garden while the ones on the upper level had a balcony. The plans of all the dwellings were the same or reversed versions. There were two entries to each dwelling, one for the family and

---

21 Communication in 1983 from several present and past dwellers of the blocks of flats.
22 Hake 1977, 38.
23 SK Aerial photograph 1:6000, sheet 596, 1975.

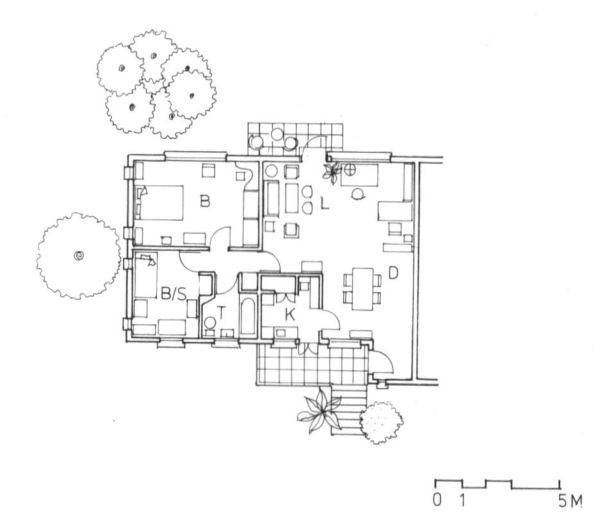

*Fig. 14.11
Employer-built flat,
Spring Valley, dwelling
plan*

*Fig. 14.12
Employer-built flat,
Spring Valley*

visitors, and the other to the kitchen for domestic staff. The main entry was through the dining area to the living room. The kitchen was next to the dining area. A door separated the two bedrooms and the bathroom from the living room. Access to the terrace and the garden was from the living room.[24] (*Figs. 14.11, 14.12*)

Within the compound, the low densities of the neighborhood are repeated. But the organization of the compound contradicts the distinction maintained

---

24 Field study in December 1983.

*Fig. 14.13
Employer-built flat,
the Hill, dwelling
plan*

*Fig. 14.14
Employer-built flat,
the Hill*

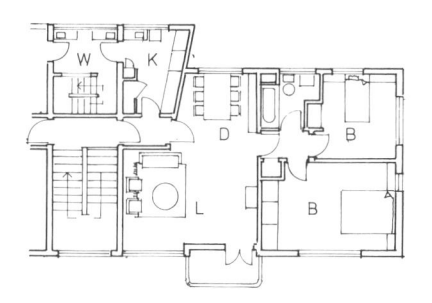

in the houses built earlier for Europeans between the more public front and the more private back side: in the compound, the dwellings are approached from one direction only, through spaces shared by other dwellers and the domestic staff. This reversal of principles is continued in the plan of the dwelling, where the entrance path and staircase are the same for family, visitors, and domestic staff, with the door to the kitchen separated only at the last moment. In relation to the dwelling, the most private spaces are not merely the bedrooms but also the terrace, accessible from the living room, on the opposite side of the building from the entrance.

The Nairobi Hill dwelling was located in a block of flats built later on the inner suburban belt near the city center.[25] In Nairobi Hill on the ridge next to the city center, railways officers already had their detached houses at the turn of the century when Nairobi was founded. After the Second World War, the proximity of the city center intensified the land use of the area. The dwelling studied was located in one of several similar blocks, constructed of concrete and with a flat roof. Each block had three floors with two dwellings on each floor, with the entrance to the main staircase on the ground floor. A separate service staircase provided access to the kitchens. The floor area of the flat was about 85 m. In the flat studied, entry was through a corridor to the dining area which was part of the living room. From the living-dining room, a door led to a suite of two bedrooms and a bathroom. The living room also had a balcony. Access to the kitchen was from the entry corridor and from the washing space on the landing of the service staircase. (*Figs. 14.13, 14.14*)

In the compound with the higher apartment blocks, the difference between the common external spaces and the private internal ones is more marked than in the older compound with two-storied buildings. External space on the ground is attached only to the group of dwellings but not to any single dwelling. Within the building, the entry of the family and visitors is distinctly separated from that of the domestic staff, both having their own staircase and doors to different parts of the dwelling. As a whole, the separation of different functions, common in the earlier dwellings planned for or by Europeans, is also repeated in these two flats.

Privately-built dwellings

Houses had been built with private funds since the founding of Nairobi by Europeans particularly in the hilly areas west and north of the center. These areas were located on ground adjacent to but higher than the center, with a cooler climate. They also contained houses built by employers like the Railways for their European staff. After the Second World War, the residential areas near the center began to expand further off to land earlier used for farming and hunting. These included Spring Valley, described in the previous section of post-war flats, and Upper Hill, a large residential region which Halliman and Morgan in a 1967 description of the city referred to as such because of its position on higher ground than the city center (i.e. over 5,500 feet altitude). According to Halliman and Morgan, Upper Nairobi in 1967 was

> the best residential area and contained the majority (82 per cent) of the Europeans . . . The typical dwelling is a one-family detached house

---

25 Nairobi and District Topographic Map 1:2500, sheet NE 13/A, 1955; SK Aerial photograph, 1:6000, sheet 2210, 1975; field study in December 1983.

of one storey built of stone under a tile roof with separate servant's quarters on a plot of a quarter of an acre or more although the number of flats has increased in the inner districts. Much of the area consists of ridges separated by deeply cut wooded valleys which gives a pleasing aspect to these parts and the fertile red soil permits attractive gardens to be developed. The valleys are difficult to cross and roads tend to follow the line of the ridges towards the centre of the city making tortuous any journey across the area.[26]

In the *Master Plan* of 1948, this area had been zoned for residential purposes[27] but the plot subdivision presented coincided only in fragments with the one illustrated in the map of 1955.[28] In this map, the predominant house type was a detached house. Two privately-built dwellings were selected for the study, a detached house from Spring Valley and a row house from Upper Hill.[29]

The Spring Valley detached house was located on a fenced private plot with an extensive garden.[30] In addition to the main building built of stone blocks and with pitched roofs, there were two separate additional structures: a building with a guest room and storage space, and the rooms for domestic staff. The property was owned by a private individual and rented on an annual contract, for example, to expatriate families. The floor area of the dwelling was about 180m. The main entry was from the forecourt with space for parking several cars, to a hall with access to the dining room, the kitchen and kitchen storage, and to the bathroom with toilet. Adjacent to the dining room was the studio or library whose door earlier had opened directly from the hall; this door had been closed by the present occupants and a new doorway constructed to the dining area. The living room was connected to the dining room with a wide opening. Access to the bedrooms was through a door from the dining area. There were three bedrooms, one of which had been converted by the present dwellers from a storage space, and a bathroom with a toilet, all grouped around a small second living room. This space also had a door to the terrace, and had been converted into a habitable space from the corridor-like space it had been when the present dwellers moved into the house. (*Figs. 14.15, 14.16*)

The dwelling contained three functional areas which could be separated from each other by locked doors: the kitchen and laundry area adjacent to the entrance hall, the living and dining room with the library, and the

---

26 Halliman and Morgan 1967, 106.
27 MP 1948, maps, e.g. Existing Population Distribution.
28 Nairobi and District Topographical Map 1:2500, sheet NE 12/B, 1955.
29 Statements referring to the origin of the dwellings and to the time of their construction were based on indirect data such as information on the development of these areas in general and on the typical house types; these have neither been confirmed nor contradicted due to lack of direct data on the planning and building histories of the houses. The Spring Valley detached house had obviously been extended and converted several times, also during the residence of the present dwellers, but the original form of the house could not be reconstructed on the data available. It is possible that the Upper Hill row house was built later, after independence.
30 SK Aerial photograph 1:6000, sheet 596, 1975.

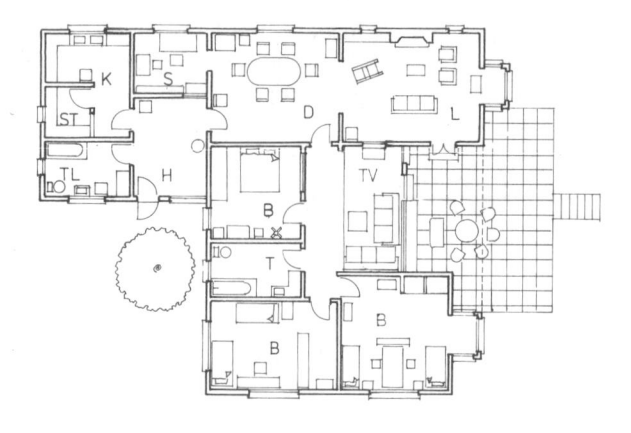

*Fig. 14.15
Privately-built
detached house,
Spring Valley,
dwelling plan*

*Fig. 14.16
Privately-built
detached house,
Spring Valley*

bedrooms with the family room and bathroom. All the changes the present dwellers had made emphasized the distinction between the three areas; this was particularly clear in the change of the position of the door to the library and in the conversion of the storage into a bedroom. In the changes, the old character of the house had not been lost: the fireplace, the bay window, and the door to the partly roofed garden terrace gave a particular identity to the living room and, since it dominated the dwelling, to the whole interior.

The Upper Hill dwelling was situated at one end of a five-unit row house, built on a relatively large plot near one of the major roads. The plot contained land shared by the different dwelling units and small individual private

*Fig. 14.17
Privately-built row
house, Upper Hill
dwelling plan*

*Fig. 14.18
Privately-built row
house, Upper Hill*

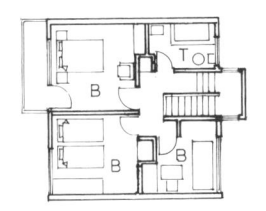

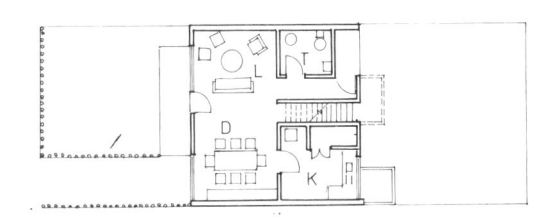

gardens in both the front and the back of the dwelling. The house had a modern outlook with its flat roof and a balcony on the front facade. At the time of the study, the owner of the whole row house was a private company which utilized the dwellings as employer-housing. The dwelling had two stories with a total floor area of about 95m. The rooms of the domestic servants were all situated in a separate building at the back of the plot. Entry to each dwelling unit was through a front garden directly to the living room which was combined with the dining area. The only access to the kitchen and to the kitchen storage was from the dining area. In back of the living room was a toilet, a corridor leading to the back door, and the staircase

CHAPTER 14 COLONIAL EUROPEAN DWELLING FORMS ■ 273

leading to the upper level. On the upper level, there were two bedrooms with windows to the front of the building – one with a balcony – and a smaller

The back door was not accessible from the front gate and could not easily be utilized as a second entry; also, the fact that both entries led to the living room minimizes its usefulness for that purpose. Inside the dwelling, all the activities in the house necessarily involve or occur in the living room: even the entry to the kitchen is totally controlled. The only pattern distinctly related to the dwellings planned for Europeans was the separation of public rooms, such as the living room, from private rooms, such as the bedrooms.[31]

---

[31] This also puts some doubt on whether the house had, in fact, been planned for Europeans; however, the location supported the presupposition.

15 African dwelling forms

Although many Africans working in early colonial Nairobi were housed by their employers either in shared rooms built by big companies like the Railways or on compounds in the European housing areas as domestic staff, the majority of the population lived in unplanned areas at the edge of the city. The notion of planned areas for Africans did not arise until the early 1910s when the inadequacy of the uncontrolled village settlements generated a discussion on the question of a new "native location," and its realization took almost a decade. The idea was to demolish all the illegally built areas and force the inhabitants to move to the native locations to ensure that living conditions were not below the standards set by the municipality. Pumwani, the first of the native locations, was established only in 1920.[1]

The Africans living in colonial Nairobi were of two main kinds. Some groups followed more rural ways of life, practiced traditional religions or Christianity, and originated from the rural areas around Nairobi; their stay in town was usually temporary. In the early decades, their practices of dwelling in Nairobi may well have resembled rural ones.[2] Some groups followed more urban ways of life, practiced Islam, and usually originated from the coastal Swahili culture; the small group of Sudanese army veterans may be identified as belonging to the same group. Of the two, the more urbanized groups were smaller in number, but their role in the city was more significant than their numerical proportion. The Pumwani Africans belonged to the urbanized groups.[3]

The residential areas of the urbanized Africans were perceived by the Europeans as places of illegal activities; from the beginning, prostitution, drugs, the illegal brewing and selling of alcohol as well as the hiding of political activists have been linked to Pumwani.[4] The view of the colonialists has been repeated even in fairly recent descriptions. Thomas Akare, a

---

1   For the initial discussion on the native location, see above, chapter 10; for the establishment of Pumwani, chapter 11.
2   For an anthropological study of the traditional life of the Kikuyu, the largest single ethnic group in Kenya occupying the central highlands immediately north of Nairobi, see Kenyatta 1982, 76-84, 177-181. According to Kenyatta (p.xv), the population of the Kikuyu numbered about one million in the 1930's. Jomo Kenyatta later became the first President of independent Kenya. For more recent studies, see Lee Smith and Lamba 1981, 113-117; Andersen 1978.
3   Hake 1977, 136. Hake (p.130) translated Pumwani colloquially as "take it easy" or "relax."
4   Hake 1977, 130-133.

contemporary writer who located his novel *The Slums* in Pumwani, lets one of his characters reflect on the area:

> This place has the history of the whole town. It is the mother of Nairobi. And that is true, though some call it a two-shilling city because of these two-shilling women, others Majengo, Pumwani, Matopeni because of the mud buildings with brown rusted roofs, or Mairungi city or Miraa because of the drug . . . Yes. That is the Slums . . . A most corrupted city. A place where evil can be seen at any time of the day but worse in the night. A place with every kind of people. The richest and the poorest. A city of no shame. A place full of many bastards. Corrupt police too. A city where evils of love are hidden in buibuis and kanzus. With both married and unmarried. A city where the youngsters you see playing naked in the dust are the leaders of tomorrow. Yes. Perhaps, yes. To me this was the Slums. One of the most independent cities. Living here takes guts.[5]

Self-built dwellings: the majengo house. According to the "Survey of the problems of re-developing Pumwani Estate" prepared by E.T. Farnworth, Chief Valuer, in 1964, the original intention of the 1920 scheme of the "native location" was to provide sites of about 1,500 square feet for building a hut between 100 and 750 square feet in size – that is, with no more than 50% coverage – which would accommodate a maximum of fifteen persons per house. Occupation was to be purely temporary and restricted to the allottee and his family, with the structures deemed as movable property belonging to the holder of the site and on demand from the municipality, re-erectable on an alternative site. Additions or alterations to the building as well as subletting were illegal without permission from the Municipal Council. The Municipality leased the land from the Government for 99 years, built the roads, communal ablutions and latrines, and laid down the sites. The sites were planned by the municipality, which was part of the colonial administration, but the structures were to be built by the people themselves.[6]

A map of Pumwani from 1955 indicates a plot subdivision which differed from the one conventionally used in Nairobi *(Fig. 15.1)*.[7] In fact, the terms of allocation of the 1920 Pumwani scheme did not use the concept of plot, but that of stand to refer to the piece of land allocated for the erection of a hut or other structure.[8] In Pumwani, the pieces of land marked for building did not cover all of the land between the planned roads; a neutral belt surrounded each plot. Judging from the map, the environment was to be built

---

5   Akare 1981, 139.
6   Farnworth 1964, 3f. In the Nairobi Master Plan for a Colonial Capital (MP 1948, 18), Pumwani is mentioned as an area where the Africans built their own houses and some street plan was followed; according to the report, "discussions about the kind of quarters the African should inhabit did not probe very deep into the problems of native domestic ambitions, but they established the principle of municipal responsibility in the provision of houses."
7   Nairobi and District Topographic Map 1:2500, sheet NE 14/A, 1955. A map showing the same subdivision was also attached to Farnworth's report (1964, 17).
8   Farnworth 1964, 3.

relatively densely compared, for example, to the residential areas built by the Railways for its staff, European, Asian, and African. The arrangement of the plots with space between the buildings, however, allows for sufficient cross-ventilation and for some protection against fire hazards.

Farnworth's report did not mention whether type plans were to be followed, although an illustration text in it refers to a "typical design of existing houses: narrow corridor giving access to rooms."[9] Majengo refers to the house type originating from the coastal Swahili culture, with Mombasa as one of its centers, but extending from Lamu on the Kenyan coast in the north to Mozambique in the south; in Nairobi, Majengo has also been used to refer to the Pumwani area with the majengo houses. Traditionally, the majengo house was built of mud and wattle with palm leaf roofing. The plans have varied in different times and places, but according to Dick Urban Vestbro, all the modern variations of the plan of the urban majengo type seem to include a front veranda facing the street, a central corridor connecting the veranda and the back, and rooms symmetrically on both sides of it. In contemporary majengo houses, corrugated iron sheets have replaced the leaf roofing.[10]

In this study, the plan of the initial Pumwani building was reconstructed on the basis of an analysis of the present, much enlarged house, and in comparison with similar majengo houses. According to the owner whose father had built the original house, the core of the present building was erected in 1936.[11] The reconstructed plan of the Pumwani house – with a floor area of about 90 m – consists of a front veranda as wide as the house, a central corridor with a front door from the veranda and a back door to the yard, and four rooms of equal sizes on both sides of the corridor. The rooms have not been specified by use. Since the wash rooms and latrines were provided communally, they are not duplicated within the dwelling. Later, the core of the house studied has been extended so that at the time of the field study it contained fifteen more rooms with uses ranging from dwelling to a shop, two kiosks, an eating house and a workshop.[12] (*Figs. 15.2, 15.3*)

---

9   Farnworth 1964, 1. Quoting an undated manuscript drafted by Colonel O.F.Watkins, Deputy Native Commissioner, Hake (1977, 130) has noted that it was suggested that the houses be of the square, four-roomed type, and "owing to lack of funds they will have to be wattle-and-daub; each house should be separate." For the history of Pumwani from the first discussions of the native location in 1906 until the redevelopment plans of 1970, see Hake ibid., Chapter 9.
10 For studies on the [majengo] Swahili house, see Vestbro 1975, 23-35, on its background and contemporary variations in Dar es Salaam, Tanzania; Hoek-Smit 1976, 23-35, 42-46, on residential patterns in a majengo village near Nairobi. For a historical photograph, see e.g. Frisell 1939, 7a. The majengo house is totally different from the urban Swahili stone house of the land-owning merchants, typical, for example, to parts of Lamu and Mombasa on the Kenyan coast; for a description of the Swahili stone house, e.g. Ghaidan 1975, 43-60.
11 Communication from the owner in June 1983.
12 Field study in June 1983. For a comparison with a similar Pumwani house, measured some time between 1973 and 1981, see Barnow et al. 1983, 34, 3, 86; its differences from the dwelling studied included both front rooms used as shops (*dukas*), the latrine located at the end of the corridor and the kitchen and store replacing one of the end rooms.

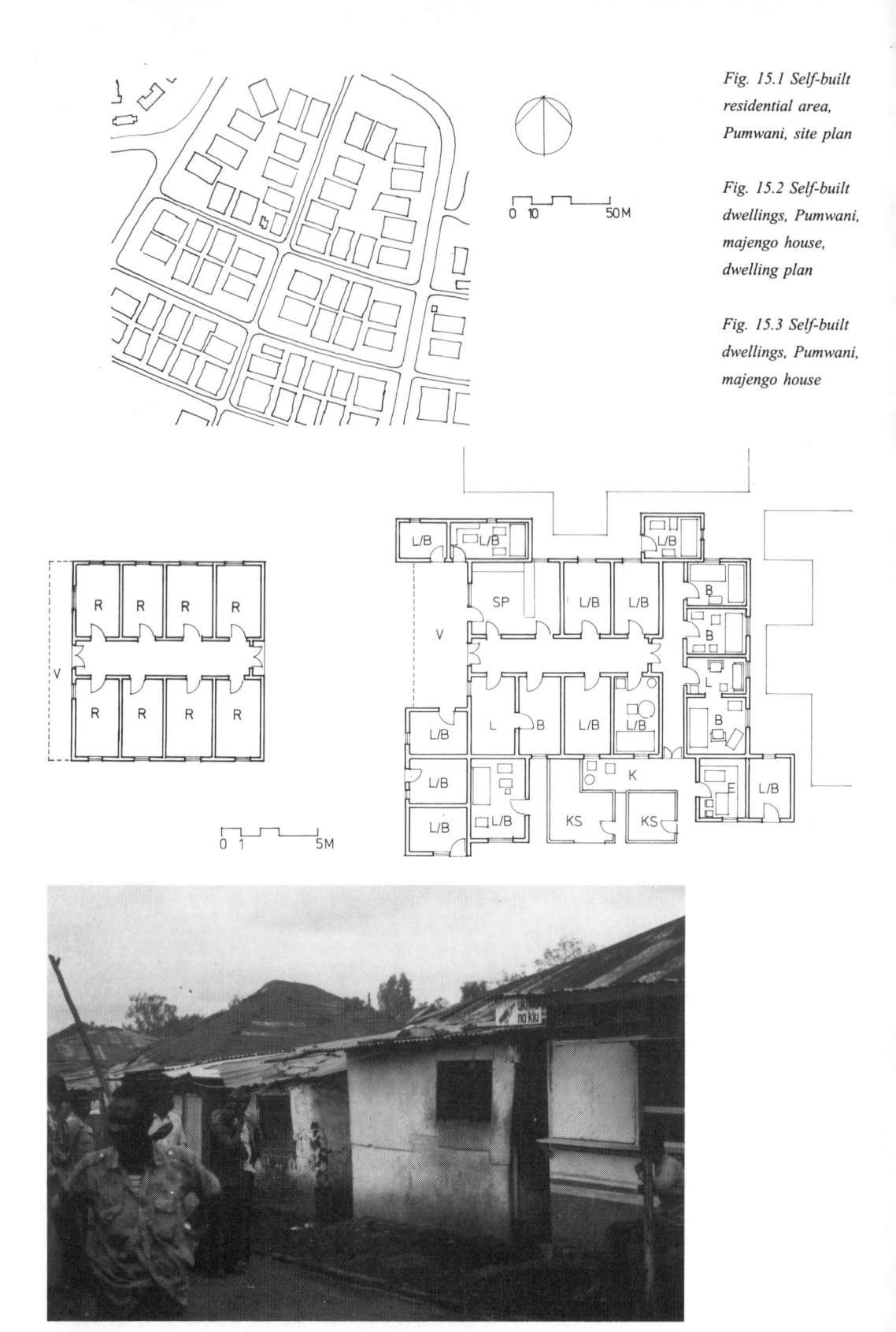

Fig. 15.1 Self-built residential area, Pumwani, site plan

Fig. 15.2 Self-built dwellings, Pumwani, majengo house, dwelling plan

Fig. 15.3 Self-built dwellings, Pumwani, majengo house

278 ■ PART IV   DWELLING FORMS IN NAIROBI

The dwelling plan with its rooms of the same size, each accessible from the corridor, is flexible: each room may be used separately or in combination with others. The form and size of the rooms enables multi-purpose uses, but also allows distinctions by function. The construction material of the walls facilitates alterations like new connections between rooms or directly to the outside. The two entrances and the width of the corridor add to the flexibility, offering the possibility of extending activities from the private rooms to the semi-private interior space and to the yard around the building.

■ 16 Asian dwelling forms

While the residence of Africans in towns was strictly limited by the colonialists, Asians were not permitted to buy land for farming and were allowed to live only in towns. The colonial powers restricted the urban areas where the Asians were allowed to build and tried to regulate the densities, but controlled neither the building types nor the building materials the Asians wished to use. In addition to housing units built by the Railways for their employees, in the first decade Asians lived in the privately developed Asian areas, located in the bazaar area in the town center, and later also in Ngara on the other side of the Nairobi River and in Eastleigh further east of the center. In colonial Nairobi, the predominant Asian house type was the courtyard house, built for joint families and tenants.

In his novel set in contemporary Nairobi, Meja Mwangi has depicted in an illuminating way the background of Dacca House, one of the courtyard houses in the River Road area in the city center:

> Dacca House has a history as long as, but much more colourful than that of any other along Grogan Road. It is older and sturdier than most. The fact that it stands erect and tough, while many others have either already perished or are in the process of sagging and crumbling all around, is a living testimony to the proud craftsmanship of just one man – old Kachra Samat, now retired to a generous mansion in the cool and quiet suburbia. Until recently Dacca House had been the flower of his youth, the fruit of his sweat. He built Dacca House with his own hands and named it after his home city on the River Ganges, thousands of kilometers across the Indian Ocean.
>
> Along with his compatriots, Kachra Samat first came to this country as a coolie engaged in the building of the great colonial railway . . . the white man had granted the Indians trade concessions and large plots of land on which to build their shops and stores. The Indians had built their shops, flourished and settled down on a more or less permanent basis.
>
> That is a long time ago, way back when the city streets were mere mud tracks, and the river behind Grogan Road, a freshwater river with fish and green snakes, dragonflies and nesting places for birds and wild ducks. Old Indians can still remember fishing in what is now a moving sewer.
>
> Like his compatriots, Kachra Samat had not built the house to let. He had toiled over it for his family to live in, in the early days when there were no rental houses in the city. It was a one-floor affair. The ground floor had been many things before finally resigning itself to being a mere second-rate garage specialising in used and stolen motor car parts.

It had started as a drapery store selling Indian textiles; then it became a bookshop, a photographic studio, a cobbler's shop, a grocery store and finally a garage. It had, however, mainly due to its poor location, escaped the fate, worse than death, that had overtaken most of the formerly Indian properties on River and Grogan Roads – that of being turned into bars and brothels after the Indians sold out to Africans . . .

Upstairs in Dacca House were the fifteen rooms for Kachra Samat's extensive family. It was built L-shaped so that every room had a door and a window opening onto the yard. In keeping with the fashion of the age, there were connecting doors between all the rooms, so that one could travel the whole L of the building without stepping outside at all. This design later proved priceless to the new landlord of Dacca House. Against the further wall of the yard were the common floor-level toilets, a bathroom with a monstrous tub which rested on four pig-iron lions' feet, and a shower room. The kitchens had been built nearest the rooms. The building was surrounded by a high stone wall topped with rows of broken glass to prevent natives from clambering over to steal. The only entrance was from Grogan Road and up the stairs through a heavy wooden door which was locked day and night during the long occupancy of Kachra Samat, his brothers, uncles, sisters and all their numerous offspring. it was a big, safe place and for thirty years it was home for the Kachra family. They worked hard in the shop below, the father as a tailor, the mother as a cashier and the young Kachras as shop attendants, and at dusk they closed shop, went upstairs and bolted themselves in their rooms for night. During the night, all communication was carried on through the connecting doors. One did not need to step outside except to go to the latrine.

As the years went by and life became progressively comfortable, more and more compatriots came from India to settle permanently, and stone buildings mushroomed along the river and up the valley . . . Almost by magic, a street took shape, one identical to many Indian streets in Dacca or New Delhi.[1]

The Asian courtyard house may be described as a building planned to accommodate a joint family, sometimes also tenants. In her study of Hindu families of urban India, Aileen D. Ross defined the joint family as

> a group of people who generally live under one roof, who eat food cooked at one hearth, who hold property in common and who participate in common family worship and are related to each other as some particular type of kindred.[2]

---

1   Mwangi 1979, 77-80. However, Mwangi's description of a bath tub seems improbable as an element in an Asian dwelling; in Nairobi, the method of purification for Asians was running water, either poured from a vessel or by using a shower.(Personal communications from local Asians in 1983; cf. Lannoy 1971, 7, on similar Indian practices.) The bath tub with its standing water was part of the British dwelling practices. The reference to New Delhi would more correctly be connected to Delhi.
2   Ross 1961, chapter 1 (quotation from p.9), referring also to studies emphasizing authority, the common way of life, common income and property, as well as mutual rights and obligations.

The Asian families living in the Nairobi dwellings studied were all Hindus and from Gujarat in western India. Of the privately-built Asian dwellings selected for the study, three were courtyard houses: two in the suburbs, in Ngara and in Eastleigh, and a third in the city center, in the River Road area. The fourth Asian planned dwelling studied was originally a detached house converted into a courtyard house, and the fifth dwelling was a semi-detached house, both located in the suburbs.

Privately-built joint family dwellings: courtyard houses

In the early years of the town, the Asian bazaar area was enlarged into the present River Road area to its east, both in the city center. By the 1910s, the Asian residential area started to extend to Ngara, to the north of the River Road area across the Nairobi River. The land-use pattern of this part of Ngara contained relatively small residential plots. As the predominant house type was the courtyard house, which entailed high plot coverage, the density was also relatively high. An aerial photograph shows a plot coverage resembling those at the edge of the city center.[3] The resulting environment was a streetscape with urban characteristics, further supported by the stone used as the building material and the scarcity of vegetation. The character of Ngara, however, differed from that of the Asian parts of the city center in its functional uniformity: large parts of it were only residential.

In the arrangement of the plots, a distinction was maintained between the front and the back. Each plot had two entries: the front entry with a veranda towards the street and the back entry from the service lane. On some plots, the house was separated from the street with a small planted garden, on others, the building line was at the front edge of the plot. The plot of the dwelling studied was approximately 21 m wide and 35 m deep, with a front garden and narrow strips of unbuilt areas on both sides of the building.

The dwelling plan of the Ngara courtyard house was organized symmetrically around the inner courtyard. The entry to the front veranda and the corridor connecting the front to the courtyard were located on the central axis. The rooms on both sides of the axis were the same. Only the entry from the back lane was off center. Four rooms opened onto the front veranda and eight ones onto the courtyard. The two front rooms on both sides of the veranda were slightly larger than the other rooms on the side of the building. The rooms on both sides of the corridor leading to the courtyard were smaller. The functions of the rooms was not specified. All the rooms had connecting doors to the adjacent rooms and to the courtyard. The courtyard was partly covered with a roof creating a gallery at the edge. The courtyard was totally paved and was used for various activities. Several small kitchens and storage rooms were located at the back of the courtyard. The kitchens were used by

---

3   SK Aerial photograph, sheet No.2210, 1:6000, 1975.

*Fig. 16.1
Privately-built
courtyard house by
Asians, Ngara,
dwelling plan*

*Fig. 16.2
Privately-built
courtyard house,
Ngara*

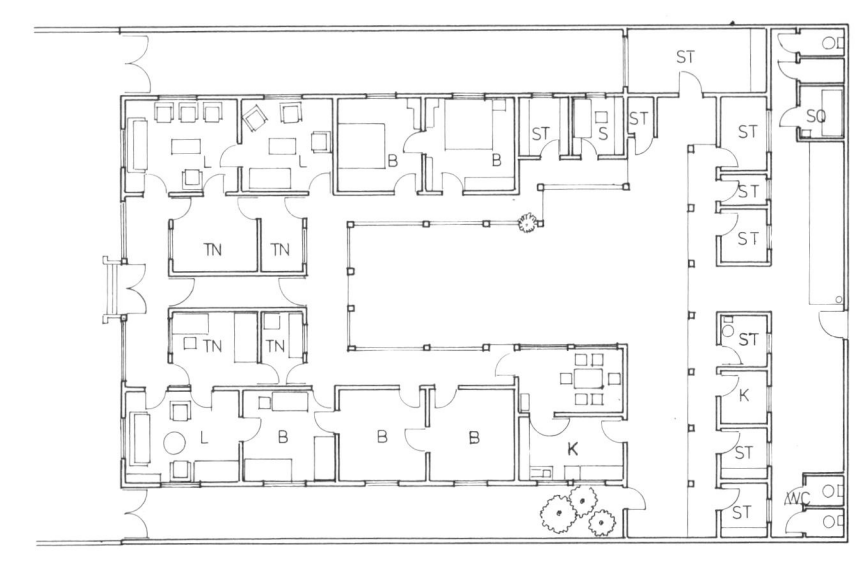

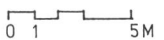

the tenant families of the initial phase. The dwelling was large, with a floor area of about 250 m, and including the courtyard space of about 160 m, it contained over 400 m of usable space. Behind the kitchens and with its own entry there was a separate back yard containing the rooms of the domestic staff as well as the washing place and latrine.[4] (*Figs. 16.1, 16.2*)

---

4   Field study in May 1983; communication from the owner of the house, a joint family member of one of the initial owners of the house.

CHAPTER 16 ASIAN DWELLING FORMS ■ 283

The plan implies that the dwelling was intended to house more than one family, not only because of the number of kitchens but also the connections provided for each room both to the courtyard and to adjacent rooms. In a sense, each room is independent of the others, and also usable independently. The major feature of the dwelling plan is the courtyard. Because of its position in the middle of the dwelling and its relative privacy, it has almost the character of an interior space; the prerequisite for this, of course, is the climatic conditions of Nairobi. The qualities of the courtyard as a room seem to be contradicted by the stone finishing of not only the facades but also the floor of the gallery and courtyard.

The Ngara house was first constructed in the 1930s by a group of Indians who joined their capital to build the house. Initially, it was occupied by the owners, their families, and tenant families, altogether some sixty to seventy persons. Each owner family had only one room, the other rooms generating income for the building of other houses for each of the owner families. The process took more than ten years to complete. After one of owners had gained sole ownership of the Ngara house, tenants continued to occupy some of the rooms, the growing joint family gradually occupying more rooms, and finally, the whole house. At its largest, the joint family consisted of the parents who had moved to Nairobi from Gujarat in the 1920s, their seven sons and their families.[5]

In many ways, Eastleigh was built according to the principles applied in Ngara. The development of the area, which was located further away in the suburbs, some three kilometers to the northeast of the city center, began after Ngara.[6] The plot subdivision of Eastleigh was a typical gridiron with the main thoroughfares named First and Second Avenue, and the perpendicular streets numbered up to Fourteenth Street. As in Ngara, the plot coverage and density is relatively high, and the outlook of the area is not suburban, as its location in the urban structure would lead us to assume, but urban. The average plot was 16 m wide and 26 m deep, with access to each plot both from the front street and from the back lane. The predominant house type was the courtyard house.[7] (*Fig. 16.3*)

The original plan of the dwelling has been reconstructed on the basis of the study of the present dwelling and in comparison with similar dwelling types in the area. As in the Ngara dwelling, the courtyard has retained its

---

5 Communications in 1983 from one of the members of the joint family and from the son of one of the tenant families.
6 Hake 1977, 38, 176. Eastleigh, formerly known as Egerton Estate and Nairobi East Township, was named after the English railway works town. The 2003 acres had been bought freehold in 1904-5, and in 1912, 654 acres were subdivided into 3332 plots. (p.255) In Barnow et al's data, the map of 1920 shows fragmentary developments in Ngara but not in Eastleigh. This map is based on the Key Plan of Nairobi Township of 22.10.1919, scale 1:10000; the authors have assessed the reliability of the information as "approximate" (Barnow et al 1983, 26, 86). Caminos and Goethert (1980, 219), however, described Eastleigh as having already been developed in the 1910's.
7 Nairobi and District Topographical Map 1:2500, sheet NE 24/B, 1955.

*Fig. 16.3
Privately-built
courtyard house
area, Eastleigh, site
plan*

*Fig. 16.4
Privately-built
courtyard house,
Eastleigh, dwelling
plan*

*Fig. 16.5
Privately-built
courtyard house,
Eastleigh*

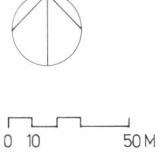

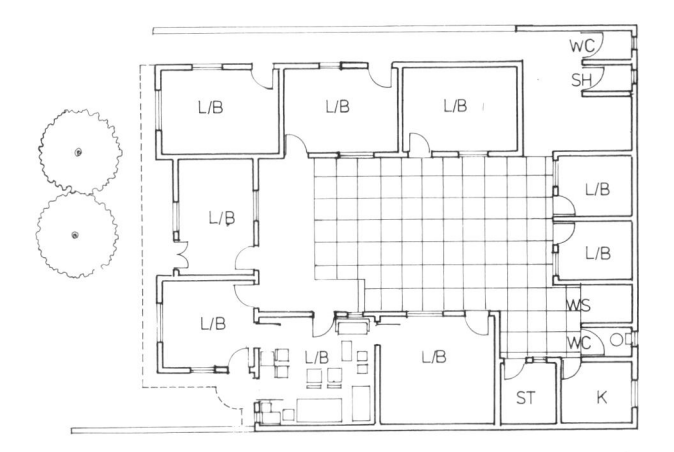

CHAPTER 16 ASIAN DWELLING FORMS ■ 285

central position in relation to the rooms whose functionas are unspecified, with the kitchen and storage at the back. However, the plan is asymmetrical, and both the front veranda and the central corridor are missing. The dwelling is also smaller than the Ngara one but large compared to the dwellings the Railways built for Asians, with a floor area of over 160 m and the additional 80 m of the courtyard.[8] (*Figs. 16.4, 16.5*)

The general appearance of the Eastleigh dwellings seems somewhat closer to European aesthetic ideas than the ones in Ngara: the Eastleigh facades are finished and painted white, not the crude Indian type stonework typical of the Ngara houses. The principles of the earlier courtyard house are maintained in the plan. The flexibility of the use of each room, both in terms of function and in terms of combination with the other rooms, is also repeated in the Eastleigh dwelling. The slightly larger room sizes even add to the flexibility. But the smaller size of the dwelling as a totality, and particularly the altered relation of the courtyard to the street, have reduced the use of the courtyard for purposes which are more strongly linked with the street, either in terms of activity or of prestige. In the Eastleigh dwelling, the courtyard is more of a back yard than in the Ngara house.

The third courtyard house studied was located in the city center in the River Road area. Defined as an Asian commercial area in the beginning of the century, this area first came about as an enlargement of the bazaar, has contained both commercial and residential activities, and was occupied predominantly by members of the Asian community until the 1970s.[9] The development involved high plot coverage and density. In the River Road area, the plots were slightly larger than those in the bazaar area (Biashara Street) in the city center, but smaller than the ones planned in the suburban Ngara and Eastleigh. The plot of the studied dwelling was about 16 m wide and 24 m deep.[10] After the Second World War, the initial one-storied buildings began to be replaced by two-storied structures of the kind the example studied represented; the dwelling studied was part of a two-story building with commercial facilities on the ground floor and residential ones on the upper floor. As the buildings of the area in general, the building in which the dwelling studied was located also covered most of the plot, with an open space in the center. Access to the plot was both from the street and from a back street. Usually the family who had shops on the street level lived on the upper level.

The River Road area differs from the Ngara and Eastleigh in that it is historically very urban: from the very beginning, the plots and the buildings were planned for mixed use. Therefore in the River Road area, the distinction

---

8   Field work in June 1983; communication from a previous dweller of the house. For a similar house type in the area, e.g. Gattoni and Patel 1973, 65.
9   Hake 1977, 175. For an analysis of a part of the River Road area, see also Moniz 1984.
10 Nairobi and District Topographic Map 1:2500, sheets NE 13/B and NE 23/D, 1955; SK Aerial photograph 1:6000, sheet No.2210, 1975; drawings of the construction of the second phase of the studied dwelling, acquired from the owner.

between public and private as well as front and back spaces was more crucial than in the purely residential areas. In terms of the arrangement of the plots, the ground floor street spaces of the buildings were indeed not only more public than those in the purely residential areas, as shops and workshops, they were also very concretely open to the public. In this sense, the development of the two-storied courtyard house in which the functions were separated on different floors with the second floor reserved for residential use, was feasible. (*Fig. 16.6*)

The plan of the dwelling studied has been reconstructed on the basis of the original plan. The dwelling is situated on the upper floor, above the shops. Access to the dwelling from the street is through a staircase on one side of the street frontage, ending on the upper level terrace which forms a courtyard. The plan contains three shops on the street level, with service space in the back yard including access to the back street, storage rooms and toilets for the shops. The back yard is open to the upper level courtyard; a staircase connects the back yard to the upper level. The upper floor plan is organized around a central courtyard so that two similar parts are formed, each with four rooms of similar sizes towards the streets and a kitchen, bath/shower, toilet, and storage space at the side of the courtyard. In the plan, there are interconnecting doors between all the rooms, and the uses of the rooms has not been specified. The present plan had been built in two phases, with the first phase containing the rooms on the street side of the courtyard, built in the 1950s, and the second phase the rooms on the back street side, built after independence. The floor area of the dwelling consists of the two parts, each about 90 m, and the courtyard of some additional 100 m.[11] (*Figs. 16.7, 16.8*)

In the River Road dwelling, the principles which were discernible in the Ngara and the Eastleigh dwellings are retained, albeit with alterations. The location on the upper floor separates the dwelling from the activities on the street, which in the Ngara dwelling had been visible all the way to the courtyard through the central corridor. In this respect, the privacy of the courtyard is increased. But because the courtyard opens into the service court of the shops on the ground floor level, the residential courtyard still is - at least to an extent - a semi-public space. When the shops are kept by the same family who inhabits the upper floor, the visual connection also enables the supervision of the work from the dwelling. The opening to the ground floor level emphasizes the division of the courtyard into two separate parts, even if within seeing and hearing distance. The multi-purpose rooms with connections to the courtyard and to the adjacent rooms, typical of the courtyard house type, also have potential for varying uses because of their relatively generous dimensions. In the River Road courtyard dwelling, however, the courtyard has a role which differs from the Ngara and Eastleigh

---

11 Drawings of the construction of the second phase, acquired from the owner; field study in May 1983; communications from members of the joint family.

*Fig. 16.6
Privately-built
courtyard house area,
city center, site plan*

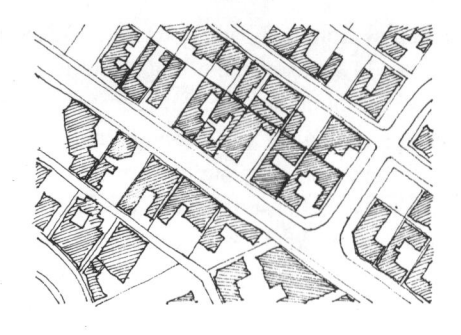

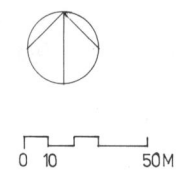

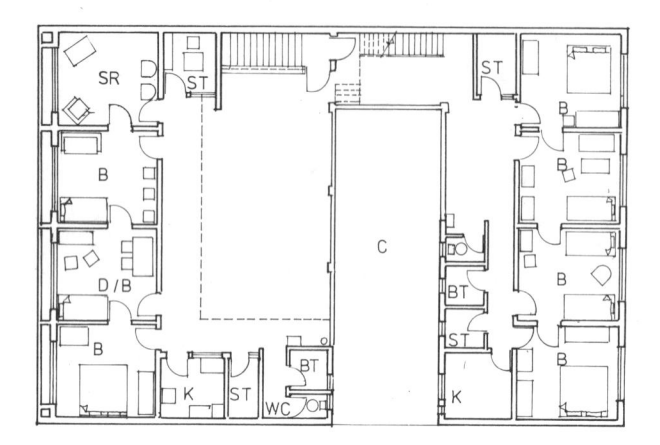

*Fig. 16.7
Privately-built
courtyard house, city
center, dwelling plan*

*Fig. 16.8
Privately-built
courtyard house, city
center*

288 ■ PART IV DWELLING FORMS IN NAIROBI

dwellings: here, the courtyard as the only point of entry is the most public part of the dwelling. The separation of the front rooms with access directly from the street via the courtyard has in the River Road dwelling plan been transformed into a more enclosed dwelling. This may be attributed to the location of the building in the city center where the ground floor shops may be used partly for the same purposes as the front rooms in the suburbs: as male guest rooms for meeting business associates and other visitors.

A detached house converted into a courtyard house. The pre-independence dwellings studied which were planned by Asians included another courtyard house which originally was a detached house, not based on a courtyard, but into which it was transformed by several extensions. The house was located in Parklands, which had been reserved for Europeans from the turn of the century until the Second World War and which later developed into an Asian area.[12] Parklands had become part of the municipality when the city boundaries were extended in 1919.[13] The plots were relatively large, following the English garden city concept similar to the one applied in the Hill area, with houses located in the middle of the plot, surrounded by gardens and by services at the back. After the change in the occupancy from the Europeans to the Asians, the initially large plots were further subdivided. The resulting plots were still considerably larger than the ones allocated for the Asians in Ngara and Eastleigh. In many houses, the main entry was elaborated with a driveway between two gates. The plot of the house studied was 30 m wide and over 70 m deep.[14] (*Fig. 16.9*)

The new Asian residential area differed significantly from the earlier Asian parts of the city. While the River Road area, Ngara, and Eastleigh, regardless of their location in the city center or in the suburbs, were urban, with high densities and plot coverage, the character of Parklands was definitely suburban. The relation of the house to its immediate surroundings became totally different from the earlier forms. A major part of the plot was covered by the garden.

The first plan of the Parklands house studied was designed by L.N. Vadgama for Mr. Singh in February 1946. The plan of the house is asymmetrical, the front elevation showing an open veranda and entry door to the right and a protruding part of the building with an adjacent small porch and entry to the left. The room in the center is marked as a sitting room, with two bedrooms on the veranda side of it, and two bedrooms and stores on the other side. Access to the back veranda and the back yard is through the front veranda entry. The kitchen and bathroom are located at the other

---

12 According to Hake (1977, 255), Parklands was among the first residential areas developed and was by 1906 housing many Government officials; after Parklands became an Asian area, Upper Parklands further to the west was restricted to Europeans.
13 Halliman and Morgan 1967, 104.
14 Nairobi and District Topographic Map 1:2500, Sheet NE 33/D, 1955. For a demonstration of the change in the plot subdivision, compare the maps of 1940 and 1950 in Barnow et al. 1983, 43, 53.

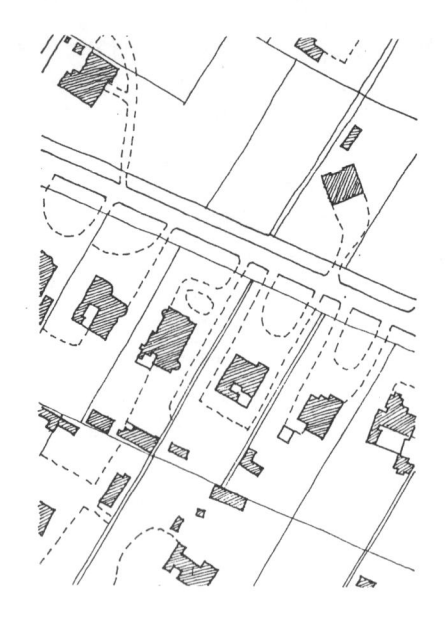

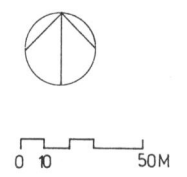

Fig. 16.9 Privately-built detached house, Parklands, site plan

Fig. 16.10 Detached house converted into courtyard house, Parklands, dwelling plan

Fig. 16.11 Privately-built detached house, Parklands

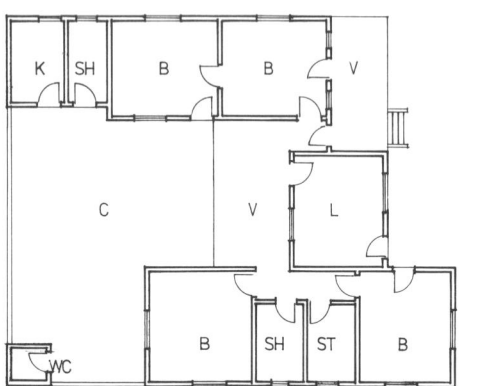

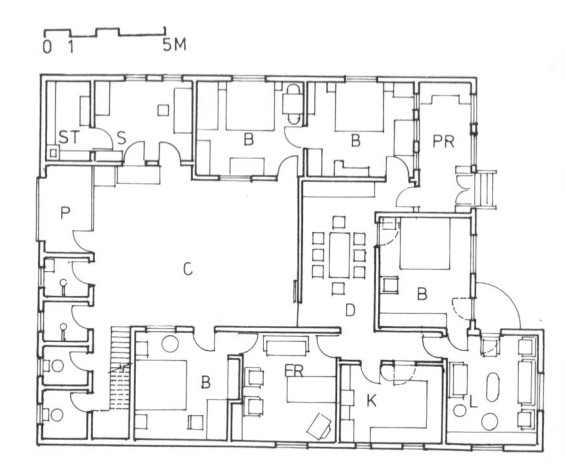

290 ■ PART IV DWELLING FORMS IN NAIROBI

side of the back yard and, in another corner, the toilet. The back yard is walled. Altogether, the floor area shown in the initial plan was about 125 m, with the verandas and the back yard accounting for an additional 170 m. Later plans show additions of a separate garage building with a store room from May 1947, and the additions of a bedroom, a second toilet, shower and laundry rooms with the extension of the kitchen from February 1955.[15] At the time of the study in 1983, several other conversions and extensions had also been made.[16] (*Figs. 16.10, 16.11*)

The organization of the initial plan of the Parklands dwelling is a combination of features from a detached house located in the suburbs with large garden plots and from a courtyard house located in a densely built urban structure with limited space. The front veranda and the positioning of windows towards the outside convey the idea of a detached house, while the several entries to different rooms in the front, the walled back yard, and the direct accesses from the rooms to the back yard suggest a dense urban context. The separation of the kitchen to the back of the house had occurred in the Asian houses planned by both the Railways and by the Asians. Some of the characteristics were similar to those present in the Eastleigh house, particularly the function of the front rooms with direct access from the outside to serve as both bedrooms (as they are named in the plan) and as rooms to receive visitors. In this sense, the plan implies that the house was to be inhabited by a joint family with several adult male members.

The joint family system was followed by many Asians in Nairobi, although before independence there were rarely more than two generations, since the Asians had come from India at the turn of the century, and usually later. The joint family provided security both in economic, social, and cultural issues; this was important for the minority who did not have any support from the colonial system, as the Europeans, or from their rural communities, as the Africans. The core of the Hindu community was the joint family, usually including three generations, sometimes unmarried uncles, cousins going to school, or relatives visiting the country for months. Analyzing Indian culture and society, Richard Lannoy emphasized that even for the modern urban joint family, the ancestral home remained "not only a symbol, but the heart of a family's sense of identity."[17]

Although the construction of Hindu houses traditionally involved religion and astrology in the selection of the site, the examination of the soil, and the planning of the house, in Nairobi the Hindus had to adjust these to the colonial context. Plots were available only in particular areas allocated for Asians, regardless of the astrological implications of the location, and, instead of

---

15 This drawing and the others referred to in the text were acquired from the owner of the house.
16 Field study in May 1983; communications from members of the joint family. Drawings of the alterations were not available.
17 Lannoy 1971, 87.

religion, building by-laws partly regulated the size and shape of the house. Ross described the interior arrangements of the dwelling of the Hindu joint family of urban India including one or more shared living or reception rooms, a worshipping room, and the kitchen, the rest being multi-purpose rooms. Each room was connected to the adjacent rooms and to the courtyard, perceived as the social space of the community living in the house. Concerns about purity and pollution influenced the location and organization of some spaces. The Pooja – the worshipping room – or the family shrine had to be accessible for daily worship but placed so that it could be guarded against unwelcome intrusion. The kitchen was seen as a sacred area, the preparation of food containing strong religious meanings. The toilet was perceived as an element causing pollution and requiring purification. A comment on Hindu houses in Singapore may be illuminating:

> The separation of toilet facilities in the Hindu Indian house . . . is more than a question of general hygiene, it is part and parcel of the religious practice.[18]

In the traditional Hindu concept of dwelling, the aspect of unpretentiousness was emphasized in several studies, regardless of the caste or income level of the family; as Reverend J.E. Padfield summarized his description of a Hindu house in India at the turn of the century:

> It is . . . the absence of comfort which (to the European) seems most conspicuous in a Hindu home.[19]

In recent decades, however, the concept may be changing. In the 1960s, the dwelling practices of the Asians living in Nairobi tended to differ depending on which part of India their family originated in. In a study on the Indian minority in East Africa based on field work in 1964, Agehanda Bharati noted that Gujarati Hindus usually lived relatively modestly, preferring to save and invest their incomes; their wealth was difficult to predict from the looks of the houses. Panjabis, however, used their income more to create pleasant dwellings with little worry about future investments. According to Bharati, most East African Asians at the time enjoyed the latest electronic gadgets.[20] But in the same study, Bharati also described the interiors of Asian dwellings in a way which contradicts the depiction of modesty:

> Most houses, cutting across all Indian communities, decorate their interior with Ravi Varma type oleographs and polychrome representa-

---

18   Beng-Huat 1988, 12. For more extensive descriptions of Hindu traditions concerning worship in dwellings, see Ross 1961, 54ff., 63; Beng-Huat 1988, 12; concerning the kitchen, Ross 1961, 54f.; Lannoy 1971, 150f.; Beng-Huat 1988, 11-14.
19   For an illustrative historical description of "an ordinary house of the fairly well-to-do Hindu in the town" in India at the end of the last century, see J.E. Padfield, *The Hindu at Home*, 1896, 16-24, quoted extensively in King 1984, 53ff.
20   According to Bharati (1970, 20, 66), the majority of the East African Indians were Gujarati-speaking Hindus, forming approximately 70% of the total Asian population.

tions of gods, goddesses, Gandhi, Nehru, Vallabhai Pate, Sabhas Chandra Bose, kings and queens of the Hindu pantheon, film actresses from the Indian screen, sectarian and national Hindu leaders from the past 400 years, and an occasional photograph of Queen Elizabeth and Prince Philip, or even Elvis Presley stuck into the frames of the aforesaid products. The walls are replete with cheap chintz, and the oleographs themselves are perfectly ghastly, super-realistic, gaudily-colored and embarrassingly banal. The choice has little to do with the economic level, for these artifacts are found among millionaire industrialists and the poorest fundis [laborers] alike. Paper flowers abound on the tables and windowsills, even when the garden around the house produces fine specimens en masse: these seem to be reserved for the house-shrines only, though even there paper flowers tend to outnumber the natural plants.[21]

Privately-built nuclear family dwellings: a semi-detached house

After the Second World War, the growing Asian community needed more housing, and, as Halliman and Morgan noted in their geographical study of the Nairobi city and region, "expansion in Parklands-Eastleigh was limited by the municipal housing in Eastlands on one side and the low density development of European-style housing on the other."[22] New housing estates for Asians were built in the area known as Nairobi South, some three kilometers south of the city center. The area was flat and had black cotton soil, which is difficult to drain, to build on, or to grow vegetation on, but the location was conveniently near the industrial area. In the plan, the streets form an incomplete gridiron, each block consisting of some 12 residential plots and a land reservation for unspecified purposes. By 1955, only a portion of the plots had been built. The plot of the dwelling studied was approximately 15 m wide and 40 m deep. The predominant house type in this area was the semi-detached house.[23]

The plan suggests a development of clusters of houses as the basis of the general organization of the area, something which had not occurred in the Asian areas built earlier. In the River Road area, Ngara, Eastleigh, and Parklands, the layout of the plots had been an issue related to surveying, a more or less mechanical allocation of land for different purposes. In Nairobi South, the roads, for example, help to create smaller blocks and the land reserves provide some potential for the construction of public spaces and buildings. The relatively narrow but deep plots implied an environment with the edges of the road largely built and the back sides developed as gardens. This combines the urban characteristics of Ngara or Eastleigh with the more

---

21   Bharati 1970, 57f.
22   Halliman and Morgan 1967, 106.
23   Nairobi and District Topographic Map 1:2500, sheet NE 4/C, 1955; field study in May 1983.

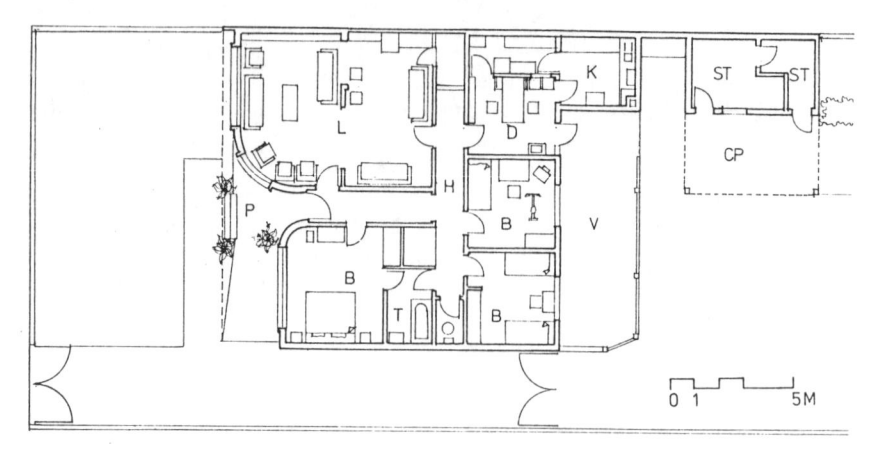

Fig. 16.12 Privately-built semidetached house, Nairobi South, dwelling plan

Fig. 16.13 Privately-built semidetached house, Nairobi South

suburban characteristics of Parklands.

The dwelling studied was a semi-detached house designed for an Asian family. According to the initial plan, the house was designed for Hassanali M. Kassam by P. Rambaldo. The plan shows the entrance through a front veranda to a passage, with a "lounge" (as the living room is called in the plan), a dining room, and an "open garden" (an internal courtyard) to its right, and the main bedroom, a bath room, and a linen store to its left. The passage from the entry ends in another passage perpendicular to it, with access to the open garden, a toilet, two bedrooms, and a "utility, breakfast and children's room" through which the kitchen, the back terrace, and two storage rooms are accessible. A separate structure contains the "boys' room" with shower and toilet, and the boiler.[24] (*Figs. 16.12, 16.13*)

Painted a dazzling white, the building with its rounded walls framing the entrance, a large picture window commanding the front view, and a flat roof conveys a modern image. This is no longer a traditional plan of an Asian dwelling. The open courtyard which is the heart of the Asian courtyard house has been reduced to an "open garden," not as a place for the joint family to gather but as a place to look at or to provide ventilation and greenery. The rooms are no longer linked to the courtyard and to each other, but separated by a neutral space, the corridor. It implies that the rooms may not be used flexibly for different purposes or by different tenants: the position of the room in the plan restricts the possible functions. This is a plan of a dwelling for a nuclear family.

Among these pre-independence dwellings planned by Asians, that of a small nuclear family differed from those of large joint families. The typical joint family dwelling had been based on the courtyard type, with interconnected and functionally unspecified rooms surrounding a courtyard located in the center and used like a room; the type related to models from India. Both in the courtyard house of the joint family and in the semi-detached house of the nuclear family, the kitchen was relatively secluded from the rest of the rooms. However, the nuclear family dwelling did not contain a courtyard, but rooms assigned for specific functions, somewhat in the manner of European models. Contrary to the plans of European dwellings in Nairobi, the different functional areas within this dwelling were not strictly separated. Thus the semi-detached dwelling may be perceived as a development of the Asian dwelling in Nairobi in the context of a change in family type from the joint family to the nuclear family.

---

24   Plan of the house, dated October 1954 and revised in December in the same year, acquired from the owner; field study. In the dwelling studied, the plan was reversed.

■ 17 "Universal" dwelling forms

Before independence, a large portion of Nairobi dwellings had been constructed by the various cultural groups for their own use, based on earlier dwelling plans which they had modified for the new context and on concepts of dwelling with which they were familiar. There were only two exceptions, albeit central ones: employer-built housing, which was, of course, momentous at the time, and public housing, steadily growing in significance particularly in the period following the Second World War until 1963. After independence, housing in Nairobi increasingly developed into an activity where the processes of planning and designing houses were detached from the future dwellers, not only in terms of actual participation but, more importantly, in terms of cultural responsiveness. The variety of concepts of dwelling particular to the real cultural composition of Nairobi began to be replaced by concepts of dwelling essentially removed from the historical and social context: in effect, by concepts of dwelling claimed to be universal.

The influence of the universal concepts of dwelling extended into much of post-independence housing. In the public sector particularly the international development aid programs were crucial; in the private sector the incentives to rent or to sell residential property were increasing parallel with the rapid population growth of the capital city. Thus the effects were concentrated on planned dwellings, that is, almost exclusively on dwellings of the middle classes, even if some of the model plans developed for low-cost housing also contained presuppositions of universality. Although in many ways the dwellings of the public sector differed from those of the private sector both in context and in design, the "universal" concepts of dwelling governing them nevertheless partially converged.

The notion of "universal" concepts of dwelling compressed two initially separate developments. One was the idea of domestic architecture as a way of promoting reform: as a means of converting one particular way of life deemed as unfit into another considered virtuous, usually specifically involving the transformation of the ways of life of the workers or ethnic groups into those of the middle classes.[1] In essence, it implied the superiority of middle class values and practices to other deviating ones, claiming them

---

1 For developments in the United States, see Wright 1981, chapters 4 and 7; in France, Paravicini 1990, chapter 9. See also above, chapter 15.

to be universal and pursuing the establishment of their position as such. The other development imbedded in the formulation was the idea of universal dwelling types: standardized residential units based on the vital minimum requirements of life functions and on pure geometric forms suitable for industrial production.[2] The idea of a new way of life, then, consisted of both the notion of the dwelling as a means of promoting the ways of life of the middle classes as the model for other social groups, and the notion of the scientific development of the model dwelling plan. In both its aspects, the reference to a new way of life implied a total change: the rejection of inherited historical models for the adoption of consciously planned models claimed as universal. For a new way of life to develop, existing customs of dwelling had to be replaced by built forms rationally planned for universal human needs.[3] In essence, dwelling was perceived as an activity which involved those aspects of human beings which were shared by all. It implied that while economic differences may result in different resources for the purchase of houses – illuminated, for example, in the notion of low-cost housing – the underlying human needs of the dwellers were fundamentally alike.

Public sector dwellings

After independence, the Kenyan Government, the National Housing Corporation, Nairobi City Council, and funding organizations such as the Housing Finance Company of Kenya with financial support from development aid organizations including the Commonwealth Development Corporation, United States Agency for International Development, the World Bank, and the International Development Agency, devised development funding plans where families with middle-range incomes could gain ownership of a house. Within this kind of frame, a large number of housing schemes have also been built in Nairobi, among them the three areas – Kibera, Umoja, and Buru Buru – from which dwellings were selected for this study. All three areas were located in the suburbs, at the time of building more or less at the outer edge of the city, but in today's (1996) situation, already surrounded by newer housing areas. The Kibera dwelling is based on the courtyard principle, while the two others are row houses, one-storied in Umoja and two-storied in Buru Buru.

The courtyard house reinvented. The new village in Kibera was one of the mortgage housing schemes financed by the National Housing Corporation and the Commonwealth Development Corporation in the early 1970s. Kibera,

---

2   On the principles and development of minimum dwellings, within CIAM (Congrès Internationaux d'Architecture Moderne, 1928-1956), see Le Corbusier 1987, 231; Gropius (orig. "Die soziologischen Grundlagen der Minimalwohnung", *Die Justiz*, vol.5, no.8, 1929) 1962, 98; Le Corbusier 1971; Giedion 1967, 696-704; Tafuri and Dal Co 1980, 246f.

3   Paul Rabinow has identified this approach of modern planning as normative, or middling, modernism, which he has defined as the attempt to create new, liberated and purified human beings, the norms and forms claimed as universal. For a historical analysis of the processes involved within French planning, see Rabinow 1989.

located in a suburban area to the southwest of the city center, is an old squatter settlement, long just outside the municipal boundary. It was developed in the 1910s by Sudanese soldiers recruited to the King's African Rifles, later veterans of the First World War. By 1933, the old Kibera area was inhabited by 251 Sudanese house-owners and by 320 non-Sudanese.[4] Like Pumwani, Kibera has all through its history been an area with strong links to the Islamic traditions of the coastal Swahili culture. Even today, the Sudanese core with its mosque has remained. In 1963, the boundary of Nairobi was extended and Kibera became part of the municipality. Since then, the squatter area has been complemented with several planned housing schemes.

The site of the residential area studied, popularly identified as Fort Jesus after the Mombasa citadel, was situated next to the old Kibera, between the railway line, which had been realigned after the Second World War, and the main thoroughfare, Kibera Drive. The site sloping towards the south-east was about 36 acres, to be built in two phases. The first phase comprised 114 dwellings and was completed in 1972. The housing exemplified by that built in the Fort Jesus scheme was not intended to replace the mud and wattle structures of the squatter areas, but, as Project Architect Andrew Wuensche defined it, "to satisfy the demands of emerging lower middle class."[5] Within the government-initiated housing schemes of Nairobi, the design of the Kibera courtyard house was and has remained an exception.

The plan of the area is based on a strict north-south gridiron, with the houses, the clusters, and the spaces between them following the geometry, the only deviations noticeable in the slight east-west modifications of the position of some clusters in relation to each other. The link to the main road is by a peripheral road which loops into the area, with parking planned as enlargements of the road. In the site plan, the two phases are separated by a valley to be developed as a recreation zone containing the main pedestrian spine as well as a nursery, a school, and a clinic. The dwelling plans were based on a 40 ft. by 40 ft. square in one level. In the system, three houses formed an L-shaped group with access from the shared entrance porch at the inside corner of the L. Four of these joined together made up a cluster of twelve dwellings. Common squares were located between the clusters. The first phase comprised 19 clusters, some modified from the system.[6] (*Fig. 17.1*) This overall arrangement of the area, according to the Project Architect, comprised a system of paths, dwelling clusters and children's play areas:

> The system that emerged has a logic in which the basic element, the dwelling, automatically generates the shape of the whole cluster, the pedestrian network, and a hierarchy of open spaces.[7]

---

4   Hake (1977, 96f.) referring to Dorothy Halliman's thesis, *Kibera: A Plan for Suburban Renewal* (1952).
5   Wuensche 1974, 312.
6   SK Aerial photograph 1:6000, sheet 603, 1975; the presentation of the project by the project architect (Wuensche 1974); field study in June 1983.
7   Wuensche 1974, 313.

The geometry, realized in a very compact form, makes the new area stand out from its surroundings. The imposed system is totally alien to the forms of the old self-built Kibera. The effect of the strict gridiron is emphasized by the characteristics of the site as a relatively even slope, without marked changes within the area. Geometry seems to dominate the plan, even though conforming to it can occur only at the expense of practicality, both on the large and on the small scale. On the large scale, for example, pedestrian paths are planned as perpendicular, i.e. urban, networks, when the context is suburban, although paths immediately outside the area follow more curved movement patterns. On a smaller scale, the cluster formation creates a congested point at the entrances to the three dwellings. Thus the purpose of producing a system – of dwellings, of clusters, of open spaces – has superseded the development of a specific plan for the building of a particular area. In this sense, the Kibera plan can be seen as an application of a model, planned to be repeated elsewhere.

The design brief required that the site be developed at a high density, with a mixture of three, four and six room dwellings. The dwellings were to be based on courtyard house plans initially designed by the colonial administration but rejected by the new designers. In the new plans, the courtyard principle was retained. In designing the type plans for the houses, the smaller houses were conceived as family dwellings and the larger ones were perceived to have a mixture of tenants. It was assumed that in the smaller houses a private garden would be appropriate, while in the six-room dwellings it would not be. Thus the same walled area could be used for all the house types. This would also allow the extension of the smaller house onto the garden area later, and give flexibility during the planning. The walled space reserved for each dwelling was about 150 m, with a floor area of about 65 m in the four-room dwellings and about 90 m in the six-room dwellings. All the rooms were gathered around a courtyard.[8] The courtyard was conceived as "a very useful extension to the house, and a means of independent access to all rooms"[9] but nevertheless a clash was seen between its role as an area for relaxation and one for household practicalities. Therefore two courtyards were planned, one relating to the living room and bedrooms, and another relating to the kitchens. The shower and toilets were located around a small corridor next to the entrance, with a space for the garbage can provided outside the dwelling. The smallest, three-roomed dwelling contained one large room, two smaller ones, and a kitchen, the four-roomed one a second large room, and the largest, the six-roomed one, two more small rooms and a second kitchen and shower. The rooms faced the main courtyard and the dwellings were relatively closed to the outside: in the group of three dwellings, one did not have any windows to the exterior, and the two others had only one each.

---

8   Dwelling plans, published in Wuensche 1974 and in Hooper et al 1974.
9   Wuensche 1974, 313.

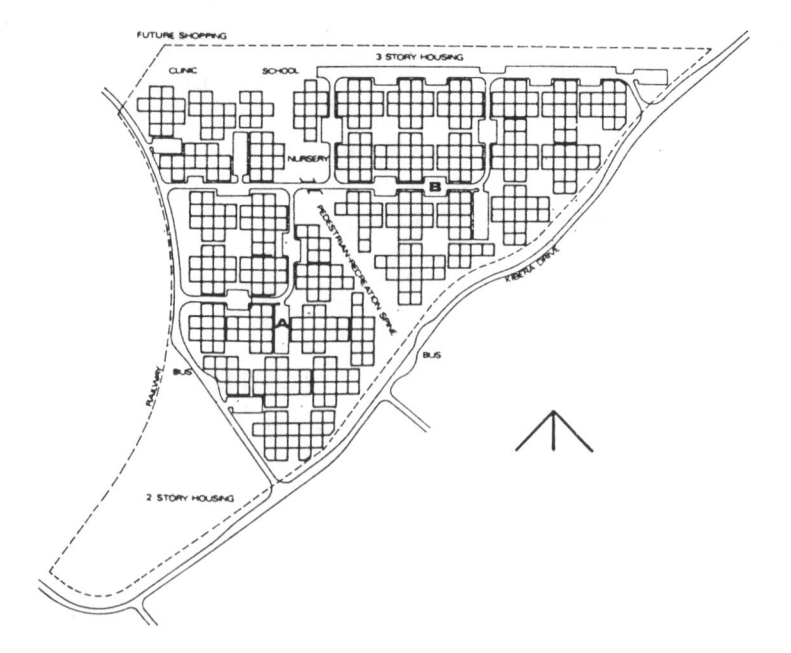

Fig. 17.1 Public sector housing, Kibera, site plan

Fig. 17.2 Public sector courtyard house, Kibera, dwelling plan

Fig. 17.3 Public sector courtyard house, Kibera

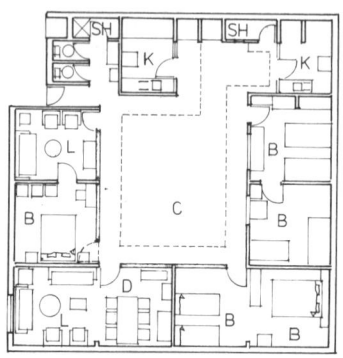

300 ■ PART IV DWELLING FORMS IN NAIROBI

The dwelling studied had been built in two phases and contained six rooms at the time of the study.[10] (*Figs. 17.2, 17.3*)

In the dwelling plan, the geometry of the site plan is repeated on a smaller scale. The plan implies a distinction of two functional zones: one zone formed by the rooms for habitation – living room(s), bedrooms, and the main courtyard – and the other by the services – the kitchens, the service courtyard, the toilets and showers, and the refuse. Between the two zones is the point of entry. The design of the zone around the main courtyard is based on almost a complete symmetry, with the position of the partition walls, doors, and windows aligned. The only deviation of the symmetry is caused by the entrance. Because of the almost total enclosure of the dwelling from the exterior, the plan makes not only the rooms but also the courtyard into relatively private spaces. This has consequences on the environmental character of the area in general. Despite the relatively high densities and coverage, the common spaces between the buildings are not urban places for gathering, but rather land left over in the geometric system.

One- and two-story row houses. With the extension of Nairobi's boundaries in March 1963, Eastlands to the east of the city center became one of the areas of expansion.[11] The older parts of the Eastlands had been predominately filled by African residential areas like Kaloleni and Makadara built by the City Council and large employers, among them the Railways. Before the extension of the boundary, according to the census of 1962, 70% of the 155,000 Africans of Nairobi were living in Eastlands.[12] The extended Eastlands was flat treeless land on black cotton soil, at the edge of the Athi Plains. It was to be the main area of development for residential areas built with public funds.[13] Thus it also became the area into which much of the development aid related to housing the middle classes was directed.

Within Eastlands, one of these areas was Umoja Estate, some 7 km east of the city center, beyond the Outer Ring Road. Umoja Estate was planned as the first low-income housing project in Nairobi financed by the Housing Guarantee Program of USAID, the United States Agency for International Development. The first phase was started in 1975 and consisted of 3,000 single story units with one to three rooms in row houses.[14] The site – previously a sisal farm[15] – is flat treeless land, the plains extending to the horizon. The general land use of the Umoja Estate may be seen from an aerial photograph: located between the Ring Road and the main internal road, fingers of roads create a repetitive pattern. In each finger, the uniform one-storied

---

10 Field study in June 1983.
11 Halliman and Morgan 1967, 98f, esp. the map on the boundary changes since 1900.
12 Halliman and Morgan 1967, 106.
13 On the plans concerning post-independence Nairobi residential areas financed by the Government or the Municipality and supported by international development agencies, see e.g. Emig and Ismail 1980, 62.
14 Hoek-Smit 1983, 1.
15 Map of Nairobi 1:50000, sheet 148/4, 1975.

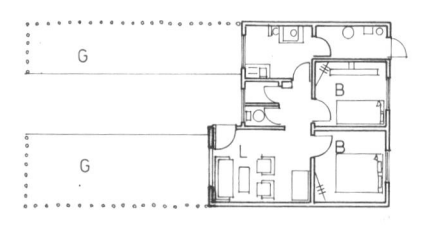

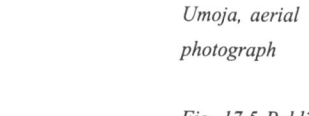

Fig. 17.4 Public sector housing, Umoja, aerial photograph

Fig. 17.5 Public sector row house, Umoja, dwelling plan

Fig. 17.6 Public sector row house, Umoja

302 ■ PART IV   DWELLING FORMS IN NAIROBI

row houses are built on both sides of road loops formed into elongated hexagons. In addition to the roads, the plan does not provide other common spaces within the area.[16] (*Fig. 17.4*)

The dwelling studied was located in the middle of the Umoja Estate phase I.[17] All the dwelling plans within Umoja I were the same. Each dwelling has access to a front and a back yard. The front entrance with space provided for a garden and a car port, leads directly into the living room. To its back is one of the bedrooms, with a door connecting the two. A corridor from the living room leads to the kitchen, with the shower and toilet on one side of the corridor, facing the front of the house, and a second bedroom on the other side, facing the back. The kitchen storage space also provides access to the back yard. The back yard boundaries of the opposite row houses meet. According to the plan, the yards are not walled. The dwelling was planned to be built in two phases. The first phase included the wet core, the storage room, and one bedroom, with a floor area of about 24 m. The second phase contained the living room and another bedroom, together accounting for about 22 m, and adding up to a total of 46 m. According to the present dwellers, this phasing had also been followed in building the dwelling studied. (*Figs. 17.5, 17.6*)

In the Umoja dwelling plan, the difference between the front and the back of the house is visible in the external spaces: the front yard is articulated and attached to the living room, while the back yard is attached to the kitchen and storage activities. This distinction, however, is not followed in the internal organization of the dwelling, where the windows both of main spaces like the living room and of secondary spaces like the shower and the toilet are to the front. The entrance to the living room is also the only entrance; in the plan, the back yard cannot be used as a second entrance because it lacks access to a public space. Evidently the organization of the plan has been influenced by the phasing and by the intention of locating the connections to the common pipes so that they may be easily maintained. For this, the wet core has been positioned in the front of the house, on the more public side of the building, and the bedrooms on the back, on the more private side.

The other dwelling studied was situated on Buru Buru Estate, a housing development project constructed (by the time of the field study) in five phases between 1973 and 1983 by the Commonwealth Development Corporation in cooperation with the Kenyan Government and the Nairobi City Council. The area is located some 6 km east from the city center, between the Rabai Road and the Outer Ring Road. The first phase of 920 units was completed between September 1973 and July 1974.[18] The first two phases consisted of units with three to five rooms, some single story, some double story.[19] After the field

---

16 SK Aerial photograph 1:6000, sheet 773, 1975; field study in June 1983; Nairobi Road Map 1:20000, 1981.
17 Field study.
18 *Sunday Nation*, March 11, 1973.

study, new phases of residential areas have been built adjacent to the earlier Buru Buru areas. The dwelling selected for this study, a maisonette with four rooms on two floors, was from phase four.

The dwelling studied was located in one of the clusters of two-storied row houses around a space reserved for a playground, connected to the internal loop road of the residential area with a cul-de-sac. At the edge of the cluster, four row houses formed a small square with some common space in the center. The row houses were white stucco and had red tile roofs reminiscent of a modern Spanish village. The area had been completed fairly recently before the field study. The row houses were situated in the middle of the plot so that each dwelling had access to a walled front yard with space for a garden, and a car port, and also to a back yard with a washing place and space for household activities. The entrance from the outside was directly to the living room. A space for dining was attached to the back of the living room. On the ground floor, there was also a smaller room, the kitchen, a toilet, the staircase to the upper floor, and a door to the back yard, all accessible from the corridor. A door separated the corridor from the living room. On the upper floor, there were two bedrooms, a smaller and larger one, both with built-in cupboards, a toilet, a boiler, and a shower. In area, the upper floor was smaller than the ground floor. According to the plan, the back yard was open to the common green area.[20] (*Figs. 17.7, 17.8*)

In the plan of the row house, the front and the back are clearly distinguished. Visitors enter from the front yard which is articulated with brightly painted walls, a built-in seat and a garden, and which provides the opportunity to identify the car with the dwelling. The seat at the entry suggests functions earlier performed by a veranda: a place to communicate with neighbors, to meet casual visitors, or to welcome guests. The back yard is for secondary and more private activities. The arrangement enables the use of the living room and the front garden separately from the rest of the dwelling, with a door in between. The rest of the ground floor is, according to the plan, accessible from the back. The back door is a second point of entry, available both for the tenant or domestic staff. The ground floor bedroom may easily be let out because of the back entrance and the ground floor toilet. The different functional areas are clearly separated. The area reserved for meeting visitors can be closed off. The kitchen and the ground floor room can be used independently of the rest of the dwelling. The upper floor has the character of the family suite, even though the separation from the ground floor is not by a door which could be locked but by an open staircase.

In some respects, the organization of the two dwelling plans studied resembled each other. Both the Umoja and the Buru Buru dwellings were located in row houses on self-contained plots, contained front and back yards,

---

19 Menezes 1978, 34. For the area plan of Buru Buru II and an example of a dwelling plan, see Barnow et al 1983, 74.
20 Field study in June 1983.

Fig. 17.7 Public sector row house, Buru Buru, dwelling plan

Fig. 17.8 Public sector row house, Buru Buru

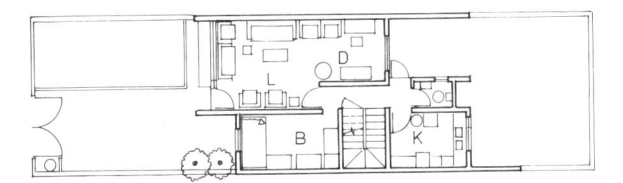

and involved the living room as the space to enter the dwelling. There were also differences: the separation of the front yard and the living room from the other spaces in the Buru Buru dwelling is not followed in the Umoja dwelling where the separation is at most partial. The differences were clearest in relation to the distinctions between the front and the back: in the Umoja dwelling, this distinction was disregarded while in the Buru Buru dwelling it was further emphasized by the separating door between the living room and the rest of the dwelling and by the functional distinction in the two stories.

In western analyses of newly independent African countries, the middle classes were perceived not only as an insurance for continuity, because of their support of the status quo and western values, but also as the real motors of development and modernization.[21] In creating a middle class in Kenya, housing was seen as one of the key elements. Particularly in the 1960s and early 70s, public housing programs and development aid policies favored middle income groups.[22] The notion of dwellings as a vehicle in the creation of a middle class also involved the planning and design of the dwellings; this aspect had already been important in the reform movements. Then, emphasis had been given to improvements in health conditions towards a better way of life. In the newly independent Kenya, according to Richard Stren, housing plans and projects received much national publicity, and on the symbolic level, modern forms were considered appealing. Within this context, modern dwellings for African families were seen as visible evidence of the progress from a colonial society to a modern African state: "by living in more modern structures, it is implied that Africans are themselves more modern."[23] Peter Marris[24] noted similar tendencies in his study of a rehousing project in Lagos, Nigeria:

> The rehousing estate . . . was not designed to accommodate an existing pattern of life. It attempted to reform it, to retrieve human dignity from surroundings felt to be degrading. New standards of space and amenity, and a separate dwelling for each household, would encourage people to take pride in their homes, and adopt the accepted symbols of a progressive society. But in effect, if not intentionally, these reforms encouraged a much more radical change in social patterns. Well-spaced streets with shrubs and garden could only be provided where the residents would be a long way from their work and their relatives, and they could only pay for this suburban life at the sacrifice of other claims upon their resources. Households became isolated from their wider family groups, and obligations to their kin were much more difficult to fulfil. The estate, therefore, encouraged a new interpretation of social values, in which privacy, independence and domestic comfort displaced traditional loyalties.[25]

According to Marris, the slum clearance scheme of the center of the capital was pursued so insistently primarily not because of its unhealthy conditions or overcrowding, but because the area was seen as a national disgrace, "for the scorn [it] must arouse in visitors from those nations which for centuries had exploited, ruled and patronized West Africa."[26] It was a question of national pride and of the symbols which the Nigerians attached to their intentions rather than to their present conditions. Thus in terms of national symbols, the rapid Africanization of the government (which in Kenya took

---

21 See e.g. Davidson 1978, 314; Lloyd 1973, 63-70; Magubane 1976, 190ff.
22 See e.g. Stren 1972, 88; Chana 1984, 18; Elkan and Zwanenberg 1975, 670. For similar tendencies in other African ex-colonial countries, e.g. Blair 1971, 231. Recently, this may have changed towards more low-cost solutions, see e.g. Williams 1984, 179.
23 Stren 1972, 81.
24 Marris 1962, 118ff.
25 Marris 1962, 132.
26 Marris 1962, 119.

place after independence) increased the demands on modern housing, that is, demands on housing with the proper image, as an external symbol for the other members of the international community. But the symbolic aspect of housing has also been connected to the internal relationships, those within the country. For the middle classes, the modern dwellings served as a means of identifying themselves as a new group and as different from the older groups of Kenya. In this sense, the modern dwellings of the middle classes have been linked both to international and to national symbols. In terms of both, the notion of modern planned dwellings carried the appropriate meanings for the middle classes.

From the point of view of the "aid-giving" countries, the notion of dwellings as a means of creating a middle class in Kenya was supported both by the argumentation of the western reform movements, oriented for over a century towards workers and ethnic groups, and by the theories of modernization, oriented towards the economically less-developed (i.e. Third World) ex-colonial countries. In this context, the notion of scientific research as the basis of the new forms of dwelling was central. Science was seen as a method of discovering, analyzing and formalizing the needs and functions of the universal human being. The concept of scientific research denoted expertise of and by professionals, involving legislation, norms, standards, and formal education. In each of these, the western approaches were the ones accepted as scientific, as those of the experts. Referring particularly to the planning education given in England and directed towards the "developing," often ex-colonial countries, Anthony D. King has aptly described this the

> subtle process of cognitive colonialism [where] values, language, methods and professional ideologies are largely transplanted.[27]

Thus the values imbedded in the scientific approaches become to be taken for granted: they are not identified as part of a system of values but considered to be objective, outside the realm of values. In the establishment of the values as self-evident, the issue of economic control over the production of the research has been crucial. Through the scientific studies used in the formulation of the aid programs, the development aid agencies have ensured that their values would continue to form the policies of the countries "receiving" the aid.

In the context of development aid programs, then, the modern planned dwellings thus fulfilled the goals of the "aid-receiving" countries, within which the newly established middle classes as the civil servants participating in the administration of the aid supported the construction of housing areas with the attained symbolic qualities. In addition, they fulfilled the goals of the "aid-giving" countries, within which the notion of universality as a scientific approach to planning houses and the particular external forms which

---

27 King 1980, 217.

this resulted in was accepted as the unquestioned basis.

In relation to contemporary urban concepts of dwelling in Kenya, approaches which emphasize a self-evident Euro-American perspective necessarily remain inadequate. In a critical review of research on African urbanism, Azuka A. Dike has emphasized that the majority of Euro-American Africanists tend to perceive socio-cultural change as linear progression towards western urbanism, failing to recognize that most urban Africans consider their rural abode as their home.[28] Examples from various African countries suggested that significant features distinguishing African families from Euro-American ones included the importance of the larger kin group beyond the nuclear family, of children more to the kin group than only to the parents, and the care and respect for the elderly.[29]

A more focused study, Lucy Jayne Kamau's analysis of the symbolic aspects of modern middle class houses in Kibera, Nairobi, indicated that the dwellings were oriented around social interaction with kin and friends from the family's rural home area, vital to urban survival. Kamau perceived the living room as the stage for the social life of the family, both functionally and symbolically, particularly for the male members of the family. For the families studied, eating and drinking involved symbolic meanings, eating attached to the expression of a close relationship. Around the sofa area, eating and drinking were social occasions, while eating for nourishment was not, food being consumed rapidly and accompanied with minimal conversation. In Kamau's study, bedrooms were functionally important but socially unimportant, while the kitchen was regarded functionally as a space used exclusively by women and children and symbolically as negative: shameful and private. As a totality, the dwelling was seen not as a domestic haven of the parents and children, but as the place for the family - and the male head in particular - to identify themselves as members of a larger group.[30]

Private sector dwellings

At independence, the colonial "closed" housing system was replaced by an "open" housing market. Although, as Anthony D.King has described the

---

28 Dike 1979, 19ff. See also Elkan 1973, 113.
29 Kayongo-Male and Onyango 1984, 6-10, 32-37; their book was based on anthropological studies in the sub-Saharan parts of Africa on a general level. On the effects of modern urban renewal projects on family life, see Marris 1962.
30 Kamau 1978. The study was based on interviews of the occupants and on observations on the use of dwellings as part of a larger research project of the Housing Research and Development Unit at the University of Nairobi, conducted in 1972. The houses were detached or semi-detached units based on European models. No identification of the houses was given, but indirect information suggests that they were not part of the Fort Jesus courtyard house area included in this study. As far as I know, Kamau's study is the only one involving an anthropological analysis of Kenyan middle class domestic spaces within a contemporary urban context; she emphasized that the generalizations should be understood as tentative.

situation in colonial cities in general,

> clearly, the building of the colonial city, from the seventeenth to the twentieth centuries, created, either for colonial landlords or others, surplus values, whether in speculative development or as rent,[31]

the "opening" of the market after independence seems to have been even more profitable. It involved the transformation of property into an exchangeable commodity, in a sense into a more universal form of exchange than the colonial property with its particular socio-cultural connections. The commodification of the land and the buildings improved the opportunities of those social groups with capital for investment. In this process, how the built environment was planned and designed was significant. The market determined which houses were more in demand and which of their characteristics were desired: the housing market was more "open" for those houses which conformed to the demands of the market. More precisely, the housing market was differentiated to cater to each income level. Housing in the high quality private sector, owned by companies and affluent individuals, met the demands of the economically influential groups.

In Nairobi, these dominant groups have been the national, increasingly "westernized" élites and the expatriates dominated by western international upper middle class groups. Peter C. Lloyd has described the national élites of the African countries as comprising the professionals, the bureaucrats, and the businessmen, almost invariably Western-educated and with an "overt life-style [which] has far more in common with an international 'middle-class' standard than with their traditional homes."[32] The expatriates include embassy personnel, experts of international organizations, employees of multinational corporations or of smaller companies; they serve on the visiting staff of the university or of a ministry of the government. They stay in the city for a limited time, from a few months to several years. In the Nairobi census of 1979, out of a total population of about 830,000, some 20,000 (less than 2%) were registered as Europeans.[33] Their salaries tend to be much higher than those of the locally employed, and they maintain a way of life that "the African envies even though he may not wish to emulate it in every detail," as Lloyd described the Nigerian situation.[34] As one example of expatriates, we may refer to a study on experts engaged in development aid programs. In describing the external symbols of status of Finnish development aid experts in Tanzania and Zambia in the late seventies, Olli Alho distinguished a quality car of western make, often a Mercedes-Benz, one or two domestic servants, a detached house equipped more to a European than to an African standard, membership in an exclusive club, hobbies uncommon among

---

31 King 1985, 27.
32 Lloyd 1975, 546.
33 Census of Nairobi 1979, quoted in O'Connor 1983, 116.
34 Lloyd 1973, 133.

Africans like hunting, sailing, deep-sea fishing, tennis, squash, billiards, and a relatively liberal use of cash.[35]

The housing demands of the market in the private sector, then, centered around the western-oriented upper middle class concepts of dwelling: in effect, concepts of dwelling claimed to be universal. This involved both the symbolic and the practical aspects, and was related to the two developments discussed earlier, dwellings as instruments of reform and universal dwelling types. The universal concepts of dwelling applied in the private housing sector in Nairobi after independence may also be perceived in relation to the processes of globalization involving a homogenization of particular aspects of cultures within increasingly integrated systems of international economy, technology, and policy.[36] In these processes, the "universal" dwellings may be seen as ways to transfer the ways of life, the images and the ideologies produced by the modern industrial free market economies of the west.[37] The presence of expatriates, for example, in the Nairobi of the 1980s, was the result of particular histories which are rooted in colonialism. The "global dwelling types" they preferred not only served their immediate practical and symbolic needs, but also supported the continuity of Euro-American values and world views within the ex-colonial society, in essence, the continuity of the ideological power structure.

In Nairobi, the privately built dwellings were usually constructed on individual plots, were privately owned, and were located in the suburbs from the north to the southwest of the city center, including areas like Parklands, Spring Valley, Lavington, Upper Hill and Nairobi South. House types range from detached houses to row houses and apartment blocks. Three privately produced dwellings were selected for the study: a serviced flat in the city center, and two suburban dwellings, a two-storied row house in Kileleshwa and a detached house in Lavington. Of these, the flat and the row house have been built for renting, while the detached house has been built for the owner's own use but possibly for selling later.

Dwellings for rent: a flat and a row house. The serviced flat studied was located at the edge of the city center on a compound attached to a major hotel.[38] The surroundings were relatively urban, with shops, hotels, offices, workshops, and various cultural services in the vicinity; however, there were few residential activities outside the hotel and the blocks concerned. Situated at the edge of the city center, the density of the area was lower than in the commercial center, but the density within the site was relatively high. The development was constructed in two phases, completed in 1978. The compound contained six blocks of flats and two blocks of offices. The first phase included the blocks of flats with a total built-up area of about 9,300

---

35   Alho 1980, 104.
36   On processes of cultural globalization, see e.g. Featherstone 1990, King 1991.
37   Cf. the bungalow, King 1984, 259ff.
38   SK Aerial photograph 1:6000, sheet 2210, 1975.

Fig. 17.9 Private sector flat, city center, dwelling plan

Fig. 17.10 Private sector flat, city center

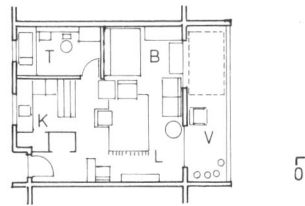

m and a block of offices of about 2,000 m. The second phase consisted of a second block of offices and a swimming pool, about 1,660 m. In the site plan, the 6 to 8-storied blocks were grouped around a central courtyard.[39]

The blocks of flats contained 6 different types of dwellings from one-room studios to flats with 3 bedrooms and a study. Two of the blocks contained only studios and one-bedroom flats.[40] The dwelling studied was a studio with a floor area of about 42 m with an additional 10 m balcony, the smallest of the offered dwelling types. The entry to each dwelling was from an external balcony on one side of the building, connected to the ground floor with a staircase. In the dwelling plan, the kitchen and the bathroom were situated towards the access balcony and the studio space and an adjacent private balcony towards the central courtyard. The studio space contained a built-in bed and closets in a recess. An open counter connected the kitchen to the living room.[41] (*Figs. 17.9, 17.10*)

---

39 Chana and Devji 1981, 1.02.
40 Chana and Devji 1981, 3.01.
41 Field study in August 1983.

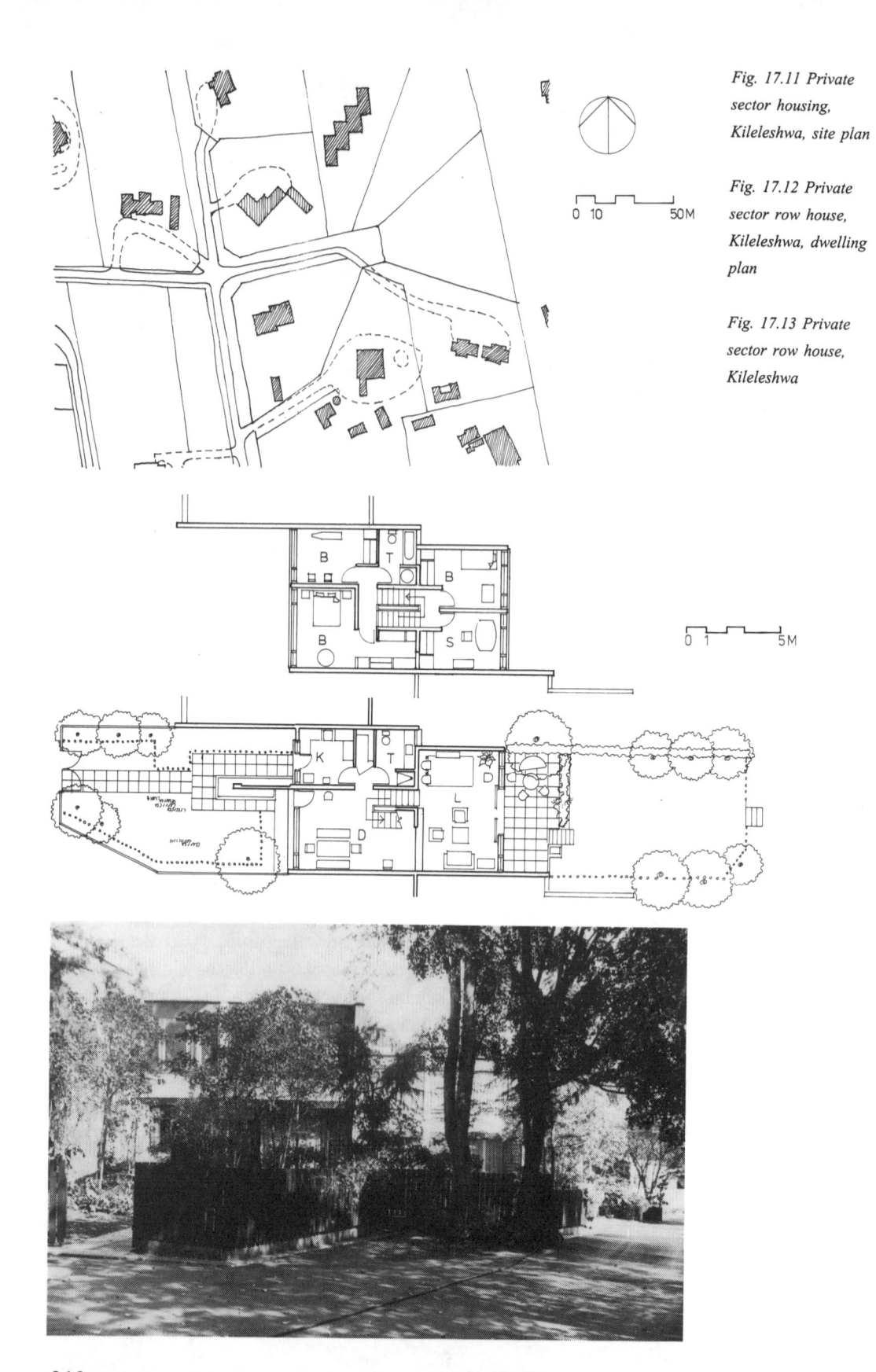

Fig. 17.11 Private sector housing, Kileleshwa, site plan

Fig. 17.12 Private sector row house, Kileleshwa, dwelling plan

Fig. 17.13 Private sector row house, Kileleshwa

Within the dwelling, distinctions between front and back or public and private were maintained by the position of the service spaces on the common balcony side. With the small windows high up, the dwelling turned its back on the common walkway immediately adjacent to the dwelling. On the central courtyard side, the private balcony formed a protective zone for the interior towards the other dwellings. The functional distinction of the studio space into the living space, eating counter, and sleeping area was only partial: with the small floor area, the functions necessarily integrated.

The dwelling studied in a row house, privately built for renting, was located in Kileleshwa, a suburb some 3 to 4 km west of the city center, part of Upper Nairobi described earlier in the section on colonial privately built dwellings by Europeans. After independence, the area has experienced changes as the unbuilt plots are being developed into multi-family occupation, essentially row houses with several dwelling units. While the earlier detached houses were situated on relatively flat land, the unbuilt parts were situated on ridges with more difficult building conditions. These plots began to be developed in the 1970s. The houses were planned for renting, sometimes with the owner occupying one of the dwellings.

Located on a ridge by the Kirichwa Kubwa River, the plot of the row house studied was sloped. Entry to the plot was from the upper end, with the dwellings receding towards the river. The staggered plan formed semi-private front gardens for each dwelling. The rooms for the domestic staff were in a separate building situated furthest from the entry. The unbuilt part of the plot was developed as gardens, with the parts near the dwellings divided by walls. The row house consisted of four relatively large dwellings, planned on the basis of two stories with split levels.[42] (*Fig. 17.11*)

In the front garden, the entry to the dwelling was divided into two, with the entry for the family and visitors separated by a wall from that to the kitchen. The main entry was to the dining room, located on the same level with the kitchen, the kitchen store and a bathroom. Visually accessible but a half level lower was the living room and the terrace in the garden. Upstairs, a half level from the dining room were two bedrooms, and another half level up, two other bedrooms and a second bathroom with a boiler. The main bedroom on the top floor also contained a dressing space. The floor area of the dwelling was about 140 m. (*Figs. 17.12, 17.13*)

In the dwelling plan, the separation of the spaces used only by the family from those also used by visitors or by the domestic staff was organized by the separate entries and by the level differences. The dining room was the meeting point of the three spheres. The combined main and service entrances, together with the location of the kitchen made the front yard into a semi-private area. Thus the back yard with its terrace, large garden and access to the living room became the more prestigious of the two yards.

---

42 Field study in November 1983.

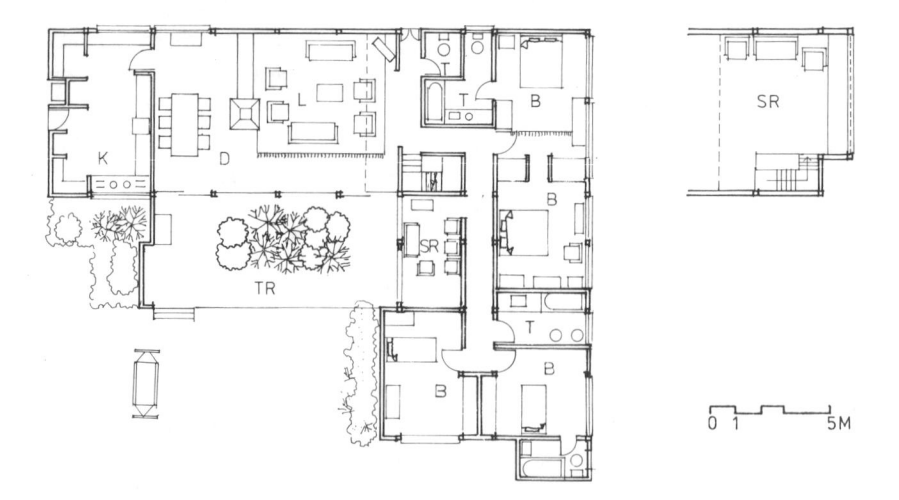

Fig. 17.14 Private sector detached house, Lavington, dwelling plan

Fig. 17.15 Private sector detached house, Lavington

Dwellings for sale: an owner-occupied detached house. The detached house studied was located in Lavington, a suburb by road some 8 km northwest of the city center. The area has been mostly developed after independence. In the maps illustrating the situation in 1948, attached to the Master Plan, the area – about five times the size of the city center – is totally undeveloped, with just a handful of buildings. The density of Lavington was low.[43] The predominant building type was the detached house on a large garden plot,

---

43 MP 1948., e.g. Buildings and Open Spaces Distribution. The undeveloped land can also be seen in the Nairobi and District Topographic Map 1:2500, sheets NE 32/C and NE 22/A, 1955.

314 ■ PART IV   DWELLING FORMS IN NAIROBI

slowly being complemented by row houses. The houses in the area were relatively large; the plot sizes seemed smaller than, for example, in Spring Valley.[44] The dwelling studied was a detached house, designed by an architect and built in the 1970s.

The plot was located on a ridge, with entry to the house from the upper end of the slope. The plan of the dwelling was enclosed towards the entry and open towards the garden. The entrance led to a small lobby opening into the living room. A dining area was at the other end of the living room, with an adjacent kitchen. Large windows connected the living room to the terrace. A guest toilet was adjacent to the lobby. A small second living room was located on the upper floor, constructed as a balcony and reached by stairs. The kitchen also had a direct entry from the outside, next to the car port and the rooms of the domestic staff. The study and the four bedrooms formed a separate wing, with a private bathroom attached to two of the bedrooms and a third bathroom was accessible from the corridor. Altogether the floor area of the dwelling was about 240 m, with a terrace of about 45 m.[45] (*Figs. 17.14, 17.15*)

In the dwelling, the front and the back of the house were distinct, with the entrance front closing itself towards the outside. The private terrace was sheltered from the exterior by the house and the garden. Inside, the more public living room, the living room balcony, the dining room, and the terrace formed an entity which was separate from the private bedrooms. In two bedrooms, the privacy was emphasized by the attached bathrooms. The public spaces were open and flowed into each other, but within the private sphere, there was only one connecting door between the bedrooms, the other links occurring through a neutral space, the corridor. The kitchen was planned so it could also be usable separately from the rest of the dwelling.

The privately produced post-independence dwelling plans studied had some common features. In all three, the entry side of the dwelling or house emphasized the privacy of the dwelling spaces. On this side were the service functions like the kitchens and bathrooms. The spaces for meeting friends were situated in the back of the dwelling, away from the entrance. In the two multi-roomed dwellings, the bedrooms were separated from both the living rooms and the service spaces. Thus the general organization of the dwelling plan in the three cases accentuated the distinctions of the privacy of the dwelling both externally, in its relation to the outside and internally, between the relations of the rooms for different functions.

In the context of the Nairobi of the 1980s, "universal" concepts of dwelling were introduced to the housing market through three separate but related arenas. These were, first, the middle-class dwelling produced with support from international development aid programs, second, the symbols attached

---

44 SK Aerial photograph 1:6000, sheet 598, 1975; field study in July 1983.
45 Drawing acquired from the owner; field study in July 1983.

to modern housing within the national policies of the newly independent ex-colonial countries, and, finally, the influence of the international community of expatriates, creating a demand for particular kinds of dwellings and simultaneously providing a subtle but constant basis of comparison for the local inhabitants. The origins of each arena were in frames of thinking which could be described, on a very general level, as Anglo-American, and which were also supported by, for example, by a whole range of global processes, including locally available media such as books, movies, advertisements, and magazines. In relation to housing, the Anglo-American concepts of dwelling were both presented and referred to as models. In this sense, access to Anglo-American concepts of dwelling was not only about a discussion of the principles but also about the adoption of specific practices.

In his study on working class housing in England between 1850 and 1914, M.J. Daunton indicated that middle class housing has historically differed from that of working class housing, partially because middle class houses have been more spacious, but also because of the different meanings attached to each space, the living room in the front seen by the working classes as the formal, public and symbolically important space, and by the middle classes as the setting for everyday life.[46] John Burnett has noted that after the Second World War, working class houses and middle class houses have been increasingly converging, both in terms of space and in terms of amenity standard; however, whether this implied a convergence in terms of spatial uses and meanings, remained open.[47] For the United States, Irwin Altman and Martin Chemers presented an "anthropological" - as they called it - analysis of an American home. Within the dwelling, the living room faced the front, was perceived as the place for entertaining and had a formal character, while the kitchen faced the back and was also used as an informal living space. The bedrooms were seen as private and individualized, the bathroom as nonpersonal and austere.[48]

In comparison, neither the English nor the American studies referred to seemed to have a direct correspondence with the Nairobi dwellings. The clear distinction between the front of the house as the public, formal, and symbolic spaces, and the back as the private, informal, and secular spaces, seemed unrelated to the organization of the dwellings studied. In the plans of the Nairobi dwellings for the local middle classes, the rooms at the front of the building were presented as public, but also as informal and as holding symbols of prestige. The back was planned for secular domestic purposes, but not for

---

46 Daunton 1983, 277-282.
47 Burnett 1986, 319.
48 Altman and Chemers 1984, chapter 8. While Altman and Chemers acknowledged the absence of a homogeneous American society and the existence of a variety of dwelling types built in America, they nevertheless suggested some qualities which they perceived as common to ethnic, regional and socioeconomic groups within the United States, particularly in the case of the "American homes" defined in the study as present-day middle class suburban dwellings for nuclear families.

private informal gatherings among family and close friends; even the entry could only be from the front. In the plans for the expatriate market, the rooms towards the entry were neither public nor prestigious. In one house, the dining area near the entry could be used for more informal gatherings, but in all three dwellings the spaces in the back – the living room and the terrace attached to it – were the loci of public activity within the dwelling, the spaces conveying symbols of prestige. In the plans, the dwelling functioned as a barrier between the social functions of the family and the world outside the dwelling. This was enforced by the organization of the plot: the entry to the house was separated from the road by a gate, a driveway, a garden, a car port, and possibly some plants immediately outside the house, all providing a protective layer around the privacy of the dwelling.

The main characteristics adopted in Nairobi from the Anglo-American dwelling models were those related to the location of the houses, the amount of space, and the standard of amenities. These dwellings were located in suburban areas with low densities, private gardens, and in neighborhoods with relatively homogeneous selection of residents. The amount of space and the amenities offered were better than in older dwellings, and, in the case of the expatriate market, reaching or sometimes exceeding English and American standards. In essence, they compared well with the luxury houses of England which Burnett has described as houses with the greatest advances in respect of

> comfort and convenience, represented by improved heating systems, better fitted and equipped kitchens, bathrooms and WCs properly incorporated into the house-plan, more electric power outlets and increased storage space, including storage of the car.[49]

---

49 Burnett 1986, 325.

■18 Dwelling practices in Nairobi, 1983

The discussion of the dwelling forms of Nairobi – colonial European, African, Asian, and "universal" – was complemented with an anthropological approach to the Nairobi dwelling cultures, based on documentation, observations, and interviews in 1983. In terms of floor area, the dwellings varied greatly, the smallest units being about 20 m and the largest over 300 m. The analysis of the dwelling plans indicated significant differences in the use of space between the smallest and the larger dwellings. In the one- and two-room dwellings, external areas were much used as an enlargement and the use of the internal areas was relatively undifferentiated; this included the smallest dwelling units in landhies and in the majengo house and courtyard houses used as tenements (with rented rooms), inhabited by families and single persons with incomes closer to the lower end of the incomes of dwellers in this study. The integrated use of internal space was also observed in the one-room dwelling inhabited by a single person with an income closer to the higher end of incomes of the dwellers in this study. In larger dwellings, the use of space was more differentiated and mostly confined to the interior. Observations on the smallest dwelling units were therefore not included in the discussion of the cultural differentiation of space, that is, the dwelling practices. Sixteen of the twenty dwellings discussed earlier, then, were included in this section: eight dwellings inhabited by African families, five by Asians and three by Europeans.

African dwelling practices

Dwellers and dwellings. Of the eight African dwellings inhabited by Africans, four accommodated a nuclear family, two a single-parent family, one a couple without children and one was shared by several single persons. In addition to their own children, two families had one or two young relatives living with them. The occupations of the dwellers included two departmental level directors, one at a parastatal and the other at a private company, two university lecturers, two clerks in senior positions, the owner of a kiosk, a laboratory nurse, two secretaries, and four university students; there were also housewives, some working part-time. Two of the families employed domestic servants, and two others had a relative who participated in the cooking, household work, and taking care of children. Of the eight houses, five were employer-housing built before independence, and three involved development aid programs, of these, two were owner-occupied and one was rented.[1]

Entry, back yard, and veranda. In the dwellings built before independence, the plans had included two or three entries, the main entry at the front and a back entry through the back yard or veranda to a back lane or garden. In the dwellings built after independence, two had two entries each, while the third one was a courtyard dwelling with one entry only. In these dwellings, the back entries had been securely bolted and were normally not used at all. In one of the buildings, the unwalled back yard was not used, for example clothes dried in the front yard. Several persons interviewed gave security as the main reason for the bolting, the fragile locks of the back entry having attracted unlawful entries by thugs. The control of only one entry was perceived as more secure. In practice, each dwelling had only one entry regardless of the original form of the building.

The gardens attached to three of the row houses were used for growing economy plants; two families also kept chicken in the back yard. The verandas were used mainly for storage and for the protection of valuable articles such as the TV-antenna in one veranda. In the dwelling with the courtyard, it was used in some ways like a room, for example for sewing to order with a machine kept in the courtyard, and in other ways like a back yard, for example for drying clothes on lines.

Living room and dining area. Inside the dwelling, the specialization of the rooms somewhat varied depending on the plan. In all cases, however, the largest room nearest the entry and with a visual connection to the front of the building was used as a living room; in the one exception, the room used as a living room had no windows.[2] The focus of the living rooms was commonly the sofa area, with a sofa, two easy chairs, and side tables; in two dwellings, the sofa area contained two sofas in addition to the easy chairs. In all the dwellings, the sofa area was its best furnished, most generously spaced and most articulated area. In most dwellings, a dining table was located in another area in the same room, but usually this part of the room was not articulated. In some dwellings, the area had a dining table set with matching chairs and an embroidered table cloth, in others, there was maybe only one chair next to the table set against the wall. Whether it was used for dining, working, or other purposes, was not clear. (*Figs. 18.1, 18.2*)

Bedrooms. Compared to the living rooms, the bedrooms were furnished relatively barely. The master bedroom usually had a double bed, sometimes

---

[1] These may be compared to two surveys made of two areas involving development aid programs, in Umoja (Hoek-Smit 1983) and Buru Buru (Menezes 1978), according to which respectively 70%/77% of the occupants were nuclear families with or without relatives living in the same household, and only 7%/22% were bachelor households. In general, the dwellers in the two areas were of the highly educated minority, with the heads of family predominantly in civil service, clerical or educational jobs or as professionals. Of the wives, about 66%/73% were in full-time employment, in teaching, secretarial jobs or as professionals.

[2] The verandas on both sides of the room had been converted into habitable spaces.

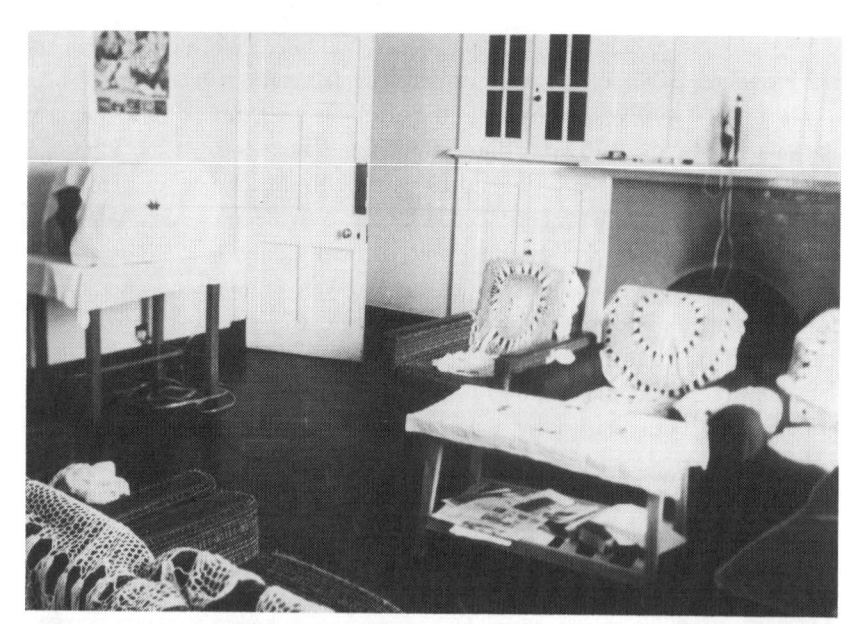

Fig. 18.1 Living room of African family in the Hill

Fig. 18.2 Living room with dining area of African family in Buru Buru

with an infant's cot or bed, the clothes stored in the built-in closets provided or on clothes lines crossing the room. In one dwelling, each of the spouses had their own bedroom, both furnished equally barely, with only the bed in the middle of the room and clothes stored on lines. In another, the largest bedroom contained both the parents' double bed and two children's beds. The other bedrooms were shared by the children and sometimes also by their ayah (young relative who takes care of the children). In these dwellings, these rooms were usually quite congested, with the bunk bed and other beds covering most of the floor space, and often more than one child to each bed. Sometimes there was no other furniture. Clothes and other items were stored in boxes on shelves or under the beds, or on clothes lines and on pegs on

Fig. 18.3 Bedroom and storage of clothes of African family in the Hill

Fig. 18.4 Master bedroom of African family in Upper Hill

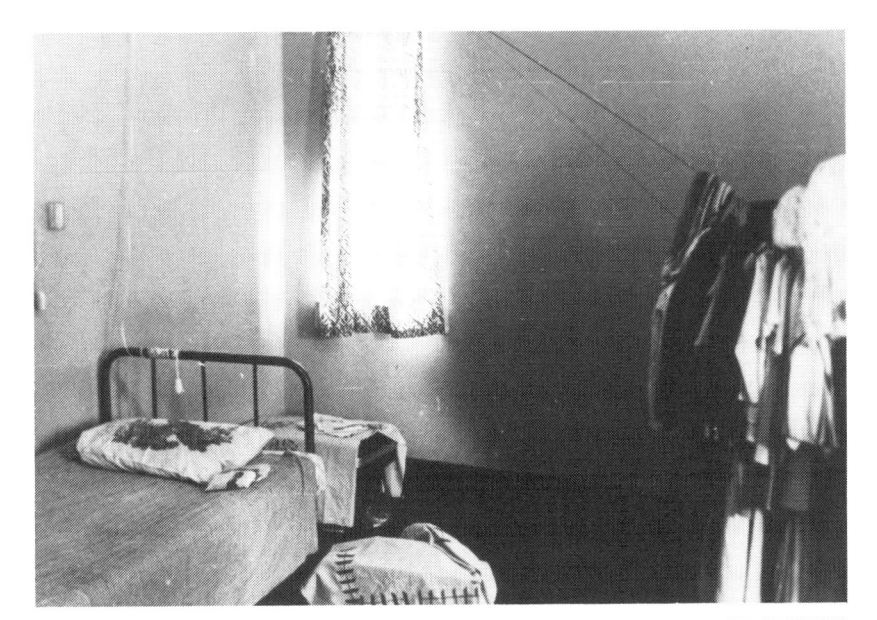

the wall. In two dwellings, the children had been provided with a work table in the bedroom; this was unusual, but may be also have been due to the ages of the children. In one dwelling, the finest bedrooms had been allocated to the children, with the parents sleeping in a much smaller room converted from a room originally planned for domestic servants. In all the bedrooms, the curtains were closed for protection against sunlight and were opened on request only to allow more light for observation and the photography of the room. (*Figs. 18.3, 18.4*)

Other rooms. Three of the dwellings had rooms rented to a tenant; in one of them, the tenant was also related to the family. In a row house where part of the veranda had been converted into a bedroom, this bedroom was used

Fig. 18.5 Kitchen of African family in Kibera

by the ayah of the family, also related to them; incidentally, the only entry to the dwelling was through this room. In another row house, the third bedroom was reserved for overnight guests or relatives; it was kept in prime condition and was not used for other purposes when there were no guests. The family would have preferred the guest room to be located on the ground floor, for reasons including both the prestige and the convenience of the visitor.

Kitchen. In most of the dwellings, the entry to the kitchen was through the living room; there were two exceptions, one through an entry hall and the other through a courtyard. The kitchens usually had little built-in furniture. The three finest ones in the study were fully equipped kitchens with stoves, built-in storage space and a refrigerator. The common standard varied from a gas stove and a working table to a simple portable gas cooker on the table top. All the dwellings had sinks with running water. Older dwellings had a flue open to the sky for cooking with an open fire. The older dwellings also usually had a separate kitchen storage room or pantry. (*Fig. 18.5*)

Shower/bathroom and toilet. Three of the dwellings contained a bathroom with a tub and five had a shower with cold water. In all, these were separate from the toilets, two of which were located in separate buildings; this occurred in the oldest houses. Neither of these spaces was in any way articulated, with the items in both kept to a minimum. The doors were kept closed at all times; in one or two cases, the smell was distinctive. In general, the toilets in particular were considered extremely unpleasant spaces. Some dwellers also remarked that the showers tended to flood at times.

Totality. In general, the living room was clearly the most important space in the dwellings studied. It was the space where guests were entertained and the kin gathered. It contained the largest variety of furniture and was articulated with pictures and decorations. It was more open to the outside than the other rooms, both functionally in terms of activities immediately outside the entry and symbolically in terms of accessibility to guests. The living room also functioned as a block between the outside and the rest of the dwelling. The bedrooms were separate from the living room, and often contained only the beds and the clothes stored. The kitchen, and the walled back yard when there was one, were service spaces, necessary in practical terms but marginal in symbolic terms. This applied even more to the shower or bathroom and the toilet which were closed off from the rest of the dwelling and mentally screened from outsiders' view.

Exceptions. However, there were two dwellings to which these characteristics applied at most only partially: the semidetached and row houses of the Railways built in the 1930s. In both, the plan of the house hindered the use of the living room in the way described above. In the semidetached house, the entry was to a large hall with direct access to the living room, two bedrooms, the kitchen, and the back yard; in this plan, the living room was not as central as in the other dwellings. In the Railways row house, the original plan had been totally transformed by the conversion of the verandas, the initial bedroom becoming the largest room and entered through the previous veranda converted into a small bedroom. After the transformation, the living room became windowless, therefore unusable as a bedroom, and the largest room with the two windows on different sides continued to be used as a bedroom. In terms of dwelling practices, without a more detailed knowledge of the particular practices of the family descriptive analyses were difficult to make.

Asian dwelling practices

Dwellers and dwellings. Of the five Asian dwellings studied, four accommodated a joint family and one a nuclear family. In the joint families, the oldest generation was represented by one to three persons who had moved to Nairobi from India, some in the 1920s, some in the 1940s. The younger generations included one or two of their children with their families. The composition of the joint family varied, but in the dwellings studied the one with the largest number of members included, for example, the owner of the house and his wife, their two unmarried daughters, the eldest son, his wife and his five children between 1 and 8 years of age. Four of the five families employed domestic servants for washing, gardening, and security; some of them lived on the same plot, others did not. One of the families had an African teacher as a tenant. The occupations of the dwellers included owners of shops and industrial enterprises, self-employed professionals such as physicians, engineers, and architects, as well as university students. The dwellings inhabited by Asians included three houses built as or converted into courtyard houses, a detached house, and a semidetached house, the earliest built in the 1930s and the newest in the 1970s. All were owner-occupied.

Entry. The relation of the houses to their surroundings varied: two houses were somewhat exposed to the street, with only a low wall separating them, but the three others were more withdrawn. Of the three, one was located on the upper floor of a building with commercial activities on the street level, and accessible only by a staircase behind an inconspicuous door. The other two were situated on large walled plots guarded by security personnel. All dwellings originally had more than one entry, but at the time of the field study, in three of them the other entries had either been bolted or, in one case, blocked totally with concrete. Gardens with economic and decorative plants adjoined four of the five houses.

Living rooms, family rooms and the courtyard. In houses with a specific living room for receiving guests, it was usually directly accessible from the entry space. The living room – the formal sitting room – was conventionally used for receiving guests and for family gatherings, but when the number of visitors at a time was larger, it tended to be used more by the men. Usually there was more than one space used as a living room. In one dwelling, there was a second living room next to the first one, to be used by female guests and family members in these kinds of situations. For prestigious guests, either visiting or staying overnight, the bedroom of the oldest male held the most weight symbolically; it could also be used for conducting business affairs, although this was not common. In exceptional situations where the number of guests was high, the courtyard was also used for entertaining guests, especially for eating meals. (*Figs. 18.6, 18.7, 18.8*)

In everyday life, the courtyard was the living room of the persons staying in the house all day, including the women not working outside the home, the smaller children, school children in the afternoons, and domestic staff. Various kinds of activities took place there, from grinding grains by hand, hulling beans, and cleaning vegetables to washing the dishes, hanging clothes out to dry, and children's play. The religious plant tulsi was usually grown in a pot kept in the courtyard. The courtyard usually had no furniture. In two of the houses, the dining room – which as a specified space was not traditionally part of an Asian dwelling – had become the family living room, where the family gathered and where closer family friends were invited.

"Bedrooms". In general, the bedrooms in a dwelling with a joint family were used both for sleeping and working and as private living rooms. The bedrooms conventionally had connecting doors both to the adjacent rooms and to the courtyard or another common space, normally kept open. The oldest male of the family usually had his own bedroom, and in some dwellings the wife slept in the same room, in others not. The allocation of the bedrooms varied according the needs of the individual family members; for example,

Fig. 18.6 Courtyard of Asian family in Ngara

Fig. 18.7 Living room and master bedroom of Asian family in the city center

Fig. 18.8 Formal living room of Asian family in Parklands

Fig. 18.9 Shrine of Asian family in Nairobi South

the grandmother might sleep with the smaller children, a child preparing for important exams could be given a bedroom for the duration of the study period, or a person suffering an illness could be allocated a more peaceful room. Young married couples had a room of their own, with the woman (who had moved in with the husband's joint family) using the same room as her private living room for meeting friends. The distribution of rooms was flexible: for example, they would be changed to accommodate visiting relatives who could stay for several months. The family members, however, attached no special meanings to a particular room and expressed a willingness to adjust to each new situation in terms of the possible change of rooms; children even seemed to enjoy the changes. (*Fig. 18.10*)

Shrine, prayer room. A shrine or a prayer room was observed in all the Asian family dwellings. The shrines were in places protected from the more public activities of the dwelling, such as kitchen storages, and were used daily by the different family members. A separate prayer room had been arranged in one dwelling. (*Fig. 18.9*)

Kitchen, shower room and toilet. In the Asian families, the kitchen carried special meanings. Food preparation and cooking was done exclusively by family members, usually by the women. The food preparation had to follow religious principles, with particular procedures and vessels. All five dwellings

Fig. 18.10 Rooms with connecting doors of Asian family in the city center

Fig. 18.11 Kitchen of Asian family in Lavington

contained a fully modernized kitchen with built-in storage space, electric stoves, and refrigerators, but in one of them, the old kitchen with its simple cooking devices placed directly on the floor was the only one in daily use. The kitchen storage was usually a separate room, and in three dwellings, the kitchen storage was also the place where the religious altar was placed, explained by the privacy of the room. Shower rooms and toilets were separate from each other. (*Fig. 18.11*)

Extreme examples. The dwelling in which the traditional practices were most clearly followed was the upper floor courtyard dwelling in the city center: it had the character of humbleness: the furniture was simple, relatively small in size, with only the necessities. The dwelling which most deviated from the traditional practices was the house built in the 1970s. The living room and dining area were based on an open plan, the bedrooms (each en suite) accessible from a separate corridor.

Totality. In the Asian dwellings, the two dominant characteristics were the network of connections between the rooms and the flexible use of the rooms. Most of the rooms had more than one door and were used for more than one function. The most important single space was the courtyard which gathered the spaces both visually and functionally; corridors were few and short. Functional multiplicity also implied responsiveness: for example, visitors

Fig. 18.12 Terrace of European single person in Kileleshwa

Fig. 18.13 Living room and dining area of European family in Spring Valley

Fig. 18.14 Children's bedroom of European family in Spring Valley

could be met on various levels of formality and informality, depending on the visitor and the purpose of the visit. Except for the head of the family, the members were not attached to a particular bedroom; their identity was independent of the personalized space. In general, the furniture and the decorative elements of the dwellings could not be used to decipher the economic status of the family: even affluent families lived in modest surroundings.

European dwelling practices

Dwellers and dwellings. Of the three dwellings inhabited by expatriate Europeans, one accommodated a nuclear family with three children, one a couple without children, and one a single person. All three families employed one or more domestic servants for cooking, household work, and/or gardening; none had tenants. One of the dwellings involved employer-housing, the two others were rented from private owners. Two of the dwellings – the detached house and the flat – had been built before independence, and the row house had been built less than five years earlier. All three dwellings were located on relatively large plots which were fenced, one of them guarded around the clock.

Entry. The relation of the dwelling to its immediate surroundings was similar in all three dwellings. On the entry side, the emphasis was on practicalities like the car port and the separation of the entries of the family and guests from that of the domestic staff. Although the entry was visible from the kitchen, the dwellings were to an extent closed towards the entry side.

Living room, dining area and terrace. In the dwellings inhabited by the Europeans, the living room adjoined the dining area. There were two focuses: the sofa set with two easy chairs and a coffee table or side tables, arranged to form a group, in one dwelling around the fireplace, and the large dining table. Both spaces were articulated with furniture, carpets, electronic devices, potted plants, books, and various decorative items, such as Africana artefacts like bead ornaments, head rests, and masks in one of the dwellings. In the European dwellings, the living room was the place for gathering both for family members and for their visitors.[3] The dining room was used for family breakfasts and meals and for entertaining guests at dinner parties. In all the three dwellings, the terrace with its outdoor furniture and garden were used as extensions of the living room; during the dry season, the terrace was used more than the living room inside the dwelling. (*Figs. 18.12, 18.13*)

---

3 Cf. Alho's study (1980, 72f.) indicated that in Tanzania and Zambia in the late 1970's among Finnish expatriates, visiting and various kinds of social exchange was relatively high, more frequent, informal and spontaneous than it had been for the same persons back home in Finland.

Fig. 18.15 Kitchen of European family in Spring Valley (flat)

Bedrooms and other rooms. In the dwellings inhabited by Europeans, the bedrooms were furnished as extensively as the living room and dining area. The bathroom and storage space for clothes were connected to the bedrooms. Particularly the children's bedrooms were highly personalized spaces. In these dwellings, the bedrooms formed a separate entity, either in a wing which could be locked or on the upper levels. All three dwellings also included a room used for working at home; in two, they were rooms planned as bedrooms, in the third a space adjoining the dining area. (*Fig. 18.14*)

Kitchen. The kitchens in the houses inhabited by Europeans were equipped with complete stove and oven systems, refrigerators, built-in kitchen sinks and cupboards, and had ample space for the storage of both food stuffs and crockery, including a pentry in two dwellings. In two dwellings, the kitchen entry was separate. The kitchen was the one room where the domestic staff worked in the dwelling for longer periods of time. (*Fig. 18.15*)

Bathroom and toilet. All three dwellings had bathrooms combining the bathtub and the toilet, located adjacent to the bedrooms. Two of the dwellings also had a second bathroom, the row house with a shower and toilet; in both cases these were located near the kitchen and the entry area.

Totality. In the European dwellings studied, both the living room with its dining area and the bedrooms were articulated spaces, with functionally varied furniture and decorations like pictures on the wall, small artefacts, carpets, and colorful curtains. To an extent, this was also true of the kitchens and the bathrooms. The spatial organization was related to two main activity types. The more public activities included the gathering of family members and the entertainment of guests, particularly adults, and were more concentrated in the living room, dining area, and terrace. The more private activities included functions such as individual work, resting, or, for the children, meeting a close friend, and usually occurred in the bedroom or the work room. Separate from these were the kitchen and bathroom, used by all members of the family at different times of day. The kitchen, the bedrooms and bathroom were rarely visited by adults outside the family.

Comparisons of dwelling practices

The spatial organization of the African, Asian, and European expatriate dwelling practices varied considerably. In the African dwellings, the focus of activity was the living room, with the bedrooms, the kitchen, and the toilet serving as secondary and more receded areas, used only during particular times of the day. The adult male sphere comprised the living room, dominated the use of the rest of the dwelling. In the Asian dwellings, the activities were more dispersed to all the rooms and to different times of day. The distinctions between the rooms were made less on the basis of the unchanging function of the room and more on the basis of the situation and by adjustments made temporarily, for example, by closing the door between two rooms. The formal and religious distinctions affected the use of the dwelling. In the European expatriate dwellings, the functions were differentiated somewhat on the basis of age groups, the adult activities focused on the living-dining areas and the work room and the children's activities centered in their own bedrooms.

In general, the rooms in the European expatriate dwellings studied had more furniture and decorations than those of the other groups. In the Europeans' dwellings, the difference between the level of articulation of the living room and the bedrooms was smaller than that observed in the dwellings inhabited by the African families and in many of the dwellings inhabited by the Asian families.

In all three groups, the immediate surroundings of the dwellings were utilized, but in different ways. In the African dwellings, the emphasis was more on growing edible plants and chicken, and on practical activities like washing and drying clothes. In some dwellings, the entrance areas and courtyards were also used for gathering, especially in the evening. In the Asian dwellings, the courtyard was used almost like a room, for all kinds of activities from preparing food and eating to work, children's play, and meeting informal visitors. According to information given by the dwellers, earlier the entry areas of the houses were also used in a similar fashion, but this has changed in the last decades. In the European expatriate dwellings, the use of the entry side was mostly related to practicalities attached to household work, and just occasionally (and only in the row house studied) to functions like children's play. The activities were concentrated on the side opposite the entrance, on the terrace attached to the living room and the garden as its extension, actively used particularly for the consumption of beverages and for small meals, both among family members and with guests during the daytime and in the evenings.

Dwelling patterns

On the basis of the study of dwelling forms and practices, three patterns of dwelling could be discerned: the gate pattern, the chain pattern, and the wing pattern. The patterns of dwelling should not be perceived as models with direct correspondence to empirical cases, but rather as theoretical constructions somewhat in the manner of Max Weber's ideal types.[4] In this study, the notion of dwelling patterns includes both the ways of living in the dwellings and the dwellings as the physical frame, emphasizing the interdependence between the two. The concept of dwelling pattern could be described as the cultural way of "living" the dwelling.

The gate pattern. The most dominant characteristic of the dwelling with a gate pattern is the identification of one room as a center of activity. This room is like a gate, and the persons in the room can also function as gate-keepers, controlling the whole dwelling. Often the "gate room" is the living room, dominated by the male adults of the family. This is the space where the head of the family meets with his kin and friends and where all the issues of the social group are discussed together. The wife and the children can also participate. The focus of the dwelling is the living room, the rest of the dwelling serves only specific purposes and times of the day. Bedrooms are for sleeping at night, and kitchens, showers and toilets are best hidden, to be used only for the particular functions. The back yard is seen as an extension of the service spaces, and used only if walled and the entry from the outside is closed. In the plan, the essential prerequisite of the gate pattern is the restriction of the points of entry to one. Among the dwellings studied this was achieved by bolting or otherwise closing off the other entrances except the one leading to the living room. The dwellings studied following the gate pattern were inhabited by Africans. (*Fig. 18.16*)

The chain pattern. The dominant features of the dwellings following the chain pattern were the number of connections between the rooms, often through a courtyard, and the lack of functional distinctions between the rooms. The connections form spatial chains which may be used in various ways adjusted to the particular needs of the situation. Connections between the

---

4   Weber 1949, 90-93.

Fig. 18.16 The gate pattern

Fig. 18.17 The chain pattern

Fig. 18.18 The wing pattern

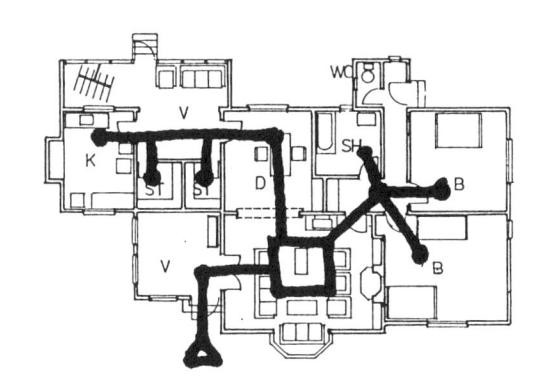

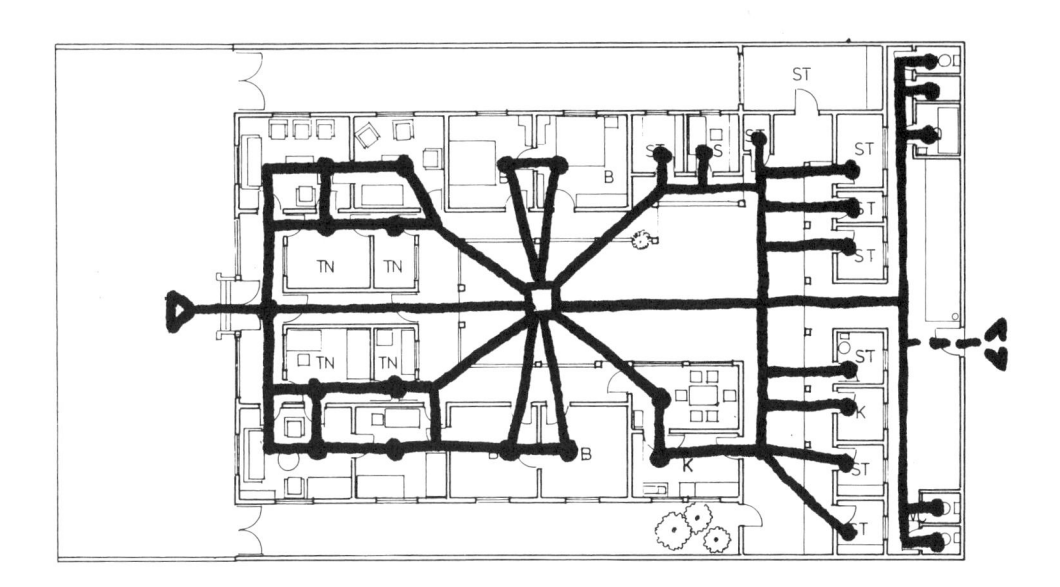

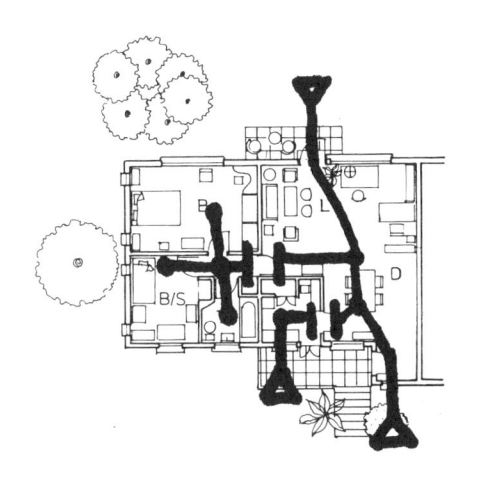

CHAPTER 18 DWELLING PRACTICES IN NAIROBI, 1983 ■ 333

rooms enable the establishment of temporary combinations. Corridors are few and short. In the chain pattern, most of the rooms are used both as living spaces and as bedrooms. There are two or more living rooms, including the enclosed courtyard. Bedrooms are not assigned to individuals, except the room of the head of the family. The location of the religious altar is not determined by the prestige of the room but by the possibility of privacy during prayers. Among the dwellings studied the courtyard house, attached to the joint family living in the house, was the common example of the chain pattern. The dwellings studied following the chain pattern were inhabited by Asians. (*Fig. 18.17*)

The wing pattern. The wing pattern may be described as a dwelling with wings which can be spatially separated and which function independently from each other. The core of the wing pattern is the living-dining room, with two wings, one containing the spaces attached to the bedrooms and the other containing the spaces attached to the kitchen. The living-dining room core is that part of the dwelling where family members meet with each other and with guests; domestic staff may also work in the area. The bedroom wing with the bedrooms and the bathroom is the area restricted to family members only, for privacy not only from visitors or domestic servants but also from each other. A corridor separates each bedroom from the others. At night, the door to the bedroom wing is kept locked to control entry to the wing. The kitchen wing contains the kitchen, its storage spaces, and access to the outside, that is, a separate entry; this part of the dwelling is for the use of domestic staff. The wing may be locked off from the rest of the dwelling by a door. The plan with a wing pattern requires that there is more than one entry and that the spatial organization is based on independently functioning parts. The dwellings studied following the wing pattern were inhabited by Europeans. (*Fig. 18.18*)

In conclusion, the patterns identified in the practices of Nairobi dwelling studied here were not strictly connected either to specific dwelling types or to the dwellers the planners of the dwellings had envisaged. The courtyard house was the one dwelling type with more direct links with one of the patterns, the chain pattern, but in the dwellings studied, of the four courtyard houses only two had retained their original planned form, the other two having been converted to conform to the patterns of dwelling of the later inhabitants. However, the patterns identified in Nairobi seemed to be linked to specific cultural groups: the gate pattern to African, the chain pattern to Asian, and the wing pattern to European dwelling practices.

PART FIVE

CULTURAL INTERPRETATIONS
OF BUILT FORMS

■ 19 Interpreting the built forms of Nairobi

The built forms of contemporary Nairobi contain not only the present but also fragments of earlier Nairobis. Reading the built forms, we may be able to understand something of its past realities. An interpretation of the present built forms, however, cannot be reduced to a single cohesive history (or story) of their origin, nor was this attempted. At the same time, the significance of the notion of the past, of histories, was emphasized in the interpretation. In any urban context, the existence of particular built forms – and of the meanings and practices attached to them – normally influences the introduction of new built forms; in a sense, the already existing built forms can be seen as a system which tends to accept some new forms and reject others. The latent meanings carried by the existing built forms can be said to have the potential to generate new possibilities, new built forms not contemplated before, while some of the earlier possibilities are lost. In this sense, the histories of the built forms of Nairobi were tied to the interpretation of the contemporary reality.

A genealogy of the present

Initially, Nairobi was conceived as a railway town. The interests of the Railways governed not only the selection of the triangular site near the old caravan route passing Nairobi River, at the edge of the Athi Plains and the foot of the hills, but also the shape of the railway, its two bends maximizing the area to be controlled by the Railways. The location at the junction of the plains and the hills established for the future of Nairobi its geographical duality. The first plans of 1898 and 1899 indicated the dominance of the Railways areas in the town as it was conceived. After the railhead reached Nairobi, however, the town began to evolve in ways which the Railways could no longer control. In the first plans, the administrative functions and the commercial activities were located near the railway station, but the move of the Protectorate Headquarters to Nairobi and the springing up of the Indian bazaar shifted the focus of the town further away from the station. Government Road (today Moi Avenue) which connected the station with the government offices and the bazaar became the most important street of Nairobi at the turn of the century and has retained some of its significance to the present.

The character of Nairobi in the very first years was a combination of two disparate elements: the railway area based on practical considerations and the congested Indian bazaar. From the beginning, European urban practices were imposed on the areas inhabited by members of other cultures: since they did not conform to European sanitary conceptions, the Indian bazaar in the town core and several African villages in the surroundings were repeatedly burned down by the administrators. The insecurity of the location assessed as insanitary first discouraged private investments in urban land, but within a few years, the plots in the center of town and large portions around it had been sold to enterprising individuals. Control of plot subdivision and development was minimal. To protect the interests of the Europeans, spatial and economic restrictions were adopted, the habitation and ownership of land by Asians confined to segregated areas within the town. Through the urban forms of Nairobi, the cultural, political, technological, and economic dominance of the Europeans was strengthened and maintained. In this context, the Asian contribution to urban development was tolerated, while the Africans were perceived as essentially pastoral.

After the First World War, European settlers gained more influence in relation to the colonial administration. The population growth made the extension of the town boundary imperative, and new housing areas were opened for Asian habitation to the north/northeast and, for Africans, on the plain to the east/southeast of the town center. Thus an urban pattern which had emerged, largely unplanned, during the first decades of the history of Nairobi, was not only preserved but expanded. One of the instruments employed by the European-dominated municipality was town planning and more particularly the zoning of areas for different purposes, allowing the politically increasingly difficult issue of areas segregated on the basis of race or ethnicity to be transformed into the "unpolitical" issue of areas differentiated on the basis of technical standards. The culturally biased criteria inherently in favor of the European community were perceived as universal and were not questioned.

In the context of the continuous population growth and consequent housing shortage in Nairobi, dwellings were a means of attracting employees. Social distinctions were produced in employer-built dwelling forms as meticulously as in the urban forms, as the interwar examples selected from the Railways dwelling units indicated. The European directors' quarters were located in prestigious areas with microclimatic advantages, restricted to Europeans, on large individual garden plots, in roomy detached houses with modern comforts. Dwellings built for Asian clerical staff were located in less prestigious areas with higher temperatures, restricted to Asians, on more densely built shared plots, in smaller semi-detached or row houses with more elementary sanitation. The all-male shared dwellings provided for the African laborers were located in densely built barracks next to the work area, fenced off from the rest of the town and constantly controlled, in rooms offering no privacy or protection against heat or cold, and with shared basic sanitary facilities. On the basis of the dwellings studied, the colonial dwellings built for Europeans reflected values attached to the English middle classes, those built for Asians conformed to recommendations on housing for the English working class, while those built for Africans most resembled the racially segregated barracks in South African mining towns. In contrast, in dwellings built by the Asians and Africans for themselves, the aspect of distinction was subdued, the versatility of the plans and the urban locations instead suggesting possibilities of adjusting to various combinations of dwellers and forms of dwelling.

During the interwar years, the character of the urban form of Nairobi changed form the earlier "wild west" appearance into a more urban and culturally more European town. It was due partly to the erection of large public buildings in the town center, including the Law Courts, the Railway Headquarters, the Municipal Offices, and the City Market, partly to the large-scale rebuilding of the Indian bazaar, and partly to the construction of the extensive tarmac road system which connected the garden suburbs to the center. The increase of commercial activity could be observed in the development of Delamere Avenue (today Kenyatta Avenue) as a wider and more European type major street to challenge the leading role of Government Road. An area with a distinct Indian character, integrating the diverse activities of the Asian community, had evolved around River Road, between Government Road and Nairobi River. Just blocks from the main streets, however, large areas of land still remained mostly undeveloped, implying the concentration of the urban core.

After the Second World War, the global situation altered British policies towards their colonies. Industrial development, discouraged in the 1920s and 30s to protect the British economy, became an essential part of the colonial policies. The weakening influence of the British in South Asia, due, among other things, to the independence of India, the "jewel in the crown," changed the direction of British interests in their African colonies. For Nairobi, it meant elevation to the status of a colonial capital: from a European outpost in the middle of the African wilderness to one of the showcases of British overseas policies. The planning and production of the urban forms of Nairobi was seen as the means of developing the industrial bases, injecting modern values and practices, and creating common symbols. Built forms were perceived as instruments in the transformation of the disparate groups with contradictory goals into a modern society committed to the progress of the country. The *Master Plan* of 1948 united the goals and the built forms: the planners suggested the establishment of a civic center, the construction of a network of modern roads, and the building of neighborhoods as social assimilators. For the realization of the social intentions, the production of family dwellings for Africans was seen as central. Although blocks of flats as a novel form of dwelling were introduced to Nairobi in the 1940s, older models were still widely followed in the dwelling forms.

From the perspectives of the Africans and Asians in Nairobi, the new colonial policies implied measures of increased control. The possibilities of participating in the economic progress of the city were mostly open only to those who were willing to submit to the cultural practices of the dominant European community. During most of the 1950s, a large portion of the control was directed through built forms, in operations such as restrictions or denials of access, limitations of use, and demolitions of structures defined as illegal. In terms of meanings attached to the urban forms, the conversion of public urban spaces into spaces of detention, even if only temporarily, left an unforgettable imprint in the minds of the Africans living in Nairobi during the Emergency.

During the two decades following the Second World War and preceding the independence of Kenya, the European character of Nairobi which had been established earlier was strengthened. The realignment of the railway and the construction of the new highway (today Uhuru Highway) in its place changed the traffic flows and some of the main points of entry to the city center. Delamere Avenue, which earlier connected only the European suburbs on the western Hill to the core, now also became the major link from the European suburbs on the north and southwest, the industrial area, and to national traffic from the Mombasa-Kisumu highway. This pattern has been retained until today. The new residential areas built for African families on publicly owned land in Eastlands were perceived by the colonial Europeans as models of African urban ways of life and, together with the industrial area, began the extension of the built area towards the east. At the same time, the older suburbs grew towards the north and the west.

From its past, then, the capital of the newly independent country inherited a pattern of built forms which had been produced by the cultures of the dominant Europeans and, to a much lesser extent, of the Asians. Ingrained in its built forms were urban practices and meanings which continued to reproduce the past cultures despite the end of colonialism. Moreover, the new elites of the country had largely adopted the values of western Europe. In independent Kenya, modernization – already promoted by the colonialists – was seen not only as the vehicle for well-being but was also linked to the processes of nation-building and to the acceptance of the country, on an equal basis, among other nation-states in the international community. To indicate international membership, the built forms of the new nations necessarily conformed to their symbols, applied historically in similar situations throughout the world. These included institutional buildings such as those of the parliament and government departments to express democratic and sound administration, a business and commercial center with high-rise office buildings and hotels to indicate modernity, the university to imply interest in the advancement of the society, modern planned residential areas to show social consciousness, and the demolition of conspicuously situated squatter settlements to denote the will to erase "underdevelopment." Nairobi's urban development was perceived as the necessary prerequisite to establish its position in the global economic network.

During the first two decades following independence, Nairobi emerged as a modern metropolis modeled on western principles of planning: a leading city in East Africa, a gateway between the First and Third Worlds, and an internationally important center. Its infrastructure was improved, including the street and highway network, the communication systems, and the international airport. The substantial extension of the city boundaries enabled the future development of the metropolitan area. Although decentralization was introduced in the *Metropolitan Growth Strategy* of 1973 as the basis of regional planning, the established pattern of functional segregation and zoning was largely continued. In the city center, government buildings were erected in the City Square south of the central open area between the Law Courts and the Parliament Building, making Harambee Avenue and Haile Selassie Avenue by 1983 into the two most modern major streets in Nairobi. The Kenyatta Conference Center became the new landmark of the city, not only because of its location next to the Law Courts, or because of its easily identifiable built form, but because it was perceived as an expression of the new international role of Nairobi and Kenya, the meeting point of people from all over the world on common concerns ranging from global problems of habitat to women's issues and the yearly Safari Rally. Another focus of government buildings was established on top of the Hill, beyond Uhuru Park next to Uhuru Highway. Together, the two concentrations of prominent buildings formed an axis which much resembled the civic center which had already been suggested in the *Master Plan* of 1948. The prestigious locations around the City Square and Uhuru Park also attracted international hotels.

In addition to the administrative core, the commercial and business center of the city also expanded. The southern part of Government Road with its palm trees and double lane system referred to modern African capitals more clearly than the narrower northern part of Government Road with its arcade-lined shop fronts or Kenyatta Avenue with its mixture of old and new buildings. In comparison with the decades preceding independence, the focus of development in the city center moved southward from Kenyatta Avenue, and by the 1980s, new structures were also erected on the unbuilt eastern edge of Uhuru Highway. The university area with its modernistic buildings around a central green was established in the northernmost triangle and expanded to the other side of Uhuru Highway. All around the center and in the subcenters, particularly in Westlands on the Uhuru, individual old buildings were also replaced by new high-rise structures. In general, the character of the newest parts of the city center began to resemble that of a modernized city center anywhere in the world, easily accepted by the international community of expatriate residents and tourists but culturally inaccessible to large sections of local citizens.

The city grew rapidly towards the east: new residential areas were established in Eastlands. In areas earlier restricted to Europeans, the subdivision of plots increased densities and diversified the available dwelling forms from the conventional detached houses to row houses and blocks of flats. At the same time, the areas with a distinct Asian character were being transformed: old courtyard houses based on Asian concepts of dwelling were being converted into tenements with one-room dwellings and shared facilities, and rented to African families. The adoption of built models perceived as universal also occurred in dwelling forms. The dwellings produced in the public sector during the 1960s and 70s were directed to the emerging middle classes perceived as essential in nation-building. As the studied indicated examples, the dwelling forms typically repeated western models, not only in the internal organization but also in the location and external forms of the residential areas, following standards required by the international development agencies involved in the production of these areas. Within the private sector, the preferences of the expatriates began to influence the types and standards of dwellings built for letting or for later sale.

Among foreigners involved in development aid and cooperation programs, Nairobi was seen as an urban conglomeration in an under-developed or developing country: the unfortunate consequence of uncontrolled immigration from the rural areas, in the future resulting in chaos, if strong measures were not immediately adopted. Intervention with help from western countries with the financial resources and expertise was seen as vital. According to the dominant development aid policies from the 1960s well into the 80s, cities were undesirable places for habitation – a conception coinciding with that referred to by idealists and philanthropists in 19th century Europe. From this perspective, the most conspicuous built forms of Nairobi were the unauthorized settlements built for the people with the lowest incomes.

The built forms of contemporary Nairobi are products of historical cultural processes. Earlier, the European colonizers preferred European built forms and practices, and defined the forms and practices of the other cultures as unauthorized, insanitary, or illegal. Through interventions on the production and use of built forms, they legitimized not only their own cultural frame by establishing it as universal, but also their right to intervene on other cultural practices and forms. Within interventions involving western experts, funds, or development agencies, these policies have also been continued after independence, the overt colonial hubris transformed into technical standards defined as universal and unpolitical. In this sense, the historical layers of contemporary built forms continue to produce western cultural practices. However, urban practices and the meanings the different cultures attach to them also participate in cultural production. The built forms carry not only the manifest meanings implanted in them by the planners and builders of the original environment, but also latent meanings, "other" possibilities, open to the different groups of people "living" the city. All through the history of Nairobi, the built forms have been "lived" in various ways, some of which have been defined as legal, others as illegal. In this sense, the historical layers of contemporary Nairobi have produced and continue to produce a diversity of cultural practices and meanings. It is through a study of the cultural diversity both in the production of the built forms and in the practices and meanings attached to them that this interpretation of Nairobi's built forms was developed.

Concepts of Nairobi

Before its founding, the surveyors and engineers of the Railways perceived Nairobi as a European foothold in the middle of Africa, a small town erected around the station for the various activities of the Railways. The view was dominated by practical considerations, based on common British models of establishing similar stations in varying locations around the world: a kind of embryonic modernism. The occurrence of several outbreaks of plague during the first years of the town increased the colonizers' interests in regulating buildings and their use. Both the regulations on sanitation and the proposals on segregation advocated the perception of Nairobi as a town with problems which can be solved to everyone's satisfaction by conforming to standards like those adopted in the rapidly growing industrial towns in Britain during the latter half of the 19th century. Segregation as a solution for emergent problems had already been utilized in the plans of Victorian country houses and was easily adjusted for town planning; its racial foundation in Nairobi reflected the contemporaneous attitudes of the colonizers towards the "non-British" as lower on the universal ladder of development and civilization, therefore separate. The establishment of the municipal form in the 1920s and 30s largely reinforced the earlier views of Nairobi. From the points of view of administration and planning, the town was still about problems, to be solved pragmatically with measures similar to those used in Britain and its colonies. In this sense, the official views of Nairobi until the Second World War may be described as reflections of the modernist concept of the city. Other views were also presented, but more subdued. In descriptions implying a romanticist approach, the exotic characteristics were most often connected to nature and the indigenous people, or to the daring life styles of the carefree Europeans, but usually not to Nairobi as a place.

A change in how Nairobi was perceived may be discerned after the Second World War, first formulated in the *Master Plan* of 1948. Instead of identifying only individual problems in need of solutions, Nairobi was approached as a totality, its built forms seen as potential instruments in the social and cultural transformation of its citizens and civic life. The goal was to support the modernization of the society towards the more developed civilizations of Europe represented by Britain. The emphasis was on characteristics defined as universal, but articulated further than the versions of the interwar years. The civic center, the commercial and business center, the residential neighborhoods, the industrial area, the recreational areas, and the road network were planned on models imported from the more advanced countries for the benefit of the whole society. The overall universalism of the approach prevented any identification of local functions or built forms, much less of culturally different priorities. During the final decades of British colonialism in Kenya, then, the dominant view of Nairobi was one of modernism. By contrast, adventure novels included more romantic notions, seeing the disharmonious built forms of the different cultural groups as exotic and as settings for strangely dangerous events.

Independence altered notions of what Nairobi was about, both for the Kenyans and for those with interests in intervening in the changes of Nairobi. The elite of the newly independent country saw its capital as the gateway to the international community: an indication of the equal status of the nation among other nations, therefore necessarily containing a modern western-type city center, fine suburbs, and the infrastructure to connect them. This concept of Nairobi resembled the one promoted during colonialism: in both, the notion of modernity was expressed in the universality of the built forms. But contrary to the earlier concept, the Nairobi of independent Kenya was also seen as a symbol of the uniqueness of the country and its people, not so much in terms of the urban forms as a totality, but in terms of individual public buildings which were identified as symbols of the city, both in theory – as the general request for the development of a "national" architecture for the newly independent African countries indicated – and in practice, in Nairobi particularly in the Kenyatta Conference Center. However, for many of the expatriates involved in development programs, Nairobi represented a rapidly growing conglomerate beyond control, its squatters seen mostly as seriously lacking in sanitary and technological standards, difficult to improve and impossible to regulate. The expatriates' moralism towards the unauthorized settlements excluded these areas as a viable local solution with social, cultural and economic advantages for those living there. In both the Kenyan and the expatriates' views of Nairobi, then, characteristics understood as universal predominated, implying a modernist concept of the city. In the Kenyan perceptions, they also included the notion of built forms as national symbols, suggesting a romanticist view of Nairobi.

In this study, the built forms of Nairobi were approached as cultural, suggesting a hermeneutic concept of the city. Within this frame of interpretation, the built forms were perceived as culturally different ways of "living" the city: the study discusses different cultural practices and the meanings attached to them. The culturally shared territories of the city comprised built forms where the African, Asian and European cultural practices of Nairobi meet, sometimes intertwining, but without integration. The culturally privileged territories of the dwellings comprised of built forms where the practices and meanings of one culture predominated but sometimes in built forms originally planned for another culture. All through the history of Nairobi, beyond the official statements and the adventure stories has been the everyday life of different communities, different cultures, their urban and dwelling practices anchored in the microhistorical realities. In this sense, the built forms of Nairobi represented the cultural concept of the city.

■ 20 Towards cultures

When built forms are approached as cultural, that is, as traces of the meanings the different cultures have attached to them, the art historical object of study is not the physical entity as such, but its relations to a society within a particular historical context. This concept of built forms may be connected to the Braudel-inspired notion of a particular kind of spatiality involving the slow but continuous change of the built city, identified above, in chapter one. Compared to architectural and art histories focused on the plan, designer or construction of individual buildings or areas, the cultural approach opens new possibilities. The study of a built form also throws light on the cultures of the society of which it is part: art history approaches cultural history.

The traditional basis of art history as the study of the material and visual reality can function as a point of reference to which non-material aspects may be anchored. The spatial histories of a city are also, in a sense, social histories of its various cultures. The materiality of the built forms makes it possible to connect insights from different fields of study such as planning history, geography, urban anthropology, urban sociology, and social and economic history. At the same time, the cultural frame of interpretation serves to reject claims of unproblematic objectivity, which sometimes have been attached to the notion of the material reality.

In the study of the built forms of Nairobi, the cultural approach brought to focus processes, areas, and communities neglected or undervalued in descriptions of its earlier architectural and planning histories. The historical processes of the changes of the urban and dwelling forms were the concrete visual frame to which the forms of life of the different cultures were attached. The city center as a culturally shared built form and the dwellings of the middle-classes as culturally privileged built forms have earlier received less attention than the organization of land use and traffic, from geographers and town planners, or the problems of squatter areas and their solution by publicly funded housing, from sociologists and architects. Perhaps the most fruitful insight was the notion of multiple cultures as essential elements in the study of built forms; yet this enlargement must be seen as merely a beginning towards the writing of multiple culturally oriented histories of built forms in Nairobi. My view as a European expatriate had its limitations, buttressed by the European bias in part of the reference material. I see the study of the histories of built forms of Nairobi from a multitude of cultural perspectives, particularly local ones, as a program for future research. This does not imply writing culturally, ideologically, or politically biased histories, but searching for truly plural voices in history. The difficulties related to the sources on built forms, also exposed in this study, should not be perceived as a discouragement but as an incentive both to preserve and utilize more thoroughly the existing material, and to extend research to previously unidentified sources. In this respect, for example, two sources used in this study seem promising for more comprehensive studies: historical photographs of built forms and the varied and well-kept archives of the Railways.

More generally, for the objects of art history the cultural concept of built forms suggests a shift in focus. Within the modernist frame of interpretation, the object of study has been the built form as a planned physical entity: its objectively measurable material characteristics. Within the romanticist frame of interpretation, the object of study has been the built form as the expression of ideals and intentions: its subjectively experienced symbolic characteristics. In both, the built form was the focus, its characteristics seen as self-evident. Within the hermeneutic frame of interpretation, however, the focus is not the built form as such, but the meanings attached to it by different communities. Because these meanings may be and frequently are multiple, even contradictory, the built forms emerge as potentially ambiguous.

For research in art history, this opens up new problematizations, new objects of study, and new sources. The issue of art as the expression of supposedly universal aesthetic values may be reformulated, for example, into the issue of the meanings of art for different communities in a particular historical context, involving analyses of the concepts of meaning and art. Redefinitions of the concept of art have already been explored by artists, with developments also valuable for art history. For the study of built forms, the new definitions entail the re-examination of the foundations of the art historical study of built forms, of the frames within which knowledge about built forms is possible, and of their culturally bound histories. In this connection, the cultural approach to built forms should not be seen as a solution in any sense of the word, but as an instrument to generate questions, pose problems, and expose elements of the underlying presuppositions of the different art historical research orientations.

In relation to built forms, the questioning of universal aesthetic values as the self-evident point of departure of art historical research leads to the redefinition of the concept of architecture, not as subjectively experienced, but as contextual: cultural and historical. Within this frame, aesthetic values can be approached as aspects of a particular culture. This opens new objects of study, including built forms perceived as meaningful for a specific community but earlier, within the notion of universal aesthetic values, excluded as "ordinary" (not exceptional), "vernacular" (not designed), or "without architectural quality" (not appreciated). Particularly for the study of cities, it also suggests the necessity of culturally multiple interpretations of a shared urban form: for example, the variation of meanings the built forms of the city center carry for the different cultures "living" the city. For this kind of art historical study, the sources connected to the planning, design and production of the urban forms are insufficient; equally important are documents on how the built forms have historically related to the different cultures. In terms of methodology, this may involve the dissolution of rigid disciplinary boundaries.

Multiculturality is here used to refer not to the variations of ethnically or racially distinguishable communities in global metropolises such as London, New York, Paris, or Hong Kong, but to the notion of differences in cultural practices and meanings within any urban entity. In emphasizing the cultural differences within a particular city, the extent of the variation is relative to the context. Thus also cities like Helsinki – with a history usually presented as culturally static, a population seen as homogeneous (if the seven per cent minority of Swedish-speaking Finns, otherwise similar to the majority, is excepted), and minimal immigration – can be perceived as multicultural, with communities like Helsinki-born urbanites and first-generation citizens, inhabitants of the city center and of the suburbs, low-income and high-income groups, and numerous others.

The notion of multiculturality involves not only an understanding of cultures perceived as others, but also a language to express the otherness. Language, however, is part of a culture. In discussing the understanding of other cultures in the social sciences, Charles Taylor has argued that universalistic views have rejected the notion of otherness and pursued an "objective" approach, external to all cultures, while subjectivist views have promoted empathy and the adoption of the other's perspective as the solution. The danger of the first is ethnocentricity, and of second incorrigibility. Taylor has suggested that understanding otherness implies a particular language:

> It will almost always be the case that the adequate language in which we can understand another society is not our language of understanding, or theirs, but rather what one could call a language of perspicuous contrast. This would be a language in which we could formulate both their way of life and ours as alternative possibilities in relation to some human constants at work in both.[1]

In other words, what is needed is a language which does not suppress cultural differences, but indicates or even emphasizes the contrasts. Taylor's concept of a language of perspicuous contrast may be compared with the cultural approach in the interpretation of built forms in art history. In both, the notion of cultural otherness is adopted as the point of departure for a more articulate understanding not only of the others, but also of our own culture. In this sense, art history can contribute to our self-understanding.

---

1   Taylor 1985b, 125.

Appendixes

Appendix 1

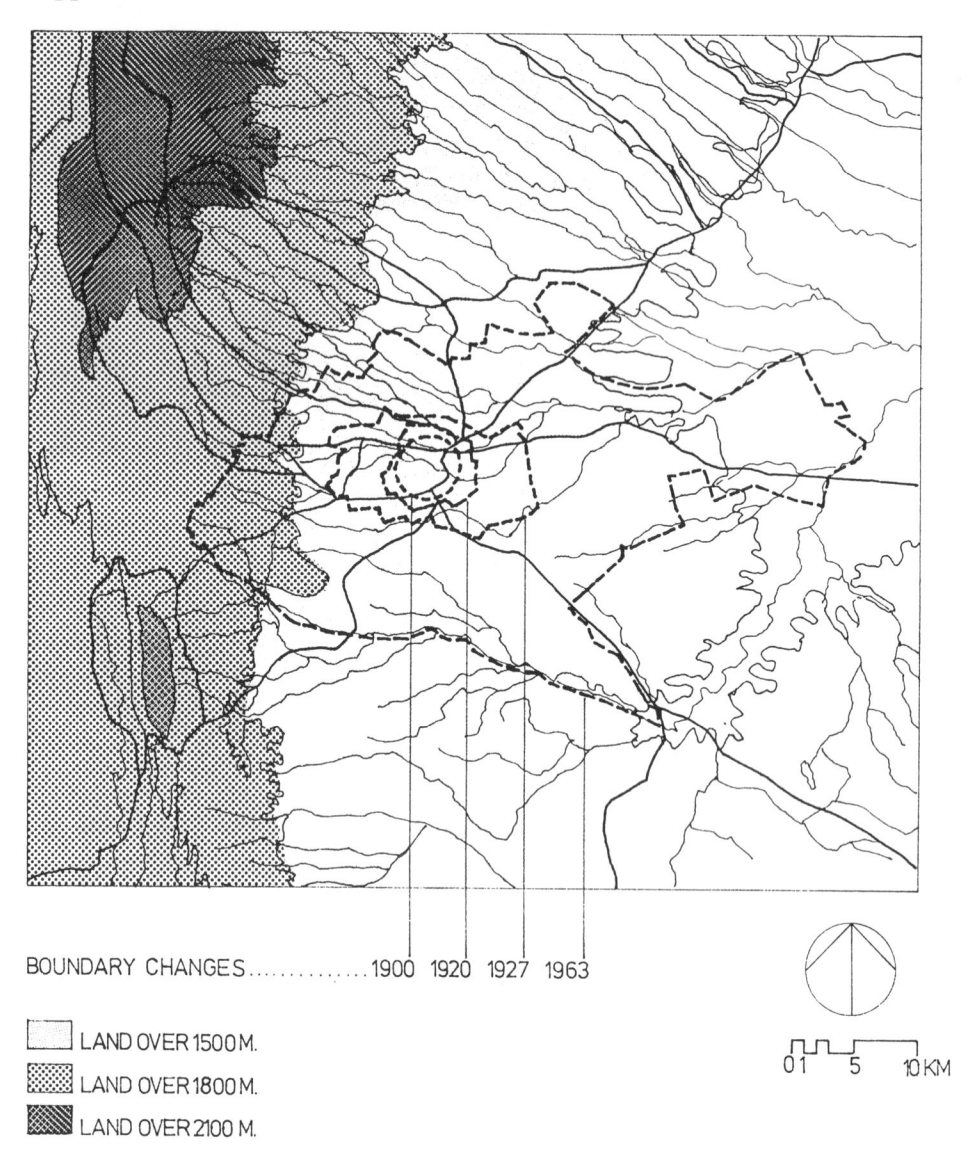

BOUNDARY CHANGES............1900 1920 1927 1963

☐ LAND OVER 1500 M.
▒ LAND OVER 1800 M.
▓ LAND OVER 2100 M.

0 1   5   10 KM

Appendix 2

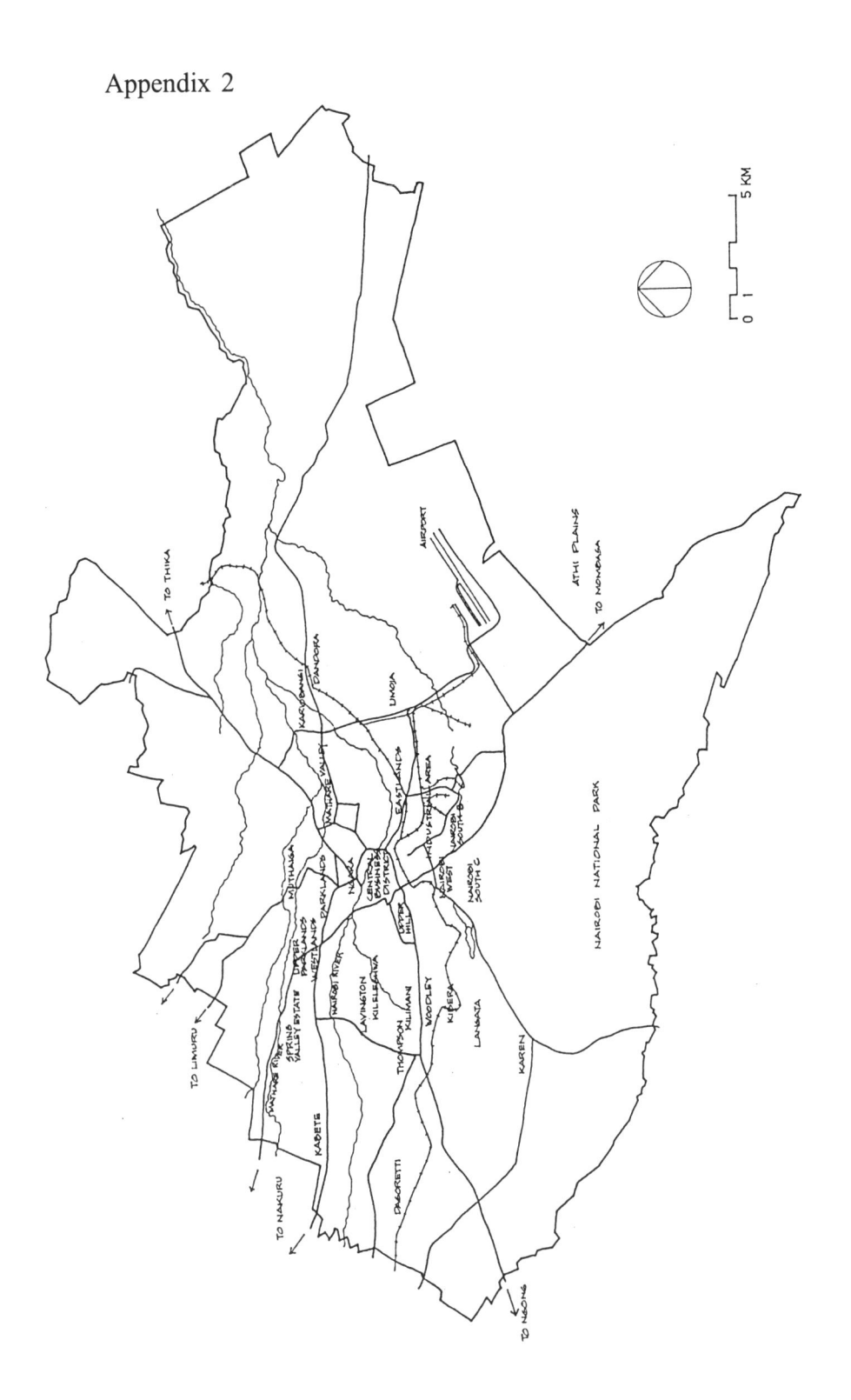

Appendix 3

TEXTS OF QUOTATIONS IN THE ORIGINAL LANGUAGES

Part III, chapter 9:

Kirsti Gallen-Kallela: Isäni Akseli Gallen-Kallela, first edition 1964, revised edition 1992, pp.463-465:
> Nairobi . . . oli siihen aikaan, 1909-1910, pieni kylä, jossa asui noin 500 valkoihoista, loput hinduja . . . Pääkatu kulki silloin kaupungin päästä toiseen, asemalta hienoon Norfolk-hotelliin, ja sitten alkoi valtamaantie erämaan halki Fort-Hallin linnoitukseen. Katua reunustivat korkeat eukalyptuspuut . . . Pääkadun varrella sijaitsivat aaltopellistä rakennetut valkoisten kaupat . . . Poikkikatu oli kokonaan hindubasaarina; sen hökkelit oli jaettu väliseinillä kopeiksi, joiden lattiat olivat ostajan pään tasalla. Etuseinä puuttui ja kalteva lattia oli ahdettu täyteen avonaisia riisi-, maissi-, herne- ym.laatikoita . . . Kauempana oli katoksellinen ruokahalli, josta valkoiset rouvat ostivat ruokatarvikkeensa, enimmäkseen kaikenlaisia hedelmiä ja vihanneksia . . . Hindutemppeli sijaitsi pääkadun ja basaarin risteyksessä.

Kirsti Gallen-Kallela: Muistelmia nuoruusvuosiltani 1896-1931, 1982, p.49:
> Hotel Stanley Nairobissa oli vuonna 1909 kaksikerroksinen peltikattoinen Villin lännen -tyylinen talo, joka sijaitsi Nairobin pääkadun Governement Roadin varrella. Muita katuja ei siellä juuri ollutkaan . . . Stanley-hotellissa asuimme neljä viikkoa, kunnes saimme oman kodin Nairobin ulkopuolelta aron reunalta.

Part III, chapter 13:

Ronny Ambjörnsson: Kenya, 1971, p.169-170:
> Den tillfällige europeiske besökaren i Nairobi möts inte alls av stagnation och underutveckling. Tvärtom, han går ut i en stad, som kunde ligga var som helst it Europa. Överallt rivs det och byggs, gator breddas och nya hus växer upp som hötorgsskrapor ur jorden. Kasinon, hotell, bankpalats, regeringsbyggnader, polishus, parkeringshus, bensin- och försäkringsbolagens palats med valspråk på latin: Caltex House, Agip House, New Jogoo House, Prudential Assurance Building (Fortis qui prudens), Development House, Silo Park House, alla i en skön och betecknande blandning. Högst av alla reser sig, som sig bör, det tjuguvåniga Hilton Hotel från vars översta våningar man knappt kan ana ruckelstäderna långt borta i utkanterna; man är för hög för att kunna urskilja några detaljer.
> Gör man sig besvär med att gå utåt öster, förändras husen för varje kvarter. De sjunker ihop alltmer tills man befinner sig på andra sidan Nairobi River, ett avloppsdike som skiljer själva staden från de afrikanska bostadsområdena. Längs Nairobi River har afrikanerna slagit upp sina skjul av säckar och brädbitar. De väntar på jobb. En del har väntat två år, andra har väntat längre. En del har en jordbit i reservated ddär familjen väntar, en del har ingen jord alls. De bor med sin familj bakom säckarna. Dessa säckstäder utgör ingen vacker anblick, de är knappast ens pittoreska. De torde heller inte vara hygieniska . . . I Kenya rivs för att turisterna skall få luft och ljus. Men folket bor kvar på samma plats nu under presenningar och lådor.

Appendix 4

DESCRIPTIONS OF THE DWELLINGS STUDIED

Table 1: The number of houses studied, defined according to their time of construction and to their location within the urban structure.

	Time of construction:			total
Location:	1899-1940	1940-1963	1963-1983	
city center	1	1	1	3
ring around city center	5	1	–	6
suburban	1	5	5	11
total	7	7	6	20

In table 1, the city center was defined as the area within the boundary formed by the Nairobi River, the railway yard, and Uhuru Highway. The ring around it included Ngara, Pumwani, and the Upper Hill area, within approximately a two-kilometer radius. Areas beyond that were considered suburban.

Table 1 indicates that of the dwellings studied built before 1940, only one was located in the area presently regarded as suburban (Eastleigh). In the urban structure of the pre-1940 city, the present ring around the city center was "suburban", but within walking distance of the city center.

Table 2: The number of houses studied, defined according to their time of construction and to the house type.

	Time of construction:			total
Type:	1899-1940	1940-1963	1963-1983	
detached house	1	2	1	4
semi-detached	1	1	–	2
row house	2	1	3	6
courtyard house	2	1	1	4
flat	–	2	1	3
majengo	1	–	–	1
total	7	7	6	20

Table 2 indicates how the dwellings studied differed in terms of the house type. Flats were not built before 1940. Of the three row houses built during independence one had a single floor, one two floors, and the third was a split level house.

Table 3: The number of dwellings studied, defined according to the cultural group that the dwellings were originally planned for and according to the cultural group they were inhabited by during the study.

	Dwellers in 1983:			total
	Kenyan-African	Kenyan-Asian	expat.-European	
Planned dwellers:				
1899-1940:				7
.African	2	-	-	
.Asian	3	1	-	
.European	1	-	-	
1940-1963:				7
.African	-	-	-	
.Asian	-	3	-	
.European	2	-	2	
1963-1983:				6
.Kenyan-African	3	-	-	
.Kenyan-Asian	-	-	-	
.expatriate	1	1	1	
Total	12	5	3	20

Table 3 indicates that of the dwellings studied, five had originally been planned for Africans, six for Asians, and nine for Europeans. Altogether eleven houses had been both planned for and were in 1983 inhabited by the same cultural group: five by Kenyan-Africans, three by Kenyan-Asians, and three by (expatriate-) Europeans. Nine houses had originally been planned for a cultural group different from the one occupying it at the time of study.

Table 4: The number of houses studied, defined according to house ownership and to the dwellers.

	Ownership:			total
	Employer housing	Owner-occupied	Rented	
Dwellers:				
Kenyan-African				12
.fam./single	6	-	-	
.fam.+tenant/s	-	3	-	
.tenants only	-	-	3	
Kenyan-Asian				5
.family	-	4	-	
.fam.+tenant	-	1	-	
expat.-European				3
.fam./single	1	-	2	
total	7	8	5	20

In table 4, of the six units of employer housing inhabited by Kenyan-Africans, in four the dwellers were employees of the Railways, one of the University, and one of a private company. Of the three units of rented housing inhabited by tenants only, one had several one- or two-room dwellings, and another housed three single persons sharing. Of the four owner-occupied dwellings inhabited by Kenyan-Asians, three of the dweller families were joint ones.

Table 4 indicates that among the dwellings studied, the major groups were employer housing among the Kenyan-Africans, owner-occupied housing among the Kenyan-Asians, and rental housing among the expatriate-Europeans.

Table 5: The number of houses studied, defined according to dwelling types and dwellers.

Dwellings:	Dwellers: Kenyan-African	Kenyan-Asian	expat.-European	total
detached house	1	2	1	4
semi-detached	1	1	-	2
row house	5	-	1	6
courtyard house	2	2	-	4
flat	2	-	1	3
majengo	1	-	-	1
total	12	5	3	20

In table 5, of the two courtyard houses inhabited by Kenyan-Africans, one had been originally built by Kenyan-Asians for an extended family and had been later converted into a multi-family house. The other had been built for Kenyan-Africans; in Nairobi, the type is an exception among government funded housing, but relatively much studied after construction.

Illustration Sources

Unless otherwise indicated, the illustrations are by the author.

Andreasen 1987: 13.12
Autonews 1983: 8.6, 10.2, 11.1, 11.2
Barnow 1990: 10.1, 13.15, 13.16
Barnow et al 1983: 8.2, 11.13, 13.21
Blair 1980: 12.16
Chana 1984: 13.11
City of Nairobi Map and Guide 1978: 6.15, 8.9
Ann Creager: 13.3, 13.3
Emig and Ismael 1980: 8.1, 11.5, 11.6, 13.6 - 13.9
Etherton 1971: 13.2, 13.10
Frisell 1939: 11.3
Gallen-Kallela Museum: 9.2
Halliman and Morgan 1967: 8.4, 9.1, 13.1
Huxley and Curtis 1980: 8.7, 8.8
Kenya Insight Guide 1985: 12.17, 13.22
Master Plan 1948: 8.3, 12.1 - 12.13
National Geographic 1950: 12.15
O'Connor 1983: 13.13, 13.14
Postcard: cover, 11.7 - 11.12, 12.14
Slide (commercial): 13.17, 13.19
Tiwari 1981: 8.5

Sources

The bibliography includes only sources directly used for reference. Documents quoted from other sources are indicated in the notes. The dwelling owners' names have been omitted at their request, to protect their privacy. In the bibliography, published diaries, letters and memoirs, and works of fiction are listed separately.

Abbreviations

KR/PA   Kenya Railways, Architects' Department Plan Archives
MP 1948   Nairobi Master Plan 1948: Thornton White et al 1948
SK   Survey of Kenya

Unpublished material

Gallen-Kallela Museum Archives, Espoo (Finland):
    Photograph collection, Africa section
    Slide collection of paintings

Kenya Railways, Nairobi (Kenya):
    Architects' Department Plan Archives: Dwelling and site plans

Survey of Kenya, Nairobi (Kenya):
    Aerial photographs of Nairobi

University of Nairobi, Nairobi (Kenya):
Faculty of Architecture, Design and Development:
    Housing Research and Development Unit Archives:
    *Chana, T.S., and Z.H.Devji. *Norfolk Towers Phase I Flats: A User-Reaction Study.* 1981.
    *Chana, T.S., P.Houlberg, J.Hagger, G.J.de Kruijff and A.Rwomire. *Evaluation of the Site and Services Programme in Kenya.* Draft. 1979.
    City Council of Nairobi (Building) By-Laws, 1948, ("Planning"). 1949.
    *Farnworth, E.T. *A Survey of the Problems of Re-Developing Pumwani Estate: A report submitted to the Nairobi City Council.* 1964.
    *Hoek-Smit, Marja C. *Housing Preferences of Middle Income Tenant Housing Households in Umoja Estate, Nairobi, Kenya.* Prepared for the Housing Development and Research Unit, Nairobi City Council. 1983.
    *Hooper, Charles, Philip Mein, Muindi Mulili & George Ochola. *Kibera New Village, Nairobi: A Selective Appraisal of a Courtyard Housing Scheme.* 1974.
    *Menezes, Leonie. *BuruBuru: A Social Study.* 1978.
    *Morrison, Hunter. *Mathare Valley Report: A Case Study in Low Income Housing.* Draft. Nairobi, 1972.
    *Soni, P. *Notes on Planning and Building Low Cost Housing in Kenya.* Nairobi, 1983.
    *Stren, Richard. *Urban Development in Kenya and Tanzania: A Comparative Analysis.* Working Paper No.147, Institute for Development Studies, University of Nairobi, Nairobi, March 1974.

Faculty Library, Theses:
    *Moniz, Anthony Mervyn. *Urban Mixed Land Use.* B.Arch.thesis, University of Nairobi, Department of Architecture, 1984.
    *Soni, Praful Naran. *On Self-Help in a Site and Service Project in Kenya.* M.Arch.Thesis, Massachusetts Institute of Technology, Department of Architecture, 1980.

Private archives:

Bruce Creager's archive, Nairobi (Kenya):
Mimeographed papers and newspaper clippings on Nairobi planning and housing, from the Standard, the Daily Nation, and the Sunday Nation, 1971-1982

Dwelling owners' archives, Nairobi (Kenya):
Dwelling plans

Anja Kervanto Nevanlinna's archive, Helsinki (Finland):
Measured drawings of 20 dwellings, 1983
Photographs of Nairobi, 1980-89
Field study notes, 1983

Published maps

Survey of Kenya, Map Office, Nairobi (Kenya):
Maps of Nairobi

University of Nairobi, Nairobi (Kenya):
Faculty of Architecture, Design and Development:
Department of Land Development Map Archives:
Maps of Nairobi

Newspapers and other printed material

The Standard, Nairobi, 1983
Daily Nation, Nairobi, 1973, 1983
Sunday Nation, Nairobi, 1983
African Business, London, 1983
Autonews, Nairobi, 1983
National Geographic, Washington D.C., 1950

Postcards, purchased in Nairobi in 1980-1989

Published diaries, letters and memoirs; satirical articles

Blixen, Karen. *Out of Africa*. (Orig.1937.) Penguin, Harmondsworth, 1954.
Blixen, see also Dinesen.
Cell, John W., ed. *By Kenya Possessed. The Correspondence of Norman Leys and J.H.Oldham 1918-1926*. The University of Chicago Press, Chicago, 1976.
Dinesen, Isak (Karen Blixen). *Letters from Africa 1914-1931*. (Orig. Breve fra Afrika 1914-24 and Breve fra Afrika 1925-31, 1978.) Ed. Frans Lasson. Picador/Pan Books, London, 1983.
Frisell, Hjalmar. *Leva farligt i Afrika*. Bonniers, Stockholm, 1939.
Gallen-Kallela, Kirsti. *Muistelmia nuoruusvuosiltani 1896-1931*. Weilin+Göös, Espoo, 1982.
Gallen-Kallela, Kirsti. *Isäni Akseli Gallen-Kallela*. (Orig.1964-65.) Ed. Kaari Raivio. WSOY, Helsinki, 1992.
Huxley, Elspeth, and Arnold Curtis, eds. *Pioneers' Scrapbook: Reminiscences of Kenya 1890 to 1968*. Evans, London, 1980.
Leys, Norman. *Kenya*. (First edition 1924.) Fourth edition. Frank Cass, London, 1973.
Meinertzhagen, Richard. *Kenya Diary, 1902-1906*. (orig.1957.) Eland Books, London, 1983.
Ngugi wa Thiong'o (James Ngugi). *Detained: A Writer's Prison Diary*. Heinemann, Nairobi, 1981.
Ng'weno, Hilary. *With a Light Touch*. Stellascope, Nairobi, 1982.

Fiction

Akare, Thomas. *The Slums*. Heinemann, London, 1981.
Mwangi, Meja. *Going Down River Road*. Heinemann, London, 1976.
Mwangi, Meja. *The Cockroach Dance*. Longman, Nairobi, 1979.
Naipaul, V.S. *In a Free State*. Penguin, Harmondsworth, 1973.
Ngugi wa Thiong'o. *A Grain of Wheat*. (Orig. 1967.) Heinemann, London, 1982.
Ruark, Robert. *Uhuru*. Corgi, London, 1962.
Ruark, Robert. *Something of Value*. Doubleday, Garden City (N.Y.), 1955.

Bibliography

Abu-Lughod, Janet. *Rabat: Urban Apartheid in Morocco*. Princeton University Press, Princeton, 1980.
Abuor, C. Ojwando. *White Highlands no More*. Pan African Researchers, Nairobi, 1973.
Alho, Olli. *Kehitysyhteistyöasiantuntija vieraassa kulttuurissa*. (A Study of Finnish Development Experts in Africa.) Jyväskylän yliopisto, etnologian laitos, tutkimuksia 12, Jyväskylä, 1980.
AlSayyad, Nezar. Urbanism and the Dominance Equation: Reflections on Colonialism and National Identity. In *Forms of Dominance: On the Architecture and Urbanism of the Colonial Enterprise*, ed. Nezar AlSayyad. Avebury, Aldershot, 1992.
Altman, Irwin and Martin M.Chemers. *Culture and Environment*. Cambridge University Press, Cambridge, 1984.
Ambjörnsson, Ronny. Kenya. In *Etiopien, Kenya, Tanzania, Zambia: Fyra resor*, eds. Ronny Ambjörnsson, Lars Ardelius, Björn Håkansson and Agneta Pleijel. Författarförlaget, Stockholm, 1971.
Amis, Philip. Squattere eller lejere: Kommercialiseringen af uautoriserede boliger i Nairobi. In *Boligsproblemet i den Tredje Verden*, ed. Finn Barnow. Kunstakademiets Forlag, Kobenhavn, 1987.
Andersen, Kaj Blegvad. *African Traditional Architecture: A Study of the Housing and Settlement Patterns of Rural Kenya*. Oxford University Press, Nairobi, 1978.
Andreasen, Jörgen. *Urban Development and Housing in Kenya*. Background Paper No.1, Royal Danish Academy of Fine Arts, Copenhagen, 1987.
Andrews, Paul, Malcolm Christie and Richard Martin. Squatters and the Evolution of a Lifestyle. *Architectural Design*, vol.43, No.1, 1973.
Bacon, Edmund N. *Design of Cities*. (Orig.1968.) Revised edition. Thames and

Hudson, London, 1975.
Barnow, Finn. *Kolonistens by: Studier af urbanisering og byplanlaegning i den tredje verden.* Kunstakademiets forlag, København, 1990.
Barnow, Finn et al. *Urban Development in Kenya: The Growth of Nairobi 1900-1970.* School of Architecture, Copenhagen, 1983.
Barthes, Roland. *The Rustle of Language.* (Orig. Le bruissement de la langue, 1984.) Basil Blackwell, Oxford, 1986.
Baudrillard, Jean, et Marc Guillaume. *Figures de l'altérité.* Descartes, Paris, 1992.
Bedarida, François. The Growth of Urban History in France: Some Methodological Trends. In *The Study of Urban History*, ed. H.J. Dyos, Edward Arnold, London, 1968.
Benevolo, Leonardo. *The History of Modern Architecture. Vol.I: The Tradition of Modern Architecture.*(a) *Vol.II: The Modern Movement.*(b) Routledge & Kegan Paul, London, 1971.
Beng-Huat, Chua. Adjusting Religious Practices to Different Housing Forms in Singapore. *Architecture and Behavior*, Vol. 4, No. 1, 1988.
Berlin, Isaiah. *Vico and Herder.* Hogarth, London, 1976.
Berlin, Isaiah. *Against the Current.* Clarendon, London, 1979.
Berlin, Isaiah. *The Crooked Timber of Humanity.* Fontana, London, 1990.
Bharati, Agehananda. A Social Survey. In *Portrait of a Minority: Asians in East Africa*, eds.Dharam P.Ghai and Yash P.Ghai. Revised edition. Oxford University Press, Nairobi, 1970.
Bhaskar, Roy. *A Realist Theory of Science.* Harvester Wheatshef, London, 1978.
Blacker, J.G.C. Population Growth and Urbanization in Kenya. In Bloomberg and Abrams: *United Nations Mission to Kenya on Housing.* Prepared for the Government of Kenya, United Nations, Commissioner for Technical Assistance, Department of Economic and Social Affairs, 1965.
Blair, Thomas L. Shelter in Urbanising and Industrialising Africa. In *Shelter in Africa*, ed.Paul Oliver. Barrie & Jenkins, London, 1971.
Blair, Thomas. Education for Habitat. *Architectural Association Quarterly*, vol.12, No.1, 1980.
de Blij, Harm, and Esmond Martin, eds. *African Perspectives.* Methuen, New York, 1981.
Bloomberg, Lawrence N., and Charles Abrams. *United Nations Mission to Kenya on Housing.* Prepared for the Government of Kenya, United Nations, Commissioner for Technical Assistance, Department of Economic and Social Affairs, 1965.
Bonte, Pierre, and Michel Izard, eds. *Dictionnaire de l'ethnologie et de l'anthropologie.* Presses Universitaires de France, Paris, 1991.
Boudon, Raymond, and François Bourricaud. *Dictionnaire critique de la sociologie.* Presses Universitaires de France, Paris, 1986.
Bourdieu, Pierre. *Outline of a Theory of Practice.* (Orig. Esquisse d'une théorie de la pratique, précédé de trois études d'ethnologie kabyle, 1972.) Cambridge University Press, Cambridge, 1977.
Brake, Michael. *The sociology of youth culture and youth subcultures.* Routledge & Kegan Paul, London, 1980.
Braudel, Fernand. *The Mediterranean and the Mediterranean World in the Age of Philip II.* (Orig. La Méditeranée et le Monde Méditerranéen á l'epoque de Philippe II, 1949.) Vol.1, Second revised edition. Fontana, London, 1986.
Braunfels, Wolfgang. *Urban Design in Western Europe: Regime and Architecture, 900-1900.* (Orig. Abendländische Stadtbaukunst: Herrschaftsform und Baugestalt, 1976.) University of Chicago Press, Chicago, 1988.
British Library Catalogue of Printed Books II. 1975.
de Bruijne, G.A. The colonial city and the post-colonial world. In *Colonial Cities*, eds. Robert Ross and Gerard J.Telkamp. Martinus Nijhoff, Dordrecht, 1985.
Burnett, John. *A Social History of Housing 1815-1985.* Second edition. Routledge, London, 1986.
Caminos, Horacio, and Reinhard Goethert. *Urbanization Primer.* MIT Press, Cambridge (Mass.), 1980.
Carter, Harold. The Map in Urban History. *Urban History Yearbook 1979.* Leicester University Press, Leicester, 1979.
Cassirer, Ernst. *An Essay on Man: An Introduction to a Philosophy of Human Culture.* Yale University Press, New Haven, 1944.
de Certeau, Michel. *Heterologies: Discourse on the Other.* Manchester University Press, Manchester, 1986.
Chana, T.S. Nairobi: Dandora and Other Projects. In *Low-income Housing in the Developing World*, ed. G.K.Payne, John Wiley, London, 1984.
Chana, T., and H. Morrison. Housing systems in the low income sector of Nairobi, Kenya. *Ekistics*, Vol.36, No.214, 1973.
Choay, Françoise. *L'urbanisme, utopies et réalités.* Coll. Points, Seuil, Paris, 1965.
Choay, Françoise. *The modern city: Planning in the 19th Century.* Seuil, Paris, 1969.
Choay, Françoise. *La règle et le modèle: Sur la théorie de l'architecture et de l'urbanisme.* Seuil, Paris, 1980.
Choay, Françoise. Pensées sur la ville, arts de la ville. In *Histoire de la France urbaine, Tome 4: La ville de l'âge industriel*, ed. Maurice Agulhon. Seuil, Paris, 1983.
Choay, Françoise. Conclusion. In *Morpho-

logie urbaine et parcellaire, éd. Pierre Merlin. Presses Universitaires de Vincennes, Saint-Denis, 1988.

Clarke, John, Stuart Hall, Tony Jefferson and Brian Roberts. Sub-Cultures, Cultures and Class. In *Culture, Ideology and Social Process*, eds. Tony Bennett, Graham Martin, Colin Mercer and Janet Woollacott. Open University Press, London, 1981.

Clifford, James. Introduction: Partial Truths. In *Writing Culture: The Poetics and Politics of Ethnography*, eds. James Clifford and George E.Marcus. University of California Press, Berkeley, 1986.

Conzen, Kathleen Neils. Community Studies, Urban History, and American Local History. In *The Past Before Us*, ed.Michael Kammen. Cornell University Press, Ithaca, 1980.

Conzen, M.R.G. The Use of Town Plans in the Study of Urban History. In *The Study of Urban History*, ed. H.J. Dyos. Edward Arnold, London, 1968.

Conzen, Michael P. Town-plan analysis in an American setting: cadastral processes in Boston and Omaha, 1630-1930. In *The Built Form of Western Cities*, ed. T.R .Slater. Leicester University Press, Leicester, 1990.

Cox, Richard. *Kenyatta's Country*. Hutchinson, London, 1965.

Crampe-Crasnabet, Michèle. *Cordorcet, lecteur des Lumières*. Presses Universitaires de France, Paris, 1985.

Daunton, M.J. *House and Home in the Victorian City: Working-Class Housing 1850-1914*. Edward Arnold, London, 1983.

Davidson, Basil. *Africa in Modern History*. Penguin, London, 1978.

Davis, Mike. *City of Quartz: Excavating the Future in Los Angeles*. Verso, London, 1990.

Dike, Azuka A. Misconceptions of African Urbanism: Some Euro-African Notions. In *Development of Urban Systems in Africa*, eds. R.A. Obudho & Salah El-Shakhs. Praeger, New York, 1979.

Dossal, Marian. *Imperial Design and Indian Realities: The Planning of Bombay City 1845-1875*. Oxford University Press, Bombay, 1991.

Dreyfus, Hubert L. *Being-in-the-World: A Commentary of Heidegger's "Being and Time", Division I*. MIT Press, Cambridge (Mass.), 1991.

Dreyfus, Hubert L., and Paul Rabinow. *Michel Foucault, Beyond Structuralism and Hermeneutics*. Harvester Wheatsheaf, New York, 1982.

Dumont, Louis. *Essais sur l'individualisme: Une perspective anthropologique sur l'idéologie moderne*. Coll. Points, Paris, 1985.

Dyos, H.J. Agenda for Urban Historians. In *The Study of Urban History*, ed. H.J. Dyos, Edward Arnold, London, 1968.

Eco, Umberto. Does Counter-culture Exist? (Orig. Sette anni di desiderio, 1983.) In *Apocalypse Postponed*. Flamingo, London, 1995.

Ehrlich, Cyril. Economic and Social Developments before Independence. In *Zamani, A Survey of East African History*, ed. B.A. Ogot. East African Publishing House, Nairobi, 1974.

Eley, Geoff. De l'histoire au 'tournant linguistique' dans l'historiographie anglo-américaine des années 1980. *Genèses* 7, 1992.

Elias, Norbert. *The History of Manners. The Civilizing Process, Vol.1*. (Orig. Über den Prozess der Zivilisation, 1939.) Pantheon, New York, 1978.

Elkan, Walter. Circular Migration and the Growth of Towns in East Africa. In *Third World Employment, Problems and Strategy*, eds. Richard Jolly et al. Penguin, Harmondsworth, 1973.

Elkan, Walter, and Roger van Zwanenberg. How People Came to Live in Towns. In *Colonialism in Africa 1870-1960, Vol.4: The Economics of Colonialism*, eds. Peter Duignan and L.H. Gann. Cambridge University Press, Cambridge, 1975.

Emig, Sören, and Zahir Ismail. *Notes on the Urban Planning of Nairobi*. Royal Academy of Fine Arts, School of Architecture, Copenhagen, 1980.

Escobar, Arturo. Planning. In *The Development Dictionary*, ed. Wolfgang Sachs. Zed Books, London, 1992.

Esteva, Gustavo. Development. In *The Development Dictionary*, ed. Wolfgang Sachs. Zed Books, London, 1992.

Etherton, David. *Mathare Valley, a case study of uncontrolled settlement in Nairobi*. Housing Research and Development Unit, University of Nairobi, Nairobi, 1971.

Evenson, Norma. *Paris: A Century of Change, 1878-1978*. Yale University Press, New Haven, 1979.

Fanon, Franz. *The Wretched of the Earth*. (Orig. Les Damnés de la terre, 1961.) Grove Press, New York, 1963.

Featherstone, Mike, ed. *Global Culture: Nationalism, Globalization and Modernity*. Sage, London, 1990.

Finkielkraut, Alain. *La défaite de la pensée*. Coll. Points, Gallimard, Paris, 1987.

Fischer, Claude S. Toward a Subcultural Theory of Urbanism. *American Journal of Sociology*, vol. 80, No.6, 1975.

Fischer, Claude S. *The Urban Experience*. Harcourt Brace Jovanovich, New York, 1976.

Fletcher, Banister. *A History of Architecture*. Ed. John Musgrove. 19th ed. Butterworths, London, 1987.

Foucault, Michel. *The Order of Things. An Archaeology of the Human Sciences*. (Orig. Les Mots et les choses, 1966.) Routledge, London, 1970.

Foucault, Michel. *The Archaeology of Knowledge*. (Orig. L'Archéologie du savoir, 1969.) Routledge, London, 1972.

Foucault, Michel. *Discipline and Punish: The Birth of the Prison*. (Orig. Surveiller et punir: Naissance de la prison, 1975.) Penguin Books, Harmondsworth, 1979.

Foucault, Michel. *Power/Knowledge*, ed. Colin Gordon. Pantheon Books, New York, 1980.

Foucault, Michel. Space, Knowledge, and Power. In *The Foucault Reader*, ed. Paul Rabinow, Penguin Books. Harmondsworth, 1984.

Fox, Richard G. Rationale and Romance in Urban Anthropology. In *City Ways*, eds. John Friedl and Noel J.Chrisman. Thomas Y.Crowell, New York, 1975.

Franklin, Jill. *The Gentleman's Country House and its plan, 1835-1914*. Routledge & Kegan Paul, London, 1981.

Furedi, Frank. The African Crowd in Nairobi: Popular Movements and Elite Politics. In *Third World Urbanization*, eds. Janet Abu-Lughod and Michael Hay, New York, 1979.

Gadamer, Hans-Georg. *Philosophical Hermeneutics*. University of California Press, Berkeley, 1976.

Gadamer, Hans-Georg. The Problem of Historical Consciousness. (Orig. Le Problème de la conscience historique, 1963.) In *Interpretive Social Science, A Second Look*, eds. Paul Rabinow and William M. Sullivan. University of California Press, Berkeley, 1987.

Galaty, John, and John Leavitt. Entry 'Culture', 2.Les théories, In: *Dictionnaire de l'ethnologie et de l'anthropologie*, eds. Pierre Bonte et Michel Izard. Presses Universitaires 1991.

Gans, Herbert J. *People and Plans*. Basic Books, New York, 1968.

Gans, Herbert J. *The Urban Villagers: Group and Class in the Life of Italian-Americans*. Revised edition. Free Press, New York, 1982.

Gaskell, Ivan. History of Images. In *New Perspectives on Historical Writing*, ed. Peter Burke. Polity Press, Cambridge, 1991.

Gattoni, George and Praful Patel. *Residential Land Utilization. Case Study: Nairobi, Kenya*. MIT Press, Cambridge (Mass.), 1973.

Geddes, Patrick. *Cities in Evolution: An Introduction to the Town Planning Movement and to the Study of Civics*. (Orig.1915.) Ernest Benn, London, 1968.

Geertz, Clifford. *The Interpretation of Cultures*. Basic Books, New York, 1973.

Gellner, Ernest. *Culture, Identity, and Politics*. Cambridge University Press, Cambridge, 1987.

Gellner, Ernest. *Reason and Culture: The Historic Role of Rationality and Rationalism*. Blackwell, Oxford, 1992.

Ghai, Dharam P. An Economic Survey. In *Portrait of a Minority: Asians in East Africa*, eds. Dharam P. Ghai and Yash P. Ghai. Oxford University Press, Nairobi, 1970.

Ghai, Dharam P. and Yash P.Ghai, eds. *Portrait of a Minority: Asians in East Africa*. Revised edition. Oxford University Press, Nairobi, 1970.

Ghai, D.P. Some Aspects of Social and Economic Progress and Policies in East Africa, 1961 to 1971. In *Zamani: A Survey of East African History*, ed. B.A.Ogot, East African Publishing House, Nairobi, 1974.

Ghaidan, Usam. *Lamu: A Study of the Swahili Town*. East African Publishing House, Nairobi, 1975.

Giddens, Anthony. *Central Problems in Social Theory*. University of California Press, Berkeley, 1979.

Giddens, Anthony. *The Constitution of Society*. Polity, Cambridge, 1984.

Giedion, Sigfried. *Space, Time and Architecture: The Growth of a New Tradition*. Fifth revised edition. Harvard University Press, Cambridge (Mass.), 1967.

Ginzburg, Carlo. Geschichte und Geschichten: Über Archive, Marlene Dietrich und die Lust an der Geschichte. In *Spurensicherungen: Über verborgene Geschichte, Kunst und soziales Gedächtnis*. Klaus Wagenbach, Berlin, 1983.

Ginzburg, Carlo. *Clues, Myths, and the Historical Method*. (Orig. Miti emblemi spie: morfologia e storia, 1986.) Johns Hopkins University Press, Baltimore, 1989.

Girouard, Mark. *Life in the English Country House*. Penguin, Harmondsworth, 1980.

Government of Kenya. *Development Plan 1979-1983*. Government Printer, Nairobi, 1979.

Grafmeyer, Y. and I.Joseph, eds. *L'Ecole de Chicago, Naissance de l'écologie urbaine*. Aubier, Paris, 1984.

Gropius, Walter. Sociological Premises for the Minimum Dwelling of Urban Industrial Populations. (Orig. Die soziologischen Grundlagen der Minimalwohnung, 1929.) In Walter Gropius, *Scope of Total Architecture*. Collier, New York, 1962.

Gugler, Josef. Urbanization in East Africa. In *Urban Challenge in East Africa*, ed. John Hutton, East African Publishing House, Nairobi, 1972.

Habermas, Jürgen. *La technique et la science comme "idéologie."* (Orig. Technik und Wissenschaft als Ideologie, 1968.) Gallimard, Paris, 1973.

Habermas, Jürgen. *The Philosophical Discourse of Modernity*. MIT Press, Cambridge (Mass.), 1987.

Hake, Andrew. *African Metropolis: Nairobi's Self-Help City*. Sussex University Press, London, 1977.

Hall, Peter. *The World Cities*. Third Edition.

Weidenfeld and Nicolson, London, 1984.

Hall, Peter. *Cities of Tomorrow: An Intellectual History of Urban Planning and Design in the Twentieth Century.* Basil Blackwell, Oxford, 1988.

Halliman, Dorothy M., and W.T.W. Morgan. The City of Nairobi. In *Nairobi: City and Region*, ed. W.T.W. Morgan. Oxford University Press, Nairobi, 1967.

Hammarstrom, Ingrid, and Thomas Hall. Perspectives on 'Svensk stad'. *Urban History Yearbook 1983.* Leicester University Press, Leicester, 1983.

Hannerz, Ulf. *Exploring the City.* Columbia University Press, New York, 1980.

Hannerz, Ulf. Delkulturerna och helheten. In *Kultur och medvetande: en tvärvetenskaplig analys*, ed. Ulf Hannerz, Rita Liljeström and Orvar Löfgren. Akademilitteratur, Lund, 1982.

Hannerz, Ulf. *Cultural Complexity: Studies in the Social Organization of Meaning.* Columbia University Press, New York, 1992.

Harvey, David. *Social Justice and the City.* (Orig.1973.) Basil Blackwell, London, 1988.

Hauser, Arnold. *The Social History of Art. Vol.III: Rococo, Classicism and Romanticism.* Routledge & Kegan Paul, London, 1962.

Hebdige, Dick. *Subculture: The Meaning of Style.* Methuen, London, 1979.

Hill, M.F. *Permanent Way. Vol.1, The Story of the Kenya and Uganda Railway.* East African Literature Bureau, Nairobi, 1949.

Hoek-Smit, Marja C. *The Future Planning of a Majengo: Swahili Village-Masuku.* Housing Research and Development Unit, University of Nairobi, Nairobi, 1976.

Holston, James. *The Modernist City: An Anthropological Critique of Brasilia.* University of Chicago Press, Chicago, 1989.

Hooper, Charles. *Design for Climate: Guidelines for the Design of Low Cost Houses for the Climates of Kenya.* Housing Research and Development Unit, University of Nairobi, 1975.

Hutton, John, ed. *Urban Challenge in East Africa.* East African Publishing House, Nairobi, 1972.

Huxley, Elspeth. *White Man's Country: Lord Delamere and the Making of Kenya.* (a) Vol.1, 1870-1914. (b) Vol.2, 1914-1931. (Orig.1935.) Chatto and Windus, London, 1968.

Izard, M. Entry 'Culture', 1.Le problème. In *Dictionnaire de l'ethnologie et de l'anthropologie*, eds. Pierre Bonte et Michel Izard. Presses Universitaires de France, Paris, 1991.

Jameson, Fredric. *Postmodernism, or, The Cultural Logic of Late Capitalism.* Verso, London, 1991.

Jung, Carl G. Approaching the Unconscious. In *Man and His Symbols*, eds. Carl G.Jung et al. Picador, London, 1964.

Kamau, Lucy Jayne. Semipublic, Private and Hidden Rooms: Symbolic Aspects of Domestic Space in Urban Kenya. *African Urban Studies*, vol. 3, 1978.

Kayongo-Male, Diane, and Philista Onyango. *The Sociology of the African Family.* Longman, London, 1984.

Kenya Insight Guide 1985, eds. Mohamed Amin and John Eames. APA Publications, Singapore, 1985. Second edition, 1990.

Kenyatta, Jomo. *Facing Mount Kenya: The Traditional Life of the Gikuyu.* (Orig.1938). Heinemann, Nairobi, 1982.

Kervanto (Nevanlinna), Anja. *Arkkitehtuurifilosofisia kytkentöjä: Arkkitehtien käsityksiä ympäristön laadusta.* (Architecture in Philosophical Context.) Teknillinen korkeakoulu, Arkkitehtiosasto, Yhdyskuntasunnittelun laitos, Julkaisu A 31, Otaniemi, 1987.

Kimani, S.M. The Structure of Land Ownership in Nairobi. *Canadian Journal of African Studies*, Vol.VI, No.iii, 1972.

Kimani, S.M. Location and Functional Structure of Shopping Centres in Nairobi. In *Urbanization and Development Planning in Kenya*, ed.R.A.Obudho. Kenya Literature Bureau, Nairobi, 1981.

King, Anthony D. *Colonial Urban Development: Culture, Social Power and Environment.* Routledge & Kegan Paul, London, 1976.

King, Anthony D., ed. *Buildings and Society.* Routledge and Kegan Paul, London, 1980.

King, Anthony D. Colonial architecture and urban development: Reconversion of colonial typologies in independent India. *Lotus international* 34, 1982.

King, Anthony D. *The Bungalow: The Production of a Global Culture.* Routledge and Kegan Paul, London, 1984.

King, Anthony D. Colonial Cities: Global Pivots of Change. In *Colonial Cities*, eds. Robert Ross and Gerard J.Telkamp. Martinus Nijhoff, Dordrecht, 1985.

King, Anthony D. *Urbanism, Colonialism, and the World-Economy: Cultural and Spatial Foundations of the World Urban System.* Routledge, London, 1990.

King, Anthony D., ed. *Culture, Globalization and the World-System: Contemporary Conditions for the Representation of Identity.* Department of Art and Art History, State University of New York at Binghamton, and Macmillan, London, 1991.

Kostof, Spiro. *The City Shaped: Urban Patterns and Meanings Through History.* Thames and Hudson, London, 1991.

Kristeva, Julia. *Étrangers à nous-mêmes.* Coll. Points, Gallimard, Paris, 1988.

Kuhn, Thomas S. *The Structure of Scientific Revolutions.* Second, enlarged edition. University of Chicago Press, Chicago, 1970.

LaCapra, Dominick. *History & Criticism.*

Cornell University Press, Ithaca, 1985.
Langer, Susanne K. *Feeling and Form: A Theory of Art*. Charles Scribner's Sons, New York, 1953.
Lannoy, Richard. *The Speaking Tree: A Study of Indian Culture and Society*. Oxford University Press, London, 1971.
Le Corbusier. *La Charte d'Athènes*. (Orig.1957.) Coll. Points, Minuit, Paris, 1971.
Le Corbusier. *The City of Tomorrow*. (Orig. Urbanisme, 1924.) Architectural Press, London, 1987.
Lee Smith, Diana, and Davinder Lamba. Man/Environment Interaction: The Rural Family and its Home Environment. In *Urbanization and Development Planning in Kenya*, ed. R.A. Obudho. Kenya Literature Bureau, Nairobi, 1981.
Lefebvre, Henri. *Critique de la vie quotidienne. Tome III: De la modernité au modernisme*. L'Arche, Paris, 1981.
Lefebvre, Henri. *The Production of Space*. (Orig. La production de l'espace, 1974.) Blackwell, Oxford, 1991.
Lemon, Anthony, ed. *Homes Apart: South Africa's Segregated Cities*. Paul Chapman, London, 1991.
Lévi-Strauss, Claude. *Structural Anthropology 1*. (Orig. Anthropologie structurale, 1958.) Penguin, Harmondsworth, 1963.
Lévi-Strauss, Claude. *Structural Anthropology 2*. (Orig. Anthropologie structurale 2, 1973.) Penguin, Harmondsworth, 1976.
Lewis, Oscar. *The Children of Sánchez: Autobiography of a Mexican Family*. Penguin, Harmondsworth, 1961.
Lewis, Oscar. Urbanization without Breakdown: A Case Study. In *City Ways*, eds. John Friedl and Noel J.Chrisman. Thomas Y. Crowell, New York, 1975.
Lloyd, Peter C. *Classes, Crises and Coups*. Paladin, London, 1973.
Lloyd, Peter C. The Rise of New Indigenous Elites. In *Colonialism in Africa, 1870-1960, Vol.4, The Economics of Colonialism*, eds. Peter Duignan & L.H. Gann, 1975.
Magubane, Bernard. The Evolution of Class Structure in Africa. In *The Political Economy of Contemporary Africa*, eds. Peter C.W. Gutkind & Immanuel Wallerstein. Sage, Beverly Hills (Calif.), 1976.
Malombe, Joyce. The Role of Government and Users in the Provision of Low Income Housing in Nairobi, Kenya. *Open House International*, Vol.17, No.1, 1992.
Marescotti, Luca. Les représentations actuelles du territoire: "la parcellaire urbain". In *Morphologie urbaine et parcellaire*, éd. Pierre Merlin. Presses Universitaires de Vincennes, Saint-Denis, 1988.
Marris, Peter. *Family and Social Change in an African City: A Study of Rehousing in Lagos*. Northwestern University Press, 1962.
Mauss, Marcel. *The Gift*. (Orig. Essai sur le Don, 1950.) Routledge, London, 1990.
Mayer, Harold M., and Richard C. Wade. *Chicago: Growth of a Metropolis*. The University of Chicago Press, Chicago, 1969.
Memon, P.A. Kenya. In *African Perspectives*, eds. Harm De Blij and Edmond Martin. Methuen, New York, 1981.
Memon, P.A. The Growth of Low-Income Settlements: Planning Response in the Peri-Urban Zone of Nairobi. *Third World Planning Review*, Vol.4, No.2, May 1982.
Merlin, Pierre, éd. *Morphologie urbaine et parcellaire*. Presses Universitaires de Vincennes, Saint-Denis, 1988.
Miller, Charles. *The Lunatic Express: An Entertainment in Imperialism*. Ballantine, New York, 1971.
Mohl, Raymond A. The new urban history and its alternatives: some reflections on recent U.S. scholarship on the twentieth-century city. *Urban History Yearbook 1983*. Leicester University Press, Leicester, 1983.
Moore, W. Robert. Britain Tackles the East African Bush. *National Geographic*, vol.48, March 1950.
Morris, A.E.J. *History of Urban Form*. George Godwin, London, 1979.
Morrison, Hunter. Popular Housing Systems in Mombasa and Nairobi, Kenya. *Ekistics*, Vol.38, No.227, 1974.
Mumford, Lewis. *Culture of Cities*. (Orig. 1938.) Harcourt Brace Jovanovich, New York, 1970.
Mumford, Lewis. Machinery and the Modern Style. (Orig. from The New Republic, 1921.) In *Roots of Contemporary American Architecture*, ed. Lewis Mumford. Dover Publications, New York, 1972.
Muthesius, Herman. *The English House*. (Orig. Das Englische Haus, 3 vols., 1904-5.) Crosby Lockwood Staples, London, 1979.
Muthesius, Stefan. *The English Terraced House*. Yale University Press, New Haven, 1982.
Nevanlinna, Anja Kervanto. Culture, way of life, and power - concepts for research in architecture. *Nordic Journal of Architectural Research*, Vol.5, No.3, 1992.(a)
Nevanlinna, Anja Kervanto. Kaupunki, kommunikaatio, valta. *Synteesi*, Vol.11, No.4, 1992.(b)
Nevanlinna, Anja Kervanto. Huomautuksia kaupungista, kommunikaatiosta, vallasta. *Synteesi*, Vol.12, No.2, 1993.(a)
Nevanlinna, Anja Kervanto. Mistä kaupungissa on kyse: Kaupunkikäsitysten ja niiden representaatioiden ehdoista. *Tiede ja edistys*, Vol.18, No.4, 1993.(b)
Norberg-Schulz, Christian. *Genius Loci: Towards a Phenomenology of Architecture*. Academy Editions, London, 1980.
Obbo, Christine. *African Women: Their Strug-*

gle for Economic Independence. Zed Press, London, 1980.

Obudho, R.A. Urban Primacy in Kenya. In *The Spatial Structure of Development: A Study of Kenya*, eds. R.A.Obudho and D.R.F.Taylor. Westview Press, Boulder (Colo.), 1979.

Obudho, R.A. Historical Perspective of Urbanization. In *Urbanization and Development Planning in Kenya*, ed. R.A. Obudho, Kenya Literature Bureau, Nairobi, 1981.

O'Connor, Anthony. *The African City*. Hutchinson, London, 1983.

Ogot, Bethwell A. Kenya Under the British, 1895 to 1963. In *Zamani: A Survey of East African History*, ed. B.A.Ogot. New edition. East African Publishing House, Nairobi, 1974.

Olsen, Donald J. *The City as a Work of Art: London, Paris, Vienna*. Yale University Press, New Haven, 1986.

Paravicini, Ursula. *Habitat au Féminin*. Presses Polytechniques et Universitaires Romandes, Lausanne, 1990.

Paulsson, Gregor. *The Study of Cities: Notes about the hermeneutics of urban space*. Munksgaard, Copenhagen, 1959.

Paulsson, Gregor. *Svensk stad. Vol.1, Liv och stil i svenska städer under 1800-talet. Vol.2, Från bruksby till trädgårdsstad*. (Orig.1950.) Studentlitteratur, Lund, 1971.

Pirie, G.H. Kimberley. In *Homes Apart: South Africa's Segregated Cities*, ed. Anthony Lemon. Paul Chapman, London, 1991.

Porphyrios, Demetri. Notes on a Method. *Architectural Design*, Vol.51, No.5/6, 1981.

Rabinow, Paul. *Reflections on Fieldwork in Morocco*. University of California Press, Berkeley, 1977.

Rabinow, Paul. *French Modern: Norms and Forms of the Social Environment*. MIT Press, Cambridge (Mass), 1989.

Rasmussen, Steen Eiler. *London: the Unique City*. (Orig.1934 in Danish.) Revised and abridged edition. Penguin, Harmondsworth, 1960.

Reulecke, Jürgen, and Gerhard Huck. Urban history research in Germany: its development and present condition. *Urban History Yearbook 1981*. Leicester University Press, Leicester, 1981.

Ricoeur, Paul. *History and Truth*. Northwestern University Press, Evanston, 1965.

Ricoeur, Paul. *Hermeneutics and the Human Sciences*. Cambridge University Press, Cambridge, 1981.

Roche, Daniel. Urban History in France: Achievements, Tendencies and Objectives. *Urban History Yearbook 1980*. Leicester University Press, Leicester, 1980.

Rodger, Richard. Urban History: Prospect and Retrospect. *Urban History*, Vol.19, No.1, 1992.

Rorty, Richard. *Philosophy and the Mirror of Nature*. Basil Blackwell, London, 1980.

Rosberg, Carl G., and John Nottingham. *The Myth of "Mau Mau": Nationalism in Kenya*. Praeger, New York, 1966.

Ross, Aileen D. *The Hindu Family in its Urban Setting*. University of Toronto Press, Toronto, 1961.

Ross, Marc Howard. *Grass Roots in an African City: Political Behavior in Nairobi*. MIT Press, Cambridge (Mass.), 1975.

Ross, Robert, and Gerard J.Telkamp. Introduction. In *Colonial Cities*, eds. Robert Ross and Gerard J.Telkamp. Martinus Nijhoff, Dordrecht, 1985.

Sachs, Wolfgang, ed. *The Development Dictionary*. Zed Books, London, 1992.

Said, Edward W. *Orientalism*. Penguin, Harmondsworth, 1978.

Said, Edward W. *The World, the Text, and the Critic*. Vintage, London, 1983.

Said, Edward W. *Culture & Imperialism*. Vintage, London, 1993.

Seidenberg, Dana April. *Uhuru and the Kenya Indians: The Role of a Minority Community in Kenya Politics 1939-1963*. Heritage Bookshop, Nairobi, 1983.

Sennett, Richard. *The Fall of Public Man*. Vintage, New York, 1978.

Sitte, Camillo. City Planning according to Artistic Principles. (Orig. Der Städte-Bau nach seinen künstlerischen Grundsätzen, 1889.) In *Camillo Sitte: The Birth of Modern City Planning*, eds. George R. Collins and Christine Crasemann Collins. Pizzoli, New York, 1986.

Skinner, Quentin and his Critics. *Meaning & Context*. Ed.James Tully. Polity Press, London, 1988.

Slater, T.R., ed. *The Built Form of Western Cities*. Leicester University Press, Leicester, 1990.

Söderholm, Stig. Kamera kenttätyössä: kuvadokumentit ja visuaalinen metodiikka. In *Kulttuurin kenttätutkimus*, toim. Päivikki Suojanen ja Lassi Saressalo. Tampereen kansanperinteen laitos, Julkaisu 9, Tampere, 1982.

Soja, Edward W. *The Geography of Modernization in Kenya: A Spatial Analysis of Social, Economic, and Political Change*. Syracuse University Press, Syracuse, 1968.

Soja, Edward W. The Geography of Modernization - A Radical Reappraisal. In *The Spatial Structure of Development: A Study of Kenya*, eds. R.A.Obudho and D.R.A. Taylor. Westview Press, Boulder (Colo.), 1979.

Soja, Edward W. *Postmodern Geographies*. Verso, London, 1989.

Spivak, Gayatri Chakravorty. *In Other Worlds*. Routledge, London, 1988.

Stichter, Sharon. The Formation of a Working Class in Kenya. In *The Development of an African Working Class: Studies in Class Formation and Action*, eds. Richard Sandbrook and Robin Cohen. Longman, London, 1975.

Stren, Richard. The Evolution of Housing Policy in Kenya. In *Urban Challenge in East Africa*, ed. John Hutton. East African Publishing House, Nairobi, 1972.

Sutcliffe, Anthony. Introduction: Urbanization, Planning, and the Giant City. In *Metropolis 1890-1940*, ed.Anthony Sutcliffe. Mansell, London, 1984.

Swainson, Nicola. *The Development of Corporate Capitalism in Kenya 1918-1977.* University of California Press, Berkeley, 1980.

Tafuri, Manfredo, and Francesco Dal Co. *Modern Architecture.* Academy Editions, London, 1980.

Tagg, John. *Grounds of Dispute: Art History, Cultural Politics and the Discursive Field.* Macmillan, London, 1992.

Taylor, Charles. Philosophy and its history. In *Philosophy in History*, eds. Richard Rorty, J.B. Schneewind and Quentin Skinner. Cambridge University Press, Cambridge, 1984.

Taylor, Charles. *Human Agency and Language. Philosophical Papers, Vol.1.* Cambridge University Press, Cambridge, 1985.(a)

Taylor, Charles. *Philosophy and the Human Sciences. Philosophical Papers, Vol.2.* Cambridge University Press, Cambridge, 1985.(b)

Taylor, Charles. Interpretation and the Sciences of Man. (Orig.1971.) In *Interpretive Social Science: A Second Look*, eds. Paul Rabinow & William M.Sullivan. University of California Press, Berkeley, 1987.

Taylor, Charles. The hermeneutics of conflict. In *Meaning and Context: Quentin Skinner and his Critics*, ed. James Tully. Polity, London, 1988.

Thornton White, L.W., L. Silberman, and P.R. Anderson. *Nairobi Master Plan for a Colonial Capital, A Report Prepared for the Municipal Council of Nairobi.* His Majesty's Stationery Office, London, 1948.

Tignor, Robert L. *The Colonial Transformation of Kenya = The Kamba, Kikuyu and Maasai from 1900 to 1939.* Princeton University Press, Princeton (N.J.), 1976.

Tiwari, R.C. The Origin, Growth and the Functional Structure of the Central Business Districts of Nairobi. In *Urbanization and Development Planning in Kenya*, ed. R.A. Obudho. Kenya Literature Bureau, Nairobi, 1981.

Todorov, Tzvetan. *Nous et les autres: La réflexion française sur la diversité humaine.* Coll. Points, Seuil, Paris, 1989.

Toulmin, Stephen. *Cosmopolis: The Hidden Agenda of Modernity.* University of Chicago Press, Chicago, 1990.

Touraine, Alain. *Critique de la modernité.* Fayard, Paris, 1992.

Trzebinski, Errol. *The Kenya Pioneers: The Frontiersmen of an Adopted Land.* Mandarin, London, 1985.

Tylor, Edward B. *Primitive Culture.* (Orig. 1871.) Gordon Press, New York, 1974.

Vattimo, Gianni. *The End of Modernity: Nihilism and Hermeneutics in Postmodern Culture.* Johns Hopkins University Press, Baltimore, 1988.

Vestbro, Dick Urban. *Social Life and Dwelling Space: An Analysis of Three House Types in Dar Es Salaam.* University of Lund, College of Architecture, Department of Building Function Analysis, Report No.2, 1975.

Veyne, Paul. *Comment on écrit l'histoire, suivi de Foucault révolutionne l'histoire.* Coll. Points, Seuil, Paris, 1978.

Virtanen, Keijo. *Kulttuurihistoria - tie kokonaisvaltaiseen historiaan.* Annales Universitatis Turkuensis C 60, Turku, 1987.

Wallerstein, Immanuel. *The Politics of the World-Economy.* Cambridge University Press, Cambridge, 1984.

Wallerstein, Immanuel. Culture as the Ideological Battleground of the Modern World-System. In *Global Culture: Nationalism, Globalization and Modernity*, ed. Mike Featherstone. Sage, London, 1990.

Wallerstein, Immanuel. *Unthinking Social Science: The Limits of Nineteenth-Century Paradigms.* Polity, Oxford, 1991.

Weber, Max. *The Methodology of the Social Sciences.* Free Press, New York, 1949.

Weisner, Thomas S. Kariobangi: A Case History of a Squatter Resettlement Scheme in Kenya. In *A Century of Change in Eastern Africa*, ed. W.Arens. Mouton, The Hague, 1976.

Werlin, Herbert H. The Hawkers of Nairobi: The Politics of the Informal Sector. In *Urbanization and Development Planning in Kenya*, ed.R. A. Obudho. Kenya Literature Bureau, Nairobi, 1981.

Williams, David G. The Role of International Agencies: The World Bank. In *Low-Income Housing in the Developing World*, ed. G.K. Payne. John Wiley & Sons, London, 1984.

Williams, Raymond. *Culture and Society 1780-1950.* Pelican, Harmondsworth, 1963.

Williams, Raymond. *Culture.* Fontana, London, 1981.

Williams, Raymond. *Keywords: A vocabulary of culture and society.* Fontana, London, 1983.

Wilson, Elizabeth. *The Sphinx in the City: Urban Life, the Control of Disorder, and Women.* Virago Press, London, 1991.

Wirth, Louis. Urbanism as a Way of Life. (Orig. in American Journal of Sociology, 1938.) In *City Ways*, eds. John Friedl and Noel J.Chrisman. Thomas Y. Crowell, New York, 1975.

Wittgenstein, Ludwig. *Philosophical Investigations.* (Orig. Philosophische Unter-

suchungen, 1953.) Basil Blackwell, Oxford, 1958.
Wittgenstein, Ludwig. *On Certainty*. (Orig. Über Gewissheit, 1969.) Basil Blackwell, Oxford, 1974.
Wolff, Janet. *The Social Production of Art*. Second edition. Macmillan, London, 1993.
Worsley, Peter. *The Three Worlds: Culture and World Development*. Weidenfeld and Nicolson, London, 1984.
von Wright, Georg Henrik. Wittgenstein on Certainty. In *Problems in the Theory of Knowledge*, ed. G.H.von Wright. Martinus Nijhoff, the Hague, 1972.
von Wright, Georg Henrik. *Minervan pöllö*. Otava, Helsinki, 1992.

Wright, Gwendolyn. *Building the Dream: The Social History of Housing in America*. MIT Press, Cambridge (Mass.), 1981.
Wright, Gwendolyn. *The Politics of Design in French Colonial Urbanism*. University of Chicago Press, Chicago, 1991.
Wuensche, Andrew. Low Cost Housing, Kibera, Nairobi. *Architectural Design*, Vol.44, No.5, 1974.
Zwanenberg, R.M.A. van. *Colonial Capitalism and Labour in Kenya 1919-1939*. East African Literature Bureau, Nairobi, 1975.
Zwanenberg, R.M.A. van, and Anne King. *An Economic History of Kenya and Uganda 1800-1970*. Macmillan, London, 1975.

Name Index

Abercrombie, Patrick 172
Abrams, Charles 219, 220, 221
Abu-Lughod, Janet 57
Abuor, C. Ojwando 81, 82, 128, 129, 151, 199, 200
Ainsworth, John 92, 98, 107, 109, 126
Akare, Thomas 82, 275f
Alho, Olli 83, 309, 310, 329
AlSayyad, Nezar 75
Altman, Irwin 316
Ambjörnsson, Ronny 216, 248f
Amis, Philip 63
Andersen, Kaj Blegvad 83, 275
Anderson, P.R. 79, 158
Andreasen, Jörgen 238, 239
Andrews, Paul 63
Aradeon, David 65, 245

Bacon, Edmund N. 21
Baker, Herbert 64, 65, 140, 142
Bakhtin, Mikhail 8
Barnow, Finn 80, 81, 95, 109, 110, 117, 119, 121, 137, 144, 155, 167, 179, 180, 181, 185, 186, 188, 204, 226, 232f, 238, 240, 243, 249, 252, 263, 277, 284, 289, 304
Barthes, Roland 23
Baudrillard, Jean 42
Bedarida, François 21, 22
Benevolo, Leonardo 21
Beng-Huat, Chua 292
Berlin, Isaiah 27, 28, 30, 37, 38, 47, 48, 49,
Bharati, Agehanda 83, 292, 293
Bhaskar, Roy 26, 50
Bishop of Uganda 131
Blacker, J.G.C. 204, 209, 220
Blair, Thomas L. 103, 228, 306
Blixen, Karen 67, 81, 82, 85, 123, 214, 129, 140; see also Isak Dinesen
Bloch, Marc 46
Bloomberg, Lawrence N. 219, 220, 221
Bonte, Pierre 36
Boudon, Raymond 28, 61
Bourdieu, Pierre 26, 51
Bourricaud, François 28, 61
Brake, Michael Paul 40
Bransby-Williams, G. 107, 111, 116, 118
Braudel, Fernand 22, 46
Braunfels, Wolfgang 31
de Bruijne, G.A. 57, 63
Buchanan, Colin 227, 230
Burnett, John 261, 264, 316f

Caminos, Horacio 64, 194, 214, 215, 284
Carter, Harold 86

Carter, W. Morris 147
Cassirer, Ernst 33, 49
Cell, John W. 97, 117, 124, 128
de Certeau, Michel 42
Chana, T.S. 63, 82, 221, 222, 237, 238, 239, 306, 311
Chemers, Martin 316
Choay, Françoise 19, 29
Christie, Malcolm 63
Church, Arthur F. 93, 114
Churchill, Winston 106, 107
Clarke, John 40
Clifford, James 23
Conzen, Kathleen Neils 28
Conzen, Michael P. 86
Conzen, M.R.G. 86
Cox, Richard 82, 211, 214, 222, 249
Crampe-Crasnabet, Michèle 28
Cranworth, Lord 117
Curtis, Arnold 96, 103

Dal Co, Francesco 297
Daunton, M.J. 316
Davidson, Basil 81, 204, 306
Davis, Mike 40
Delamere, Lord 81, 106, 113, 131, 139, 146, 203
Devji, Z.H. 82, 311
Dike, Azuka A. 83, 308
Dinesen, Isak 81, 83, 129; see also Karen Blixen
Dossal, Marian 57
Dostoyevski, Feodor 8
Dreyfus, Hubert L. 50, 51, 52, 75
Dumont, Louis 28, 30
Dyer, Thornly 189
Dyos, H.J. 20

Eastwood, B. 257
Eco, Umberto 36
Ehrlich, Cyril 187
Eley, Geoff 45
Elgin, Lord 129
Elias, Norbert 36
Eliot, Charles 105
Elkan, Walter 115, 116, 129, 133, 189, 190, 193, 204, 237, 306, 308
Ellis, Sergeant 91
Emig, Sören 63, 80, 83, 93, 96, 141, 142, 143, 144f, 165, 180, 181, 227, 228, 230, 231f, 301
Engels, Friedrich 39
Escobar, Arturo 28
Esteva, Gustavo 28, 61

NAME INDEX ■ 365

Etherton, David 63, 214, 215, 225, 237, 238, 239
Evenson, Norma 29

Fanon, Franz 66
Farnworth, E.T. 81, 137, 223ff, 276f
Featherstone, Mike 310
Feetham, Justice R. 133, 134, 136, 139, 140
Finkielkraut, Alain 30
Fischer, Claude S. 40
Fletcher, Banister 64, 65, 141, 142
Foucault, Michel 20, 42, 45, 46, 51, 52, 55, 56, 75
Fox, Richard G. 19
Franklin, Jill 261
Frisell, Hjalmar 81, 126, 275
Frost, Richard 188, 189
Furedi, Frank 146

Gadamer, Hans-Georg 32, 50, 51, 52
Galaty, John 36
Gallen-Kallela, Akseli 81, 84, 112, 113
Gallen-Kallela, Kirsti 81, 112, 113, 148
Gans, Herbert J. 40
Gaskell, Ivan 24
Gattoni, George 63, 64, 286
Geddes, Patrick 21
Geertz, Clifford 19, 26, 43, 44, 45, 47, 52
Gellner, Ernest 28, 30, 38
Ghai, Dharam P. 81, 82, 187, 237, 240
Ghai, Yash P. 81, 82
Ghaidan, Usam 277
Giddens, Anthony 19, 45
Giedion, Sigfried 21, 297
Ginzburg, Carlo 30, 43
Girouard, Mark 261
Goethert, Reinhard 64, 194, 214, 215, 284
Grafmeyer, Y. 20
Grindley, William 222
Gropius, Walter 297
Gugler, Josef 204
Guillaume, Marc 42

Habermas, Jürgen 28
Hake, Andrew 63, 79, 106, 107, 108, 109, 111, 116, 117, 118, 119, 121, 133, 134, 135, 136, 137, 139, 140, 141, 143, 146, 148, 157, 171, 179, 181, 187, 188, 192, 193, 194, 195, 201, 202, 215, 216, 221, 222, 223, 225, 227, 237, 139, 264, 265, 267, 275, 277, 284, 286, 289, 298
Hall, Peter 21, 178f, 181, 227, 264
Hall, Thomas 21
Halliman, Dorothy M. 63, 79, 98, 99, 101, 107, 109, 111, 120, 134, 136, 140, 148, 149, 161, 186, 204, 205ff, 210ff, 229, 249, 270, 271, 289, 293, 298, 301
Hammarstrom, Ingrid 21
Hammond, Lt.Col. F.D. 258
Hannerz, Ulf 20, 40
Hardinge, Arthur 150
Harvey, David 20
Hauser, Arnold 30, 42, 48
Hebdige, Dick 40
Heidegger, Martin 50

Herder, J.G. 37, 38, 48, 49
Hill, M.F. 81, 91, 92, 94, 95, 96, 97, 98, 101, 103, 105, 106, 107, 109, 110, 122, 126, 127, 128, 129, 132, 134, 257, 258
Hoek-Smit, Marja C. 82, 275, 301, 319
Holston, James 34
Hooper, Charles 82, 299
Huck, Gerhard 20
Hussell, T. 228
Hutton, John 225
Huxley, Elspeth 81, 82, 96, 97, 103, 106, 109, 110, 113, 114, 127, 128, 130, 131, 139, 148

Ismael, Zahir 63, 80, 83, 93, 96, 141, 142, 143, 144f, 165, 180, 181, 227, 228, 230, 231f, 301
Izard, Michel 36, 62

Jameson, Fredric 20
Jameson, F. Walton 140
Jeevanjee, A.M. 103, 108, 119. 120, 121, 122, 124, 134
Johnston, Sir Harry 109, 110
Joseph, I. 20
Jung, Carl G. 33, 49

Kamau, Lucy Jayne 83, 308
Kayongo-Male, Diane, 83, 308
Kenyatta, Jomo 83, 275
Kervanto (Nevanlinna), Anja 27; see also Nevanlinna
Kimani, Samson M. 62, 118, 227, 228, 234ff
Kimathi, Dedan 150
King, Anne 81, 91, 93, 129, 130, 137, 147, 157, 191, 192, 193, 195, 216
King, Anthony D. 20, 23, 34, 46, 55, 57, 75, 96, 261, 292, 307, 308, 309, 310
Kostof, Spiro 54
Kristeva, Julia 42
Kuhn, Thomas S. 26

LaCapra, Dominick 37
Lamba, Davinder 83, 275
Langer, Susanne K. 31, 33, 49
Lannoy, Richard 281, 291, 292
Le Corbusier 297
Leavitt, John 36
Lee Smith, Diana 83, 275
Lefebvre, Henri 19, 27
Lemon, Anthony 265
Lévi-Strauss, Claude 37, 38, 39, 43
Lewis, Oscar 39
Leys, Norman 82, 92, 97, 117, 124, 125, 127, 128, 135, 136, 146
Linstrum, Derek 65
Lloyd, Peter C. 306, 309
Lugard, F.D. 109, 156
Lutyens, Edwin 140

Mabin, A. 265
Magubane, Bernard 306
Malombe, Joyce 221, 222, 239
Manyatta, Dam 216, 217, 218
Marescotti, Luca 86
Markus, Otto 106

Marris, Peter 83, 216, 306, 308
Marshal, R.W. 228
Martin, Richard 63
Marx, Karl 39
Mathu, Eliud 191
Mauss, Marcel 38
Mayer, Harold M. 86, 87
Mbogua, J.P. 225
Mbotela, Tom 200
Meinertzhagen, Richard 81, 103, 111, 112
Memon, P.A. 63, 181, 188, 204
Menezes, Leonie 82, 304, 319
Merlin, Pierre 19
Merville, Roberts 222
Miller, Charles 81, 97, 101, 156
Milner, Lord 132
Mohl, Raymond A. 20
Molesworth, Guildford 91, 92, 93
Moniz, Anthony Mervyn 81, 286
Moore, W. Robert 82, 158, 196
Morgan, W.T.W. 63, 79, 98, 99, 101, 107, 109, 111, 120, 134, 140, 148, 149, 161, 186, 205, 207f, 210ff, 229, 270, 271, 289, 293, 301
Morris, A.E.J. 19
Morrison, Hunter 63, 214
Morrison, Major 117
Moyne, Lord 146
Mumford, Lewis 21
Muthesius, Herman 261
Muthesius, Stefan 261
Mwangi, Meja 82, 280, 281

Naipaul, V.S. 66
Nevanlinna, Anja Kervanto 27, 36, 86; see also Kervanto
Ng'weno, Hilary 218
Ngugi wa Thiong'o (James Ngugi) 82, 156, 188, 189, 203
Norberg-Schulz, Christian 31
Northey, Sir Edvard 130, 133, 258
Nostvik, K.H. 245
Nottingham, John 81, 121, 127, 136, 137, 138, 191, 192, 194, 195

O'Callaghan, F.L. 95
O'Connor, Anthony 62, 241f
Obbo, Christine 81, 216
Obudho, R.A. 62, 81, 157, 238,
Ochieng, Philip 216
Ogot, Bethwell A. 81, 128, 129, 146, 147, 191, 194
Ohanga, B. Apolo 191
Oldham, J.H. 82, 117, 128
Olsen, Donald J. 28
Onyango, Philista 83, 308
Orde Browne, Major G.St.J. 189

Padfield, Reverend J. E. 292
Paravicini, Ursula 296
Parker, Mary 109, 116, 118, 119, 136, 137
Patel, Praful 63, 64, 286
Patterson, Colonel 97, 105
Paulsson, Gregor 20f
Perham, Dame Margery 156

Pirie, G.H. 265
Porphyrios, Demetri 54
Preston, R.O. 96, 97

Queen Victoria 121

Rabinow, Paul 20, 45, 51, 52, 57, 75, 297
Radford, Dr. 106
Rasmussen, Steen Eiler 31
Reulecke, Jürgen 20
Ricoeur, Paul 42, 50, 54
Roche, Daniel 20
Rodger, Richard 20, 21f
Rorty, Richard 44
Rosberg, Carl G. 81, 121, 127, 136, 137, 138, 191, 192, 194, 195
Ross, Aileen D. 281, 292
Ross, Marc Howard 81, 116, 194, 195, 226
Ross, Robert 57
Rousseau, J.-J. 43
Rozenthal, A.A. 228
Ruark, Robert 82, 197, 199
Rubia, Charles 213

Sachs, Wolfgang 61
Said, Edward W. 42, 62, 65, 66
Salisbury, Lord 91
Seaton, Henry 146
Seidenberg, Dana April 81, 97, 118, 130, 133, 192, 195
Sennett, Richard 40
Silberman, L. 79, 158
Simpson, W.J. 108, 118, 119, 121
Sitte, Camillo 121
Skinner, Quentin 50
Slater, T.R. 19
Soan, John 141
Söderholm, Stig 87
Soja, Edward W. 20, 62, 81, 212, 225, 234, 236
Soni, Praful Naran 63, 142, 178, 214, 222, 239
Sorre, Max 21
Spivak, Gayatri Chakravorty 42
Stichter, Sharon 81, 158, 193
Stren, Richard 187, 189, 190, 191, 194, 215, 216, 220, 306
Sutcliffe, Anthony 29
Swainson, Nicola 81, 157

Tafuri, Manfredo 297
Tagg, John 25, 87
Taylor, Charles 27, 32, 44, 45, 48, 50, 52, 347
Taylor, H.B. 122
Telkamp, Gerard J. 57
Thornton White, L. 79, 119, 158, 172, 187, 195
Tignor, Robert L. 93
Tiwari, Ramesh C. 91, 101, 111, 118, 155, 161, 185, 209
Todorov, Tzvetan 42
Tönnies, Ferdinand 38
Toulmin, Stephen 27, 28
Touraine, Alain 28
Tribe, M.A. 221
Turner, Borden 128

Tylor, Edward B. 37, 42
Trzebinski, Errol 81, 106, 126

Unwin, Raymond 264

Vaillat, Léandre 57
Vasey, Ernest 190
Vattimo, Gianni 32, 42, 43, 44, 45
Vestbro, Dick Urban 275
Veyne, Paul 42, 52
Vico, Giambattista 37, 48
Virjee, Suleiman 124
Virtanen, Keijo 79
Visram, Allidina 117
Vukovitch, A. 228

Wade, Richard C. 86, 87
Wallerstein, Immanuel 28, 36, 37, 75
Waring, E.L. 137
Watkins, Lt.Col. O.F. 277

Weber, Max 28, 47, 52, 332
Weisner, Thomas S. 63, 215, 216
Werlin, Herbert 190, 193, 213, 214
Whitehouse, George 91, 95, 114
Williams, David G. 306
Williams, Raymond 36, 38
Wilson, Elizabeth 40
Wirth, Louis 40
Wittgenstein, Ludwig 25, 26, 50
Wolff, Janet 54
Worsley, Peter 39, 61
Woodley, F.G.R. 158
von Wright, Georg Henrik 26, 30
Wright, Gwendolyn 57, 296
Wuensche, Andrew 82, 298, 299

Zwanenberg, R.M.A. van 81, 91, 93, 115, 116, 127, 128, 129, 130, 133, 137, 138, 147, 157, 189, 190, 191, 192, 193, 195, 204, 216, 237, 306

Place Index

Accra Road 231
Ainsworth Bridge 165, 169, 233, 244
All Saints Cathedral 155
Asian Bazaar, see Indian Bazaar

Bahati 187, 188, 194, 235
Banana 214
Banda Street 168; see also Portal Street
Bazaar Street 102, 103, 106, 111, 207f, 248; fig. 8.9; see also Biashara Street
Bernhard Estate 204
Biashara Street 68, 103, 106, 229, 248, 252; fig. 13.19; see also Bazaar Street
Bombay 57, 265
Bondeni 194
Box Estate 214
Brasilia 34
Brazil 34, 219
Britain 76, 131, 158, 159, 178, 185, 202, 343
Burma Market 199f
Buru Buru 82, 240, 297, 303ff, 319; figs. 5.14, 17.7, 17.8, 18.2

California 221, 225
Canberra 166, 167; fig. 12.9
Cape Town fig. 12.9
Carton City 214
Cathedral of the Holy Family 149, 155, 166
Chamberlain Road 259; see also Mara Road
Chicago 39, 86, 207
Chiromo 175, 243, 244
City Center 74, 157, 205, 207, 209, 231, 243, 244ff, 252f, 280, 286ff, 310f, 341; figs. 12.1, 12.6, 13.1, 13.8, 13.9, 13.15, 13.16, 13.22, 16.6-16.8, 17.9, 17.10, 18.7, 18.10
City Hall 209, 245
City Hall Way 155, 209, 231, 246, 248
City Market 149, 154, 155, 339; fig. 12.15, 13.19
City Park 186
City Square 149, 155, 207; fig. 13.1
Congo 219
Country Bus Station 202, 214

Dagoretti 215, 230
Dagoretti Corner 243
Dagoretti Road 111, 205
Dandora 230, 234, 239; figs. 13.11, 13.12
Dar es Salaam 277
Delamere Avenue 165, 168, 195, 197, 198, 339, 340; figs. 12.13, 12.14; see also Kenyatta Avenue, Sixth Street
Delhi 34, 46, 281
Delhi Road 261; see also Park Road

Desai Road 261; see also Ngara Road
Dhobi (washermen) Quarters 107, 111
Donovan Maule Theatre 188
Doonholm 236

East African Highway 165, 167, 169, 177
East African Lighting Offices fig. 12.12
Eastlands 187, 201, 205, 206, 207, 214, 221, 224, 236, 252, 293, 301, 340, 341; fig. 5.13
Eastleigh 117, 143, 175, 194, 205, 206, 235, 242, 243, 280, 282, 284ff, 289, 293; figs. 16.3-16.5; see also Egerton Estate, Nairobi East Township
Egerton Estate 284; see also Eastleigh
Eliot Street 102, 155; fig. 8.8; see also Wabera Street
England 109
Europe 67, 76, 78, 161
European Bazaar 99, 100, 122; fig. 8.5

Finland 78, 329
First Avenue 208, 284; see also Haile Selassie Avenue, Whitehouse Road
First Street 96
Fort Hall Road 186, 230, 231, 261; see also Muranga Road
Fourteenth Street 284
Fort Jesus 82, 298; see also Kibera

Ghana 219
Gorofani 187, 188
Government House 109, 112, 123, 124, 141, 142, 175, 252
Government Road 99, 102, 103, 109, 111, 118, 121, 122, 126, 142, 149, 150, 153f, 155, 165, 168, 197, 198, 203, 207, 229, 244, 245, 246, 248, 253, 337, 339; figs. 8.7, 10.2, 11.1, 11.2, 11.3, 11.4, 11.9, 12.16; see also Harry Thuku Road, Moi Avenue, Station Road
Grogan Road 208, 215, 280f; see also Kijabe Road, Kirinyaga Road
Gujarat 78, 282, 284

Haile Selassie Avenue 168, 207, 208, 209, 229, 244, 341; see also First Avenue, Whitehouse Road
Harambee 221, 229
Harambee Avenue 68, 244, 341; figs. 5.2
Harare 141
Hardinge Street 150f, 155; fig. 11.10; see also Kimathi Street
Harry Thuku Road 244; see also Government Road

PLACE INDEX ■ 369

Helsinki 57, 347
Highlands 110, 129, 132, 147, 236
Hill 98, 99, 100, 101, 109, 111, 115, 121, 140, 142, 143, 150, 155, 165, 166, 167, 169, 175, 186, 189, 207, 231, 234, 235, 243, 252, 239, 269f, 289, 340, 341; figs. 14.1-14.3, 14.13, 14.14, 18.1, 18.3
Hilton Hotel 248
Hong Kong 118, 347

ICEA Building 69; fig. 13.18
India 34, 76, 78, 96, 97, 121, 126, 127, 131, 140, 281f, 292, 339
Indian Bazaar 99, 105, 106, 109, 111, 112, 114, 116, 117, 118, 122, 124, 142, 149, 167, 168, 280, 282, 337, 338, 339; fig. 8.5
Indian Ocean 56, 91
Industrial Area 164, 169ff, 205, 207, 232, 235, 236, 243

Jamhuri 221
Jamia Mosque 69, 142, 149, 154; fig. 12.15
Jeevanjee Gardens 253
Jericho 201, 236
Jerusalem 201, 236
Juja 235

Kabete 144, 232
Kabete Road 143, 144
Kaburini 136, 137, 202, 214, 215
Kaloleni 170, 175, 194, 236, 301; fig. 5.11
Karen Blixen House fig. 5.12
Karen 140, 205, 230, 267
Kariobangi 215
Kariokor 136, 139, 194
Karura Forest 215; figs. 13.3, 13.4
Kassarani 230
Kenya Center (East African Center) 164, 166, 167, 168, 169, 177, 183, 186, 233, 244; figs. 12.7, 12.9
Kenya Parkway 165; fig. 12.8; see also Princess Elizabeth Highway, Uhuru Highway
Kenyatta Avenue 68, 150, 203, 207f, 209, 229, 242, 245, 246, 248, 253, 339; fig. 13.8; see also Delamere Avenue, Sixth Street
Kenyatta Conference Center 65, 245, 246ff, 247, 248, 341, 344; figs. 13.20
Khoja Mosque 149, 153
Kiambu 165, 204, 249
Kiambu Distruct 204
Kibera 76, 80, 82, 136, 165, 215, 221, 232, 243, 297ff, 308; figs. 17.1-17.3, 18.5
Kibera Drive 298
Kijabe Road 208; see also Grogan Road
Kikuyu Road 93
Kileleshwa 136, 137, 143, 235, 243, 309, 313; figs. 17.11-17.13, 18.12
Kilimani 140, 143, 175
Kilimanjaro Avenue 259
Kimathi 150, 221; see also Hardinge Street
Kimathi Street 209, 248
Kimberley 265
Kingsway 208; see also University Way
Kingsway Camp 199

Kinyango 214
Kirinyaga 214
Kirinyaga Road 208; fig. 5.7; see also Grogan Road
Kitui Village 214
Koinange Street 151, 168, 229, 246; fig. 13.19

Lagos 216
Lake Victoria 56, 91, 121
Lamu 277
Lamu Road fig. 5.9
Langata 140, 205, 230
Langata Road 234
Lavington 175, 243, 310, 314f; figs. 17.14, 17.15, 18.11
Law Courts 142, 148, 155, 165, 166, 229, 245, 247, 339, 341; figs. 11.13, 12.12, 13.20
Limuru 197
Loita Street 209
London 31, 57, 77, 91, 141, 172, 265, 347
Lower Parklands 143, 174, 175
Lusaka 179
Lutheran Church 246

Machakos 98, 114
Madaraka 221
Majengo, see Pumwani
Makadara 204, 236, 301
Makongeni 171, 175, 187
Mara Road 259; see also Chamberlain Road
Maringo 201, 236
Masikini 136, 137
Mathare River 194
Mathare Valley 63, 194, 202, 214, 215, 216, 217f, 235, 237, 238f, 249; fig. 13.10
Mbotela 187, 188, 236
McMillan Memorial Library 149, 154; fig. 12.15
Mecca 67
Moi Avenue 68, 242, 244, 248, 253, 337; figs. 5.1, 13.7, 13.17; see also Government Road, Station Road
Moktar Daddah Street 231
Mombasa (village) 136, 137
Mombasa (city) 91, 97, 105, 114, 121, 277
Morocco 57
Mount Kenya 67, 91
Municipal Market fig. 5.6
Muranga Road 244, 261
Muthaiga 76, 117, 134, 140, 143, 175, 189, 197, 204, 205, 232, 267
Muthuri 214
Muthurwa (Landhies) 139, 143, 175, 202, 264; figs. 14.8-10

Nairobi East Township 284; see also Eastleigh
Nairobi House 150
Nairobi National Park 205
Nairobi River 70, 93, 98, 99, 100, 109, 111, 116, 121, 135, 153, 165, 202, 208, 209, 214, 215, 229, 231, 234, 243, 248, 280, 282, 337, 339
Nairobi South 204, 205, 206, 235, 293ff, 310; figs. 16.12, 16.13, 18.9
National Theatre 188, 189

New Delhi 140, 166, 167, 281; fig. 12.9
New York 57, 347
Ngara 135, 143, 154, 174, 201, 229, 235, 236, 244, 252, 261, 264, 288ff, 289, 293; figs. 14.4-14.7, 16.1, 16.2, 18.6
Ngara Road 111, 261; fig. 5.8; see also Desai Road
Ngong Road 144, 175, 230, 243
Ngong Hills 67
Nkrumah Lane 209, 229
Norfolk Hotel 112, 123, 149, 189, 196, 198, 249; fig. 11.8
Norfolk Towers 82
North America 76, 78
Nyasaland 117

Ofafa 201
Outer Ring Road 234, 239, 243, 301, 303

Pakistan 97
Pangani 136, 138, 143, 147, 174, 175
Paris 29, 57, 167; fig. 12.9
Park Road 231, 261; see also Delhi Road
Parliament Building 189, 248, 341
Parklands 97, 109, 111, 121, 134, 143, 175, 204, 205, 206, 235, 242, 243, 267, 289ff, 293, 310; figs. 16.9-16.11, 18.8
Peponi Road fig. 5.10
Portal Street 168; fig. 12.15; see also Banda Street
Pretoria 140, 167; fig. 12.9
Princess Elizabeth Highway 165, 186, 253; see also Kenya Parkway, Uhuru Highway
Pumwani 76, 81, 116, 136f, 139, 143, 147, 175, 202, 219, 221, 222ff, 225, 236, 275ff, 298; figs. 5.9, 13.5, 15.1-15.3

Rabai Road 303
Rabat 57
Racecourse Road 143, 196
Railway Headquarters 142, 149, 155, 339; fig. 12.12
Railway Station 95, 98, 141, 149, 337; fig. 11.7
Railway Club 109
Rhodesia 141
Ridgeway Estate 232
Rio de Janeiro 57
River Road 68, 129, 149, 153, 167, 168, 207f, 214, 234, 248, 252, 280, 282, 285, 286ff, 293, 339
Roman Catholic Church 109
Ruaraka 230

Sadler Street 168
Salisbury 141
Sclaters Road 93
Second Avenue 284
Second Street 96
Sergeant Ellis Avenue 155
Shauri Moyo 147
Singapore 292

Sixth Avenue 102, 103, 126, 142, 149, 150, 153f, 155; figs. 8.8, 11.2, 11.10
South Africa 65, 110, 114, 137, 140, 158, 161, 171, 265
Spring Valley 140, 205, 232, 243, 267, 270f, 310, 315; figs. 14.11, 14.12, 14.15, 14.16, 18.13-18.15
Stahere 187
Standard Street 155
St.Andrew's Church 246
Stanley Hotel 112, 113, 151, 198, 203, 209; figs. 9.2, 13.18
Starehe 139
Station Road 96, 101, 111, 121, 126, 253
St.Paul's Church 246
Swamp Parkway 165, 186, 233
Synagogue 246

Tanganyika 191, 219; see also Tanzania
Tanzania 83, 212, 277, 329; see also Tanganyika, Zanzibar
Thika 234
Thika Road 186, 243
Thompson Estate 140, 175, 204
Tom Mboya Street 68, 168, 208, 209; fig. 5.3; see also Victoria Street
Torr's Hotel 151
Town Hall 142, 155, 166

Uganda 108, 110, 118, 156, 191, 212, 219
Uhuru 221
Uhuru Highway 186, 203, 207f, 209, 229, 230, 231, 234, 242, 244, 245, 249, 253, 340, 341; see also Kenya Parkway, Princess Elizabeth Highway
Uhuru Park 231, 245, 341
Umoja 82, 240, 297, 301ff, 319; figs. 17.4-17.6
United States 39, 296, 316
University 246
University Way 208, 209, 229, 233; see also Kingsway
Upper Hill 144, 175, 271, 272, 310; figs. 14.17, 14.18, 18.4
Upper Nairobi 205, 206, 207, 270
Upper Parklands 140, 165, 175, 205, 267, 289

Victoria Street 103, 111, 153, 168, 203, 208; see also Tom Mboya Street

Wabera Street 155; see also Eliot Street
Washington D.C. 167; fig. 12.9
Westlands 140, 144, 175, 189, 341
Whitehouse Road 168, 208; see also First Avenue, Haile Selassie Avenue
Wilson Airport 229, 232

Zambia 63, 83, 241, 329
Zanzibar 108, 118, 150, 191
Zimbabwe 141
Ziwani 194

FINNISH HISTORICAL SOCIETY

The Finnish Historical Society, founded in 1875, is the main scientific society of historians in Finland. The core of the membership comprises the most eminent of Finnish scholars active in research.

Publishing is the prime function of the Society. Its publication series are *Historiallisia Tutkimuksia* (Historical Research, monographs in Finnish and Swedish, 196 issues so far), *Historiallinen Arkisto* (Historical Archives, shorter studies in the form of articles in Finnish, 107 issues so far), *Studia Historica* (monographs in English and in German, 55 in number), *Bibliotheca Historica* (doctoral dissertations in Finnish, Swedish, English and German, 18 volumes in number), *Käsikirjoja* ("Handbooks" including the Finnish Historical Biblio-graphies 1544–1990), and a series of *Suomen historian lähteitä* (Finnish historical Sources). At present, the Society publishes some 20 to 25 volumes each year.

The Society is responsible for international relations in its field and is also involved in editing the joint Nordic review *Scandinavian Journal of History*.

Historical studies in English and German published by the Finnish Historical Society in the 1990s

STUDIA HISTORICA

34 *Anssi Halmesvirta,* The British Conception of the Finnish 'Race', Nation and Culture, 1760 – 1918. 1990. 324 pp. ISBN 951-8915-28-8.

35 *Harri Siiskonen,* Trade and Socioeconomic Change in Ovamboland, 1850 – 1906. 1990. 269 pp. ISBN 951-8915-30-X

36 *Maria Suutala,* Tier und Mensch im Denken der deutschen Renaissance. 1990. 321 pp. ISBN 951-8915-34-2.

37 *Ilkka Nummela,* Stadstruktur und Bodenwert – Eine Studie über die Industrialisie- rungsperiode in Kuopio (Finnland) (1875 – 1914). 1990. 416 pp. ISBN 951-8915-35-0.

38 *Steven D. Huxley,* Constitutionalist Insurgency – Finnish 'Passive Resistance' against Russification as a Case on Nonmilitary Struggle in the European Resistance Tradition. 1990. 284 pp. ISBN 951-8915-40-7.

Yrjö Kaukiainen, Sailing into Twilight – Finnish Shipping in an Age of Transport Revolution, 1860 – 1914. 1991. 429 pp. ISBN 951-8915-41-5.

Eero Kuparinen, An African Alternative – Nordic Migration to South Africa, 1815 – 1914. 1991. 487 pp. ISBN 951-8915-45-8.

Heikki Mikkeli, An Aristotelian Response to Renaissance Humanism – Jacopo Zabarella on the Nature of Arts and Sciences. 1992. 196 pp. ISBN 951-8915-58-X.

Kari Väyrynen, Der Prozess der Bildung und Erziehung im finnischen Hegelianismus. 1992. 311 pp. ISBN 951-8915-53-9.

Martti Pärssinen, Tawantinsuyu – The Inca State and Its Political Organization. 1992. 462 pp. ISBN 951-8915-62-8.

Antti Häkkinen, Just a Sack of Potatoes? – Crisis Experiences in European Societies, Past and Present. 1992. 240 pp. ISBN 951-8915-63-6.

Kirsi Saarikangas, Model Houses for Model Families – Gender, Ideology and the Modern Dwelling – The Type-Planned Houses of the 1940s in Finland. 1993. 403 pp. ISBN 951-8915-65-2.

Christian Krötzl, Pilger, Mirakel und Alltag – Formen des Verhaltens im skandinavischen Mittelalter. 1994. 393 pp. ISBN 951-8915-92-X.

Veli-Matti Rautio, Die Bernstein-Debatte – Die politisch-ideologischen Strömungen und die Parteiideologie in der Sozialdemokratischen Partei Deutschlands 1898 – 1903. 1994. 377 pp. ISBN 951-8915-94-6.

Arto Luukkanen, The Party of Unbelief – The Religious Policy of The Bolshevik Party, 1917 – 1929. 1994. 1994. 274 pp. ISBN 951-710-008-6.

Juhani Koponen, Development for Exploitation – German Colonial Policies in Mainland Tanzania, 1884 – 1914. 1994. 740 pp. ISBN 951-710-005-1.

Kaija Tiainen-Anttila, The Problem of Humanity – The Blacks in the European Enlightenment. 1994. 367 pp. ISBN 951-710-007-8.

Maija Kallinen, Change and Stability – Natural Philosophy at the Academy of Turku, 1640 – 1714. 1995. 439 pp. ISBN 951-710-001-6.

Kari Saastamoinen, The Morality of the Fallen Man – Samuel Pufendorf on Natural Law. 1995. 179 pp. ISBN 951-710-003-5.

Hannes Saarinen, Bürgerstadt undAbsoluter Kriegsherr. Danzig und Karl XII. im Nordischen Krieg. 385 pp. ISBN 951-710-031-0.

Screen, John. E. O., The Finnish Army 1881–1901 – Training the Rifle Battalions. 315 pp. ISBN 951-710-032-9.

BIBLIOTHECA HISTORICA

4 *Seppo Sivonen,* White-collar or Hoe Handle – African Education under British Colonial Policy, 1920 – 1945. 1995. 264 pp. ISBN 951-710-016-7.

7 *Henrik Knif,* Gentlemen and Spectators – Studies in Journals, Opera and the Social Scene in Late Stuart London. 1995. 302 pp. ISBN 951-710-021-3.

8 *Esko Heikkonen,* Reaping the Bounty: McCormick Harevesting Machine Company Turns Abroad, 1878–1902. 1995. 319 pp. ISBN 951-710-022-1.

9 *Tuomas Lehtonen.* Fortuna, Money, and the Sublunar World – Twelfth-century Ethical Poetics and the Satirical Poetry of the Carmina Burana. 1995. 185 pp. ISBN 951-8915-027-2.

16 *Virve Manninen,* Sozialismus oder Barbarei? Der Revolutionäre Sozialismus von Rosa Luxemburg 1899–1919. Ill. 212 pp. ISBN 951-710-047-7.

18 *Anja Kervanto Nevanlinna,* Interpreting Nairobi – The Cultural Study of Built Forms. Ill. 371 pp. ISBN 951-710-049-3.

OUTSIDE OF SERIES

Jukka Nevakivi (Ed.), Neutrality in History / La neutralité dans L'histoire – Proceedings of the Conference of the History of Neutrality organized in Helsinki 9 – 12 September 1992. 1993. 335 pp. ISBN 951-8915-66-0.

Matti Klinge, The Finnish Tradition –Essays on Structures and Identities in the North of Europe. 1993. 264 pp. ISBN 951-8915-71-7.

Rauno Endén (Ed.), Yleisradio, 1926–1996. History of Finnish Broadcasting. Hard cover. Ill, 350 pp. ISBN 951-710-040-X, Price FIM 180-

The price of each publication is FIM 120 unless otherwise specified.

Finnish Historical Society
Arkadiankatu 16 B 28
FIN-00100 Helsinki
Finland
Tel. +358+9+440 369
Fax + 358+9+441 468
E-mail: enden@shs.pp.fi

Distributor:
Tiedekirja
Kirkkokatu 14
FIN-00170 Helsinki
Finland
Tel. +358+9+635 177
Fax + 358+9+635 017